The Children's Picture Atlas in Colour

The Children's Picture Atlas in Colour

Revised Edition

Hamlyn

London · New York · Sydney · Toronto

First edition 1965 Revised edition 1971 Revised edition 1978
Second impression 1980
Published by
The Hamlyn Publishing Group Limited, Astronaut House, Hounslow Road, Feltham, Middlesex, England
by arrangement with Western Publishing Company, Inc.

© Copyright 1960 Golden Press, Inc. All rights reserved
Text © Copyright First edition 1965 Golden Pleasure Books, Ltd
Text © Copyright Revised editions 1971, 1978 Western Publishing Company, Inc.;
in association with The Hamlyn Publishing Group Ltd.

ISBN 0 600 37142 5
Printed in Czechoslovakia
51087/8

Contents

In this atlas we have tried to present a fair and balanced picture of the world, its countries, and its peoples. We have not stressed the divisions that occur, because the future well-being of the peoples of the world depends on what unites, not on what divides them. All people, whatever their race, colour, religion, or political beliefs, have one thing in common: they are all citizens of one world. The well-being of one is the well-being of all.

SPECIAL SECTION OF STATISTICAL MAPS
RICHARD EDES HARRISON

Maps on pages 8—9, 130—131, 132—133, 227, 321, 385, 446—447, 494, 495 are copyrighted by Georg Westermann Verlag. They are produced from the *Westermann Bildkarten* Lexicon by arrangement with Georg Westermann Verlag.

Introduction

Never before has the world presented greater contrasts than it does today, when modern jets land at airports only a few miles from villages that have developed little since the Stone Age.

Certainly there are no more hidden continents or mysterious islands to be discovered and the frontiers of exploration now lie in Space or beneath the sea. And yet, though faster and faster aircraft are bringing the most distant parts of the world ever closer to us, this closeness only underlines the tremendous contrasts of the world, and the fascination of foreign lands, people, and customs. For the people of the world live their lives very differently, and in conditions that vary from the cold of the polar regions to the intense heat of deserts and tropical jungles. Some live securely in highly developed modern states, surrounded by modern aids and comforts. Others are faced with a permanent threat of starvation and disease. Some live in countries where the number of motor cars causes serious traffic-jams and delays. Others have never even seen a train, or an aeroplane.

It is these contrasts which this Atlas sets out to show: the deserts, jungles, cities, plains, and also – and just as important – the people of the world, where they are and what they do.

This is Europe

Europe is part of the Old World. On its eastern side it is joined on to Asia, and it is often grouped with Asia in the term Eurasia. In fact Europe is sometimes spoken of as a peninsula of Asia. It has been the rule to trace the eastern boundary of Europe along the Ural mountains, but the Urals have never been an effective natural barrier – least of all today when the determined efforts of the USSR to forge Siberia and European Russia into a single unit are making the Urals more and more meaningless as a frontier.

Unlike the solid mass of Asia, Europe is a peninsula thrust between the Atlantic and the Mediterranean, or, more accurately, numbers of peninsulas, with sea inlets between them – the Baltic, the North Sea, the English Channel, the Adriatic, and so on. This gives a very complicated coastline. In no other part of the world are sea and land so markedly intermixed as they are throughout Europe.

The fact that Europe lies in an area of moderate temperature makes the interplay of sea and land all the more important. The parallel of 50° North runs approximately through Penzance, Amiens, Frankfurt, and Prague. Only a very small part of Europe lies within the Arctic Circle, and even here, under the moderating influence of the North Atlantic Drift, the sea is ice-free throughout the year. Europe is the only continent with a mild climate. Its position on the globe and the influence of the sea mean that, except in the most eastern part of the continent, there are no great contrasts of heat and cold, no barren deserts. The whole of Europe, excluding Euro-

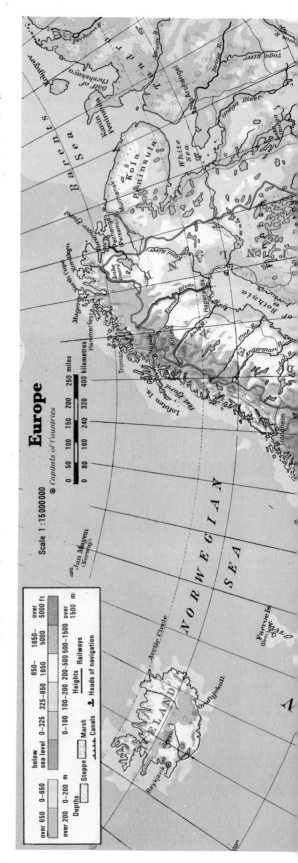

9

A group of happy Norwegian children, dressed in national costume, dancing in a meadow by the side of Hardanger Fiord.

pean Russia, has an area of 2,200,000 square miles (5,697,800 sq km), i.e. 4 per cent of the world's land surface. It is everywhere populated and exploited.

From North Cape in the extreme north of Norway to Cape Matapan at the southernmost tip of Greece the distance is only 2,400 miles (3,860 km), while from west to east, from Cape Finisterre to the mouth of the Danube, the distance is no more than 2,000 miles (3,220 km). Thus all parts of Europe are readily accessible. In addition there are numerous rivers which have played a considerable role in the development of trade throughout the continent.

Its population of about 472 millions is 12 per cent of the world's total. That means there is an average of 21 persons per square mile (8 persons per sq km) compared with 17 (6 per sq km) in Asia and less than 3 per square mile (1 per sq km) in North America – making the smallest continent the most densely populated as, in fact, Europe's population exceeds that of Africa or the Americas.

The states of Europe vary between great modern industrial countries like Britain and Federal Germany, and tiny principalities like Monaco, Liechtenstein, Andorra, San Marino and, of course, the Vatican State.

Mountains and Plains

Europe is not very mountainous. The average height of the continent is only 1,000 feet (304 m) above sea level. The Alps, the dominant heights of Europe, are modest in extent compared with the Andes and The Rockies, and modest in height compared with the Himalayas.

They stretch for 750 miles (1,200 km) from Nice in the south of France to Vienna in Austria, and altogether they include a dozen peaks over 12,000 feet (3,660 m). The Alps are less worn down by weather than older mountains, and beneath their jagged peaks are ice-bound hollows, and lower still, wooded slopes and deep valleys. The great valleys lead up to the famous passes: the Mont Cenis between France and Italy, the Great St Bernard and Simplon between Switzerland and Italy, the St Gotthard in Switzerland on the road leading to the Italian lakes, and the Brenner Pass between Austria and Italy.

Other mountain ranges are less crag-

Falun in Sweden has one of the oldest copper mines in the world. Mining has been going on here since the year 1230.

gy. The Pyrenees run between France and Spain, and their highest peak, the Pico de Aneto, is only 11,168 feet (3,400 m) in height. The Apennines run down the whole Italian Peninsula and continue in Sicily. The highest peak of these mountains, which are, in fact, an extension of the Alps, is Monte Corno in the Gran Sasso d'Italia, 9,574 feet

Many Italian towns have remained almost unchanged through the centuries: San Gimignano.

A characteristic Greek landscape scene: small villages scattered at the foot of mountains.

(2,900 m). On the flank of the Apennines are famous volcanoes: Vesuvius near Naples, Etna in Sicily, and Stromboli, a small island north of Sicily.

An extension of the Alpine system runs through the Balkans into Greece. On the eastern side of the Danube is a more detached extension, the Carpathians. The Carpathians are the largest mountain system in Europe after the Alps, covering 72,000 square miles (186,470 sq km), though not rising above 9,000 feet (2,740 m). This range flanks the Great Plain of Hungary.

In other parts of Europe the mountains are not disposed in elongated ranges but in great masses such as the Massif Central in France, the Vosges on the left bank of the Rhine, the Grampians in Scotland, and the mountains of Scandinavia. Such mountains are lower and less dense than the ranges. They rise in great rounded masses, worn down by the weather, and some of their lower slopes are heavily wooded. Often coal seams are found beneath the foothills. Bordering them are often great plains, like that of Lorraine, which adjoins the Vosges.

The two important plains in Western Europe are the sharply marked Plain of Lombardy, watered by the River Po; and, less clearly marked, the plain which

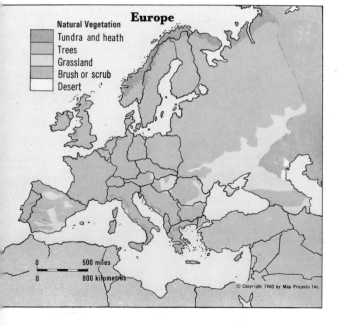

Europe

Natural Vegetation
Tundra and heath
Trees
Grassland
Brush or scrub
Desert

0   500 miles
0   800 kilometres

© Copyright 1960 by Map Projects Inc.

gradually develops from the lesser uplands of Western Europe and sweeps across northern France and Germany, extending over Denmark, Finland, the lowlands of Sweden and southern England.

There are also two important plains in Eastern Europe: the Great Plain of Hungary, and the North European Plain, which is an extension of the one that runs through France and Germany. Bohemia (the western part of Czechoslovakia) is an intermediate zone, being an undulating plateau over 1,000 feet (300 m) above sea level surrounded by mountains of a little more than 4,000 feet (1,220 m) in average height.

To understand the great variety of the European landscape we must keep in mind the manner of its formation. The Alps are among the youngest mountains in Europe. They were thrust up between 50 and 70 million years ago, and that is not long enough for the rocks to have been worn smooth by wind and weather, or the peaks to be rounded. Masses like the Grampians on the other hand were thrust up more than 400 million years ago. Once they possessed the forbidding craggy outline of the Alps, but over the ages they have been steadily weathered and scarred by deeper and broader valleys, and now have a rounded outline.

Amongst the agents in this weathering process the glaciers have played a major part, particularly those of the great Ice Ages, the last of which occurred some 20,000 years ago. Ice caps formed in Northern Europe, notably in Scandinavia and north-western Britain, and extended at their maximum to the Thames valley in the west and across the German and Polish plains to Bohemia and the Carpathians in the east. To the south the glaciers flowed outwards on

Fishing is very important to the economies of the countries of southern Europe. Tunny fishing off the coast of Sardinia.

both sides from the Pyrenees and the Alps. These glaciers acted like giant files, scraping the land they flowed over. When the ice eventually receded, it left behind deposits and depressions, the latter of which, filling up with water, remained as lakes. The lakes of the Alps, Finland, and Norway were formed in this way.

Hungarian agriculture is based on the collective farm system. Long-horned cattle are grazed on the Hungarian Plain.

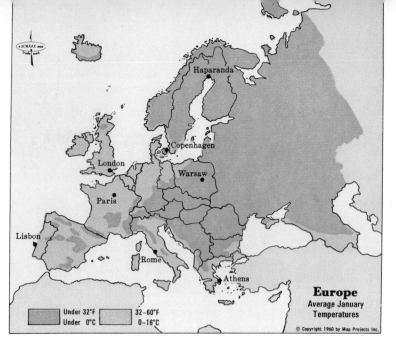

This map shows the range of January temperatures in Europe. The effects of the warm North Atlantic Drift raise winter temperatures along the west coast of northern Europe, while the continental climate depresses temperatures in central Europe. This accounts for the fact that London has a higher average January temperature than Warsaw.

The Climate, Coasts and Seas

The nature of the coasts varies greatly in Europe. In mountainous regions the coast rises steeply, as in Portugal, Italy, and Norway. Where there are plains, on the other hand, the coast consists of a gently shelving and easily eroded beach which often needs to be protected by breakwaters. The Atlantic Ocean washes the coasts of Europe from Gibraltar to Scandinavia, and the warm North Atlantic Drift is felt as far as the north of Norway.

The Mediterranean is made up of a series of deep basins in which there are numerous islands, the most important being the Balearic Islands (Majorca, Minorca, Ibiza), Corsica, Sardinia, Sicily, Crete, and Cyprus. The Mediterranean is so enclosed by the land that it is practically tideless. Consequently coastal erosion by the sea proceeds much more slowly. As the Mediterranean is warm, the water evaporates quickly, making it more salty than other seas. It

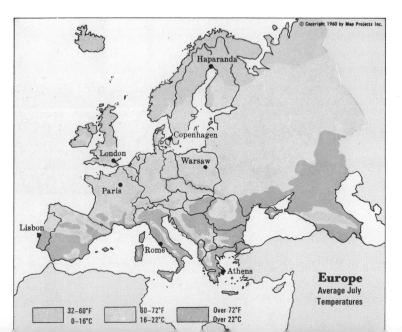

This map shows the range of July temperatures in Europe. Westerly winds, cooled by the Atlantic, depress the summer temperatures along the west coast of northern Europe. As the land absorbs heat more quickly than the sea, central Europe is warmer than western Europe in summer.

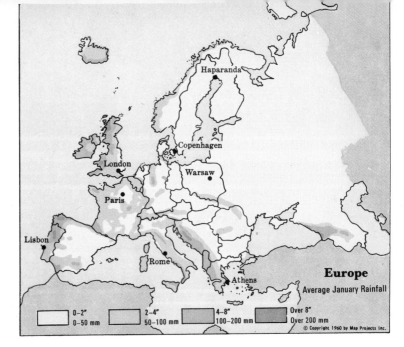

This map shows the range of January rainfall in Europe. Prevailing westerly winds bring rain to the Atlantic coast of Europe. Most rain falls in southern Europe during the winter.

has been calculated that if the Strait of Gibraltar were stopped up, the Mediterranean would dry out completely in less than 8,000 years.

The climate of Europe is much less variable than that of other continents. This is partly due to its position about half-way between the Equator and the North Pole. But in this area, often called the temperate zone, the prevailing wind is from the west. The west wind brings moisture and, because of the warm Gulf Stream or North Atlantic Drift, warmth. Thus, the summers are less hot and winters less cold on the western side of the land mass than on the eastern side of Eurasia.

In this way the sea exercises an influence far into the interior of Europe, particularly in the north. In fact, we can distinguish three climatic zones. In Western Europe, where the influence of the sea is greatest, we have the true maritime climate. In central Europe and farther east the influence of the sea progressively diminishes, and there is what is called the continental climate. In the south the influence of the sea is only felt in winter, and that is the season of rains. During the summer, depressions do not

This map shows the range of July rainfall in Europe. The influence of the westerly winds is again felt on the Atlantic coast of Europe. The relatively high rainfall in central Europe is caused by sporadic summer storms.

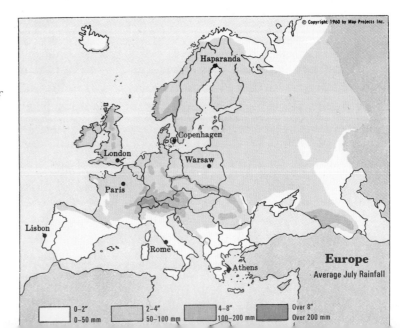

Winter in Siberia. Sharp contrasts characterise the continental climate.

penetrate into the Mediterranean regions, and summers are hot and dry. This is called the Mediterranean climate.

The maritime climate, extending over nearly all of Western Europe, is characterised by abundant rain, which falls at frequent intervals throughout the year (though slightly more often in autumn), by constant changes in the weather, and the absence of clearly marked seasons and extremes of heat and cold. With this climate rivers such as the Thames and Rhine have streams which are more or less uniform, as rainfall is fairly evenly spread over the year.

The continental climate extending over Central and Eastern Europe, is characterised by more uneven rainfall, which reaches its maximum in brief summer storms, and by the sharp contrast between summer and winter, divided by a very short spring and autumn. In these conditions such rivers as the Vistula flow very unevenly, being frozen during the winter and at their height in spring, when they are swollen by the thaw and heavy rains. Pine forests or grassland are the typical vegetation of this particular kind of climate, especially in the great steppes of Eastern Europe.

The Mediterranean climate, extending across Southern Europe, is characterised by hot summers and mild winters (though sudden cold spells do occur), and by definitely seasonal rainfall – occurring in heavy downpours, chiefly in winter. The summer is extremely dry. Dryness and heat together account for the arid appearance of the plains and low plateaus of the Mediterranean regions. The influence of this kind of climate on the rivers, on vegetation, and on agriculture is decisive. The flow of rivers is extremely variable. Vegetation is chiefly characterised by protection against drought. Trees are evergreen with small waxy leaves – olives and ilexes, for instance. They very rarely grow to a great height but form thick undergrowth. The maquis in Corsica is an example.

The Rhine rises in the Swiss Alps. Its winding course stretches in all some 850 miles (1,370 km). After flowing for a considerable distance in Switzerland, it turns northwards, and for a while forms the frontier between Germany and France, then flows on through Germany, and finally crosses into Holland. Here it empties into the North Sea, forming a large delta with several arms.

The flow of the Rhine is steady, making navigation possible. Thanks to great improvements during the last 100 years or more, big lighters can be towed as far as Basle, thereby giving Switzerland an outlet to the sea. The Rhine is linked by canal to the Rhône, which flows into the Mediterranean. Another canal joins it to the Marne, a tributary of the Seine, which flows into the Channel; the Seine in turn is similarly joined to the Loire. Lastly, one of the tributaries of the Rhine, the Main, is joined by canal to the Danube, and thus to the Black Sea. These important rivers and their connections thus make up a great system of international inland waterways, which link the North Sea with the Mediterranean and the Atlantic with the Black Sea.

The Rhine flows through some of the most productive industrial regions in all Europe, and carries more traffic than any other river in the world.

The Danube is a still longer river than the Rhine, flowing some 1,700 miles (2,730 km) from its source in Germany to the Black Sea, yet from the viewpoint of navigation it is much less important. This is for two reasons. First, it flows through a less populated, much less industrialised part of Europe in a direction unfavourable for trade. Secondly, the flow varies greatly with the seasons. In the spring, when the snow melts, the current is so strong that it is a hard task for tugs to tow lighters upstream. In addition, the river is often frozen over in winter.

There are 3,020 miles (4,832 km) of navigable rivers and canals in Holland.

The hot summers and mild winters of the Mediterranean make it an ideal tourist centre.

UNION OF SOVIET SOCIALIST REPUBLICS

Europe
miles
0   100   200   300   400   500
0   160   320   480   640   800
kilometres
© Copyright 1960 by Map Projects Inc.

CASPIAN SEA

IRAN

IRAQ

SYRIA

LEBANON

BLACK SEA

Sea of Azov

T U R K E Y

Bosporus

Dardanelles

Rhodes

Aegean Sea

Crete

ROMANIA

BULGARIA

GREECE

Ionian Sea

FINLAND

White Sea

Lake Ladoga

Gulf of Finland

Gulf of Bothnia

Baltic Sea

POLAND

CZECHOSLOVAKIA

HUNGARY

YUGOSLAVIA

ALB.

Adriatic Sea

S W E D E N

Berlin

GER. DEM. REP.

AUSTRIA

SAN MARINO

I T A L Y

Sardinia

Tyrrhenian Sea

Sicily

MALTA

MEDITERRANEAN

TUNISIA

N O R W A Y

VESTERALEN ISLANDS

Arctic Circle

GER. FED. REP.

SWITZ.   LIECHT.

MONACO

Corsica

BALEARIC ISLANDS

ALGERIA

NORWEGIAN

SEA

FAEROE ISLANDS

SHETLAND ISLANDS

ORKNEY ISLANDS

NORTH SEA

DENMARK

NETH.

BELG.

LUXEMBOURG

FRANCE

ANDORRA

SPAIN

MOROCCO

ICELAND

GREAT BRITAIN

English Channel

Bay of Biscay

PORTUGAL

Strait of Gibraltar

NORTHERN IRELAND

IRELAND

A T L A N T I C   O C E A N

70°

60°

50°

40°

30°

20°

10°

0°

10°

20°

30°

20°

30°

40°

50°

45°

40°

35°

50°

45°

40°

35°

60°

55°

60°

55°

50°

40°

30°

20°

10°

0°

10°

20°

18

Peoples of Europe

The ancient Bronze Age peoples of Europe were pushed to the west by invading tribes from the east who usually had more unified civilisations and more powerful iron weapons.

The Celts are an example of such early inhabitants. Their descendants in our day include the Bretons (Brittany), the Irish, Welsh, Scots, and the people of the Isle of Man and Cornwall. These Celtic people all live on islands or peninsulas in Western Europe, where they were forced by stronger tribes from the east.

Each of these groups of Celts had its own language. Some of these languages have disappeared, while others, such as Breton, Welsh, and Gaelic, may still be heard.

The Romans, in the days of their greatness, ruled and colonised much of Europe, especially the south and west. The French, the Spanish, Portuguese, Italians, and Romanians speak languages of Latin origin.

In Britain the invading Angles, Saxons, and Danes wiped out almost all trace of the Roman tongue and culture. Similar invasions wiped out Latin in other parts of Europe where Rome had ruled peoples of different languages and cultures.

Many of the 'Barbarians' that invaded the Roman Empire were of Germanic stock. They are represented today by the English, Dutch, German, and Scandinavian peoples.

After the Germanic invasions, tribes that spoke Slavic languages came from Asia and settled in Eastern Europe. Descended from them are the Russians, Poles, Czechs, Slovaks, Serbs, Croats, Slovenes, and Bulgarians.

Thus we see that today the three great

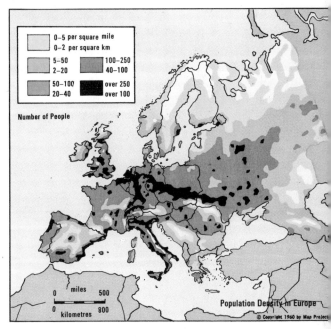

Number of People

0–5 per square mile	
0–2 per square km	
5–50	100–250
2–20	40–100
50–100	over 250
20–40	over 100

miles 500
kilometres 800

Population Density in Europe

© Copyright 1960 by Map Project

language and cultural groups of Europe are the Romance (derived from Latin), the Germanic, and the Slavic.

The influence of the culture of ancient Rome is still shown in the alphabet we use: all the countries of Western Europe use the same alphabet that the Romans did. When the Slavs invaded Europe, Roman culture had lost much of its influence. But it was still strong enough to give its alphabet to the most westerly

In their mountain villages, Bulgarian women still wear traditional national costume.

Copenhagen is one of the most beautiful cities of Northern Europe. This view shows the centre of the city.

Slavs: that is, the Poles, Czechs, and Slovenes.

The tribes of the east, however, did not adopt the Roman alphabet. In the ninth century the monk Cyril invented an alphabet based on Greek as well as Roman letters. This Cyrillic alphabet is the one used today by the Serbs, Croats, Bulgarians, and Russians.

There are also several smaller groups of European peoples. The modern Greeks long ago drove out or conquered

These traditional flat loaves of bread are sold in the street markets of Spain.

the original inhabitants and settled in Greece. They still live there and on the nearby Aegean Islands. In ancient days far-flung Greek colonies were scattered over the Mediterranean Sea, especially in Sicily and Italy. The name 'Naples' (*Napoli*) comes from two Greek words meaning 'New City'.

Today there are many descendants of the Greeks scattered from Spain to Istanbul. But the language and way of life of these early Greek settlers have been assimilated with those of the populations that came after them.

Other smaller groups are the Finns and the Hungarians. The Finns, whose culture now is very like that of the Scandinavians, have a quite different language. It is related to Estonian and to Hungarian. Both of these peoples also have their own language and way of life.

Besides the Hungarians in Hungary, groups of Hungarians are found also in Yugoslavia and in Romania. The Turks, who once conquered all Europe as far as Vienna, are now confined to an area around Istanbul in the south-east of Europe. They have their own language and culture. So have the Albanians who live in the rugged uplands north-west of Greece.

Most Europeans are fair-skinned. Many of those who live in the north are tall and have blue eyes and light hair. Southerners tend to be shorter with dark eyes and hair.

Thousands of years have gone by since the first men came into Europe. In that time tribes have conquered tribes and nations have conquered nations. Victors and vanquished have mingled and intermarried. And the blood of Greek and Roman, Celt, German, and Slav is now widely spread throughout the whole continent of Europe.

The Houses of Parliament and Big Ben: the political hub of Great Britain.

The Principal Cities of Europe

London, the greatest city in Europe, was originally built by the Romans at the lowest crossing point of the Thames. No other city can approach the variety of London, a quality stemming from the fact that it is not only a great centre of population and the cultural centre of the British Isles, but also the political hub of Britain and the Commonwealth, and a great industrial and commercial city.

Most of London has been built over the last 100 years, but there are many historic buildings, including the Tower, Westminster Abbey, St Paul's Cathedral, etc. Perhaps the most famous physical feature of London is its parks, which bring something of the countryside right into the very heart of the enormous urban area.

London is the leading industrial concentration in Britain; 21 per cent of all British workers are employed in the London area, chiefly in light industry. The great Port of London is the largest port in the United Kingdom, covering 92 miles (148 km) of the tidal Thames. It includes the container docks at Tilbury. The building of container ships, with their whole containers which can be moved rapidly from ship to lorry or train at special port termini, has also meant that many smaller ports in Britain, with container facilities, now handle a larger share of her trade.

Well over 7 million people live within Greater London, which stretches 21 miles (34 km) from north to south and 15 miles (24 km) from east to west. However, in the heart of this great expanse is the original City of London, measuring a single square mile (2½ sq km). This tiny area is one of the greatest commercial and banking centres of the world, the home of the Bank of England, the Stock Exchange, and many great banks.

Copenhagen is the capital of Denmark. It is one of the most beautiful cities in Europe, famous for its canals, statues and historic buildings.

Stockholm, the capital of Sweden, with its modern industry, fast motorways and prosperous buildings, has replaced Copenhagen as the commercial focus of Scandinavia.

Rotterdam is situated 19 miles (30 km) inland, connected with the sea by a deep-water canal called the New Waterway. At present Rotterdam handles more than three-quarters of Holland's trade, and forms – together with its satellite ports, Schiedam, Vlaardingen, and Hoek van Holland (the Hook of Holland) – the chief port in all Europe. Europoort is the largest artificial harbour and one of the busiest ports in the world. It handled 34,000 sea-going vessels and about 300,000 barges in 1975. 310 sea-going vessels are able to use its facilities simultaneously, and in 1975, 300,000,000 metric tons of seaborne cargo were handled. This included

The statue of Hans Christian Andersen's famous Little Mermaid, Copenhagen, Denmark.

330,000 containers unloaded from ships.

Thousands of ships call every year at Rotterdam, where many shipping companies have their headquarters.

Though Paris is a great political and economic centre, its chief claim to fame is in the field of culture, of which it can be truly stated to be among the capitals of the world. The art collections of the Louvre and the Museum of Modern Art are unrivalled.

Much of the inimitable atmosphere of Paris comes from the river Seine which runs through it, and among the most famous landmarks are the Gothic cathedral of Notre-Dame, the enormous palace of the Louvre, the church of Sacré-Coeur in Montmartre, the Arc de Triomphe commemorating Napoleon's victories, and the Eiffel Tower. The tree-lined boulevards of Paris are some of the most beautiful streets ever built.

Built on seven hills on the banks of the Tiber, Rome is the capital of Italy and also embraces the independent Vatican City, the centre of the Roman Catholic Church.

Rome – the Eternal City – is richer in historical remains than any other place in the world. Contrasting with such buildings as the Forum and Colosseum of classical days are the many splendid palaces and churches of the Renaissance, the most outstanding of which is St Peter's. This was chiefly the work of Michelangelo, who also painted the ceiling of the Sistine Chapel in the Vatican. The work was started in 1508 and took four years to accomplish. It is generally regarded as one of the greatest artistic works of all time.

No capital city is more important than Moscow, the capital and greatest city of the Soviet Union. The administrative

Europoort, Rotterdam. The world's largest artificial harbour and a leading container port.

A general view across Rome – the Eternal City.

and governmental departments are concentrated within the Kremlin, the historic centre of the Russian State. It was from the Kremlin that Ivan the Terrible united the whole of Russia, becoming the first Czar. He and his successors imported architects from Italy, Germany, Holland, and England to design and build palaces and churches and monasteries. Despite this, the Kremlin is essentially Russian – blending European with Asiatic.

Most of residential Moscow is modern, and today the city is also a great centre of industry.

Apart from the historic legacy of the Czars, Moscow has one world-famous landmark that is twentieth-century and entirely Soviet – the Tomb of Lenin in Red Square, which is the great shrine of modern Russia.

The traditional skyline of Paris has been transformed recently by modern building.

The Kremlin, Moscow, once the palace of the Czars and now the centre of the Soviet State.

An example of one of the effects of glaciation on landscape: lakes and islands in Finland.

Northern Europe

Of the four Scandinavian states the two largest, Norway and Sweden, form a long peninsula attached in the north to Finland and Russia. Denmark, another peninsula, is attached to Germany. Iceland is an island formerly belonging to Denmark. The shores of these countries are washed by four seas: the Baltic Sea, the North Sea, the Atlantic Ocean, and the Arctic Ocean.

The outstanding physical feature consists of the backbone of mountains which runs from north to south along the entire length of the peninsula, between a height of 3,000 feet (900 m) and 8,000 feet (2,440 m). During the great Ice Ages these were deeply scored by glaciers, which cut out fiords – deep inlets, shallow at the seaward end – and innumerable islands, along the Atlantic coast. Some of the mountains still have small glaciers.

Agriculture cannot be carried out over large areas of northern Scandinavia, due

ARCTIC OCEAN

BARENTS S

North Cape

Hammerfest

Varanger Fiord

Kirkenes

ICELAND

Isafjordur
Siglufjordur
Olafsfjordur
Akureyri
Seydisfjordur
Neskaupstadur
Breida Fiord
HvitaR.
Thjorsa R.
Vatnajokull
(Glacier)
Reykjavik
Hafnarfjordur
FlaxaBay

72°
66°
70°
64°
68°

miles
0   100
kilometres
0   160

24°   22°   20°   18°   16°   14°

ATLANTIC OCEAN

NORWEGIAN SEA

LOFOTEN ISLANDS

Arctic Circle

Senja
Tromso
Kautokeino
Ivalo
Lake Inari

Hinnoy
Harstad
Narvik
Kiruna
Muonio
Kittilä
Muonio R.

Vest Fiord
Bodo
Sulitjelma
Malmberget
Porjus Gallivare
Lonsdal
Kuusamo

Mo
Hemnesberget
Haparanda
Kemi
Pudasjärvi
Oulu
Lulea

Vega
Lake Stor
Boliden
Ronnskar
Skelleftea
Raahe
Kajaani
Iisalmi
Lake Pielinen

Leka
Mosjoen
Roa Lake

UNION OF SOVIET SOCIALIST REPUBLICS

Namsos
Steinkjer
Levanger
Vilhelmina
Lycksele
Asele
Umea

Trondheim Fiord
Kristiansund
Molde
Trondheim
Fannrem
Ostersund
Vaasa
Lake Keitele
Kuopio
Lake Kalla

Alesund
Tynset
Sveg
Sundsvall
Harnosand
Kristinestad
Lake Päijänne
Varkaus
Savonlinna
Mikkeli
Lake Saima

Dombas
Lake Näsi
Tampere
Heinola
Imatra
Lappeenranta

Sogne Fiord
Sarna
Bollnas
Soderhamn
Pori
Valkeakoski
Hämeenlinna
Lahti
Kouvola
Lake Ladoga

Voss
Gol
Ringsaker
Trysil
Elverum
Hamar
Alvdalen
Mora
Malung
Falun
Gavle
Rauma
Riihimäki
Kotka

Bergen
Odda
Honefoss
Eidsvoll
Borlange
Sandviken
Uusikaupunki
Turku
Salo

Rjukan
Drammen
Oslo
Sunne
Eda
Arvika
Fagersta
Avesta
Uppsala
Porkkala
Helsinki

Haugesund
Rauland
Kongsberg
Notodden
Horten
Moss
Karlstad
Karlskoga
Vasteras
Koping
Sundbyberg
Solna
ALAND ISLANDS
Gulf of Finland

Skien
Tonsberg
Sarpsborg
Fredrikstad
Eskilstuna
Lidingo

Stavanger
Porsgrunn
Larvik
Halden
Orebro
Sodertalje
Stockholm

Flekkefjord
Bygland
Katrineholm
Finspang

Egersund
Farsund
Arendal
Lillesand
Kristiansand
Vanersborg
IJddevalla
Trollhattan
Lidkoping
Skovde
Motala
Nykoping
Norkoping

Lindesnes
Skagerrak
Falkoping
Alingsas
Linkoping

Goteborg
Molndal
Boras
Huskvarna
Jonkoping
Vastervik
Visby
Gotland

Hjorring
Skene
Varberg
Varnamo
Oskarshamn

Thisted
Dronninglund
Halmstad
Vaxjo
Kalmar
Oland

Lemvig
Aalborg
Hobro
Markaryd
Karlshamn

Ringkobing
Holstebro
Viborg
Randers
Hoganas
Karlskrona

Silkeborg
Aarhus
Helsingor
Halsingborg
Kristianstad

DENMARK
Vejle
Horsens
Fredericia
Roskilde
Landskrona

Esbjerg
Kolding
Odense
Copenhagen
Zealand
Malmo

Sonderborg
Fyn
Svendborg
Naestved
Ystad

Nakskov
Falster
Trelleborg
Bornholm

Lolland

NORTH SEA
Kattegat

BALTIC SEA

N. AFRICA

GER. FED. REP.
GER. DEM. REP.
POLAND

10°   14°   18°   22°   26°

Northern Europe

miles
0   50   100   150   200
kilometres
0   80   160   240   320

⦿ National Capitals

Inset (above): This map shows the relationship of northern Europe to the European continent.

© Copyright 1960 by Map Projects Inc.

to the adverse physical factors of steep slopes, poor soils and the harsh climate. Apart from localised grazing and hay cropping round the settlements, it is only in the southern parts of these countries and throughout Denmark that extensive farming can be practised. Crops in the northern latitudes ripen owing to the fact that the continual daylight of the summer months compensates for the absence of hot sunshine.

Of the four Scandinavian states, Sweden, with an area of over 170,000 square miles (440,000 sq km), and 8.1 million inhabitants, is the largest, and the richest. Agriculture in the southern region is able to supply most of the country's food requirements.

Industry is very varied, including the mining of iron, copper, and other metals, and the exploitation of the country's timber, much of which is exported in the form of pulp for paper-making. The energy needed for industry is derived from hydro-electric power stations. Exports include machinery, cars, and precision electrical goods, furniture and iron ore.

The chief trading port is Göteborg at the northern end of the Kattegat from which ships sail through the Skagerrak to reach the North Sea.

The capital, Stockholm, besides being the political and administrative centre, has, like London, acquired a considerable amount of industry, particularly in the new electrical products.

Norway has a population of almost 4 millions, fewer than either Sweden or Denmark. Though there is a broad area in the south-east where farming is possible, over 70 per cent of the total area is barren, and 20 per cent of the remainder forest. On the other hand the Atlantic coast is deeply indented, there being

Oslo, the capital of Norway, is beautifully situated at the head of a fiord. The royal palace is in the background.

A Lapp woman working on reindeer hide from which boots will be made.

some 12,000 miles (19,200 km) of fiords and consequently Norway has always been a maritime country, with fisher-farmer settlements all along the rugged coast.

Of the working population 1.8 per cent is engaged in fishing, either for cod and herring off the coast, or for whales in the

Antarctic. Norway possesses the fourth largest merchant fleet in the world, after Liberia, Japan, and Britain. Fish-products and the products of Norway's forests, particularly woodpulp, are principal exports. Norway has some iron ore, and some recently discovered off-shore oil deposits at Stavanger. There is a growing amount of heavy industry, particularly in electro-chemical machinery. Mining and manufacturing employ 34 per cent of the working population. These industries are powered by hydro-electricity and exports include chemicals, fertilizers and transport equipment.

In the far north of Norway occurs the phenomenon of the Midnight Sun – in summer the sun does not set for eleven weeks. This region, called Lapland, is inhabited by the Lapps, who live off their large herds of reindeer.

Oslo, the capital, with a population of under half a million, is beautifully

Another example of the effects of glaciation. Sogne Fiord, Norway. The fiords were formed when valleys carved by glaciers were filled with sea water at the end of the Ice Age.

Göteborg is an industrial and shipbuilding town as well as being Sweden's chief port.

Stockholm, Sweden, is built on islands. Men still fish with these round nets in the heart of the city.

A Danish farmhouse. Agriculture plays a vital part in the economy, although the number of farm workers has declined rapidly.

situated at the head of a fiord, 80 miles (130 km) from the sea. Besides being an administrative and commercial centre, it is an industrial town, with shipbuilding yards and factories producing a wide range of goods, including textiles, paper, sail-cloth, hardware, etc.

Denmark, which became a member of the EEC (European Economic Community) in 1973, stands at the entrance to the Baltic, and provides a stepping stone between northern Europe and Germany. With an area of over 16,000 square miles (43,000 sq km) it has a population of 5 million people, about a quarter of whom live in the capital.

Denmark is low lying and flat, its soil is rich, and it is accordingly above all an agricultural country. The surplus produce – butter, milk, eggs, and bacon – is exported to nearby industrial countries. There are few countries in the world where the soil is so intensively cultivated or where stock-breeding and dairy production have reached so high a standard. This is partly due to the very high standard of education of those who work on the land, and also to the advanced system of co-operative marketing. Denmark

Hydro-electric plants use the steep mountain streams of Scandinavia to generate electricity for homes and factories.

produces one-third of the butter sold in the world.

Industry is developing in spite of the need to import a large proportion of raw materials needed. Food processing, engineering, glass, textiles and agricultural machinery are the biggest industries.

29

Copenhagen, the capital, is situated on the low-lying eastern shore of the island of Zealand. It is an old town which has suffered much destruction in the course of its long history, but it has always been quick to recover.

Finland has always been a border country between two worlds. From the Middle Ages to 1808, Finland was under Swedish domination. Then the country came under Russian rule, and did not become entirely independent until 1917.

Finland is mainly a country of forests and lakes. The climate is more continental than that of Sweden. Although the cultivated area is only 9 per cent of the total land area, agriculture is one of the main occupations. Rye, barley, spring wheat and vegetables are the chief crops.

More than a tenth of the country is occupied by lakes, some of vast size. At the turn of the century, lakes and marsh-

Denmark exports cheese and other dairy products all over the world.

land occupied a quarter of the country, but the marshes are progressively being reclaimed. Finland is the most forested

Nine per cent of the total area of Finland is cultivated, but agriculture is one of the main occupations of the people. Only 51 per cent of the population lives in towns.

The town of Rovaniemi in Finland lies exactly on the Arctic Circle. This picture shows that modern life goes on even in these northern latitudes.

country in Europe, and the greater part of its industry is concerned with wood-products, such as paper and plywood, prefabricated houses, etc. Finland is also famous for high-quality domestic goods, such as furniture, glass, textiles, etc. Finland has iron and copper deposits and these are processed using hydro-electricity in growing manufacturing areas. Helsinki is the capital, and the other large towns are Tampere and Turku. The lakes, linked by canals, provide a great system of inland waterways mainly for transporting timber. The Finns have an extensive fishing industry, and have recently started making ice-breaker ships.

With the whole country lying within a few degrees of the Arctic Circle, Iceland may be regarded as the most northerly country of Europe. It is a mountainous country with few trees and with an ice-

Norway possesses the fourth largest merchant fleet in the world. Only a small percentage of the total land area is suitable for cultivation, and this is confined to narrow strips in deep valleys and around fiords and lakes.

The fisheries form the basis of Iceland's economy. The men catch the fish and women workers do the sorting and cleaning.

Two Danish children play in a public garden in Copenhagen.

These Icelandic children are the descendants of Viking settlers.

Finnish lumbermen collect logs on Lake Päijänne, one of the 'Finger Lakes' of Finland.

field covering one-eighth of its surface. It is chiefly famous, however, for its many volcanoes and hot springs or geysers. Today the power of these geysers has been harnessed and one Icelander in four has his house heated from this source; while, in greenhouses similarly heated, bananas grow. Sulphur springs and lakes of boiling mud are common in volcanic districts. Earthquakes are frequent.

With little cultivable land, and no minerals the Icelanders' chief income is from fishing. To protect her only natural resource she is trying to extend her fishing rights round her coast.

About 84,000 people are concentrated in the capital, Reykjavik, a modern port in the south-west of the island, where an aluminium plant began production in 1969.

Cattle grazing beside a Scottish loch: some of the finest cattle in the world are bred in Scotland.

Western Europe

The British Isles

On 1 January 1973, Great Britain signed the Treaty of Rome and became a member of the EEC. This community of nine European nations is pledged to achieve full political, economic and monetary union by 1980. Born out of the devastation of two world wars, the ideal of a united Europe has dominated European politics for the past two decades. Great Britain, while remaining faithful to traditional friendships and alliances, is eager to play a full part in Europe.

In few other countries is there such a variation of landscape as in the British Isles. Looking at a map of the island, it would be difficult to guess the outline of its three divisions – England, Scotland and Wales.

Scotland is sharply divided into the Highlands and the Lowlands. The Highlands of Scotland are famous as areas of great natural beauty and for the cattle bred there. The Highlands include Ben Nevis, which at 4,406 feet (1,340 m) is the highest mountain in Great Britain. However, most of the population, industry, and agriculture of Scotland is concentrated in the Lowlands, and along the eastern coast where the oil industry is developing.

Wales presents an almost solid block of mountains, whose highest peak, Snowdon, is 3,560 feet (1,085 m) high. Other regions in Great Britain which are extensively hilly are Northumberland, Cumbria, Derbyshire, Devon, Cornwall, and parts of Yorkshire.

The south and east of England consists of plains interspersed with modest ranges of hills like the North and South

Downs, the Cotswolds, the Chilterns, the Quantocks and the Mendips.

London reflects the whole history of England; it is immense and was for long the largest city in the world. The population of Greater London is at present almost 8 million. The London of the City and the West End is known to all. The Port of London extends down the Thames to Tilbury, and includes the vast new container port there. Today less and less cargo is coming into the Pool of London and the warehousing area is scheduled for redevelopment.

No place in Britain is more than 100 miles (160 km) from the sea, and this fact has shaped British history, in the same way as it has always influenced the climate. The climate of Britain is well-known: frequent rather than heavy rainfall, no great extremes of temperature, a tendency to fog and cloud. All this is the result of the fact that the sea is so close to all parts of the British Isles.

Historically, the sea has brought the various races that became the British – Celts, Romans, Angles, Saxons, Danes, and Normans – and the sea also inspired Englishmen to rove the world, establishing trade, creating colonies, and building empires. Britain has a coastline of 5,000 miles (8,000 km) – twice as long as France.

Today most of the former British Empire has achieved independence – generally within the Commonwealth. But the maritime tradition continues, and the British merchant fleet is the third largest in the world, with a tonnage of 31 million tons.

Out of all British workers, only 3 per cent are employed on the land or in fishing, compared to France's 20 per cent, and 23 per cent in Italy. Of all the agricultural land of Britain, about a third

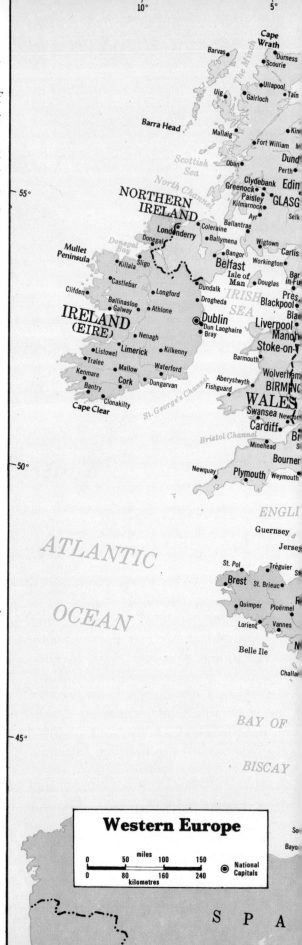

Inset (above): This map shows the relationship of western Europe to the European continent.

Britain has long been among the world leaders in the peaceful uses of atomic energy. The nuclear power station at Bradwell opened in 1962 and produces 300 megawatts of electricity.

is under the plough, mostly in the lowlands of the south and east. The rest consists of pastures, moorlands, etc. In any case the moist climate makes the country unsuitable for growing wheat except in the south-east. Accordingly many farmers go in for dairy-farming, poultry, and vegetables. Though British farming is excellently organized and highly productive, the large population means that Britain can supply only two-thirds of her own food needs.

British fisherman bring in over a million tons of fish a year, much of it from the shallow Dogger Bank in the North Sea and limited waters round Iceland. The principal fishing ports are Hull, Grimsby, Aberdeen, Yarmouth, Lowestoft, and Fleetwood.

The principal industrial regions of Great Britain are: (A.) The Midlands, Yorkshire, and Lancashire. The northern part specialised largely in textiles: wool in Leeds, Bradford, Halifax, and Huddersfield; cotton in Manchester and other Lancashire towns. However, with the advent of artificial fibres, more and more textile mills are being converted to other light industries. Heavy industry exists too, shipbuilding for instance, at Birkenhead and Barrow-in-Furness, and steelworks at Sheffield and Rotherham. Coal is mined in the Yorkshire-Nottinghamshire field, and recently a whole new very deep seam has been discovered round York and Selby. Round Birmingham, in the midst of what is known as the Black Country, engineer-

A chequered pattern of small fields, gently rolling hills – the unmistakably English countryside of Cornwall.

Ebbw Vale in the South Wales coalfield. High quality coal is mined in this area.

ing and hardware manufacture are centred. A vast range of goods, especially metal goods, are produced in this great manufacturing area and in the neighbouring towns of Wolverhampton and Walsall. Coventry and surrounding towns specialise in cycles and cars, while Sheffield is famous for its cutlery. Liverpool serves as the chief port for this region, though the Manchester Ship Canal enables sea-going ships to reach Manchester, 30 miles (48 kms) inland.

(B.) South Wales. This area is chiefly famous for its coalfields, which produce hard, smokeless coal of the highest quality, and for its great steel industry, located at Port Talbot, Cardiff, and elsewhere. The tinplate industry of Swansea and Llanelly consumes much of the steel and also uses imported tin ore. This area also has several large oil refineries.

(C.) The north-east region of Tyne and Wear and Cleveland is famous for iron and steel manufacture, shipbuilding, making oil rigs and an important chemicals industry, and coal is mined on Tyne and Wear Side.

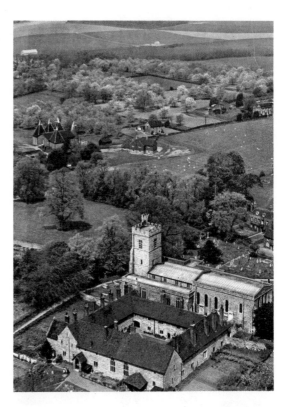

Lush meadows and a fine church in the south of England. The park-like landscape is the result of centuries of skilled farming. The buildings with sharply pointed roofs in the background are oast houses. They are used for drying hops.

37

The growth of container ports, like Tilbury at the mouth of the Thames, has led to the phasing out of traditional docking methods.

(D.) The Clyde. A wide range of manufactures is concentrated in Glasgow and its neighbouring towns, including textiles, heavy engineering, cars, aero and marine engines, chemical products, and iron and steel. Shipbuilding was the main industry along the Clyde but now oil rig construction is developing.

(E.) London. Until recently there was relatively little industry in London. Its importance was in the first place political and administrative, but it has always been a commercial centre. It has also for long been a world-famous financial centre, that is to say a great centre of banking, insurance, and the buying and selling of shares on the Stock Exchange. It has grown rapidly as an industrial centre. Heavy industries include car manufacture and cement. Light industries, such as radios, refrigerators, computers, clothing and food processing have developed. In the past twenty years industry has been moving out of London to the ring of new towns surrounding it. Also the administrative work of government departments has been moving to development areas to take employment out of London.

Besides the industrial areas already described, there are many other smaller industrial centres. One of these is Bristol which houses an important aircraft industry including Concorde.

Cumbernauld in Scotland is an example of a new town where modern planning methods have been put into operation.

A piper leading a wedding procession in Scotland.

Most of London's exclusive shops are found in Bond Street.

Oil in Britain

The recent discovery of oil and natural gas, in extensive deposits in the North Sea, is very important for Britain. Many British and overseas oil companies have shares in specific areas of the North Sea and are now prospecting and commencing production.

The North Sea itself is the biggest obstacle to be overcome: the continental shelf is very deep for standing rigs on; the

A refinery in Wales. Until North Sea oil, Britain depended on imports from the Middle East.

weather can be atrocious; the work is very dangerous; and the work-force has to remain isolated for weeks at a time. This makes prospecting and production a very different matter from land drilling and much more expensive.

Oil began to go ashore for the first time at the end of 1975, when 1.1 million metric tons were landed at Grangemouth in Scotland. By the end of 1978, Britain will have one quarter of all her needs (15–20 million tons) and by 1980, with an estimated production of 95–115 million tons, Britain is expected to have a surplus.

Natural gas, from the North Sea, has been used for several years by householders and industry in many parts of Britain. In 1975 it accounted for 17 per cent of fuel consumed in Britain.

Apart from simply providing fuel, the discovery of oil off Britain has meant: the establishment of new industries for making rigs, girders, pipes and much complex equipment; export of these to other oil producing countries; and new jobs for people, especially in Scotland, where 50,000 people employed in oil, can hope for a new prosperity.

Peat from peat bogs is a very widely used fuel in Ireland. Only ten years are needed to form peat from decaying vegetation.

The discovery of oil in British offshore waters has led to the setting up of many new industries.

Ireland

Ireland, with its soft, humid climate, is traditionally a country of grassland for livestock rearing, peat-bogs, and potato fields. The island is divided into the Republic of Ireland (Eire) and Northern Ireland (Ulster), which is part of the United Kingdom.

O'Connell Street, Dublin. This elegant capital city is world famous for the quality of its Georgian architecture.

The Republic of Ireland is much the larger of the two territories. But Northern Ireland is far more densely populated: 1½ million people in 5,461 square miles (14,143 sq km) compared to Eire's 3 million in 26,600 square miles (68,893 sq km).

Until recently there was very little industry in Eire, which joined the EEC in 1973, but there has been an increase in the interest from other European countries, notably West Germany, and today there is a growing volume of industry in the Irish Republic.

In Northern Ireland, which is part of the United Kingdom, industry has developed, especially round Belfast, the capital. The principal industries are shipbuilding, linen, and artificial textiles. These are suffering in the 1970s because of continuous civil strife in the province.

There is a great contrast between Dublin and Belfast. Dublin is still an essentially eighteenth-century city, and was the capital of Ireland before its division in 1920. Belfast, on the other hand, grew during the nineteenth century.

Windmills are a traditional feature of the Dutch landscape, though they are rapidly being replaced by modern pumping machinery. The pumps are necessary to prevent flooding.

The Benelux Countries

The three Benelux countries, Belgium, the Netherlands (Holland), and Luxembourg, have a total area of only 25,930 square miles (67,158 sq km), but they are the most densely populated countries in Europe, with over 23 million inhabitants. If they are taken as one unit they constitute the fourth richest economic power in the world.

Since 1948, when a customs union was formed, the Benelux countries have been moving steadily towards full union, thereby setting an example to the other members of the European Common Market.

Holland and Belgium are often bracketed together as the Low Countries. A good deal of the coastlines of both countries can be as much as 10 feet (3 m) below sea-level, the sea being kept at bay by sea-walls or dykes. About a quarter of Holland's arable land has been reclaimed from the sea – these reclaimed lands are called polders. The centre part of the Belgium-Holland coast is occupied by the extensive deltas of the Rhine, the Meuse, and the Scheldt.

In the southernmost region of the Benelux group we find the hills and forests of the Ardennes, whose average height is less than 1,600 feet (490 m).

Luxembourg has for long been an independent Grand Duchy. It consists of a plateau furrowed by valleys and wedged in between France, Germany, and Belgium. With an area of 1,000 square miles (2,600 sq km) it has a population of about 352,700. It is rich in iron ore and the mining and smelting of this metal is, with agriculture, the chief industry.

The capital, in which over a fifth of the population lives, is also called Luxembourg. Besides being the seat of government it is the seat of the High Authority of the European Coal and Steel Community, a body which co-ordinates the production and marketing of coal and steel in Luxembourg, Belgium, the Netherlands, West Germany, France, Italy, Britain, the Irish Republic, and Denmark.

Belgium. This tree-lined canal runs from Bruges to Damme.

A barge with a cargo of flowers passing a tulip field in Holland. The flowers are of secondary importance, whereas the bulbs are a major source of revenue.

Eighteenth-century houses in Amsterdam, one of the most beautiful cities of Northern Europe.

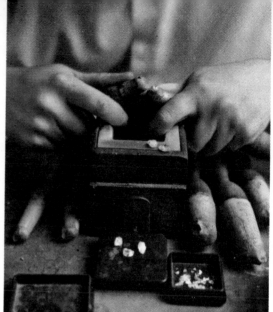

Rotterdam is an international centre for diamonds. Great skill is needed to cut and polish them.

Belgium

Belgium only became an independent country in 1830. The kingdom is a union of two peoples: the Flemings from the north (Flanders), and the Walloons from the southern provinces. The Flemings speak their own language, Flemish, while the Walloons are French-speaking.

The capital, Brussels, with over 1 million inhabitants, is situated in the middle of the country, where the two groups meet. It is now the headquarters of the EEC.

Belgium is above all an industrial and commercial country. Industry goes far back into the past, beginning with the old linen weavers of Flanders, and the armourers of Liège.

Like England, Belgium has its Black Country, which is centred on a line running from Mons through Charleroi, Namur, Huy, Seraing, to Liège. Alongside the pits of the coalfields are great blast furnaces and steel-works, chiefly at Charleroi and Liège. There are also glass-works and vast chemical factories. On the Campine coalfields are zinc and glass-works, cement-works, brick-yards, and factories for the making of chemical fertilisers.

Weaving is still a great industry in Flanders – though today all kinds of fibres are used, not only the traditional linen, at Ghent, Bruges, and Verviers.

Belgium is intensively cultivated and crop yields are high. The principal crops are wheat, rye, oats, barley, sugar-beet, flax, potatoes, and hops. Even so, Belgium, like England, has to import great quantities of foodstuffs. The greater part of Belgium's trade passes through Antwerp, one of the best equipped ports in Europe.

The Netherlands

Hard-working, conscientious, thrifty and business-like, the Dutch are equally at home on land and sea, and signs of their energy and enterprise are everywhere apparent. On the two great estuaries of the Scheldt, and the Maas, on the Waal, and inland on the innumerable canals, a constant traffic may be seen which exceeds that of the railways. Rotterdam and Amsterdam are ports of world-wide fame, providing evidence that this small country is of greater importance in the business world than many a big one.

Dutch agriculture, like Belgium's, is intensively developed and the yield per acre high, and, in fact, farming here plays a decidedly bigger part in the nation's economy than it does in Belgium. The soil of the polders is very rich. The two principal occupations are dairy-farming and market gardening and flower growing. A considerable amount of butter and cheese is exported, and large quantities of bulbs.

With a population of over 13½ millions and an area of some 13,000 square miles (33,800 sq km), (960 per square mile or 400 per sq km), Holland is quite incapable of producing all the food she needs.

Over the centuries the Dutch have fought a running battle with nature in order to reclaim more and more land from the sea, and then to defend what they had reclaimed. In particular, during this century, the map of Holland has undergone a marked change owing to one of the greatest enterprises ever undertaken by civil engineering, the reclamation of a large part of the former Zuider Zee. The idea, already projected in the seventeenth century, was put into operation a generation ago. This large but shallow estuary, covering an area of 2,000 square miles (5,180 sq km), was enclosed by a dam 18½ miles (29 km) long across the entrance, making it into an inland lake. By pumping the water out three huge polders have already been formed, adding some 410,000 acres

The main square at the heart of Brussels. With the establishment of the headquarters of the EEC Commission, Brussels has grown and prospered.

(166,000 hectares) to Holland's soil. Another polder is being reclaimed which will add another 14,800 acres (60,000 hectares) to the soil, making a total area of nearly 850 square miles (2,200 sq km). The name Zuider Zee has now been dropped, the remaining water being called Ijssel Meer. The Ijssel Meer is a fresh-water lake vital for irrigation.

The Delta project to dam the Scheldt and Lower Rhine estuaries is even more exciting. Under this, four massive dams and three secondary dams will close all but two of the deep-sea inlets of the Delta. The two left will serve the ports of Antwerp and Rotterdam. A great adjustable storm-barrier has been built near Capelle-on-the-Ijssel, north-east of Rotterdam, with sluice gates that can be lowered when the waterlevel is very high. The principal dams across the Haringvliet will also have adjustable sluices, and a small lock. The sluices are necessary to allow the tide waters to pass through the dams.

A small farmhouse in the Tarn gorge in southern France.

In addition three huge sluices are being built on the lower Rhine, which will control the distribution of fresh water, some of which will be directed into Lake Ijssel, which is part of the former Zuider Zee. Fresh water has been mentioned several times: it must be remembered that land reclamation by itself is valueless unless there is fresh water available for irrigation, since wherever land is below sea-level, as it always is in reclaimed areas, the ground-water will sometimes be salty, and therefore useless for crops.

When the project is fully completed in 1978 the coastline will have been shortened by 435 miles (700 km), the danger of floods in the south-west of Holland will have been reduced, and the area's fresh-water supply assured. Also, once the roads along the dams have been completed, the area, formerly rather iso-lated, will be opened up for development.

If her industry is prosperous, Holland is, still more, a commercial country. The Dutch have always been a great maritime nation and trade was greatly furthered by Holland's long rule over the greater part of the East Indies. Moreover, the Rhine, which reaches the sea in Holland, is itself a great commercial highway.

Amsterdam, the capital, and Holland's oldest and second largest port, is peculiar in that it is not the seat of government. The political and administrative centre is The Hague. Amsterdam is a world-famous centre of the diamond trade.

Rotterdam, under the name of Europoort, is the principal port of the Netherlands and the second largest in the world after New York. Its rise dates from the great development of the industry of the Rhineland and the great increase of traffic on the Rhine towards the end of the nineteenth century.

Many other towns in the Netherlands have large industrial developments, for example Eindhoven and Hilversum.

The greatest advance to the Netherlands' economy in recent years has been the discovery of huge amounts of natural gas off the coast north of Rotterdam.

France

Of all the countries of Europe, France is the one which presents the greatest variety of scene and climate.

There are three main areas: the first comprising two high mountain ranges – the Pyrenees in the south, and the Alps, running down from Mont Blanc (in Savoy) to the Mediterranean coast along the Italian frontier. There are also lower

The rich alluvial farmland of the lower Seine consists of soil washed down by the river.

mountain ranges – the Vosges, between France and Germany – and the Jura Mountains, running into Switzerland. There are broad lowlands in the north and west, and between the heights and the lowlands, a plateau, that reaches its greatest height in the Massif Central, and rises in its highest peaks to over 5,000 feet (1,500 m). Uranium is being worked in the Massif Central, and near La Rochelle.

With an area of over 200,000 square miles (550,000 sq km), France is the largest country of Western Europe and a great agricultural country. Ten per cent of the population is employed in agriculture. Much of the mountainous country is forested, but many of the lower slopes are used as pastures. In the lowlands, all branches of farming prosper, partly because of large subsidies given to the peasant part-time farmers all over France. On the arable land, a great deal

of wheat is grown. Vines are cultivated all over France but the most important areas are the regions of Champagne, Burgundy, and Bordeaux.

Paris, built on the banks of the Seine, is the principal city of France, and one of the great capitals of Europe. Paris has many historic buildings – the cathedral of Notre-Dame, the Law Courts, the Louvre, etc., but much of the city is of nineteenth-century origin: including the famous Boulevards and the even more famous Eiffel Tower. The growth of Paris was restricted for many years after 1840 by a ring of fortifications round the city. Since their demolition at the end of the First World War, the city has expanded rapidly, so that many of the population of more than 8 million live in fairly modern suburbs, where there is an expanding underground rail network. Few other major European states are centred so completely round their capitals as

A glacier on Mont Blanc, the highest mountain in Western Europe.

France is. Something of a gulf has always existed between the Parisians and the people from the provinces.

Industry and Trade

In the past most of France's industry was concentrated in the northern half of the country, because of the past reliance on coal and iron supplies at their source for the development of heavy industry. However, with oil now being important as a source of power, with increased transportation, and mobility of labour, industrial centres have become established over nearly all parts of France.

Today, 70 per cent of France's coal comes from the extreme north-west and the large iron ore mines are in the north-east in Alsace-Lorraine. Therefore it is natural that northern France is still important, for example there are great steelworks in Douai, Valenciennes, and Dunkirk. Manufactures include agricul-

tural machinery, railway equipment, chemicals, and textiles. Lille is the chief commercial centre.

Natural resources of the Alsace-Lorraine region apart from iron and some coal include potash in Alsace and salt deposits in Lorraine. Iron and steel is the most important industry in Lorraine, textiles in Alsace. The food-processing and brewing industries of this region are important. The chief town, Strasbourg, is the site of the EEC Parliament.

The Normandy region, situated between Dieppe and Cherbourg, has a large oil-refining industry. There are many petrol refineries round Rouen and Le Havre, particularly the latter. Le Havre is the chief port of the region and oil amounts to nine-tenths of its imports. It is also an important shipbuilding town, and its other industries include the manufacture of machinery, boilermaking, etc., and dyestuffs.

Although most of the oil used in France is imported, there is a local oilfield at Parentis in the Landes region and there are natural gas reserves in the Lacq region.

The Paris region, though without any natural resources, has, like all capitals, attracted a considerable amount of industry: in particular cars, light engineering, and consumer goods.

The chemical industry is very highly developed in the Lyons region, where four-fifths of French synthetic fibre is produced. The area is also a traditional centre of the silk industry. Other industrial towns in the Lyons region are Saint-Étienne: coal-mining, machinery, and electrical equipment; Le Creusot: armaments; Clermont-Ferrand: rubber; and Chalons-sur-Saône: copper castings.

The Toulouse region is important for aerospace industries. It is the French Concorde town.

France is the biggest producer of aluminium in Europe, and the mining and processing of bauxite (aluminium ore) is concentrated in the Marseilles region. The production of aluminium requires an enormous amount of electricity, consequently after the initial stages the aluminium is transported to factories in the Alps, and, to a lesser extent, the Pyrenees, where there is hydro-electric power.

Marseilles is one of the greatest ports of France. It imports enormous quantities of oil from the North African states, and has an important petro-chemical complex. Among its other industries, besides its part in the aluminium industry, there is shipbuilding and repair, tourism, food processing, and one of the oldest manufactures is soap.

Bordeaux is another important port, and from it large quantities of wine are shipped. Industries include the making of sulphur-phosphates and oil refining.

The UNESCO headquarters in Paris. This organisation has played a major part in improving the quality of education everywhere.

The grape harvest. The vine has one great advantage over other crops; the best wine always comes from very poor quality soil.

Jurisdiction of the corner of north-eastern France, known as Alsace-Lorraine, has frequently been disputed by France and Germany.

West Germany

With a total area not far short of 100,000 square miles (250,000 sq km) and a population of 62 million, West Germany has a fairly dense population. It is largely Protestant, though there is a majority of Catholics in Bavaria.

The northern part of the country is flat, and, in fact, on the North Sea coast rather like Holland. However, south of Brunswick, the Harz mountains rise to more than 3,000 feet (920 m); further south are the mountains of the Black Forest with the Feldberg, 4,700 feet (1,430 m), while on the Austrian frontier, the Bavarian Alps rise, in the Zugspitze, to 9,800 feet (3,000 m), this being Germany's highest mountain. Chief rivers are the Rhine (which has already been dealt with) and its tributaries the Main, Neckar, and Moselle. The other chief rivers are the Elbe, which serves the port of Hamburg and flows into the North Sea, and the Danube, which rises in the Black Forest and drains into the Black Sea. Of the many lakes, the largest, Lake Constance, is bounded by Germany, Switzerland, and Austria. The many forests in Germany are scientifically supervised by the state because of their wealth.

Industrial Germany

West Germany has shown an extraordinary power of recovery after the destruction of the Second World War. It is now the richest country of Western Europe, through the initiative of the population. For 50 miles (80 km) along the valley of the Ruhr, mines, blast-furnaces, and factories are in full production. On the Rhine a steady stream of lighters, many of them of 1,000 tons and more, are towed up and down the river. Hamburg, which suffered enormous destruction, is now restored, and once again in full activity as one of the greatest ports of Europe.

The chief industrial region of Federal Germany is the Ruhr. It employs 2.5 million workmen. 88 million metric tons of coal are produced yearly. Steel, using high quality iron ore from Scandinavia, together with its own ores, is produced at Dortmund, Duisburg, and Essen. Vast industrial complexes have developed over this whole single built-up area, which produces heavy machinery, many steel goods, vehicles, electrical and generating equipment, cables, chemical goods – in fact all the products required for great industrial expansion.

The Saar is very like the Ruhr on a smaller scale. In 1974, 9.2 million metric tons of coal was mined. Amongst its many manufactures are glassware and pottery.

The Rhineland contains many river

This coal mine at Essen in the Ruhr is only a small part of one of the greatest concentrations of industry in the world.

Medieval barons in castles like this one overlooking the Rhine, were able to enforce the payment of tolls on passing ships.

Heavy traffic on the Karlsruhe-Kassel autobahn near Frankfurt. Germany pioneered high-speed motorways in the 1930's.

ports and regional centres, including Cologne, best known for machinery, chemicals, and aluminium ware. It is near large lignite coalfields. Frankfurt and its neighbouring towns are best known for dye-stuffs, chemicals, machinery and cars; and Mannheim-Ludwigshafen, for chemicals and agricultural machinery.

There are large industrial towns in all parts of West Germany, such as Augsburg, Nuremberg, Hanover, Brunswick, Bremen, and Hamburg, which is a great port and trading centre. West Germany has oil fields in Lower Saxony.

With all this, agriculture is still very important in West Germany. In the north-west, there is a great deal of dairy-farming, and fruit-farming. In central Germany and the south are fertile farm-lands producing rich crops of wheat, bar-ley, oats, maize, sugar-beet, and

A vineyard in the Rhine valley near the Lorelei rock, famous in legend.

The Zugspitze, Germany's highest mountain, towers over this Alpine village.

Even in modern Germany old methods still survive − a Rhineland farmer ploughing with oxen.

The town of Heidelberg on the Neckar. Heidelberg is the home of one of the world's oldest universities.

potatoes. Famous wines come from the vineyards of the Rhine and Moselle valleys. Yet, even with highly mechanised farming and the extensive use of fertilisers, West Germany is quite unable to feed her large population.

Bright lights and traffic on the Kurfürstendamm, one of the main streets in West Berlin.

Most of West Berlin was rebuilt after the destruction of the Second World War.

A view of Hamburg, the largest port in Germany and one of the most important in Europe.

East Germany

The German Democratic Republic (East Germany, the DDR) has an area of 41,000 square miles (108,100 sq km) and a population of almost 17 million. Two-thirds of East Germany is devoted to agriculture, which is concentrated in two regions: the northern plain, most of which is glacial outwash sands and not very fertile; and Thuringia and Lower Saxony, which is rich farming land.

There is little coal in East Germany but, on the other hand, the country has two rich fields of lignite (brown coal). One lies in the basin of the Lower Saale in the Leipzig region, and the other in the basin of the Upper Spree.

The end of the Second World War when East Germany came under Communist rule saw her in a very bad position with regard to industry. The principal centres had always been in the west-ern part of the country to which she no longer had access. As it was, lignite and potassium salts (potash) were the only raw materials available in bulk. Nevertheless, great efforts were made at industrial redevelopment and new industry, almost all of which is State owned, accounts for 61 per cent of the national income. East Germany trades with the Communist world almost entirely. The most direct link is a pipeline from the USSR to Halle. At present East Germany ranks in the top ten industrial countries of the world.

Lignite is the most important of East Germany's resources. In fact the country is the world's chief supplier, mining 246 million metric tons a year. Lignite is used both for domestic heating and to fuel the DDR's power stations. Coke, made by a special process (itself an East German invention) from lignite, is used in the metallurgical industry, and lignite is also the raw material in the manufacture of

Body finishing plant at the Daimler-Benz factory at Sindelfingen, West Germany.

synthetic fibres and other products of the important chemical industry.

Though there is little iron-ore in East Germany, steel production, which had to start from scratch in 1945, is about 9 million metric tons a year. The chief steel works are at Halle and Eisenhüttenstadt.

Dependent on them are the mechanical engineering works at Magdeburg and Schmalkalden and the shipbuilding yards of Rostock and Wismar. Other important industries are the mining of uranium at Erzgebirge, the manufacture of optical instruments, and the world-

The high production levels in German industry are partly due to the use of modern plant.

Huge blocks of molten steel. Industry is the basis of German prosperity.

famous porcelain of Meissen.

The capital of East Germany is East Berlin (population 1 million). East Germany's second most important city is Leipzig. The annual Leipzig Fair is over 800 years old and one of the most important events in the European trade calendar. It is East Germany's principal commercial contact with its trading partners in non-communist countries.

One in nine people own a car in East Germany, one in three in West Germany.

The turbines at this coal-fired power station produce 2,000 megawatts of electricity.

The Leuna works, in Merseburg near Leipzig, East Germany, produce chemicals from coal.

The Spree at Berlin, with the industrial district on the left.

The celebrated Frankfurterallee in East Berlin was destroyed in the Second World War. It has been completely rebuilt.

Austria

The Federal Republic of Austria is all that is left of what was once a great empire. Hence its capital, Vienna, which is an important conference centre, has a population of 1¾ million, whereas there are only 7.4 million people in the whole country.

The eastern extension of the Alps occupies most of the country, with great facilities for winter sports and mountaineering. The highest peak is the Gross Glockner, 12,450 feet (3,800 m), and there are other peaks scarcely less high.

Austria can produce only three-fifths of her food. The rest has to be paid for through exports. A considerable advance has been made in industry, which is based primarily on timber and its products. Over two-fifths of Austria's 32,500 square miles (83,850 sq km) are forested; Austria comes third after Finland and Sweden in its production of timber. The most important industry derived from wood is paper-making. There is little coal, but a certain amount of lignite. Oil-wells have been working since 1936. Austria is rich in iron-ore and its export, combined with that of metal manufactures, is almost as important to the economy as that of the products of timber. Industry, chiefly centred in Vienna, Linz, and Graz, includes the manufacture of machinery, chemicals, and textiles. Austria is also one of the world's chief sources of high-quality graphite.

Great use is made of water-power, more than five-sixths of the country's electricity being hydro-electric. The rivers so far exploited for this purpose are the Inn, the Salzach, the Enns, and the Danube, which is also important for transporting industrial produce.

Until 1918 Austria was the centre of a great empire, but today her chief claim to fame is in the field of culture. Vienna, one of the most beautiful cities in Europe, is

Children playing on board one of the river craft that ply the Danube.

The cathedral of St Stephen towering above the roofs of Vienna. Situated on the Danube, Vienna is a world-famous name for its music.

famous for its university and as a musical centre. The town of Salzburg, the birthplace of Mozart, is equally famous in the world of music, and, like Vienna, is the home of an international music festival held annually.

The Viennese specialise in the very finest cakes and pastries; their cream cakes are esteemed all round the world.

Tourism is very important in Austria with 10 million visitors in 1975.

Switzerland

Switzerland has an area that is about half the size of Scotland, with a population of 6.2 million. Her central position, standing as she does between Germany, France, and Italy, makes her a country of considerable political importance.

Switzerland is strictly neutral, which is to say she does not take sides in international politics, being neither a member of NATO nor even of the United Nations, though she is considering the latter. On the other hand the International Red Cross was founded by a Swiss, and has its headquarters in Geneva. The Swiss have a 'citizens' army', which means that, though every man has to do a short period of military service, there is no standing army.

The country is divided into three main areas. South and east are the Alps, on the west the low mountains of the Jura, and between them a broad plateau which is

Collecting hay for winter fodder from rich pastures in the Swiss Alps.

the country of the lakes. The whole area contains four river basins: those of the Rhine, Rhône, Inn, and the Ticino (a tributary of the Po). The largest lakes are those of Geneva, Neuchâtel, Zürich, and Constance. The Alps are, of course, much the most important feature and attract 11 million tourists annually.

Four different languages are spoken in Switzerland, reflecting the different nationalities that have formed the Federal Republic. Nearly three-quarters of the population of 6.2 million speak German. About a fifth, living in the west, speak French, 5 per cent Italian, and 1 per cent Romansch.

Switzerland. The little church of the village of Engadine, dwarfed by the Alps.

The steep valleys of the Swiss Alps were formed by glaciers.

A typical view of the Swiss lakes. This is the town of Gunten on Lake Thun.

The Federal capital is Berne, but three other towns are bigger: Zürich, a large commercial and industrial town, has a population of 715,300. Basle, on the Rhine, is a commercial as well as a great banking centre, and Geneva is the economic centre of the south-west, and a conference centre.

Cattle graze the high pastures of the Alps in summer. The cowbells mean that they can be easily found. Dairy produce and chocolate are important Swiss exports.

Industry and Trade

Few countries can depend so much on the outside world as Switzerland. Not only does she depend on imported food and raw materials, but the tourist industry brings in much revenue.

Nevertheless, Switzerland is primarily an industrial country, and much of her industry, like watch-making, demands delicate workmanship. Her factories produce machines, precision instruments, aluminium, electrical equipment, optical apparatus, textiles, chocolate, and paper. Fast-flowing Swiss rivers provide abundant hydro-electric power. More than half the working population is employed in industry, which is concentrated in the cantons of Zürich, St Gall, and Basle.

Though Swiss agriculture is able to produce little more than half the country's needs, the pastures are so good that large quantities of dairy produce are exported. Some areas are very fertile producing vines, fruit, vegetables and cereals.

63

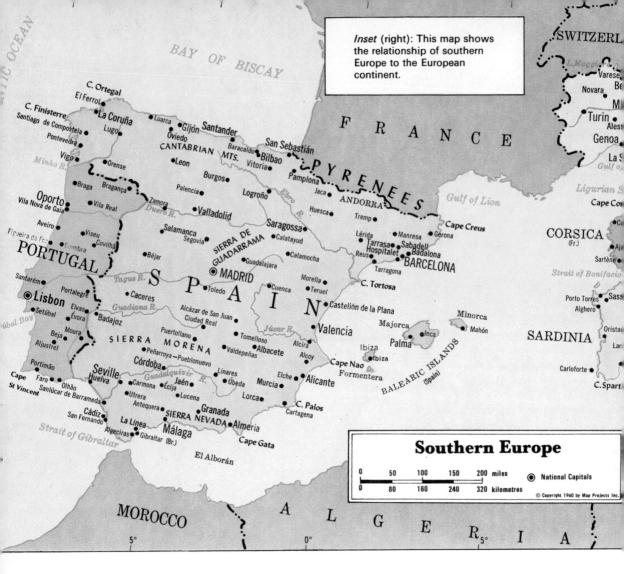

Map labels:

ATLANTIC OCEAN · BAY OF BISCAY · FRANCE · SWITZERL · L.Maggi · Varese · Be · Novara · M · Turin · Ales · Genoa · La S · Gulf of · Ligurian S · Cape Co · CORSICA (Fr.) · Aja · Sartène · Strait of Bonifacio · Porto Torres · Sass · Alghero · SARDINIA · Orista · Lar · Carloforte · C.Spart

C. Ortegal · El Ferrol · C. Finisterre · Santiago de Compostela · La Coruña · Luarca · Gijón · Santander · San Sebastián · CANTABRIAN MTS. · Baracaldo · Bilbao · Pontevedra · Lugo · Oviedo · Vitoria · PYRENEES · Vigo · Orense · Leon · Burgos · Pamplona · Jaca · ANDORRA · Minho R. · Braga · Bragança · Zamora · Palencia · Logroño · Huesca · Tremp · Cape Creus · Oporto · Vila Nova de Gaia · Vila Real · Duero R. · Valladolid · Ebro R. · Lérida · Manresa · Gerona · Aveiro · Viseu · Salamanca · Segovia · SIERRA DE GUADARRAMA · Tarrasa · Sabadell · Figueira da Fo · Covilhã · Béjar · Guadalajara · Hospitalet · Badalona · Coimbra · PORTUGAL · Tagus R. · SPAIN · MADRID · Reus · BARCELONA · Santarém · Toledo · Cuenca · Morella · Tarragona · Lisbon · Portalegre · Cáceres · Teruel · C. Tortosa · Elvas · Guadiana R. · Alcázar de San Juan · Castelión de la Plana · Setúbal · Évora · Badajoz · Ciudad Real · Júcar R. · Minorca · Beja · Moura · Puertollano · Tomelloso · Alcira · Valencia · Majorca · Mahón · Aljustrel · SIERRA MORENA · Albacete · Alcoy · Palma · Inca · Portimão · Peñarroya–Pueblonuevo · Valdepeñas · Cape Nao · Ibiza · Córdoba · Linares · Elche · Alicante · Formentera · BALEARIC ISLANDS (Spain) · Cape · Faro · Huelva · Guadalquivir R. · Jaén · Úbeda · Murcia · St Vincent · Sanlúcar de Barrameda · Olhão · Carmona · Écija · Lucena · Lorca · Carloforte · Utrera · Antequera · Granada · C. Palos · Cádiz · San Fernando · La Línea · SIERRA NEVADA · Almería · Cartagena · Algeciras · Málaga · Strait of Gibraltar · Gibraltar (Br.) · Cape Gata · El Alborán · MOROCCO · ALGERIA

Southern Europe

Scale:
0 50 100 150 200 miles
0 80 160 240 320 kilometres
⊙ National Capitals

Southern Europe

In no other part of the Western Hemisphere are the links with the past so strong and so fundamental as they are in Southern Europe. For it was in these countries, bordering the Mediterranean and Aegean sea, that western civilisation was born and developed thousands of years ago. Here classical culture faded and here too, in Italy and Spain, it was reborn again and spread throughout the world.

Southern Europe consists largely of three peninsulas, the Iberian Peninsula (Spain and Portugal), Italy, and Greece, together with the islands that belong to them. The Balearic Islands belong to Spain; Sardinia and Sicily belong to Italy. Crete and the host of islands of the Aegean and Ionian Seas belong to Greece. To these must be added Corsica, which is French, and Malta and Cyprus, both formerly British Crown Colonies and now independent members of the Commonwealth. All three peninsulas are largely mountainous: with the Pyrenees, the central Cordilleras, and the Sierra Nevada in Spain, the Apennines in Italy, and the Pindus mountains in Greece. Spain is the second most elevated country in Europe, more than half of it being

over 1,000 feet (300 m) above sea-level. The chief plains of Southern Europe are those of Andalusia in southern Spain, Lombardy in northern Italy, and Thessaly in Greece.

The Mediterranean climate is too dry to be favourable for many types of farming. Formerly Southern Europe was thickly forested, but during the centuries the trees have gradually disappeared.

When there are no trees to retain the moisture and to hold back the soil the heavy southern rain washes the soil away. This erosion has turned vast fertile areas, which have not been terraced and contour ploughed, into barren land.

But despite this, in Southern Europe more than half the working population lives on the land, though often poorly.

Spain and Portugal

The soil and climate are ideal for vines. The best wine is often made on poor soils. Spain alone has nearly 4 million acres (1.6 million hectares) of vineyards. Most of the Iberian wines are for home consumption, but the best and most famous are an important export: Port from the Douro valley in Portugal, Sherry from the Jerez region of southern Spain, and Madeira from the island of that name.

Another plant that thrives in the south is the olive. The old twisted trees, with their quivering grey-green leaves, may be seen all over the hills that fringe the northern shores of the Mediterranean. Olive oil is widely used in cooking, and large quantities are exported. Oranges and lemons are widely grown, and Spain exports large quantities of chestnuts to other European countries and to America. Other products of the south are almonds, figs, dates, peaches, tomatoes and peppers.

Wheat is the biggest crop in Spain and Portugal, next coming maize, barley, oats, rye, and rice. Barley can grow in land too dry for wheat. Oats and rye are often grown in the mountains. Rice is grown on low land capable of being flooded.

In both Spain and, more particularly, Portugal, there are large plantations of cork-oak, from whose bark comes most of the cork used in the world. And pigs graze freely in the woodlands. With less well-watered pastures than in the north, the Mediterranean countries tend to breed sheep and goats rather than cattle. Goats have a lot to do with the absence of trees in Southern Europe. Though they can thrive and produce milk in almost any country, they help to destroy forests by eating the young saplings of trees.

Some cattle are reared in the south,

The main Post Office, Madrid. This building shows the influence of the Moorish style on Spanish architecture.

but not so much for dairy-farming as for other purposes. Bulls are bred for the bull-rings of Spain and Portugal; and oxen, donkeys, and mules are widely used on the land and for transportation.

Fishing is a resource of great value to countries with poor agriculture. On the Atlantic side, Spain and Portugal are very active in this field. In Portugal fish is the most important item of diet and one of the largest of her exports. Her fishing fleet is nearly 18,000 vessels, many of which, however, are very small. Sardines and tunny-fish are tinned at the factories of Setubal. These are caught close to the coast but Portuguese fishermen sail as far as Newfoundland to fish for cod. The Spanish fishing industry is less developed, and most of the fishing is done in the Bay of Biscay, chiefly for tunny-fish.

Of the many kinds of fish found in the Mediterranean the tunny is the only one to be fished on a big scale. The others are generally consumed locally.

Avila in Spain is still encircled by its medieval defences.

In Andalusia, in the south of Spain, plantations of olive trees cover the hillsides.

Modern Industries

Many articles of everyday use are made, as in the past, by hand. In Portugal piles of hand-made pottery can be seen in any market. Artisans can still be seen painting magnificent tiles, and women can be seen lace-making. Madeira is famous for its embroidery. Spain has some mineral output of coal, iron and lead ore, copper and zinc. Portugal has mineral wealth in her coal, pyrites and kaolin deposits. Over half her power is hydro electricity.

In both countries industrial centres tend to be isolated in pockets round large cities, for example Barcelona and Bilbao in Spain, and Oporto and Lisbon in Portugal, all with some heavy manufacturing. Traditional industries such as the production of olive oil, wine and weaving still persist. However, car, textile and other new industry is growing.

The tourist industry is a great source of revenue to both Spain and Portugal. The principal areas are the Costa Brava, the Costa del Sol, and the Balearic Islands (Spain), with 34 million tourists per year and Madeira and the Azores (Portugal) with 4 million tourists.

Portuguese sardine fishing boat. Its catch is on sale on the beach.

Lisbon, a fine capital, is one of the most ancient ports in Europe. It has some shipbuilding.

The political, administrative, and cultural centre of Spain is Madrid, a city of 3.1 million inhabitants. It has also, in the last twenty years, become an industrial centre, producing electrical equipment, machinery, and chemicals. Barcelona, population 1¾ million, is the capital of the province of Barcelona. It stands in a luxuriant plain, between the mouths of two rivers.

Lisbon, the capital of Portugal, has about 1,568,000 inhabitants. It stands on the northern banks of the Tagus, about 9 miles (14 km) from the mouth. Above the mouth, the river is greatly enlarged for 10 miles (16 km) or more, making a magnificent harbour. It is the chief port. It also has an important airport. Except for the old Moorish quarter, the town was largely destroyed in the great earthquake of 1755. It was then replanned and, climbing up the slopes of a low range of hills, has long been regarded as one of the most imposing cities of Europe.

After a change of Government in 1976 Portugal's chief industries became nationalised and many of the large farms in the south have been split into smaller units.

Portugal is the world's principal cork producer. Here cork-bark is loaded on to an ox-cart.

The Azores

The Azores, a little group of volcanic islands lying more than 1,000 miles (1,600 km) out in the Atlantic, have always been looked on as a province of Portugal and as part of Europe. It was at Flores in the Azores that Sir Richard Grenville took on the whole Spanish fleet, and in the Second World War aircraft based on the Azores provided cover for the North Atlantic convoys.

The Rock of Gibraltar. Guarding the Mediterranean, it is of great strategic importance.

Gibraltar

The rocky promontory of Gibraltar, though geographically part of Spain, is an independent territory within the Commonwealth. It has been a British base for nearly two and a half centuries. 'The Rock', as it is often called, is over 1,000 feet (300 m) high and thrusts out for 2½ miles (4 km) into the Mediterranean. It commands the Strait of Gibraltar and has a naval and air base of great strategic importance. Tourism is increasing and industries to cater for this have developed. Famous features of Gibraltar are the Barbary Apes who live on the Rock. The tradition is that if they were to leave, Britain would lose Gibraltar.

Malta

Malta is a fully independent island country, 17 miles (19 km) long and 8 miles (12 km) wide, lying between Sicily and the north coast of Africa. A member of the Commonwealth, Malta was once the home of the Knights of St John and has a long history as a naval base, owing to its

Michelangelo's great cathedral in St. Peter's Square, Rome.

strategic position in the Mediterranean. The fortress town of Valletta is Malta's capital city.

Italy

Of the countries of Southern Europe, Italy, with its population of about 55 million, is the most densely populated, the most industrialised, and the most advanced in agriculture. With an area of 116,000 square miles (301,000 sq km), Italy presents four dominant geographical features: (1.) The Alps, that stand between her and the rest of Europe. (2.) The Plain of Lombardy, lying within the general confines of the continent. (3.) The relatively narrow, mountainous peninsula jutting 500 miles (800 km) into the Mediterranean. (4.) The islands of Sicily and Sardinia.

The most thickly populated districts of Italy are the Plain of Lombardy, Campania (round Rome), Apulia (in the south-east) and Sicily. The last two regions are relatively poverty stricken.

By virtue of her central position and her road and rail communications with Austria, Germany, Switzerland, and France, Italy is, of the southern countries, much the most closely integrated into Western Europe, and she is a member of the EEC.

The great Autostrada del Sol linking Italy and France is symbolic of Italy's development. This section of the road runs through the St Bernard Pass.

Venice is built on islands in a lagoon. Canals take the place of streets.
gondolas of taxis.

The Land

Of the Italian Alps, the best known are the Dolomites, which are among the most picturesque of the whole Alpine system. The great Plain of Lombardy is watered, for the most part, by the Po, whose valley is the most fertile part of Italy. Further east it is watered by the Adige and by a succession of shorter rivers flowing into the Gulf of Venice. In the foothills of the Alps are five famous lakes: Lake Maggiore, Lake Lugano, Lake Como, Lake Iseo, and Lake Garda. The climate along the Po is not unlike the climate along the middle course of the Danube, though rather warmer. The winters are cold: the average temperature at Milan being 34°F (1°C). The summers are hot and moist.

The staple food crops are maize, rice, and, in particular, wheat – which is chiefly used to make the various kinds of pasta. Pollenta, made from maize (corn) flour, is the other basic Italian food. Little bread is eaten. With one or two excep-

tions, like Parmesan cheese and Bel Paese, most of the dairy produce is consumed locally. Vines are cultivated all over Italy, largely for wine, the best-known variety being Chianti from Tuscany, though the best wines come from

This photograph was taken during the construction of the road tunnel under Mont Blanc linking Italy and France.

Piedmont in the north. Oranges and lemons are widely grown in the southernmost part of Italy, and in Sicily; olives somewhat further north. Mulberry trees are also grown in the north where their leaves, fed to silk-worms, support the local silk industry. Sheep-farming is common in the uplands.

A rice-field of the Po valley in Lombardy in northern Italy.

An orange grove on the slopes of Mount Etna in Sicily.

Industry

Since the Second World War, Italy has had an unstable economy with many changes of government. In spite of this, industry furnishes the greater part of the national income. With the exception of water power from the mountains and oil from Sicily, where the district of Ragusa is developing into one of the largest

Turin is an important centre of Italian industry, particularly the manufacture of motor vehicles, one of Italy's chief exports.

The glass-blowers of Murano have been celebrated for their skill since the thirteenth century.

European oil fields, Italy has practically no natural sources of energy. Coal from her own mines supplies only one-tenth of her needs, and to this is added natural gas, which comes partly by pipeline from the USSR. For her textile industry, wool and silk are the only products that do not come from abroad. Thus a long list of imports, including rolled iron and steel, coal, and cotton, have to be paid for by exports, shipping and tourism. Italy has 35 million visitors per year. Manufactures include motor vehicles, machinery, footwear, textiles, household electrical equipment, chemicals, and fertilizers.

The greater part of heavy industry is in the north, centred on the towns of Milan, Turin, Brescia, Genoa, and Savona. Most of the Italian textile industry is concentrated along the northern edge of the Lombardy plain below the Alps. Towns of the south, such as Naples, Terni (north of Rome), and Piombino, have limited and localised industry. Efforts are being made to bring more industry to the hitherto impoverished south: one being the opening of a steel works at Taranto.

Although great cities like Turin and Milan and great ports like Genoa are vital to the country's expanding economy, to most people Italy still means the past much more than the present or future; Venice with its canals and palaces, Florence of the Medicis, Naples with the ruins of Pompeii nearby, and above all, Rome, a thriving modern city of 3 million people, yet with the Colosseum and the Forum, the great church of St Peter's, and many other links with history.

Greece

Greece is mainly an agricultural country, but farms are small and the farmers are poor. Vineyards occupy much of the land, especially in the south, and, though much wine is made, large quantities of

A Greek shepherd boy carrying a lamb on his shoulders.

grapes are dried and sold in the form of currants and sultanas. One of the main agricultural regions is the Macedonian plain in the north, where tobacco, the chief export crop, and cotton are grown. In view of the geographical position of Greece and her many islands, it is not

Tourism plays an important part in the Greek economy. Here fishermen are preparing their nets on the island of Mykonos.

surprising that the Greeks are a maritime nation. They now have the fifth largest merchant navy in the world.

The population of Greece exceeds 8½ million, with over 2½ million in the capital, Athens. Salonika, a port and Piraeus, the port of Athens, are both of considerable importance.

Three million tourists visit the many monuments from Greece's classical past. The outstanding ones are the Parthenon and two other temples on the Acropolis on the outskirts of Athens. The Parthenon, the most famous of all Greek temples, was long left to fall into ruin. Many of its carved figures, which had fallen, were rescued by Lord Elgin. These are the world-famous Elgin marbles now in the British Museum. Piraeus, the port of Athens, handles a considerable amount of shipping. A steadily growing industry, spread over Athens and Piraeus, includes shipbuilding, the manufacture of textiles and chemicals, and food processing.

Cyprus

The island of Cyprus lies about 60 miles (96 km) from the coasts of Syria and Turkey and was, until 1960, a British Crown Colony. It is now, however, a republic, within the Commonwealth. The total population of Cyprus is about 631,700, composed of Turks living in the north-east of the island and Greeks in the rest of it.

High on the Acropolis above modern Athens stands the Parthenon, dreaming of another age.

Bratislava, on the Danube, is the capital of Slovakia.

Central and Eastern Europe

Central and eastern Europe consists of Poland, Czechoslovakia, Hungary, Yugoslavia, Albania, Romania, Bulgaria, part of the USSR, and the European section of Turkey.

The dominant physical features of this area are the mountains of the Balkans and the Carpathians. The mountains of the Balkans are an extension of the Alps. The Carpathians are the largest mountain system in Europe after the Alps.

The Carpathians flank the Plain of Hungary; the other great plain of Eastern Europe is the North European Plain that extends from France and Germany across Poland and into Russia. An intermediate zone is formed by the undulating plateau of Bohemia.

Within the Bohemian mountains is a huge area of high rolling country with very fertile soil. The heights are covered with forests, and there are rich deposits of minerals.

The Carpathians flank the great Hungarian Plain; some oil wells are sited in the outer ring, and the lower slopes are well-forested. Above the forests are pastures to which flocks are moved in summer. These mountains are covered in snow but there are no glaciers.

Sheaves of hemp, which grows abundantly in Yugoslavia. The fibre is used to make coarse textiles.

Of the two plains already mentioned, the North European Plain is composed of loose, mainly sandy materials, mostly brought down from Scandinavia by the glaciers of the most recent Ice Age, which also scattered great blocks of granite torn from the Scandinavian mountains. The plain is drained by two great rivers: the Oder and the Vistula, which empty into the Baltic.

The Hungarian Plain is the basin formed by the lower reaches of the Danube, which bisects it from north to south. The plain is made up of marshes and great areas of alluvial material washed down from the Alps and Carpathians by the Drava, Tisza, and Mures. In the centre, where the climate is dry, dust blown by winds has settled into thick layers of fine yellow-grey loess.

A characteristic Serbian church.

Poland

The bulk of Poland consists of plains and plateaus drained by the Vistula and the Oder. It is backed in the south by the Bohemian mountains and the Carpathians, rising to over 8,000 feet (2,400 m).

The plains and the plateaus fall into three groups. In the south, the Plateaus of Silesia and Little Poland and the Plain of Silesia make up a fertile farming region, and there are also rich deposits of coal, iron, zinc, lead, copper and rock salt. The second group consists of the central plains, Greater Poland, and Mazovia. The soil is less fertile, but there are minerals below: lignite and rock-salt. The third group consists of the northern plains and the Baltic ridges, sandy hills alternate with lakes and peat bogs.

The Baltic coast of Poland runs for 300 miles (480 km), from the German to the Russian frontier. The Baltic is shallow, not very salty compared with other seas, and practically tideless. There are two estuaries, one made by the Oder, which has the port of Stettin, now called Szczecin. This estuary is crossed by a number of channels and is sheltered on the seaward side by low islands, the passages between which give access to the sea. The eastern estuary is that of the Vistula.

Though the Vistula is the national river of Poland, it plays a relatively small part in the economy of the country. Its winding track and the fact that for many months in winter it is ice-bound make it unsuitable for traffic. There are two ports serving the Vistula basin: Gdansk, the old port, and Gdynia, created in 1919, which is now being expanded. Since 1945 these ports, less than 15 miles (24 km) apart, have worked in partnership.

The 'Nike' Monument and Great Opera House, Warsaw. Warsaw has been carefully reconstructed after the devastation it suffered during the Second World War.

Polish Industry

The Silesian coalfield makes Poland the third greatest coal-producing country in Europe, after the UK and West Germany and sixth in the world. Thanks to her coal, Poland, formerly a predominantly agricultural country, has turned resolutely to industry which is state owned and state run.

The seams of coal are very thick, some being 20 (6), 30 (9), and even 60 feet (18 m) in depth. They are, therefore, very easily worked. Mechanisation has been easy to introduce. The Upper Silesian coalfield, situated around Katowice, has attracted heavy industry into the same area, and there is another big plant in eastern Cracow. However, Poland is not rich in iron-ore, and heavy industry has to rely on ore imported from Sweden and the Ukraine. However, Poland is also a leading copper producer, with reserves of 10 million metric tons.

Besides having at its disposal oil, lignite, and coal, the chemical industry has access to enormous reserves of salt and sulphur.

Of other industries, textiles takes a leading place. Cotton is made at Lodz and Warsaw, and wool in Lower Silesia. Cars, shoes, glass and paper are also important.

The concentration of Polish industry in two chief regions has led to a very uneven distribution of population. The Upper Silesian region, which in area is only 4 per cent of the country, contains 15 per cent of the population. The other two industrial areas, Lower Silesia and Lodz, employ between them 60 per cent of the industrial workers.

BALTIC SEA

Gulf of Danzig

Swinoujscie
Slupsk · Gdynia
Koszalin · Gdansk
EAST PRUSSIA
Elblag
Tczew
Malbork

Szczecin
Szczecinek
Chojnice
Kwidzyn
Olsztyn
Suwalki
Augustow

POMERANIA
Dabie · Stargard
Walcz
Bydgoszcz
Grudziadz
Mlawa
Goniadz
Bialystok

GERMAN DEMOCRATIC REPUBLIC

Gorzow
Kostrzyn
Inowroclaw
Torun
Wloclawek
Plock
WARSAW
Pultusk
Ostro Mazowiecka
Ciechanowiec
Lomza

POLAND
Poznan
Gniezno
Kutno
Pruszkow
Otwock
Siedlce
Miedzyrzec

Zielona
Leszno
Grodzisk
Konin
Lowicz
Zyrardow
Ozorkow
Lodz
Piotrkow
Deblin

Sorau · Sagan
Legnica
Olesnica
Wroclaw
Wielun
Radomsko
Radom
Lublin
Chelm

Jelenia Gora
Liberec
Giant Mts.
Walbrzych
Oppeln
Czestochowa
Kielce
Ostrowiec
Zamosc

Most
Litomerice
Jablonec
Brzeg
Bytom
Sandomierz

Zatec
Carlsbad
Mlada Boleslav
Sumperk
Zabrze
Chorzow
Sosnowiec
Dabrowa
Tarnowska

Marianske Lazne
Prague
Hradec Kralove
Opava
Gliwice
Katowice
Cracow
Tarnov
Rzeszow

Plzen
Pardubice
Olomouc
Ostrava
Bielsko
Krosno
Przemysl

CZECHOSLOVAKIA
Klatovy
Pisek
Tabor
Jihlava
Prostejov
Prerov
Frydek
Mistek
Zakopane
CARPATHIAN

Budejovice
Brno
Brnzo
Gottwaldov
Zilina
Presov

Trencin
Banska
Bystrica
Roznava
Kosice

AUSTRIA
Trnava
Bratislava
Nitra
Zvolen
Lucenec
Miskolc
Nyiregyhaza
MOUNTAINS

Komarno
Nove Zamky
Levice
Salgotarjan
Eger
Mezokovesd
Satu-Mare
Baia-Mare
Darabani
Dorohoi
Botosani

Gyor
Vac
Hatvan
Hajduboszormeny
Carei
Radauti
Falticeni
Sucevea

BUDAPEST
Ujpest
Kispest
Jaszbereny
Debecen
Zalau
Dej
Bistrita
Roman
Jassy

Szombathely
Papa
Budafok
Szekesfehervar
Karcag
Torokszentmiklos
Oradea
Cluj
TRANSYLVANIA
Gheorgheni
Bacau
MOLDAVIA
Husi
Vaslui

Bakony Mts.
Veszprem
Kecskemet
Cegled
Szolnok
Salonta
Turda
Targu-Mures
Targu-Ocna
Barlad

HUNGARY
Nagykanizsa
Balaton
Kiskunfelegyhaza
Bekescsaba
Hodmezovasarhely
Brad
Alba-Iulia
ROMANIA
Tecuci

Maribor
Sostanj
Kaposvar
Szekszard
Kiskunhalas
Szeged
Mako
Deva
Sebes
Sibiu
Fagaras
Focsani

JULIAN
Kranj
Novo Mesto
Varazdin
Pecs
Baja
Subotica
Arad
Timisoara
Petrosani
Petrila
Brasov
Galati

SLOVENIA
Celje
Zagreb
Mohacs
Senta
Kikinda
Lugoj
Lupeni
Campulung
Ramnicu-Sarat
Braila

LJUBLJANA
ALPS
Sisak
Virovitica
Sombor
Becej
Caransebes
Resita
TRANSYLVANIAN
Campina
Buzau
Tulcea

TRIESTE
Karlovac
Daruvar
Apatin
Temerin
Zrenjanin
Oravita
Targu-Jiu
Ramnicu-Valcea
Targoviste
Ploesti

ISTRIA
Rijeka
Ogulin
Osijek
Novi Sad
Vrsac
Turnu-Severin
WALACHIA
BUCHAREST

Pazin
CROATIA
Bosanski Brod
Ruma
Zemun
Pancevo
Smederevo
Craiova
Slatina
Ialomita R.
Cernavoda
Constanta

Pula
Cres
Bihac
Derventa
Mitrovica
Sabac
Belgrade
Pozarevac
Bailesti
Caracal
Calarasi
Silistra

Krk
Banja Luka
Tuzla
Bijeljina
Lesnica
Valjevo
Arandjelovac
Zlot
Bor
Vidin
Lom
Corabia
Turnu-Magurele
Giurgiu
Ruse
Razgrad
Tolbukhin

Zadar
Gospic
Glamoc
Zenica
BOSNIA
Sarajevo
Kragujevac
Cacak
Rankovicevo
Zajecar
Oryakhovo
Borovan
Gigen
Nikopol
Pleven
Popovo
Kolarovgrad
Varna

Sibenik
Split
Brac
Mostar
HERZEGOVINA
Uzice
Titovo
Krusevac
Nis
Pirot
Leskovac
Lukovit
MOUNTAINS
Kazanlik
Strara Zagora
Sliven
Burgas

DALMATIA
Hvar
Korcula
DINARIC ALPS
Pljevlja
Novi Pazar
YUGOSLAVIA
SERBIA
BALKAN
BULGARIA
Kyustendil
Marek
Plain
Yambol

ADRIATIC SEA
Bileca
MONTENEGRO
Niksic
Titograd
North Albanian Alps
Vranje
Dimitrovo
Sofia
Thracian
Pazardzhik
Plovdiv
Asenovgrad
Dimitrovgrad
Khaskovo

Dubrovnik
Bar
Ulcinj
Scutari
Djakovica
Prizren
Tetovo
Kumanovo
Stip
Rhodope Mountains
Maritsa R.

ITALY
L. Scutari
Kruje
Durazzo
Tirana
Elbasan
Skoplje
Titov Veles
Prilep
Strumica

ALBANIA
Berat
Koritsa
Valona
Argyrokastron
L. Ochrida
L. Presa
Bitolj

GREECE
TURKEY

UNION OF SOVIET SOCIALIST REPUBLICS

N. AFRICA

ADRIATIC SEA
BLACK SEA
Strait of Otranto

Eastern Europe

◉ National Capitals

0	50	100	150	miles
0	80	160	240	kilometres

Inset (above): This map shows the relationship of eastern Europe to the European continent.

© Copyright 1960 by Map Projects Inc.

Polish industry has expanded rapidly since the end of the Second World War, causing many people to leave the land.

were essentially a peasant people, 50 per cent of a total population of about 34 million now lives in towns. Already 23 Polish towns have a population exceeding 110,000. The capital, Warsaw, has a population of 1.4 million. It lies on the left bank of the Vistula, and is built on a high plain and on the terraces which lead up to it. Bridges across the river connect it with its huge modern suburb of Praga on the other bank.

Seventy per cent of Poland's foreign trade is with the Communist Countries under Comecon agreements. This is an organisation similar to the EEC; offering mutual economic help within the Communist World.

Polish Farming

Before the Second World War 70 per cent of the total population of Poland lived on the land, which was very unevenly divided, with the great estates on the one hand and the small-holdings on the other. This sort of division always produces considerable extremes of poverty and wealth but it never leads to efficient farming.

The development of Polish industry has, of course, drastically affected the distribution of population. Whereas before the Second World War the Poles

The flower market at Cracow, one of the oldest towns in Poland.

Thirty-three per cent of the Polish population work on the land. Efficient farming has led to increased production.

The Land Reform Act of 1944 created 800,000 new holdings, and enlarged 250,000 existing ones. Today, the fertile soil and efficient farming methods enable Poland to supply nearly all the country's food. It produces over 8 million metric tons of rye, 6 million of wheat, and 52 million of potatoes in a year, besides large quantities of sugarbeet. 12 per cent of the industrial population work in food processing and 33 per cent of the total population are farmers.

Czechoslovakia

Geographically Czechoslovakia can be divided into three parts: Bohemia, centred on Prague, the capital; Moravia, drained by the Morava River, a tributary of the Danube; and Slovakia in the Carpathian Mountains.

Bohemia consists of an undulating plateau drained by the Upper Elbe and its tributaries, surrounded by mountains very rich in coal, lignite, graphite, and uranium.

The broad plain of Moravia consists of rich farm land in the south, while the north forms the southern end of the Silesian coalfield.

Slovakia shares with Poland the highest range of the Carpathians, the High Tatra, whose highest peak rises to over 8,700 feet (2,650 m). The mountains, which supply abundant water-power, are well forested, and also rich in iron ore and non-ferrous metals.

The old quarter in Prague.

Industry

The prosperity of the country depends, in the first place, on the old-established industries now nationalized of the western part, but recently a determined effort has been made towards the industrialisation of Slovakia.

Czech schoolchildren comparing their collections of stamps.

The most important concentration of industry is around the coalfields of Ostrava (in Silesia) and Kladno (near Prague, in Bohemia). The principal Czech iron and steel works are at Vítkovice, Kunčice, and Třinec in Silesia, Kladno, and Plzeň. There are opencast lignite works in north Bohemia. Graphite is mined in south Bohemia. Certain sands provide the raw material for the famous Bohemian glass made in the Giant Mountains. China-clay is used for the manufacture of porcelain.

Lignite is the basis of the chemical industry centred on Ústí and Most in north Bohemia, and the old textile industries are still active, cotton being produced in the Liberec region, wool and rayon at Brno (Brunn).

Folk dancing is very popular in Czechoslovakia.

A foundry at Ostrava, in Silesia. Ostrava is one of the chief coalfields of Czechoslovakia.

Since 1945 the government has been developing industry in Slovakia to take advantage of the abundant water-power and mineral wealth – including iron, copper, pyrites, and lead – to give employment to this relatively over-populated area.

Slovakia produces 80 per cent of the minerals mined in Czechoslovakia. A factory has been constructed to make aluminium goods from Hungarian bauxite, and large iron and steel and chemical works have been constructed south of Košice, the chief town of the region.

Czechoslovakia has two oil and one gas pipeline from the USSR.

Agriculture

In the past Czech farming was of two very different kinds. In Bohemia and Moravia, fertile soil, and advanced farming methods resulted in a high yield per acre. In Slovakia on the other hand, before 1939 the land was in the hands of great landowners, who used obsolete farming methods. Since 1945 a scheme of land reform has broken up the estates, and formed many state-owned collective farms.

The principal crops are wheat and barley but rye, oats, sugar beet and maize are also grown, and some fodder crops.

Prague, with a population of more than a million people, is a city of great architectural beauty. It stands on both sides of the river Vltava. On the left bank is the upper town, built round the fourteenth-century castle and the cathedral. The lower town on the right bank is a thriving industrial area producing all kinds of goods and equipment. As with other great capitals, industries tend to have their head offices there.

The Skoda works at Pilsen, Czechoslovakia. Car production is increasing and Skoda cars are exported to the West.

Fourteen bridges span the Vltava at Prague. Once called the 'golden city of a hundred spires', historic Prague is now a great industrial city.

Hungary

Hungary consists of a vast area of lowlands, flanked on the west by the Alps, and on the east by the Carpathians. West of the Danube, much of the ground is hilly. In the north are the hills of the Bakony Forest, on the southern edge of which is Lake Balaton, and further south are the Mecsék Hills, also forested. Lake Balaton is the largest lake in Hungary, about 4 miles (6 km) wide and nearly 50 miles (80 km) long. Much of the forest land is oak or beech. Beneath these hills are lignite, oil, and bauxite.

In general the climate is continental, with a long severe winter, during which Lake Balaton is frozen over. The summer is hot, in the south-east, very hot.

Agriculture and Industry

Wheat is the most important crop, though actually slightly more land is devoted to maize – which covers an area not far short of 3½ million acres. Half the arable land of the country is taken up by these two crops. A variety of other crops is grown and there are extensive vineyards around Tokay (Tokaj) and Lake Balaton in the north. Recently the wine industry has been revitalised.

Cattle, sheep, and pigs are important and one third of the population are farmers, mainly on collectivised farms.

Until 1914 Hungary had hardly any factories. The mining of lignite, coal, iron, and bauxite was developed between the two wars. It is only since 1945 that industrialisation has progressed. Besides the production of iron and steel, Hungary has a big aluminium industry, for the country has some of the largest reserves of bauxite in Europe. Hungary specialises in the manufacture of precision instruments.

The principal industrial centres are Pécs (close to the coalfield beneath the Mecsék Hills), Miskolc (engaged in iron smelting), Szeged (a textile centre near oil and natural gas deposits), Debrecen, and above all Budapest (which is at the end of an oil pipeline from Lipse).

Budapest is really two towns: Buda, the old fortified city, and the industrial and residential area of Pest.

Like Poland, Hungary has increased its industrial production rapidly since 1945. Steel is an important manufacturing industry.

All the cotton used in the textile mills of Hungary has to be imported. 62 per cent of Hungary's trade is with Comecon countries.

With a population of 2,039,000 Budapest is one of the great cities of Central Europe. It is, in fact, composed of two towns, lying on opposite sides of the Danube: Buda, the upper town on the right bank, and Pest, the lower town on the left bank. Today, as in the past, the two are very different in character – Buda remains a historical town of palaces, churches, museums, and parks. Pest is residential and, in the suburbs, industrial. As a centre of industry Budapest, like Prague, is active in almost every field.

Yugoslavia

Because of its popularity with tourists, who totalled 5½ million in 1975, Yugoslavia is, of all the Eastern European countries, the one best known to

people from the West. Yugoslavia is composed of mountain groups. In the northwest, in Slovenia, are the Julian Alps, with Triglav (9,396 feet) (2,863 m) the highest peak.

In the south-west, running parallel to the coast, is a long, mountainous range which includes the Dinaric Alps. To the east, in Serbia and Macedonia, there is a series of mountainous blocks enclosing river basins. These basins, connected by the Morava and the Vardar, form a line of communication with Salonica (Thessaloniki) in Greece. Belgrade in the north gives access to the Hungarian Plain.

Yugoslav Economy

Yugoslavia is composed of the six republics of Serbia, Croatia, Slovenia, Montenegro, Bosnia-Hercegovina, and Macedonia. 48 per cent of the population are settled on the land. Maize and wheat are the chief cereals grown in the Danube basin, and other crops of the plains and foothills are sugar-beet and grapes. The mountains provide valuable timber and grazing for large herds of cattle. Both the Dinaric and Transylvanian Alps have fine oak forests.

Minerals are plentiful. There is iron-ore in the valleys of Bosnia, bauxite on the Dalmatian coast. There is copper, lead, zinc, and mercury. Coal is rare, but lignite plentiful. To harness the water power, hydro-electric power-stations have been built. The chemical industry is fairly well developed.

Most of the industries are in the north-west. Many new factories are being built, including a modern one at Ljubljana for the manufacture of turbines and similar products. A plastics industry has been started at Split. Furni-

Dubrovnik is one of the most beautiful towns in Yugoslavia.

ture and metal construction units are manufactured near Titograd. There are carpet looms at Sarajevo and Skopje, and immense modern iron and steel works at Zenica in Bosnia.

Zagreb, capital of Croatia, and the second town in the country, is one of Yugoslavia's chief industrial and economic centres. Its character is very western, an inheritance from the days when it was part of the Austrian Empire. It consists of two parts, the old Upper Town and the modern Lower Town. The latter, with its rich buildings and neo-classical monuments, stretches down to the Sava. Among its industries are machinery, textiles and food processing. Zagreb is one of the most important railway centres of South-east Europe, where

Yugoslavia has greatly increased its tourist facilities in the last ten years.

lines from Milan, Vienna, Prague, and Budapest all converge.

Belgrade, the capital and commercial centre, is built on a spur of land at the confluence of the Danube and the Sava, which is also a point at which the Danube curves to the east. In such a position, it is obvious that Belgrade was first of all a fortress. It has suffered many attacks. As a result it has little to show of old architecture. It is a modern town, grey and sombre in its buildings. It is a transport centre linking Central Europe with the Balkans.

Ox-drawn ploughs at work in Yugoslavia.

The open-air market in Belgrade. These peasant women wait for customers for their knitting.

Photographed near Zagreb, this picture illustrates the beautiful scenery for which Yugoslavia is rightly noted.

The Danube at Belgrade.

Albania, a Mountainous Land

Albania is an inaccessible country of mountains, where packhorses are often the only transport, running north-west to south-east, reaching over 8,000 feet (2,500 m), and torrential rivers, running through deep gorges that only here and there broaden into valleys.

With abundant rainfall the country is rich in forests. The crops grown depend on the height of the land. In the valleys and on the lower slopes the vegetation is typically Mediterranean, the crops being grain, maize, sugar-beet, potatoes, fruit and rice. Higher up are the grazing lands, and then, higher still, uninterrupted forests of oaks, chestnut trees, walnuts, etc. Mineral wealth includes oil, copper, extensive coal at Valais, bitumen, iron, lignite and salt.

The production of timber and rearing of sheep and goats are the mainstay of Albania. Hitherto a backward country, it has, under the communist regime, made strenuous efforts at modernisation, both in agriculture, with a land reclamation programme since 1973, and in industry, which is completely nationalised. With Chinese help, chemical, oil, iron and steel and engineering industries are being built up, as are food processing and textiles. Until 1947, Albania was the only European country without a single railway. The first line was opened in 1950. Now there are several lines in operation, including new ones connecting factories with mines. The Tiranë-Durrës line is of particular service to the textile industry.

Tiranë and Shkodër (Scutari) are the two chief towns. Tiranë, the capital, with a population of 175,000, stands in the shelter of wooded hills. It is famous for its mosques, a survival from Turkish rule.

Seventy per cent of Albania's trade is with China.

The main government buildings in Tiranë, the capital of Albania. It is only recently that Albania has opened its frontiers to visitors from the West.

Rice is an important crop in Albania, and even the children help out in the fields. Only 15 per cent of the total area is cultivated in Albania.

A hand-loom at work. The handicrafts of Albania are still very much alive.

Romania

The southern Carpathians and the Transylvanian Alps form the backbone of Romania, rising, in the Fagaras range, to over 8,000 feet (2,500 m). These ranges form a birch- and fir-clad screen between Transylvania and the hills of the south and the Danube plain. Transylvania itself consists of hills, usually covered with orchards, and broad fertile valleys.

On the other side of the backbone, beneath the wooded foothills, stretch the plains with fields of wheat and maize, amongst which are large prairies not unlike the Russian steppes. Crops, how-

The Athene theatre at Bucharest.

ever, are at the mercy of the very uncertain rainfall. In the plains the winters are severe, the summers are very hot with occasional rain-storms.

Nearly all farms are state owned. Stock-farming depends largely on the high pastures, flocks being taken up in the summer and brought down to the villages during the long winters.

Oil is the great source of Romanian wealth; at Wallachia, at the foot of the Carpathians, and in Moldavia. However, refining exceeds production so oil is imported. Natural gas, found in Transylvania, is another very important natural resource.

Most of the petrol refineries are in the neighbourhood of Ploesti, north of Bucharest and a pipeline has been laid from there to the port of Constanta on the Black Sea and to Giurgiu on the Danube. Romania has little coal. A joint Romanian and Yugoslavian HEP plant was opened on the Danube in 1972. There are also some atomic power stations.

There are scattered deposits of iron-ore, and other minerals in meagre quantity. However, Romania is pushing

One of the lakes at Bucharest.
The Institute of Science is in the distance.

The Château of Sanaia in Romania, was built
in the late nineteenth century. It is situated at the
foot of the Transylvanian Alps.

ahead with industrialisation and mechanisation. Iron-ore and coke are imported from Russia. Agricultural machinery, steel tubes, electrical goods, cement, railway equipment, ships, cars, and chemicals are made.

The chief industrial centres are: Bucharest (the capital), Cluj, Orasul and Brasov (in Transylvania), Craiova (in Wallachia), and Resita and Timisoara (in the Banat). A new port is being built at Mangalla on the Black Sea.

Romania's trade is mostly with Comecon countries, though she has some agreements and some industrial projects with the EEC.

Bucharest, the capital (population over 1½ million) is mostly post 1945. There are big parks, broad avenues, and newly planned quarters with fine buildings.

Tourism is increasing, especially with Russians and other East Europeans visiting the Black Sea resorts.

Bulgaria

Bulgaria is one of the least well-known of the countries of Eastern Europe.

Along the frontier with Romania in the north, lies the broad plain of the Danube

St Sofia's church and the cathedral of Alexander Nevski in Sofia, the capital of Bulgaria.

The main building of a collective farm in Bulgaria. All agriculture is based on the collective farm system and enough food is produced to feed over 80 per cent of the population.

where maize and wheat are grown. On the coast is the port of Varna.

The wooded Balkan mountains, which rise to over 7,000 feet (2,100 m), run right across the country south of the Danube plain.

South of this chain are the central lowlands, through the western half of which flows the river Maritsa. Here the produce is more varied than in the north. Tobacco, cotton and rice are grown, and flowers. The biggest town here is Plovdiv, better known as Philippopolis, the centre of the textile industry. In the west of the country lies Sofia, with a population of over three-quarters of a million.

To the south and south-west of Plovdiv are two other ranges: the Rhodope mountains which rise to over 9,000 feet (2,280 m), and the highest mountains in Bulgaria – the Rila mountains, which reach 9,500 feet (2,850 m). In the valleys tobacco and sugar beet are grown.

The produce of the collectivised farms feeds over 80 per cent of the population. The commercial crops are: cotton, roses for attar of roses, fruit, and tobacco, which accounts for half of the exports.

Efforts to promote the totally nationalised industry have been handicapped by the paucity of raw materials. Lignite, manganese, lead, zinc, and copper are all Bulgaria has. Recently, however, oil has been extracted from the Balchik offshore area of the Black Sea. This is supplemented by an oil pipeline from Siberia. Nevertheless an industrial centre has been developed at Dimitrovgrad on the Maritsa using lignite and oil for the production of electricity, and an atomic power station has been built with Soviet aid at Loxlodni, on the Danube.

Cement and chemicals, including artificial fertilisers, are produced. Steel works have been started south-west of Sofia. One principal industry is weaving – much of which is done by hand at home.

Turkey in Europe

Although Turkey used to be a great European power her European possessions have shrunk, and most of her territory today is in Asia Minor.

Turkey in Europe has an area of about 9,000 square miles (23,700 sq km). It includes eastern Thrace, a pastoral land of sheep and goats, with, in the valleys, an occasional crop of tobacco, rice, or maize. The only real asset lies in the city of Istanbul, formerly Constantinople, at the entry to the Black Sea.

This former capital of Turkey, which, before that, under the name of Byzantium, was the capital of the Eastern Roman Empire, has had a long and tumultuous history. Long after the Byzantine Empire had declined, Constantinople, with its magnificent defences, held out against the Turkish advance into Europe, but finally fell in 1453. The town stands on a hilly promontory, which encloses its splendid harbour, the Golden Horn. It is full of historical remains, the most renowned being the great mosque of Santa Sophia, once the most famous church in Christendom.

There is little industry in Istanbul, but trade is brisk and tourists are plentiful.

For Turkey in Asia – see page 158

Situated on the European side of the Bosporus, Istanbul is famous in history under its earlier names: Constantinople and Byzantium.

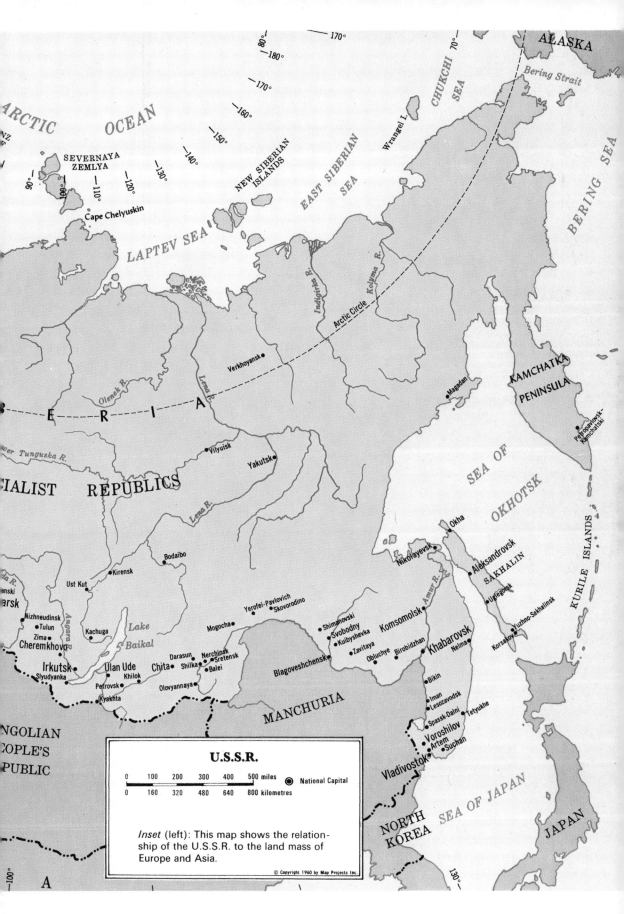

ALASKA

Bering Strait

ARCTIC OCEAN

CHUKCHI SEA

BERING SEA

SEVERNAYA
ZEMLYA

NEW SIBERIAN
ISLANDS

Wrangel I.

EAST SIBERIAN SEA

Cape Chelyuskin

LAPTEV SEA

Arctic Circle

KAMCHATKA
PENINSULA

Olenek R.

Indigirka R.

Kolyma R.

Verkhoyansk

Magadan

Petropavlovsk-
Kamchatski

Lower Tunguska R.

Lena R.

Vilyuisk

Yakutsk

SEA OF
OKHOTSK

B — E — R — I — A

CIALIST REPUBLICS

Lena R.

Okha

Nikolayevsk

Amur R.

Aleksandrovsk

KURILE ISLANDS

Bodaibo

SAKHALIN

Ugegorsk

da R.
anski
arsk

Kirensk

Ust Kut

Nizhneudinsk
Tulun
Zima
Cheremkhovo

Kachuga

Lake
Baikal

Angara R.

Mogocha

Yerofei-Pavlovich
Skovorodino

Shimanovski
Svobodny
Kuibyshevka
Zavitaya

Komsomolsk

Yuzhno-Sakhalinsk

Korsakov

Darasun
Nerchinsk
Irkutsk
Slyudyanka
Ulan Ude
Chita
Shilka
Sretensk
Balei

Obluchye Birobidzhan

Khabarovsk

Nelma

Petrovsk
Khilok
Olovyannaya

Blagoveshchensk

Kyakhta

MANCHURIA

Bikin

Iman
Lesozavodsk
Spassk-Dalni
Voroshilov
Artem   Suchan

Tetyukhe

NGOLIAN
COPLE'S
PUBLIC

Vladivostok

SEA OF JAPAN

NORTH
KOREA

JAPAN

U.S.S.R.

| 0 | 100 | 200 | 300 | 400 | 500 miles |

◉ National Capital

| 0 | 160 | 320 | 480 | 640 | 800 kilometres |

Inset (left): This map shows the relationship of the U.S.S.R. to the land mass of
Europe and Asia.

© Copyright 1960 by Map Projects Inc.

Red Square and St Basil's cathedral at the centre of Moscow.

The Soviet Union

The Union of Soviet Socialist Republics, generally denoted by its initials, USSR, is the largest state in the world. It covers one-seventh of the world's land surface. It stretches from the middle of Europe, to the eastern tip of Asia, which is only a few kilometres from the western tip of North America. The distance from west to east is such that sunrise on the frontier with Poland is eleven hours later than sunrise at the other end of the country. Travelling across the country the clocks have to be put on or back ten times. In the south the frontiers are formed by the Black Sea, Turkey, Iran, Afghanistan, China, and Outer Mongolia; in the west by Norway, Finland, the Baltic Sea, Poland, Czechoslovakia, Hungary, and Romania; in the north by the Arctic Ocean, and in the east by the Bering, Okhotsk, and Japan Seas, which lead to the Pacific. From north to south the landscape varies from tundra to subtropical deserts.

The Physical Geography of the Soviet Union

Russia is out of reach of the warming influence of the North Atlantic Drift. Almost all the water that washes her coasts is cold, and freezes in winter. Thus Russia has the severest of continental climates. Winter and summer are sharply contrasted and follow each other abruptly, as both spring and autumn are very short. In winter frost comes early and lasts for a long time. The summer is hot and stormy. The climatic differences between the various areas do not consist of how hot or how cold it may become so much as how long or how short each season may be. Beyond 50° North, winter is longer than summer. The greatest cold is encountered at Verkhoyansk, where the temperature falls to over 94°F (35°C) below zero. At the other extreme are the torrid steppes and deserts east of the Caspian Sea. The shores of the Baltic, however, are less continental in climate, and Murmansk and Petsamo, though well within the Arctic Circle, are just reached by the warm surface currents of the Arctic Ocean and are open all the winter. Other exceptions are the warm coasts of the Black Sea and the maritime provinces bordering on the Sea of Japan.

Though for the most part very low-lying, Russia has some great mountains on her periphery. The Caucasus, which lie between the Black Sea and the Caspian, are considerably higher than the Alps, having half a dozen peaks over 16,000 feet (4,870 m) – Elbruz, the highest, being 18,540 feet (5,650 m). Still higher are the Pamirs in Tadzhik at the north-western end of the Himalayas, whose heights rise to over 20,000 feet

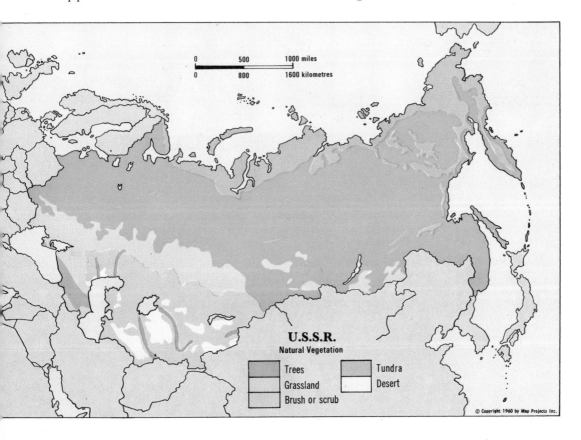

U.S.S.R.
Natural Vegetation

Trees
Grassland
Brush or scrub
Tundra
Desert

© Copyright 1960 by Map Projects Inc.

This map shows the average January temperatures in the U.S.S.R. The winters are very severe as a result of the continental climate.

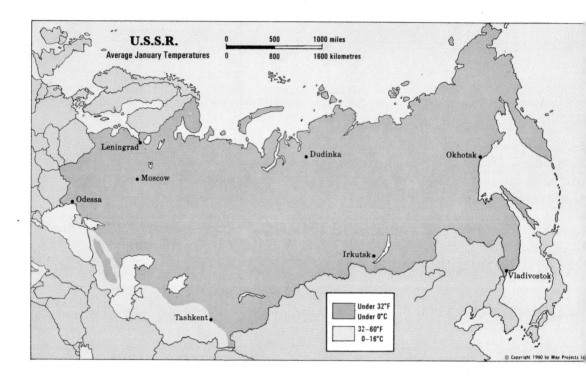

This map shows the average July temperatures in the U.S.S.R. Summers are hot, but the spring and autumn are very short.

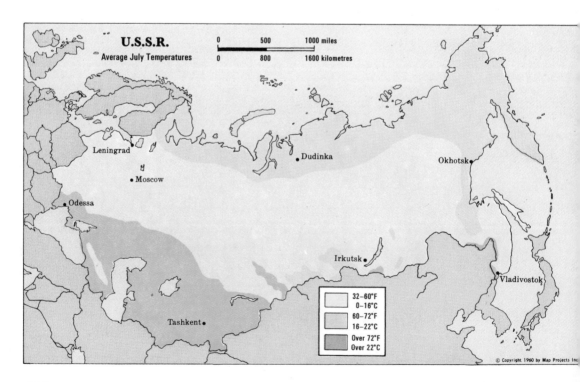

(6,000 m), and Communism peak, which reaches 24,500 feet (7,470 m), and continues eastward into the Tien Shan. Starting east of Lake Balkhash is a long mountainous area which includes the Sayan, Yablonovy, and Stanovoy mountains, the three ranges of eastern Siberia – Verkoyansk, Ceriky, and Kolyma – and finally the Kamchatka Mountains which run through the peninsula on the eastern side of the Sea of Okhotsk. Along the southern part of the Pacific coast, the Sikhote Alin range sweeps south towards Vladivostok.

By far the greater part of Russian territory consists of an immense stretch of plains or low plateaus, hardly interrupted by the gentle slopes of the Urals, reaching 5,500 feet (1,680 m). This area is drained by a number of great rivers, the Dnieper, the Volga, the Ob and Irtysh, the Yenisei, and the Lena, all of which have slow currents. In the south the dryness is an obstacle to normal river drainage. As a result we find the great inland seas, the Caspian, the Sea of Aral, and Lake Balkhash.

Vegetation varies with the latitude. In the extreme north the peaty soil is frozen in winter and produces only a scanty growth of moss and lichens. This is called tundra. South of the tundra is an enormous area of coniferous (ever-green) forests. In eastern Siberia, the forests are almost continuous down to the frontier with China. South of the forests, chiefly in the west, is the steppe. As we move towards the hotter regions, the steppe gradually gives place to scrub, in which are large patches of desert.

This map shows the range of the average annual rainfall in the U.S.S.R. The influence of the sea is again reflected in the high rainfall on the east and west coasts.

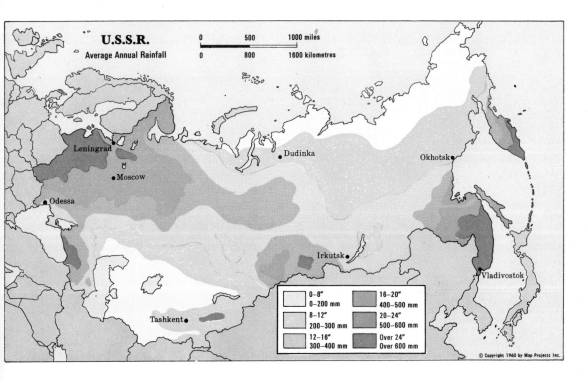

The Political and Economic Structure

More than 100 nationalities live within the Soviet Union, each maintaining its own language and culture. In the interior are Finno-Ugrians, Mongols, Tunguses; on the borders are Balts, Caucasians, Kazakhs, Kirghiz, Uzbeks, Turkomans, and many others. But in spite of their differences and the great variety of the country they live in there is a remarkable uniformity in their manner of life.

By dint of great efforts and sacrifices, Russia has succeeded, since the Revolution of 1917, in nationalising her production, and in completely reorganising the structure of the country. This is particularly remarkable when the damage by the Second World War is taken into account. The whole economic life of the country rests on a system of planned socialism. The land and all its resources, the railways and other means of transport, the banks, factories, and most of the shops are all owned by the State, which represents the workers of the country. The State co-ordinates their activities and plans development. Agricultural production is controlled by worker co-operatives. Industrial production is supervised by regional controllers. Factories making the same class of goods are grouped together in local combines.

Women shovelling wheat with wooden shovels.

Technical advances are very rapid, and the distribution of the population is undergoing a constant change with the opening of new mines, the building of new factories, the cultivation of new lands. Thousands of people moved away from their original homelands, and particularly great was the movement towards the towns. Between 1959 and 1970 there was an increase of 36 million in the urban population. Only a small amount was accounted for by boundary changes. Russia has become the second industrial power of the world, and is challenging the United States for first place.

Part of the enormous forests of Siberia. Russia has encountered great difficulties in opening-up the virgin lands of Siberia.

A happy wedding reception.

Russia is fast building new towns and rebuilding old ones. This new housing estate is in Leningrad.

The Peoples of the Soviet Union

The Soviet Union seeks to combine the idea of unity with the greatest amount of decentralisation. The population of over 262 million is divided up between 15 different Socialist Republics. Each linguistic minority maintains its own language, and government.

The largest of the Republics is Greater Russia (the Russian Socialist Federal Soviet Republic, over 6 million square miles or 17 million sq km), with a population of 134,5 million. This is itself organised on a federal basis and, though the most Russian part of the country,

The Gum Department Store in Moscow. Each of the 15 Republics is called after the major nationality that lives there.

Peasant women from one of the huge Soviet Republics which stretch across the whole of Asia.

Managers of a state farm in the Ukraine sitting down to a fine meal.

A peasant home in Byelorussia (White Russia). which lies between Poland and Moscow.

nevertheless includes 15 autonomous republics in which languages other than Russian are spoken. The RSFSR has 70 per cent of the total industrial and agricultural output of the country.

The Ukrainians form the next most important national group. With a fifth of the total population, they live in the Ukraine Soviet Socialist Republic which lies to the north of the Black Sea. With the most fertile soil in the Soviet Union, the Ukraine is often spoken of as the granary of Russia. The other Republics vary in size and importance. The Russians, Ukrainians, and White Russians are Slavs, but there are numerous other national and racial groups, like the Mongol-featured Turko-Tartars from Central Asia, the Tadzhiks from the

A group of villagers from a collective farm in Byelorussia (White Russia).

This gentle buffalo in Georgia is not at all concerned by the boy sitting on his back.

*A turbaned Uzbek in the streets of Tashkent,
the capital of the Uzbek Republic.*

*Hunters, wearing their national costume, in the
extreme east of Siberia.*

This village street scene is typical of hundreds on the fertile plains of the Ukraine.

Pamirs, the Kerilians, Estonians, Georgians, Armenians, and many others.

Fifty years ago Russia was a country of peasants, traditionally attached to the land, mostly illiterate, and so poor as to be the virtual slaves of the great aristocratic landowners. Today, over half the population live in cities, and no state in the world has a more efficient system of education than the USSR.

A long queue forms every day to visit Lenin's tomb in Red Square, Moscow.

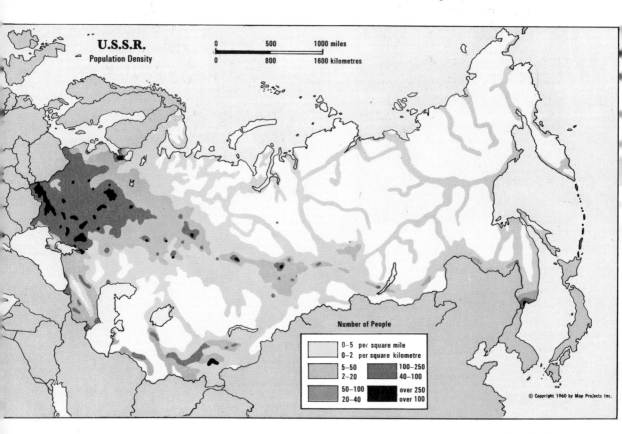

U.S.S.R.
Population Density

0	500	1000 miles
0	800	1600 kilometres

Number of People

0–5 per square mile	
0–2 per square kilometre	
5–50	100–250
2–20	40–100
50–100	over 250
20–40	over 100

© Copyright 1960 by Map Projects Inc.

The Produce of the Land

Agriculture utilises well over 2 million square miles (5 million sq km), that is to say more than one-quarter of the Soviet Union.

The bulk of arable land is in the temperate area, and the crops are mostly cereals. But it also extends into sub-tropical regions, where cotton, rice, oranges, and grapes are grown.

The steppes of Central Asia provide good grazing ground for sheep. For the rest there are the forests, which cover an area nearly twice as great as all the arable land of the country.

Cotton and flax are grown in great quantities, especially in Azerbaijan, where 70 per cent of the area is irrigated, and even hemp, the smallest of the fibre crops, amounts to about one-quarter of world production. The yearly production of timber is over 350 million cubic yards.

There are two kinds of farm in the Soviet Union – both for the breeding of dairy and stock cattle and arable farming. There is the Collective Farm and the State Farm. Collective farms are often very large, combining all the land of one or several villages. The Uzbeks, for example, have one collective farm with an area of some 150,000 acres, on which cotton is grown. It employs the workers of 3,500 families, distributed among over 70 villages. Collective farms are planned and run by the people who work on them, though plans have to be approved by the elected local authorities.

The bulk of production is sold to the state at a pre-arranged price. The remainder is sold locally for whatever price it may fetch. Of the money earned by a collective farm, part goes in tax, part is to pay expenses, and the remainder – the profit – is divided amongst the farm workers. The most skilful or experienced men earn more than the others. Managers earn two or even three times as much as ordinary labourers.

Each worker on a collective farm has his own house and, round it, a small quantity of land for his own use. He sells his surplus at the market of the collective farm, keeping the proceeds.

Apart from the collectives about one-fifth of the land farmed in Russia is under direct state ownership. Here decisions come from above. The manager is appointed by the authorities, and the labourers receive a fixed wage. State farms are generally bigger than the collectives and are run very much on factory

Stacking the straw on a collective farm in the Ukraine. This is rich farming land.

lines. Planes are used extensively for spraying crops.

The chief crops are wheat, rye, maize, sugar-beet, and potatoes. Oats and barley are grown on land unsuitable for other cereals. Cotton and fruit are grown on irrigated land in Central Asia.

In the Kirghiz Republic in Central Asia much of the newly irrigated land is devoted to cotton.

The only sub-tropical regions of Soviet Russia are the coasts of the Black Sea and the valleys and foothills of the Caucasus. In them tea is grown, vines, citrus fruits, and various crops. On the dry plains east of the Volga in Central Asia, herds of cattle are kept, and flocks of sheep and goats. Livestock are particularly good in Kazakhstan. A new breed of sheep, the 'Akharomerino', gives excellent wool.

Flax is grown in White Russia and in the neighbourhood of Moscow, while sugar-beet is grown in the Ukraine, the Caucasus, Central Asia, and the Far East. Vines are grown everywhere in the south.

Science is playing an increasing part in Soviet agriculture. Soviet scientists have succeeded in developing certain crop varieties which can grow and ripen in a very short season of 90 days. This is vital if Siberia, Russia's great Arctic 'frontier', is to be developed as the Soviet people hope.

Part of the enormous wheatfields of the Ukraine.

The Pamirs in Tadzhikistan are among the highest mountains in the world. Nomadic herdsmen as shown in this picture, use the high pastures at 12,000 ft (3,657 m) above sea level in summer.

Sunflowers are an important crop in the Soviet Union. They are used both as food and as a source of vegetable oil.

A wheatfield on the plains of Siberia.

There are large herds of goats in the Caucasus.

The harbour of Yalta in the Crimea.

Industrial Production

All industry is nationalised. Mines, oil-wells, power-stations, and factories, are all in the hands of the state, which represents the sovereign people.

The government decides what shall be produced and in what quantity. It decides when to open a new mine, when and where to build a new factory. Every detail has to fit in with a plan; usually Five Year Plans. Before a plan is finally decided there are long discussions between experts and representatives of the workers take part in them too. Once decided the plan is strictly enforced.

Each undertaking works as a separate economic unit, selling its produce to meet its expenditure. To co-ordinate their manufacture, factories of the same sort are often grouped together. Another sort of group combines industrial undertakings that are dependent on one another – as blast furnaces are dependent on mines, and as the manufacture of machinery is dependent on steel.

The Soviet's first concern after the Revolution of 1917 was to 'electrify the land' and develop heavy industry: iron and steel production, shipbuilding, heavy machinery, etc. The manufacture of consumer goods had to take second place, though greater emphasis is now being placed on them. It must be remembered that fifty years ago Russia was a very backward country, industrially, politically and in the standard of education and living.

Today Soviet Russia is second only to the United States in industrial production. She has acquired that position by virtue of her vast stores of raw material, including fuel, and by the determined effort she has made to achieve it.

Today, the Soviet Union's production of steel is second only to the United States.

Russia possesses coal, oil, natural gas, and water-power.

The most important coalfields are the Donbas, or Donetz Basin (in the southern Ukraine) with 60 per cent of the country's reserves, the Kuzbas or Kuznetsk Basin (the Upper Yenisei Valley), the Karaganda Basin in the Kazakh Republic, the Irkutsk in central Siberia, and the Basins of the Far East.

In coal production Russia comes third after the United States and China. She produces four times as much as in 1939, ten times as much as in 1928. In oil pro-duction, she comes second after North America.

The chief source used to be the Caucasus, the principal regions being Baku, Grozny, and Maikop, but about three-quarters of Russian oil now comes from the Ural-Volga area, the so-called 'Second Baku', where there are four important oilfields. Stores of natural gas are being very actively exploited in various regions. A large new oilfield has been developed in the Trans-Volga area of the Saratov. Many hydro-electrical stations incorporating irrigation schemes and

Colourful banners in Red Square urge workers to move forward together.

Russian farm machinery on display in Moscow.

Here are other examples of Russian farm equipment.

improved river navigation have been constructed. The great rivers of European Russia have little fall for the development of power, but stations built include those on the Svir and Volkhov, near Leningrad, the Kama, and the Dnieper. On the River Razdan, eight stations have been completed. Further east, big dams have been built on the Volga at Kuybyshev and on the Angara (which flows out of Lake Baikal) near Irkutsk. But as the rivers of Russia and Siberia

Selling kvass in Moscow. Kvass is a kind of beer made from fermented black bread.

are frozen in winter, heating systems have had to be installed, using either natural gas, oil, coal, or peat. There are also at least ten atomic power stations.

A craftsman at work in the Tadzhik Republic, Central Asia.

A laboratory in a Russian school. Education has played an important part in the development of the Soviet Union into a great modern state.

Russia possesses ample quantities of most of the important metals. From the Urals come iron, copper, zinc, lead, bauxite, gold, and platinum; from the Ukraine iron, manganese, and bauxite. From the Caucasus come manganese, zinc, and lead. From the Kazakh Republic come copper, lead, and zinc. Central Siberia produces zinc, lead, tin, and bauxite. The iron ore from Krivoi Rog in the Ukraine is of a very high grade. The manganese production of Georgia and the Ukraine constitutes 40 per cent of world production.

The most important iron and steel works are in the Donbas (in the southern Ukraine), at Magnitogorsk (in the Urals), and in the Kuzbas in western Siberia.

The resources of the Donbas are enormous. Besides the coal of the Donetz basin there is the iron ore of Krivoi Rog and the Kerch Peninsula in the Crimea, and bauxite, lignite, etc., all organised into a complementary industrial area. The principal towns are Donetsk (formerly Stalino): coking plant, steel works, etc.; Makeyevka: blast-furnaces and chemical industries; Lugansk (Voroshilovgrad): locomotives, heavy machinery; Zaporozhe: aluminium; Krivoi Rog: iron mines, smelting.

The Urals extend for over 1,500 miles (2,400 km) and on their flank is an oil-bearing basin that has only been partially prospected. There are more than 1,000 veins of iron-ore. One, Magnet Mountain, is linked by rail to Magnitogorsk, which contains the largest steel works in the world. New mining and manufacturing towns have developed here. Sverdlovsk, with

over 1,100,000 inhabitants, manufactures machinery and machine tools;
Chelyabinsk, special steels and ferro-
alloys, tractors, and cars; Nizhni Tagil
has large steel works, and manufactures
railway equipment. The smelting works
of the Urals have no local coal, but
natural gas has been located along the
River Ural.

Apart from these two great industrial
concentrations, the principal industrial
towns of European Russia are Leningrad, electrical machinery; Moscow and
Gorki, motor-cars; Kharkov and Volgograd, formerly Stalingrad, tractors,
locomotives, and turbines.

A chemical industry based on coal has
been built up at Novomoskovask. At
Baku and Kuibyshev, the chemical
industry is based on oil, while in other
areas it is based on wood, cellulose, or
phosphates. The raw material for the
manufacture of synthetic rubber at
Yaroslavl is alcohol. The centre of the
atomic industry is at Ust-Kamenogorsk.
Uranium is mined in Tashkent and
Armenia.

The Middle Volga is a traditional
centre of textile manufacture. Moscow is
the principal region for the manufacture
of cotton and synthetic fibres and weaving has been introduced in Tashkent in
the cotton-growing Uzbek Republic.

Food processing is increasing, with
sugar-refining in the Ukraine and
Kazakh Republics: fish-tinning on the
Lower Volga and on the coast of the Sea
of Okhotsk and meat tinning in Moscow.

Naturally there is almost every kind of
industry developing in a country so vast
as Russia. Between 1971 and 1976, 400
brand new industrial enterprises were in
production, including new atomic
plants, coalfields, oil refineries, petro-
chemical and irrigation works.

*Novosibirsk is an important industrial city that
lies at the centre of the railway system that links
western Siberia, the Kemerovo coalfield and
Altai.*

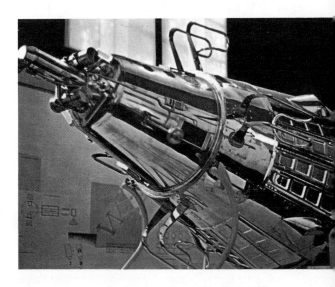

*The nose-cone of a Russian Sputnik. Russia has
scored many outstanding successes in the field of
space exploration.*

Cattle grazing on stubble on a Siberian collective farm. The Russians are making great efforts to increase their herds.

Siberia

With an area not far short of 6 million square miles (15 million sq km), Siberia is three times the size of Western Europe. A large part of it consists of fertile steppes, a continuation of the steppes of European Russia, but a much greater part makes up the largest forested area of land anywhere outside the tropics. Siberia has its coalfields and the greatest hydro-electric power-station of the country. For the Russian millions, Siberia represents the wide open spaces, just as North America did to the Europeans of the nineteenth century.

The population of this vast area is about 80 millions. The towns are expanding rapidly. Omsk is a good example. Founded in the eighteenth century, this town, lying on the River Irtysh, had a population in 1939 of 281,000 which has now more than tripled. The town still contains many one-storied houses built of wood, yet great buildings of reinforced concrete have been constructed with industrial estates constantly growing. Industry includes flour-milling and meat-packing, the tan-ning of leather, petrol refining, and the manufacture of agricultural machinery and railway equipment.

We have already spoken of the Kuzbas, the great industrial centre of western Siberia whose coalfield is the richest of the Soviet Union. That coalfield has become a centre of iron and steel production (using iron ore from the Altai), and a general centre of heavy industry. The chief towns are Novokuznetsk (formerly Stalinsk), Kemerovo, Leninsk, and Novosibirsk.

Another industrial concentration is centred on the coal basin of Karaganda, lying some 200 miles (320 km) north of Lake Balkhash. It includes smelting works, though the iron ore has to come from as far away as the northern part of the Kazakh Republic. Non-ferrous metals, including copper from the Lake Balkhash region, are also worked.

Another concentration is in central Siberia in the neighbourhood of Lake Baikal and the River Angara, which runs northward from it. Lake Baikal is longer than the Adriatic and its area is sixty times that of Lake Constance. The Angara is a great river, with rapids at several places, so that dams and hydro electric power-stations have been built. In this industrial region an important coalfield near Irkutsk is being worked, while bauxite and other non-ferrous metals are being mined on the further side of Lake Baikal. The Amur River in eastern Siberia is also the centre of an industrial area. For a considerable distance this great river forms the frontier with Manchuria, then it flows northward to the Sea of Okhotsk. The area's industries are served by the coalfields of the Bureya Mountains, Vladivostok, and the Island of Sakhalin; and by the ores of the Sikhota Alin range. Heavy industry is concentrated in Komsomolsk, Ussuriisk, and Vladivostock. Other industries depend on local timber and fish.

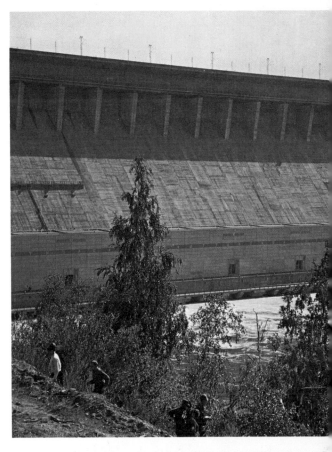

Completed in 1967, the hydro-electric power station at Bratsk, Siberia, has a capacity of 4.5 million kw.

Siberian villages usually have a frontier atmosphere.

Soviet Communications

Soviet industry is spread over an enormous area. The huge distances involved demand a highly organised system of transport.

The magnitude of these problems is illustrated by the fact that a train takes about nine days to travel the whole length of the Trans-Siberian Railway, a distance of 8,750 miles (14,080 km). Siberia has many great rivers, which would provide excellent transport were it not that, firstly, they nearly all flow northwards into the Arctic Ocean, whereas east-west transport is desired, and secondly that they freeze in winter. Even the Lower Volga, one of the most southerly stretches of river, is frozen over for three months in the year. The more northerly rivers are ice-bound for much longer. In the more western areas canals have been constructed between rivers. There is one between the Dnieper and the Bug, and the Volga is linked to the Sea of Azov on the one hand, and to the

Neva on the other, which in turn is linked to the White Sea. The cost of building these canals is enormous and frost greatly reduces their use since canal water, being almost stationary, freezes more rapidly than running water. In Russia inland water transport carries little more than 5 per cent of the goods traffic, while the railways carry 64 per cent of this traffic. New deep water ports are being built on the Black Sea.

Road transport is more hampered by spring than by winter. When the thaw comes the roads become muddy, and transport is apt to be bogged down.

There remain the railways. The construction of railways in Russia only began seriously in 1880. The highest point in pre-Revolution days was the construction of the Trans-Siberian Railway, now electrified in part, begun in 1892. This railway, which took ten years to build, is 8,750 miles (14,080 km) long – the longest railway in the world. Its

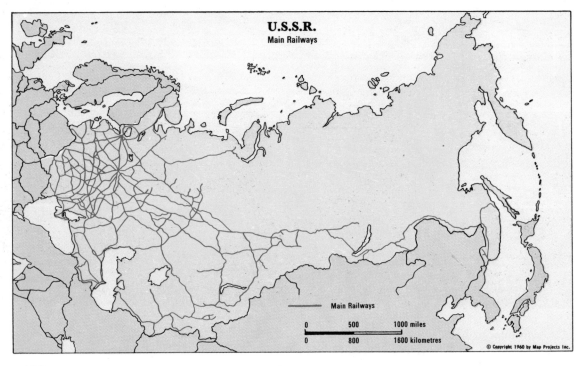

U.S.S.R.
Main Railways

Main Railways

| 0 | 500 | 1000 miles |

| 0 | 800 | 1600 kilometres |

© Copyright 1960 by Map Projects Inc.

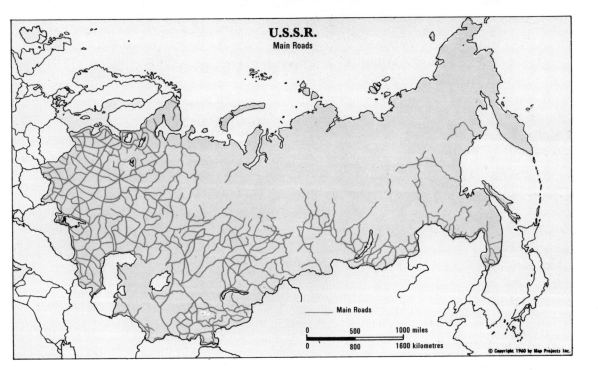

U.S.S.R.
Main Roads

Main Roads

| 0 | 500 | 1000 miles |
| 0 | 800 | 1600 kilometres |

© Copyright 1960 by Map Projects Inc.

construction marked a vital stage in the development and colonisation of Siberia.

However, in 1917, the Soviet government inherited one of the poorest railway systems in the world, and the progress of railway construction across the USSR's great distances remained slow until 1930, when the Turksib railway, running between Turkestan and Siberia, was constructed. Thus the coal, cereals and wood of the north are exchanged with the southern cotton and oil.

Joining up with the Turksib, transverse lines were constructed to connect further industrial areas. The Karaganda railway linked the coalfield of that name with the industrial concentration of the Urals.

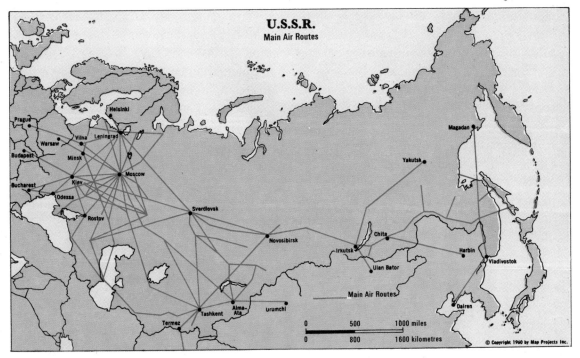

U.S.S.R.
Main Air Routes

Main Air Routes

| 0 | 500 | 1000 miles |
| 0 | 800 | 1600 kilometres |

© Copyright 1960 by Map Projects Inc.

119

Today a southern branch of the Trans-Siberian Railway links Magnitogorsk and other Ural industrial centres with the Kuzbas, passing through the northern part of the Kazakh Republic. A line linking the Russian and Chinese systems, the Trans-Mongolian, branches off from the Trans-Siberian at Ulan Ude, south of Lake Baikal, and runs to Peking, thus providing an outlet for the Angara industrial area. A second line, from the Turksib, will eventually join the Chinese railway now being constructed through the Sinkiang-Uighur Autonomous Region. A new north Siberian mainline, 2,000 miles (3,200 km) in length, from Lena to Komsomolsk will be completed by 1982.

The fortress of St Peter and St Paul, Leningrad. Formerly St Petersburg, this beautiful city, built by Peter the Great, is considered to be one of the most outstanding cities, architecturally, of Northern Europe.

Principal Towns

In 1917 only 16 per cent of the population lived in towns. The proportion has now risen to nearly 60 per cent. There are over 200 towns with more than 100,000 inhabitants, and 40 of them with more than half a million. This is largely due to the development of Russian industry, and mechanisation of agriculture.

Three types of towns are distinguishable. Firstly, the small country towns that provide market facilities for the agricultural population. Secondly, the commercial and industrial towns, usually situated beside rivers or railways. Lastly, there are the administrative towns: the capitals of the various republics, and the headquarters of regional authorities.

In some cases industrial towns are old towns that have become industrialised. These include Perm, Volgograd, and Sverdlovsk. In other cases new towns have sprung up in open country, their sites being determined by the presence of coal or other minerals. Such are Magnitogorsk in the Urals, Chelyabinsk and Makeyevka in the Donbas, and Novokuznetsk in the Kuzbas.

Minsk, the capital of White Russia, stands in an area of half-drained marshland, between the Niemen and the Upper Dnieper. At the beginning of this century, it looked like a vast, untidy, over-grown village. During the Second World War, four-fifths of it was destroyed but today it is a city of broad streets in the centre, flanked by modern houses and flats. Large factories make heavy machinery, tractors, lorries, trailers, and chemical products.

Gorki lies on the Volga at the confluence with the Oka. It is typical of the Russian river towns that mark the various stages of Muscovite expansion, when markets were set up on the rivers at a time when they were the only high-

The University of Moscow.

ways. Once important as a meeting place for the trade of Europe and Asia, its importance as a market declined after the opening of the Suez Canal. However, more recently the town has become an active manufacturing centre, in particular for tractors and motor cars.

Kiev has now been entirely rebuilt, after the damage of the last war. There are 800 completely new streets. Extend-ing to the north-west are the industrial quarters, in which mechanical engineer-ing takes a prominent place. Kiev, with its university and several scientific research organisations, has considerable status as a cultural centre.

Leningrad is a historic town. Though it has ceased to be the capital of the coun-try, it has become a great commercial and industrial centre. It has excellent

A group of women asphalt a road in Volgograd.

An Uzbek man, squatting on the ground in oriental style, enjoys a melon in the market of Samarkand.

communications. Nine railways start from it. Its port, Kronstadt, is the largest of the Soviet Union. Canals link it both to the White Sea, in the extreme north, and inland to the Volga. Its many industries include the manufacture of all equipment needed in the building of power-stations.

Leningrad is Russia's most important port. It was first built in 1703 by Peter the Great, who wanted Russia to have an outlet to the Baltic.

A power-driven barge on the Volga. The Volga is the longest river in European Russia.

Vladivostok is Russia's most important Pacific port. It stands on a gulf in the extreme south, almost on the border of Manchuria. It lies in roughly the same latitude as Marseilles, but its climate is very different. The average temperature throughout the year is only a few degrees above freezing point, the Gulf itself never freezes, but thin ice forms along the shore and remains for four months in winter. With the constant growth of Siberia and its trade with the USA and Japan, the importance of Vladivostock is increasing.

Moscow, the Soviet capital is both a historic and modern city. The historic buildings of old Moscow date from the

Most of the Siberian towns are new. Krasnoyarsk is built on the river Yenisei at the point where it is crossed by the Trans-Siberian railway. It lies in a huge clearing of the forest, and is a picturesque town, backed by rocky hills which supply the setting for a school of mountain climbing.

Though dating from the eighteenth century, Omsk has only expanded in recent years, with the agricultural development of the northern part of the Kazakh Republic. Its industries are mostly concerned with foodstuffs.

Novosibirsk is the giant amongst the Siberian towns, with a population of 1,243,000. It is built at the point where the Trans-Siberian railway crosses the river Ob and is the natural centre of communications for the coalfields of the Kuzbas. A large hydro-electric power-station, recently constructed, has added to its importance. The town is also a great cultural centre, a witness to the extent Siberia has developed as a civilised area.

The atmosphere in the market of Taskhent is decidedly oriental. Though integral parts of the USSR, the various Republics all retain their own individual character.

Much of Moscow has been rebuilt. Here are some examples of modern Russian architecture.

fourteenth century. Many of the most famous lie within the Kremlin, including the great palace of the Czars, built of white stone with great gold cupolas, and outside the Kremlin walls, in present-day Red Square, is the Cathedral of St Basil, built by Ivan the Terrible. Moscow ceased to be the capital of Russia in the seventeenth century, but since the Revolution has once again become the centre of the Russian State.

The rest of the city is of recent construction: big blocks of flats, and gov-ernment offices, theatres, museums, hotels, big stores, and, very important, the huge University.

Special residential suburbs have been built round the old town. An impressive underground railway was opened in 1935, and every quarter is served by buses or trolleybuses.

Practically every branch of industry is represented in Moscow. Prominent amongst them are mechanical engineering and light industry, such as textiles, printing, etc. Two thirds of the products

The beautiful city of Leningrad was built by Peter the Great to be his capital. At that time it was called St Petersburg.

Khan. For ages the religious centre of Central Asia, Bukhara has innumerable mosques.

Baku, which stands on a promontory of the western shore of the Caspian, is a town of over 1¼ million inhabitants. Once a Moslem town, it is now the great oil centre of the Caucasus. So rich is the land in oil, that it used to spout out spontaneously and sometimes these fountains used to burst into flames. Because of this, Baku was once regarded as a Holy City by the Parsees or fire-worshippers.

Samarkand is another of the oases once used by caravans. It was taken by Alexander the Great in 329 BC. In the Middle Ages it was a great Moslem centre. Genghis Khan sacked the town in 1220. It became Tamerlane's capital in 1370, and he made it into a fine town

Lake Ritsa, in one of the upper valleys of the Caucasus, in Georgia, is very popular with Russian holidaymakers.

of light industry consumed in Russia are manufactured in or round Moscow.

Eleven railways radiate from Moscow, and with canals in every direction, Moscow is truly the heart of European Russia.

The oriental appearance of the old towns is generally matched by that of their Moslem inhabitants.

Bukhara, with a population of 86,000, is one of the oldest towns of the Uzbek Republic. It was already a very prosperous place in the ninth century, being one of the halts on the caravan route which led to India and China. On a hill in the centre of the town is the old palace of the

A mosque in Samarkand in the Uzbek Republic.

Fishing boats on the Caspian Sea. It is from the roes of sturgeon caught here that caviar is made.

with mosques, palaces, and gardens. Today it has some factories producing textiles and machinery.

Tashkent, the capital of the Uzbek Republic, is the biggest Soviet town of the east. It stands in a wide oasis, watered by the Syr Darya and by numerous canals. It is a double town. On the one hand is the old town, with narrow, dusty streets; beside it, a new town that sprang up when the railway was built in 1898. The new town is well-planned with imposing buildings and monuments. Tashkent is an important educational centre, particularly in technology, and it has become a great industrial town, producing farming machinery, mining equipment and electrical goods for Central Asia. Tashkent is the seat of the Central Asian University. The Soviet Union's cotton research institute is situated there.

Russia's housing programme is being pushed forward as fast as possible. All houses and flats in the towns are built by the local authorities; there is no private housing.

Snow-capped Fujiyama, Japan's highest mountain, is a national symbol for Japan's people.

This is Asia

Asia is the largest of the seven continents, and in it live over 2,200 million people, more than half the population of the globe. Within its boundaries there is a greater diversity of race, territory, and climate than in any other. Looking at the map of the world it is at once obvious that Europe is really no more than a peninsula of Asia. Asia covers an area greater than that of Europe and Africa together, or the two Americas combined. It covers almost one-third of the earth's land surface.

A space-man, looking down on Asia, would see strikingly different landscapes. Asia has more mountains than any other continent. Plateaus and mountain ranges criss-cross the whole of Central Asia. The plateaus are higher than most mountains, and the peaks themselves tower very much higher still.

Those peaks are covered with ice and snow even in summer, and they rise not merely into but right above the clouds. There are half a dozen peaks 5 miles (8,830 m) above sea-level. The highest is Everest which is over 29,000 feet (8,830 m) above sea-level. It is easy to understand why this region came to be called 'the roof of the world'.

There are vast regions where there is desert. A desert belt stretches from the

Red Sea to Mongolia. Some deserts, like the Arabian, are hot all the year round, while in others, such as the Gobi Desert of Mongolia, great extremes of cold may be encountered.

Deserts and steppes cover between them more than a third of Asia. Water is so scarce that few people can live there, and these few are nomads who drive their flocks from one grazing land to another.

Immense, dark, evergreen forests cover most of Northern Asia. In this vast area there are relatively few people, mainly trappers and lumbermen. In the extreme north the forests end, giving place to tundra, a belt of which skirts the Arctic Ocean. Here the ground is frozen hard most of the year, and nothing can grow except for a few mosses and lichens.

Only a very few wandering tribes live here with their large herds of reindeer.

South of the coniferous forests are immense areas of arable and grazing land which are used for growing wheat and rearing cattle.

Further south still are the rainy tropical zones, and here, in the steaming jungle, live tigers, elephants, monkeys, and a host of tropical birds. Many millions of people live in these hot areas, most of them crowded into tiny villages along the banks of rivers, where they cultivate the rich soil. All over the world it is the general rule that the greatest numbers of people are found near water.

In Eastern Asia too, millions of people live on small farms close to the rivers. Some live actually on the water itself – in

Utilising every piece of land, Philippine farmers grow rice on carefully terraced hillsides.

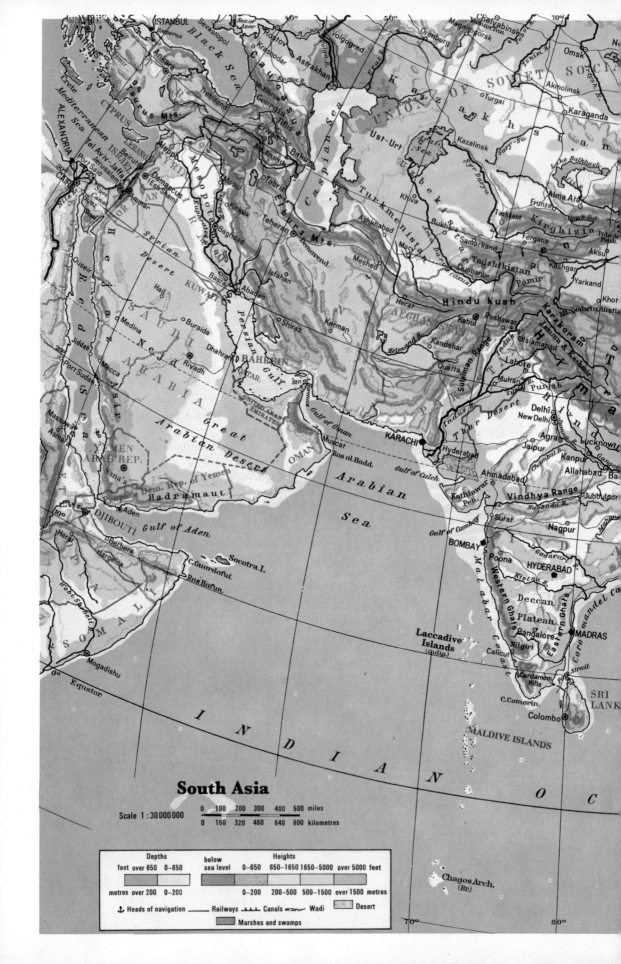

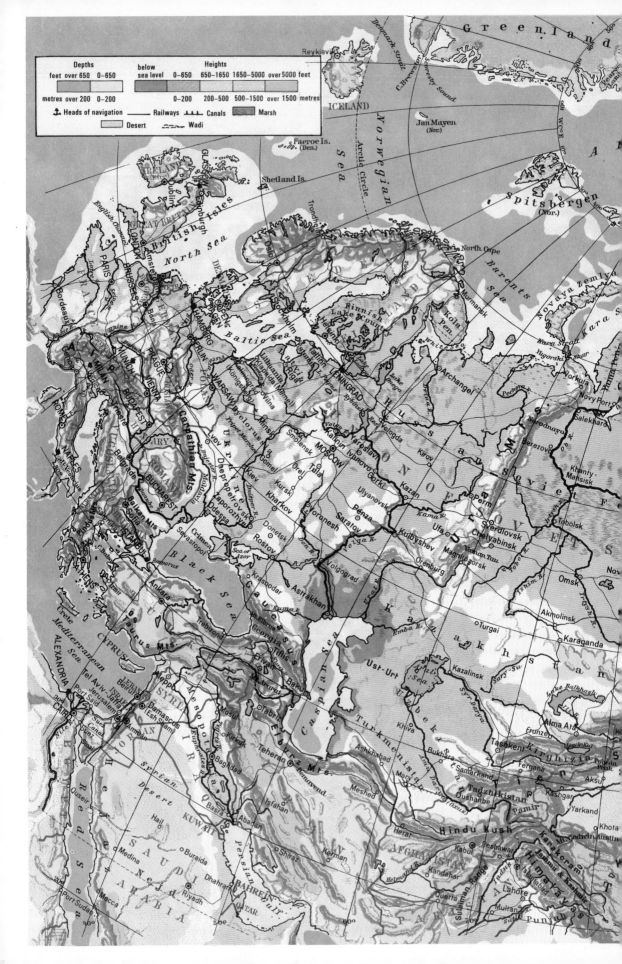

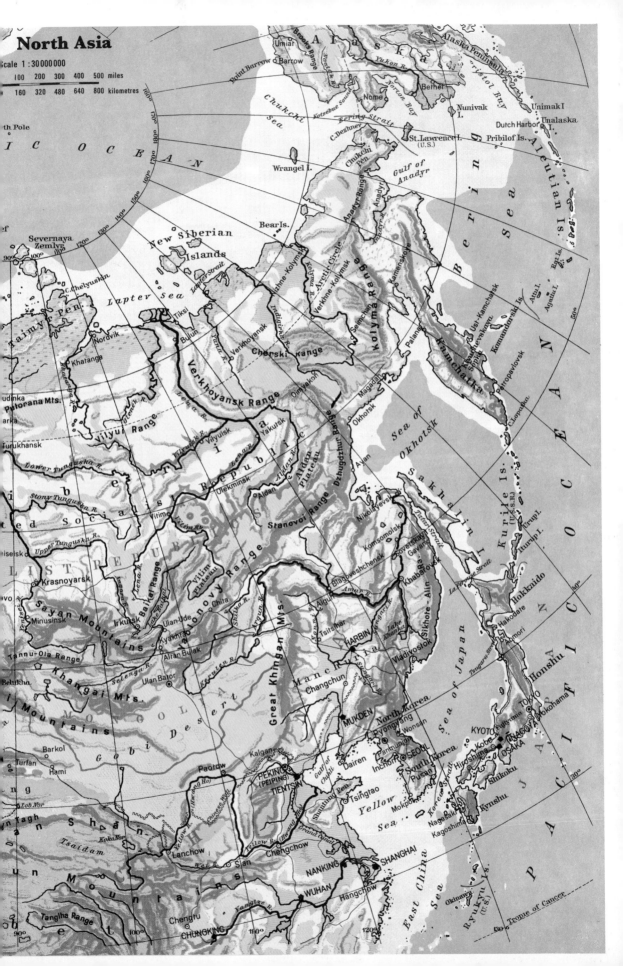

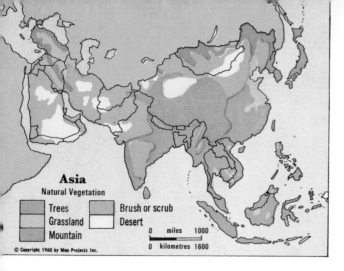

Asia
Natural Vegetation

Trees
Grassland
Mountain

Brush or scrub
Desert

0   miles   1000
0   kilometres   1600

© Copyright 1960 by Map Projects Inc.

On many of the innumerable islands of South-East Asia it rains most of the year. These islands are covered with hot, tropical jungles. In some islands, where the jungle has been cleared, rubber, coffee, sugar, tea, and spices are grown.

Asia has both the highest mountains and the lowest depressions in the world. We have already seen that the continents of Asia and Europe belong to a single land mass which is sometimes called Eurasia. Asia alone measures about 18 million square miles (46 million sq km), which is over a third of the earth's land surface. From north to south it stretches from a point within 5 degrees of the North Pole to 10 degrees south of the Equator, while from Cape Baba in Asia Minor to Cape Dezhnev on the Bering Strait occupying 163 degrees of longitude, nearly half way round the world.

boats or house-boats. There is greater crowding in the towns than anywhere else in the world; while, in contrast, Central Asia is very bare and supports only the scantiest population.

In the islands of Japan farms extend high up the sides of mountains, for the population is so dense that every inch of soil must be used to produce food. Even so, not enough is produced.

The glacier-gouged Karakoram Mountains in Central Asia contain some of the world's highest peaks.

Many seas and oceans wash the vast coastline of Asia. To the north lies the cold Arctic Ocean. The Black Sea, the Mediterranean, and the Red Sea wash the south-western shores, while to the south lies the Indian Ocean, which in the north divides into the Arabian Sea and the Bay of Bengal. To the east lies the Pacific, whose inshore branches are the South China Sea, the East China Sea, the Yellow Sea, and the Sea of Japan. Still further north is the Sea of Okhotsk and last, the Bering Sea.

The heart of Asia is a mass of great mountain ranges and high bleak plateaus. There are no fertile lowlands in Central Asia comparable to the Basins of the Mississippi, the Amazon, or the Zaire. Central Asia is not only high, cold, and bleak, but it is very, very hard to reach. The mountain ranges and plateaus of Central Asia make up the largest mountainous area in the world. Together with the deserts that lie between many of them they make Central Asia an extremely inhospitable region for any outsiders to approach.

Some of the world's greatest water systems have their sources in these moun-

Encroaching sand dunes threaten to cover this date-palm oasis in the deserts of Saudi Arabia.

tains. Melting snows from the slopes of the Hindu Kush, the Pamirs, the Elburz, the Karakoram, the Altyn Tagh, the Tien Shan, and the Himalayas, pour downwards to form great rivers. Rising in the more northern mountains the Ob, the Yenisei, and Lena Rivers flow northwards to empty into the Arctic Ocean. Few people are able to live in the cold, northern plains watered by these rivers. Other great rivers flow eastward

Wheat is raised on the treeless, hilly steppes of the Anatolian Plateau in Turkey.

Sri Lanka's warm, wet climate and rich soils favour rice cultivation.

Southern China has rugged terrain. Farms are crowded into the valleys between the craggy hills.

Monsoon rains feed the waterways along which nine-tenths of Thailand's people live.

Tropical vegetation does well, bricks and mortar less well, in this village in Bengal.

and southward from these ranges. These are the Indus, the Ganges, the Irrawaddy, the Mekong, the Brahmaputra, the Salween, the Yangtze, and the Hwang Ho. Millions of Asians make their homes in the hot, fertile valleys through which these rivers flow on their way to the Indian Ocean or the Pacific. In Western Asia the Tigris and Euphrates rise in the highlands of Turkey and flow down into the Persian Gulf. Today, as in ancient times, this river system provides water for irrigation.

Some of the rivers of Asia never reach the sea. Instead, flowing across hundreds of miles of steppes or desert they empty finally into salt swamps or into inland seas and lakes such as the Caspian Sea, Lake Balkhash, and the Aral Sea.

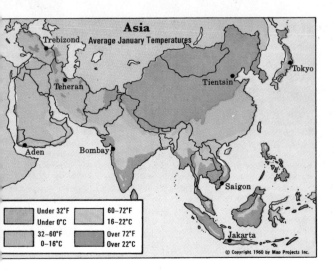

This map shows the range of average January temperatures in Asia. As the continent stretches from the Arctic ocean to the Equator, the range of temperatures is far greater than in Europe.

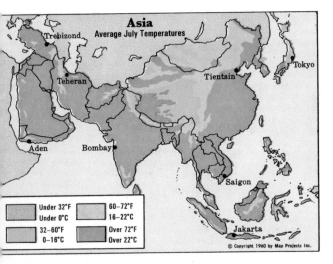

This map shows the range of average July temperatures in Asia. While the temperatures are uniformly high, the climate in south and east Asia is very different from central and west Asia because of the influence of the monsoon winds.

Climate

Stretching as it does some 5,000 miles (8,000 km) from the Arctic Ocean to the Equator, the continent is naturally affected by great extremes of climate. Asia contains some of the coldest, and hottest, wettest and driest places in the world.

The enormous area of Central Asia is over a thousand miles from the nearest sea and surrounded by high mountain chains. The warm moist air from the sea has to pass over these, and in doing so becomes chilled and loses its moisture. The only winds that do not pass over heights come from the icy polar regions. The climate of this central region is thus a severe one: the winters long and cold, the summers, except on the plateaus, hot and short. Much of the region is desert.

Northern Asia has much the same climate as Central Asia, except that it has more rainfall. Winters are extremely cold. Verkhoyansk, a village in Siberia, is the coldest inhabited place in the world.

In Southern Asia the climate is quite different. Here it is hot all the year round, except in the mountains. In the plains the temperature may reach as much as 125°F (53°C). Instead of summer and winter, there is merely a rainy season and a dry one.

The rainy season usually lasts from June to October, inclusive, and during that period it rains heavily every day. This region has the heaviest rainfall in the world. Some areas of India get more than 300 inches (7,600 mm) of rain during the wet season.

The rainy and dry seasons are caused by winds called monsoons, *monsoon* being a word of Arabic origin meaning season. The monsoons blow over all South and South-east Asia, which is sometimes called 'the monsoon region of the continent'. In winter, the monsoons blow from Central Asia towards the southern and eastern edges of the continent. Winter monsoons are dry because they blow from the land, and cold because they blow from the mountains. The summer monsoons blow inland from the sea, bringing moisture with them.

The monsoons that bring the rain are a vital factor in the lives of the millions of people living in Southern and Eastern Asia. With its coming they plant the crops on which their existence depends. Drought quickly brings people to the verge of starvation. Sometimes the monsoons are late, so that crops cannot be planted in time to ripen, sometimes the rains cause floods. In either case, the result is disastrous.

South-West Asia is an extremely dry area, with long, very hot summers. Winters are relatively mild except in the highlands of Iran. In parts of South-West Asia, winter is the rainy season, and the season for crops – moisture being more important than temperature.

Climate largely determines the way people live. In northern Siberia, for instance, the almost permanently frozen soil makes any sort of farming impossible. Therefore people must depend for their living on hunting and fishing.

In Burma the climate is warm and rainfall is abundant. In the rainy seasons floods are frequent, so the people living near rivers build their houses on piles to raise them above flood level. The warm moist climate is ideal for growing rice.

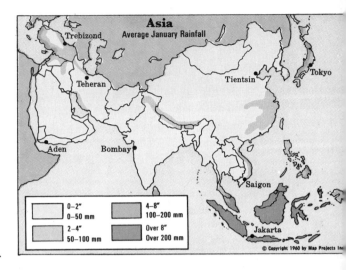

This map shows the average January rainfall in Asia. Winter monsoon winds are dry because they blow from central Asia towards the southern and eastern edges of the continent, and cold because they blow from the mountains.

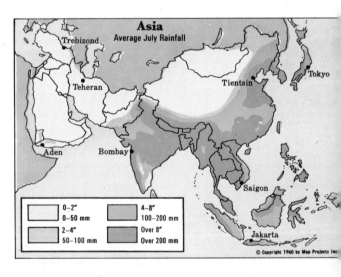

This map shows the average July rainfall in Asia. Monsoon winds blow inland over south and south-east Asia bringing moisture as far as they can reach.

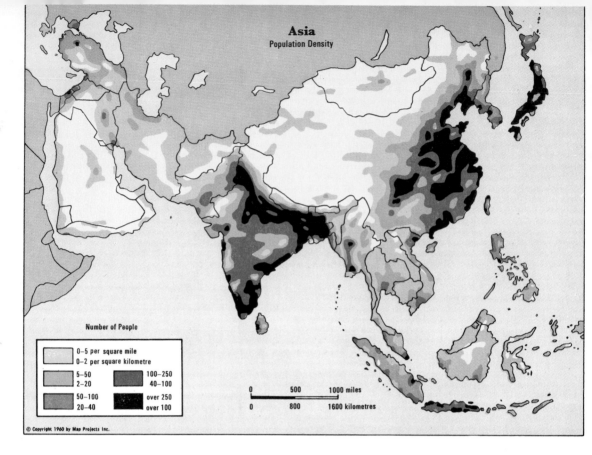

Asia
Population Density

Number of People

| 0–5 per square mile |
| 0–2 per square kilometre |

| 5–50 | 100–250 |
| 2–20 | 40–100 |

| 50–100 | over 250 |
| 20–40 | over 100 |

| 0 | 500 | 1000 miles |
| 0 | 800 | 1600 kilometres |

© Copyright 1960 by Map Projects Inc.

Peoples of Asia

With all the other contrasts presented by Asia – contrasts of climate, landscape, animal and plant life – it is only to be expected that the continent would present us with a wide variety of people. In fact, almost every racial type known in the world can be found within Asia.

There is every variety of skin colour: white, yellow, brown, black, and every intermediate shade. Within each of the colour groups there is every type of figure and feature. Thousands of years of mixing between the racial groups has created every possible combination of physical characteristics.

Even more significant are the cultural differences between the various peoples of Asia. They differ in their habits and customs, their religions, their languages, their sense of values, their arts, and their degree of education. And these differences, like the physical ones, cut across the racial lines.

In South-Western Asia, for example, most of the people are Caucasian in origin, that is, theoretically white. Yet

Turbaned Afghan men in Kabul, the capital of Afghanistan.

These men are Jordanian Arabs. Arabs are the largest group of people in South-West Asia.

there are the greatest differences both in their appearance and the way they live. Arabs, Turks, Persians, Kurds, and Israelis, all speak different languages, dress differently, follow different religions, and obey different moral codes. The Turks, Persians, and most of the Arabs are Moslems. Some of the Arabs are Christians, the Israelis are Jews. Within each religion there are many sects. Even when there is a common language, as with the Arabs, there are great differences between the desert nomads, who are shepherds, the settled farmers of the

With great toil the people of Israel have turned barren desert into flourishing farmland.

An Arab rug merchant in the market-place of Kuwait on the Persian Gulf.

more fertile regions, and the townsmen.

There are still much wider differences between the people of Southern Asia. In India alone fourteen major languages are spoken, and if every different dialect is counted the number rises to 845. In religion most Indians are Hindus, but there are also Moslems, Sikhs, Jains, Buddhists, Christians, Parsees, and others. Such cultural differences are carried on by tradition – local customs and religious observances being handed down from generation to generation.

Yet another reason is the influence of surroundings: the climate, the landscape, the nature of the soil, and the natural resources. It is obvious that people who live in cold dry prairies or deserts, as the Mongolians do, will live differently from those in a wet, tropical island like Java.

The broad rolling grasslands of Mongolia are ideal for herding livestock. To follow their herds and live on the meat and milk they produce is the traditional way of life of the Mongolians. The people of Java can stay in the same place and raise good crops on their fertile soil. They have solved the problem of growing crops in mountains by building terraces.

But Java is very crowded, and there is barely enough land to grow food for all the people and fodder for all the animals. The Javanese live chiefly on rice; they get most of their protein from fish.

Israel, in which large numbers of Jews from all over the world have settled, was formerly a land of deserts or

Hindu pilgrims bathe in the Ganges River at Benares in order to become spiritually clean.

A Pakistani snake-charmer practises his traditional, and dangerous art.

The Philippine government is trying to put education within the reach of all children.

swamps. Great efforts have been made to drain the swamps and irrigate the deserts, so that food can be produced for the settlers on the land and for those who are now creating industries.

Because the distances in Asia are so great, and the facilities for travel so limited, communities have tended to develop in isolation, with the result that each area developed a language or dialect of its own. Often two dialects of the same language are so different that the people who speak the one are unable to understand the other. A Chinese from Canton, for example, may not be able to understand his countryman, even though he comes from a village only 50 miles (80 km) away.

The fact that so many Asian people speak different dialects or languages from their neighbours has created many difficulties for their governments. In an attempt to overcome this problem some

Tibetan porters can carry loads of more than 300 lbs (136 kg) on their backs over country far too steep for any animals.

143

An old lady of Peking tends her young grandchild. In China, the natural increase in population is 2 per cent per year. Birth control is encouraged.

Since 1950, the Chinese have made great efforts to industrialise their economy. In 1970, a policy of establishing small-scale, localised industry was introduced.

countries have chosen one dialect or language to be the official one. In China, for example, the Mandarin dialect is taught to all schoolchildren. In the Philippines, where the people speak various Malay dialects, the official one is Tagalog.

This Mongol woman's ancestors once ruled a mighty empire that covered most of Asia.

Daily life in Asia is deeply affected by religion, both by its commandments and by its general influence on the outlook of the people. For instance, Hindus, because they hold the cow sacred, are forbidden to eat beef or injure cattle in any way. Some Hindus will not eat any kind of meat nor kill any living creature, even if it be a harmful one.

Asia is the great breeding ground of religions. The two great religions born in the heart of Asia are Hinduism and Buddhism. Hinduism is the religious and social system adopted by the majority of the inhabitants of India. Formerly it was chiefly responsible for the division of Indian society into castes though, in fact, the caste system is not a fundamental part of the Hindu religion. It was forbidden for Hindus to marry outside their own religious caste. Their caste also prescribed the sort of work they did, the food they might eat, and the clothes they could wear. The caste system was abolished in the Constitution of 1950.

Unlike other great world religions like Christianity or Buddhism, the Hindu religion did not have any one founder. It gradually grew over a period of 5,000 years, absorbing and assimilating all the religious and cultural movements of India. As a result there is no one great holy book like the Bible or the Koran. Hinduism, the oldest of the world's great religions, has influenced and in turn been influenced by many differing beliefs during its history – Buddhism being the most important. To many people Hinduism seems to involve the worship of literally thousands of different gods and goddesses, but, in fact, Hindus regard these as just different names for the same all-embracing God.

Buddhism has the greatest number of followers of any of the world's religions. Its founder was Gautama, the Buddha, who was born in India in 536 BC. From India Buddhism has spread, in various forms, to Tibet, China, Japan, Ceylon, and South-East Asia.

Buddhism originally grew out of Hinduism, and there is quite a large degree of similarity between them. The other great influence on Buddhism was the Taoist doctrines which came from China, though these have had the greatest influence on Japanese Buddhism.

Another group of religions arose in the south-western fringes of Asia. Christianity, an offshoot of Judaism, was born in Palestine. It spread from there to the Greek cities of Asia Minor and Rome and to the whole of Europe and to all the New World. Islam, was started by the prophet, Mohammed, in the seventh century, but its original stock was of much the same origin as Judaism and Christianity. In all these three religions, Adam was the first man, and the Koran

This Javanese man's red fez shows that he is a Moslem, as are nine out of ten Indonesians.

A Japanese father gives his child a lesson in the tricky technique of handling chopsticks.

(the Holy Book of Islam) in many respects overlaps the Old Testament. Following the Arab conquests, Islam spread right across North Africa, while in Asia it spread to Syria, Arabia, Iraq, Turkey, Iran, Afghanistan, Turkestan,

An early morning market scene in the north of Laos.

Smiling Malayan children lead a carefree life.

and what is now Pakistan. It even reached the East Indies.

Until the communists came to power in China, most of the Chinese worshipped the spirits of their ancestors. This led them to feel great reverence for the past and for traditional ways of doing things, and often made them unwilling to adopt newer and more advanced methods.

Mankind has lived in Asia from a very

A straw coolie hat shields this Vietnamese girl from the sun.

early period. Some of the oldest known fossils of prehistoric man have been found on the island of Java, in the East Indies, and near Peking in Northern China. The world's oldest civilisations are those of Asia. Chinese civilisation is nearly 5,000 years old, that of India almost as old.

Anthropologists, whose business it is to study mankind, tell us that the oldest civilisation of all, and the source of all other civilisations, was located in the region called Mesopotamia, which lies between the Tigris and the Euphrates, the two great rivers of South-West Asia.

Asia has greatly influenced the nations of the West, its greatest influence being, of course, religious. We tend to think of parts of Asia as being rather backward. But it was not always so. The great civilisations of Asia – particularly China and India – were highly developed while Europe was still primitive and barbaric. It was from Sanskrit, the classical language of India, that Greek, Latin, and in fact most of the languages of Europe were

This saffron-robed Thai youth is a Buddhist monk.

The Hindu-festival 'Under Red Curtains'.

evolved. Many inventions of great importance such as paper-making, printing, and gun-powder have come from China. The scientific knowledge of the Greeks and Romans was preserved for hundreds of years during the Dark Ages by Arab scholars. Incidentally, it was a search for a sea route to the spice markets of India that led Columbus to discover America.

A Kashmiri merchant serves his customers.

A tea-ceremony in Japan.

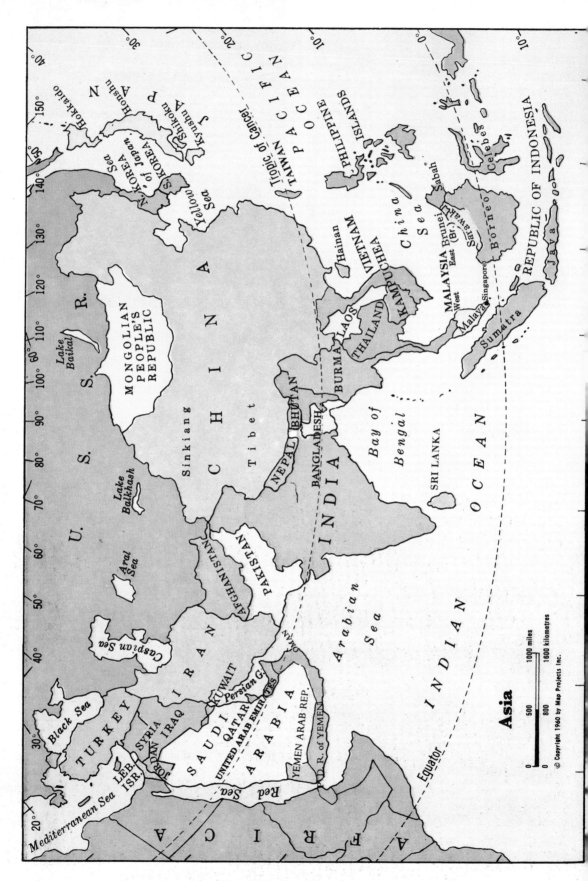

Asia

© Copyright 1960 by Map Projects Inc.

| 0 | 500 | 1000 miles |
| 0 | 800 | 1600 kilometres |

Communications

There are more than thirty countries in Asia today. The names and forms of government of many have changed since 1945. Some, like Israel, did not exist and others were under colonial rule.

In Western Europe it is easy to get quickly from one place to another over long distances because of the abundance of good roads, railways, and air services. In Asia travel is altogether different. In many places high mountains, plateaus, deserts, and jungles make it extremely difficult, if not impossible, to build roads or railways. Even where technically possible, the great distances involved make it very expensive.

In Asia there are few international railways. Millions of Asiatics have never seen, let alone travelled on, a train.

There are exceptions. In India the British built a fairly extensive and efficient railway system. And Japanese railways are among the most modern in the world.

For the most part, serviceable roads are even rarer than railways in Asia. This situation is changing, but changing slowly, and progress is inevitably uneven. Sometimes roads have been built where not even a track existed before. But enormous areas of Asia are very thinly populated, and there is little use in spending an enormous amount of money, time, and labour building a road nobody will use.

Fortunately, there has been a rapid development of air services in recent years. Several major airlines link Asia with Europe and America. There are now important airports at Tokyo, Hong Kong, Singapore, Manila, Bombay, Calcutta, Rangoon, Ankara, Bahrein, Tehran, and Kuwait. The Chinese are developing air services to the immense central area of Asia, which is the most remote part of the continent.

Means of communication in Asia differ widely as these two photographs show.

Hong Kong is one of the most densely populated cities in the world. More than 55 per cent of the population is under twenty-five years of age.

The Cities of Asia

The cities of Asia, like the landscape, climate, and people, vary very widely. Some are more than 1,000 years old, and their older quarters have remained unchanged through the centuries. Others contain the most modern buildings. Many European and American firms, besides those from the country concerned, have offices in these rapidly developing towns. And often, today, they are crowded with visitors from abroad.

Tokyo, the capital of Japan, is the largest city in the world. Besides being a great cultural and political centre, it is a great industrial one, whose exports are shipped to all the world from its great port, Yokohama, on the other side of Tokyo Bay. Industries include ship-

building, textiles, and the manufacture of motor-cars, toys, cameras, optical goods, etc. Many airlines run services to Tokyo and thousands of tourists go there every year, particularly during the cherry-blossom season.

Peking, the capital of the Chinese People's Republic, is one of the oldest cities of China. Its main industries produce steel, machinery, and textiles.

Shanghai is the largest town and seaport in China. It stands on a small river which discharges at the seaward end of the estuary of the Yangtze Kiang, and, as a port, it serves the millions of Chinese in the farms, villages, and towns of the crowded Yangtze Valley. At the beginning of this century it was entirely dominated by the offices, warehouses, and banks, of the great European trading and finance companies. Now all that has been swept away. Shanghai has the largest textile industry in China, and its other industries include shipbuilding, machinery, and food-processing.

Tientsin is another important Chinese port. Lying some seventy miles southeast of Peking, it is the commercial centre of north China. As a manufacturing town it is second only to Shanghai in the production of textiles. As a great railway centre it is the gateway to the inland region including the Chinese capital.

Shenyang (formerly called Mukden) is the chief town of Manchuria. It is one of the important manufacturing towns of China. Coal and iron are found in the vicinity, and supply the raw material for a number of industries, amongst which is the manufacture of motor-cars.

Hong Kong is a British Crown Colony on a small island off the coast of China. It is one of the busiest towns in the world. Ships from all over the world use its fine deep-water harbour. It is separated from China by only a fine natural harbour. Ferries daily bring thousands of people over to work in Hong Kong. Hong Kong lives on foreign trade. But there are many related activities such as insurance, banking, warehousing, and ship-repair.

Calcutta is India's largest town. Situated on the Ganges Delta, about 80 miles (130 km) inland from the Bay of Bengal, it is a leading manufacturing centre and the most important town on the east coast of India. One of its chief products is hessian, which is a coarse canvas made from the jute grown in the neighbourhood. But many other products including tea, coffee, rubber, cotton, and hemp are shipped from the port of Calcutta.

Minarets tower over Baghdad, capital of Iraq and formerly of a great empire.

Silk has been produced in China for thousands of years. This is a modern silk spinning factory.

151

Bombay is on the west coast of India. The second largest town of India, it is situated on an island a short distance from the mainland, with which it is connected by bridges. Bombay has one of the finest harbours in the world. It became an important cotton centre during the American Civil War, when England was unable to get cotton from the Southern States of America. It is now the leading town in India for the manufacture of cotton stuffs. With the opening of the Suez Canal, Bombay became the nearest Indian port to Europe, and its importance has stayed, even though traffic through the canal is very limited now.

Karachi, former capital of Pakistan, has grown rapidly, and now has a population of 3.5 million. Its airport is of importance, for through it pass the main routes from Europe to India, the Far East, and Australia. It is also a thriving port. Islamabad is now Pakistan's official capital.

Singapore city lies at the southern tip of the Malay peninsula. Its principal exports are rubber and tin. Trade is done

The town hall and main station in Bombay, the second largest city of India.

The bright lights of the centre of Tokyo. Tokyo is the largest city in the world.

The streets of Jakarta, capital of Indonesia, are filled with busy traffic of all kinds.

with Britain, the Commonwealth, the United States, Indonesia and South-East Asia. Singapore is now a fully independent island nation within the Commonwealth, and its great port thrives commercially.

Jakarta, a seaport on the north coast of Java, is the capital of the Republic of Indonesia and its largest town. The name Jakarta means 'important city'. During the Dutch rule of the East Indies it was called Batavia. The products of the Indonesian islands are shipped all over the world from Jakarta.

Manila is the largest and most important town in the Philippine Islands. In addition to Filipinos, the population includes large numbers of Chinese, who have settled there and become naturalised. There are also quite a number of people of Spanish extraction, for the islands were ruled by Spain until the Spanish-American War of 1898. The leading exports are copra, sugar, timber, rope, and coconut oil. Iron and chrome and precious metals are mined.

Baghdad, the capital of Iraq, stands on the Tigris river, 350 miles (560 km)

Small barges transport much of the merchandise handled in Shanghai's busy harbour.

north of the Persian Gulf. It was once the chief town of the caravan route from Europe to the Far East. The discovery of oil in Iraq has made Baghdad a town of great activity. It has a population of 1,934,000. The old part of the town lies on the right bank of the Tigris, while the modern avenues are on the left bank.

The Palace of Rest and Culture in Peking. Many former palaces are used for recreation.

Manila's location on a protected bay has helped it become one of the Orient's great ports.

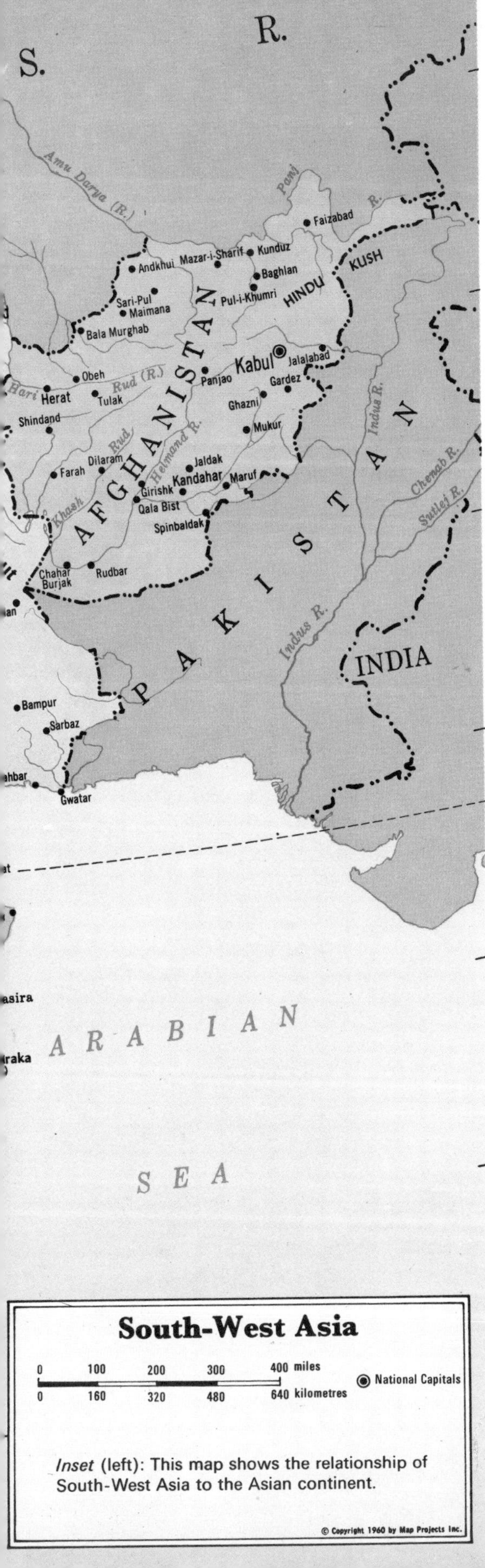

Map labels (left page):

S. R.

Amu Darya (R.)

Faizabad

Andkhui Mazar-i-Sharif Kunduz

HINDU KUSH

Baghlan

Sari-Pul
Maimana Pul-i-Khumri

Bala Murghab

Pani

Obeh Kabul Jalalabad

Hari Rud (R.) Panjao Gardez

Herat Tulak

Shindand Ghazni

AFGHANISTAN Mukur

Helmand R.

Farah Dilaram Jaldak

Girishk Kandahar Maruf

Khosh Qala Bist

Spinbaldak

Chahar Rudbar
Burjak

Bampur

Sarbaz

ahbar

Gwatar

asira

ARABIAN

iraka

SEA

PAKISTAN

Indus R.

Chenab R.

Sutlej R.

Indus R.

INDIA

South-West Asia

| 0 | 100 | 200 | 300 | 400 miles |
| 0 | 160 | 320 | 480 | 640 kilometres |

● National Capitals

Inset (left): This map shows the relationship of South-West Asia to the Asian continent.

South-West Asia

The most important difference between the Middle East on the one hand, and Southern and South-East Asia on the other, is the climate. Although part of the Middle East (the extreme south-west) is influenced by the monsoons, the bulk of the area has a Mediterranean climate, with dry summers and even a permanent drought in some areas, causing large expanses of desert. The greater part of the Arabian peninsula, Iraq, Syria, and Jordan, receives less than 10 inches (250 mm) a year. Only in the Yemen, in the south-west corner of the peninsula is rainfall more abundant, 20 inches (500 mm), due to the monsoon which strikes the mountains there.

Iran and Afghanistan, shielded by mountains both from the monsoon and Mediterranean air currents, are semi-deserts and life is largely confined to the oases.

Rainfall is much greater in the coastal regions of the Mediterranean and the mountains behind them. Jerusalem gets 25 inches (725 mm) a year, Beirut 36 inches (900 mm). It is much the same on the coast of Asia Minor, Izmir (Smyrna) receiving 20 inches (500 mm), while Trebizond, on the Black Sea, has 36 inches (900 mm). However, in these regions irrigation is often necessary in summer as the soil becomes very parched. On the Black Sea coast, although most of the rain falls in winter, meteorological conditions are more complex, and summer rain occurs also.

Because of these conditions the population is very unevenly spread. The people are largely concentrated in the more humid coastal areas. Iran has a population of about 30 million. The two great salt deserts of Dasht-i-Kavir and

Shepherds still water their flocks at the wells of Jericho, as they did in Biblical times.

Dasht-i-Lut are almost completely uninhabited. Turkey in Asia has a fairly good climate, and fertile soils, so its population is fairly evenly distributed.

South-Western Asia is occupied principally by three great races: the Iranians, the Arabs, and the Turks, united by a common religion, Islam, which originated among the Arabs.

Besides these three races there are a few small minorities that must be mentioned. The Kurds of Iraq, numbering no more than 1 million, are one of the most ancient peoples of Asia Minor, speaking an Indo-European language. Israel is peopled by Jewish settlers and refugees from many countries, but particularly from Central Europe and the Middle East. The Maronites of the Lebanon are a religious group rather than a racial one, being one of the Christian communities left in the wake of the Crusaders which have managed to survive in spite of all since the Middle Ages.

The disruption of the Ottoman Empire after the Turkish defeat in the

Jerusalem, sacred to three religions, spreads out below the Mount of Olives.

A Syrian village clings to the side of an eroded mountain for protection against raiders.

*Primitive methods of harvesting characterise
most agriculture in South-West Asia*

First World War left the map of the Middle East much as it is today.

Turkey covers a total area of 300,000 square miles (780,000 sq km) of which all but 9,000 (24,000) are in Asia.

Israel's farmers use modern machinery when the wheat crop is being harvested.

Asia Minor is extremely mountainous. It consists of a central plateau averaging over 3,000 feet (915 m) in height. Of its lakes, many of which are salt, the largest is Lake Tuz, south of Ankara. To the south and east of Lake Tuz are the Taurus Mountains, including Asia Minor's highest peak, Mount Ararat, 16,945 feet (5,165 m) high. The plateau is fringed on the north by a range of mountains sometimes called the Anti-Taurus. They are only high in the east, near the Georgian frontier, where they rise to a height of over 12,000 feet (3,650 m). There are deltaic plains along the Black Sea, the most important of which belongs to the low valley of the Sakarya, to the east of the Sea of Marmara. Two famous rivers, the Tigris and Euphrates, rise in the mountains of eastern Turkey.

Turkey

Turkey has about 44 million inhabitants. Agriculture is the chief occupation of the country, employing over 70 per cent of the total population. For the most part land is divided into small-holdings. In recent years a large-scale effort has been made to launch irrigation schemes and arrest the exhaustion of the soil. Modern methods of farming and stock-breeding have also been introduced, with excellent results. The agricultural produce of Turkey is very varied; wheat, barley, rice, cotton, tobacco, tea, olives, linseed, liquorice roots, mohair, hides and silk.

Large crops of olives are obtained in western and southern Anatolia. Turkey is one of the world's greatest producers of raisins, and a large quantity of dried figs is also exported. The production of fresh fruit and nuts is abundant.

In recent years industry has thrived. Deposits of bituminous coal, lignite, oil, iron, chromium, bauxite, manganese, and sulphur are being exploited. There are steel works, industries for the production of sulphuric acid, cement, cotton goods, and paper. Food is processed, and there are oil refineries and chemical works.

Starting south of Iskenderun, a moun-

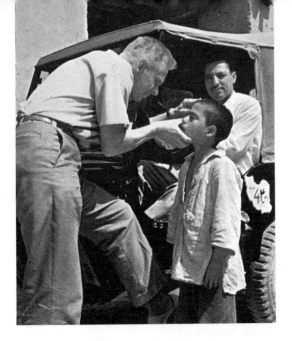

Doctors from all over the world help in the fight against disease in the Middle East.

tain range runs along the coast from Turkey through Syria, Lebanon, Israel, and Jordan. Its greatest height, Dhor-el-Khodib, is a little over 10,000 feet (3,050 m). South of Tyre, the mountains move back from the coast leaving room for several coastal plains, including the famous Plain of Sharon. East of the mountains is the long depression which contains Lake Tiberias, the River Jordan, and the Dead Sea. Further east is another mountain range which joins the

coastal range south of the Dead Sea and with it runs down to the Gulf of Aqaba.

Lebanon

The Republic of Lebanon has 2,850,000 Arabic-speaking inhabitants, a small majority of whom are Christians.

Agriculture is the chief occupation, though cultivation on only 38 per cent of the total area is limited by the mountainous nature of the country and by soil erosion. The chief products are wheat, maize, barley, olives, potatoes, sugar-beet, tobacco and fruit – particularly grapes and citrus fruits. Manufacturing, although very limited, has doubled in output in the last ten years, with food processing, clothing and the construction industry being the most important. Oil from Iraq and Saudi Arabia is refined at Tripoli.

Israel

Israel was cut out of Palestine to make a national home for the Jews. Since 1948 more than 1,500,000 Jews have emigrated to Israel. It includes the Negev, an arid area running as far as the Gulf of

Israeli schoolchildren learn about farming in the fields of their kibbutz.

Jaffa oranges and grapefruit are among the chief exports of Israel.

Shrines dot the Mount of Olives, where Jesus kept vigil in the Garden of Gethsemane.

Aqaba, giving the Israelis an outlet to the Red Sea. Since 1967, Israel has been engaged in an on-going war with neighbouring Arab countries, with shaky peace settlements at intervals.

Economic development is handicapped by an adverse balance of trade. The

As they have done since Biblical days, fishermen still fish the Sea of Galilee (Lake Tiberias).

principal unit of agriculture is the collective farm or *kibbutz*. But there is also the *mofhav* (co-operative) and some private farms. There is extensive use of irrigation, especially by the new drip method. To provide energy fuel has to be transported from abroad. Oil is piped from the Port of Eilat in the Gulf of Aqaba. It then runs via Ashkelon and Ashdod to Haifa. The Negev is rich in minerals, and chemicals are manufactured from the salts found in the water of the Dead Sea. Other industries are concerned with food-processing. Tel Aviv was founded in 1909 by Zionists. Together with Jaffa, it had a population of 362,000 in 1976. Haifa comes next with 218,000 inhabitants. Jerusalem was divided into two parts, one part belonging to Jordan, the other to Israel, until the Israelis took over control of the whole city in the 1967 war. Jerusalem is the capital of Israel, with about 304,500 inhabitants. Jerusalem is regarded as a sacred city by Christians, Jews, and Moslems.

Jordan

The Hashemite Kingdom of Jordan is only really habitable in the west, the remainder being largely desert. The population in 1976 was 2,577,000, consisting of farmers in the western part of the country, growing wheat, barley, tomatoes and citrus fruit on terraced and irrigated slopes; semi-nomads in the western sectors of the plateaus; and complete nomads living entirely on their herds. What little industry exists is limited to food-processing. Except for phosphates and potash, no mineral wealth has been discovered in the country, though it has not yet been thoroughly prospected.

Amman, population 583,000, is about 20 miles (32 km) east of the Jordan.

This Jordanian goat-herd keeps a protective eye on his herd as it crosses the desert.

Mechanised farming is little known in parts of Asia. Animals are the chief source of power in many places.

Syria

Because of physical conditions, Syria is a poor country. Except for the coastal plains and one or two other fertile areas, most of Syria consists of either mountains or deserts.

Agriculture is chiefly concentrated in the coastal plains. Receiving a fair amount of rain, they produce wheat, barley, grapes, and other fruit. There is also a certain amount of fertile volcanic soil in the Jebel Druse and Hauran areas immediately north of the Jordan frontier, and at the foot of the mountains there is a series of oases bordering the desert. The finest of these is that of Damascus, which

Irrigation with water from the Euphrates River makes this Syrian cottonfield possible.

owes its fertility to the waters of a small river coming down from the mountains. Besides growing cereal crops in considerable quantities, Syria is able to export cotton and wool. Sheep are kept largely for the sake of their wool.

Under government supervision, industry has made considerable progress since 1930. Textiles are manufactured of cotton, wool, silk, and rayon. There is also food-processing, manufacture of leather goods, cement and textiles. Damascus still pursues her ancient manufacture of damascene jewellery (inlaid gold and silver work), and woven damask with figured designs in light and shade. The country has only small deposits of minerals, phosphates, copper and manganese, though there is natural gas and oil in small amounts in the Jezirah.

Dates are an important source of food in South-East Asia. They are also a valuable export.

Oil States of the Middle East

Until the 1930s some of the oil producing countries of the Middle East were almost unheard of. They consisted of a few desert states with poverty stricken people living at subsistence level.

These people suddenly discovered that there was a fortune under their feet. The finding of oil was an event of the utmost economic importance, changing the lives of the population dramatically.

The states are Iraq, Saudi Arabia, Kuwait, Bahrein, United Arab Emirates and Iran. At first their development was slow, but the demand for oil increased as more countries became industrialized; as more vehicles were made; as more by-products from oil were discovered; as oil drilling technology improved; and as transportation of oil became more sophisticated and less costly. With all this realized, the demand from the greatest oilfields in the world reached such a pitch that by the late 1960s to 70s the oil states became some of the richest countries in the world. Their political significance in the world has increased accordingly.

The oil states are putting a great deal of their wealth into improving the lives of their people. They are building new schools, hospitals, universities and public buildings in the most luxurious styles, and attracting top people from all over the world to work in them. They are developing their agriculture in many experimental ways: using glasshouses in the desert and expensive irrigation techniques. They are even trying to plant forests in the desert.

Not only are they putting vast amounts of money into their own countries, but they are investing it in overseas countries. They realise that their oil will not last for ever, so they are making provision for their children.

Other countries are benefiting directly from the oil states' wealth. They are selling them luxury goods such as expensive cars and private planes and many other consumer goods. Foreign industry is also being attracted to these states. The importance of them is shown by the establishment of one of the first two supersonic passenger Concorde regular

The oilfield at Kirkuk in Iraq. The world's demand for oil has radically altered the political importance of the oil-producing states of the Middle East.

services from Western Europe to Bahrein.

In spite of all this wealth it will be seen from a study of the individual countries that life goes on for many as it has done throughout history.

Iraq

Iraq has an area of over 171,267 square miles (438,446 sq km). Something like half of it, lying west of the Euphrates, is part of the Syrian Desert. The Tigris and Euphrates together form a great river basin, a good deal of which is marshy. Where they flow into the Persian Gulf, a great delta has been formed which is divided between Iran, Iraq, and the small state of Kuwait. In the north-east is a range of mountains along the Turkish and Iranian frontiers which, from a height of 2,000 (600 m) to 6,000 feet (1,800 m), is covered with forests of oaks. This area and the upper Tigris basin are the only regions with an adequate rainfall.

Agriculture depends, as it always has, on irrigation. The Tigris and Euphrates

Kurd nomads wander the mountains of the Iran-Iraq border, seeking grass and water.

each have two seasons of spate a year. They rise with the winter rains and again when the snows melt in their upper reaches in spring. There are two harvests a year: autumn-sown wheat and barley; and maize, millet, rice, sesame, and cotton sown in the spring. Moreover Iraq is the greatest date-producing country of the world. Other agricultural produce includes oranges, vegetables of all sorts, and leguminous plants.

The country is backward in industry, although factories are being established with Soviet aid. Manufactures include textiles, both cotton and wool, shoes and leather goods, and food-processing. There are deposits of various metals – iron, copper, etc. – but prospecting has hardly started. Since 1927 oil has been the great source of wealth. The wells are at Kirkuk, Khanaqin, and near Basra. Crude production in 1974 was 97 million metric tons, making Iraq the world's eighth largest producer.

The ungainly camel is familiar in all desert areas – even those occupied by oil wells.

Arabian Peninsula Countries

The great square-cut Arabian peninsula, with an area of a million square miles (2.6 million sq kms), consists of a vast plateau sloping gradually down from a line of mountains along the Red Sea coast towards the Persian Gulf and the Gulf of Oman. The mountains, which average some 5,000 feet (1,520 m) in height, rise in the Yemen to over 12,000 feet (3,660 m). The only other mountains of any importance run along the coast of the Gulf of Oman, reaching nearly 10,000 feet (3,050 m) in the Jabal Akhdar.

Most of this area is extremely dry. The only part to receive a fairly adequate rainfall consists of the Yemen and the Hadhramaut, the latter being a coastal strip running half-way along the south coast, traditionally famous as a land of prosperity. Another prosperous region is along the coastal plain at the foot of the mountains in the Batina district of Oman. Inside these areas a region of dry steppes runs all round the peninsula, particularly in the Hejaz, in the west, and in the Syrian Desert, which extends into Iraq, Jordan, and Syria. The real desert is in the stony central part of Nejd, and in the sandy desert to the east and south-east.

On both steppe and desert, life is concentrated in the oases, some of which are thriving, particularly those of the Hejaz and the Hasa on the northern half of the Persian Gulf.

Saudi Arabia

The kingdom of Saudi Arabia is the dominant power of the Arabian peninsula, not because of its population, which is 7.8 million, but because of its enormous area of 927,000 square miles (2.4 million sq km), and because, in the west (the Hejaz), it includes the Moslem holy places – Jiddah, Medina, and above all Mecca – which give Saudi Arabia a certain moral authority. The country derives a great wealth from oil production which reached 412 million metric tons in 1974 making Saudi Arabia the

An oil refinery at Abadan (left). Oil is very important to the Iranian economy. A crew of Arab workmen laying an asphalt road across the Arabian desert (right).

This neat community at Dhahran, Saudi Arabia, houses the employees of a large oil company.

world's third largest producer after the USA and the USSR. The chief oilfields are at Abqaiq, ain Dar and Damman, where the original oil discovery was made in 1938. Several other fields, including some offshore deposits, are being developed. Some crude oil is refined locally, at Ras Tanura, some is transported to Bahrein for refining, some is shipped from the Persian Gulf and some is pumped through the Trans Arabian pipeline system. The government, under the name Petromin, co-ordinates oil production, exploration, and marketing and is building new refineries at Jiddah and Riyadh.

In agriculture the government has given grants for major projects of desert reclamation, including irrigation, planting windbreaks and drainage control.

Dates grow well in Medina, fruit and honey come from mountain oases, the Nejd produces cereals, coffee, limes and animal products.

Riyadh (population 300,000) is the political capital of Saudi Arabia. Great oil finances are centred here, and it is a new focus for industry and commerce in general. Mecca is the religious capital.

Kuwait

Kuwait, which has a common frontier with Iraq, enjoyed British protection from 1899 to 1961, when Britain recognised its independence. The sheikhdom is prosperous and its port, which bears the same name, and which lies on a sheltered bay, has long been a thriving market, exporting the products of the hinterland: horses, sheep, and wool. When oil was added to the list, the wealth of the country soared. Production is now over 112 million metric tons a year. Kuwait is now the world's fifth largest oil producer. The town of Kuwait now has a population of about 295,000. It is very modern and prosperous. The new mammoth tankers can be loaded from a terminal off an island off the Kuwait coast.

Bahrein

Bahrein has a population of 216,800. It is composed of islands. It was once famous for pearl fishing, but the industry has declined in recent years. The soil is rich and agriculture prosperous with dates, vegetables and dairy produce. Oil was discovered in 1932 and since then Bahrein has become a large oil-producing country. Bahrein is being developed as a major communications and industrial state. A new industry is based on aluminium smelting and future projects include expansion of marine industries and the tourist trade.

Oman and United Arab Emirates

The area to the east and south-east is divided into two sections. The larger one is the Sultanate of Oman, with an area of approximately 105,000 square miles (271,940 sq km). The other, the United Arab Emirates, formerly called the Trucial States, is on the Persian Gulf. It consists now of seven emirates. The Sultanate has a population of 750,000. Agriculture flourishes in the coastal plains and in the oases of the interior. Another resource is fishing, and trade is carried on with India. The capital is Muscat, which has lost much of its trade to the port of Matrah. Oil production began in 1967 and now it dominates the economy. Six of the seven Trucial States joined in the federation, the United Arab Emirates in December 1971, the seventh joining later. Abu Dhabi and Dubai produced 80 million metric tons of oil in 1974 making them tenth in world output.

Fishermen in Bahrein. Once famous for its pearl fishing industry, Bahrein is now a major oil-producing country.

Republic of the Yemen

The People's Democratic Republic of the Yemen has a population of 1.4 million divided into a number of governorates. Abyan long staple cotton is a major export. The town of Aden, with about 250,000 inhabitants, has an entrepôt trade in textiles, hides and coffee. However, this trade was severely affected by the Yemen Civil War and the closure of the Suez Canal, and the country is one of the poorest in the world.

A market scene in Bait al Faqih, a town of the Yemen Arab Republic.

Yemen Arab Republic

In the Yemen Arab Republic, which will eventually unite with the Republic of the Yemen, the soil is fertile on the coastal plains and in the mountain valleys. Commercial crops are cotton, coffee, tobacco, grapes and qat, a narcotic shrub. The capital is Sana'a, a town of 124,000 inhabitants, standing in the mountains at a height of 7,500 feet (2,280 m). From it a road runs down to Hodeida, the principal port, while another runs down to the more southerly port of Mocha, which gives its name to a famous variety of coffee though it is no longer exported through this port.

Iran

The kingdom of Iran, a country with an area of 630,000 square miles (1,648,000 sq km), is, like Afghanistan, much more truly part of the continent of Asia than the countries we have been dealing with. Lying between the Caspian Sea and the Persian Gulf, it consists of a central plateau surrounded by high mountains. The most important of these are the Zagros Mountains in the west and south-west and the Elburz Moun-

tains in the north, whose highest peak is Demavend, 18,900 feet (5,760 m). In the east, the Iranian plateau is separated from Afghanistan and Pakistan by the heights of Khurasan and Baluchistan.

The climate is characterised by sharp contrasts of heat and cold, severe snowy winters being followed by hot, dry summers. Grazing on the plateaus is poor. In

Child labour is common in the Middle East. This Iranian girl strings tobacco for drying.

the Azerbaijan region of the Zagros Mountains fertile basins alternate with great mountain blocks. These basins, particularly that of Lake Urmia, provide excellent arable land giving a high yield of wheat and barley, or, on some parts, cotton.

Of the country's 30 million inhabitants, 70 per cent live on the land. Large quantities of wheat are grown, as well as other cereals, such as barley and rice. Sufficient rice is grown to provide a surplus, which is exported to Oman. Fruit is grown in great variety, and considerable amounts are exported. Sugar-beet, tobacco and tea are now being grown. Of industrial crops, cotton is much the most important, about 450,000 metric tons a year being produced. Industries include car assembly, petro chemicals, steel mills, light metals, textiles and food processing. Persian rugs, and carpets, the most famous produce of the country, are still being made by hand in the traditional way at Tabriz, Hamadan, Sultanabad, Kashan, Shiraz, Kerman and Tehran. In spite of a decline in world demand, they still form one of the country's leading exports.

The country's chief source of wealth, however, is oil, found at the northern end of the Persian Gulf, and refined at Abadan. Production is more than 300 million metric tons and Iran is the world's fourth largest producer. No other export bears any comparison with that of oil. Iran also has other minerals in substantial amounts as yet undeveloped.

Afghanistan

Afghanistan is a completely inland country, covering an area of some 250,000 square miles (657,500 sq km). It is a very mountainous country, and the frontiers are, to a considerable extent, formed by mountains. But in the extreme north the frontier with Siberia follows the course of the Amu Darya (Oxus). On the Pakistan frontier is the famous Kojak Pass on the route from Kandahar to Quetta, and the still more famous Khyber Pass on the route from Kabul to Peshawar. The spine of the country is the Hindu Kush.

In a country so mountainous and so far from the sea, great varieties of temperature occur, from a maximum of 110°F (43°C) in summer, to a minimum of 14°F (−10°C) in winter. Rain falls mainly between December and April. What rain there is in summer is confined to occasional monsoon storms.

A recent estimate gives the population as around 19.6 million, all Moslems.

Except for soldiering, the only occupation of the people is agriculture. Some Afghans are settled, living in village communities in the valleys and the lower foothills of the mountains. Crops consist of wheat, barley, maize, millet, fodder crops, sugar-beet, sugar-cane, rice, cotton, and a wide range of fruits with irrigation. Still more Afghans are nomads, shifting their tents from the lower plains frequented in winter to the higher grazing grounds in summer. They breed horses, donkeys, camels, and, most of all, Karakul sheep, which go to export as 'Persian' lambskins.

Industry is in its infancy but growing with Russian and American aid. There is some cotton and wool processing and some leather-working and food processing. Mineral deposits are rarely exploited, with the exception of the coal in the Hindu Kush. Hydro-electricity is being developed. Some oil has been found in the northern region, and natural gas is piped to the USSR. Rich iron ore deposits lie unexploited west of Kabul.

169

Houseboats are a familiar sight in Kashmir, a fertile land of many beautiful lakes.

Southern Asia

The Himalayas, the world's highest mountains, form the boundary between India and Tibet.

The peninsular part of India, the Deccan, consists of ancient plateaus joined on to the main body of Asia by plains formed long ago by two great rivers. These are: in the west, the Indus which has a length of 1,900 miles (3,060 km); in the east, the Ganges, with a length of 1,560 miles (2,510 km). The latter joins the Brahmaputra, and the united rivers form an immense delta occupying the greater part of the province of Bengal – a very fertile area, but greatly overpopulated. The ridges of the Deccan are called *ghats*. The two main ridges, called the Western Ghats and the Eastern Ghats, look down on the Arabian Sea and the Bay of Bengal respectively. North of the plain is a hilly region, and north of that again the great barrier of the Himalayas. This, the greatest mountain range in the world, has formidable glaciers. In their long course of 50 miles (80 km) and more, these glaciers, like rivers, receive tributaries.

The map shows Southern Asia with major cities, rivers, and geographical features including Pakistan, India, Nepal, Bhutan, Bangladesh, Burma, Sri Lanka, and neighbouring regions.

Southern Asia

⊙ National Capitals

```
0    100    200    300 miles
0    160    320    480 kilometres
```

© Copyright 1960 by Map Projects Inc.

Inset (above): This map shows the relationship of southern Asia to the Asian continent.

The lower Himalayan slopes are forested. In depressions are the mountain states of Kashmir, Nepal, and Bhutan. Sheltered by the high mountains, these states have fertile valleys and a prosperous agriculture.

In the Near and Middle East, the climate is similar to that of the Mediterranean countries, while India and South-East Asia are dominated by the monsoons. Here, unlike the Mediterranean

area, winter is the dry season, because then the Asiatic continent is the centre of a high-pressure zone, and winds blow outwards towards the sea. In summer the pressure over the southern part of the continent is low, and moisture-laden winds blow in from the Indian Ocean or the China Sea. In their more exposed position, both India and South-East Asia receive enormous quantities of rain from the time the monsoon breaks, in May or

Whole families spend long hours in the rice-fields.

June, throughout the summer. In some areas, for instance, this rule is broken, and on the Coromandel Coast of Madras or the east coast of Annam, much rain falls in the winter.

In India, the west coast of the Deccan, Bengal, and Assam in the extreme north-east receive the heaviest rainfall – 40 inches (1,000 mm) or more in three months. One place in Assam holds the world record. Valleys sheltered from moist winds, like the valley of the Indus and the interior of the Deccan, are relatively dry, and here the soil is unproductive and the population thin. An area in the south of the Indus Basin is almost a desert. In South-East Asia, too, the rainfall varies considerably.

The most rainy parts of India and South-East Asia are covered with tropical forests. Where these have been cleared, the combination of heat, moisture, and good soil makes the plantations extremely productive, particularly for the growing of rice, which is the staple crop of the monsoon area of Asia. Abundance of food leads to high density of population, and the warm plains and deltas, like Bengal and Lower Burma, are very crowded, while the hills and plateaus are more thinly populated.

Hinduism is one of the two chief religions of Southern Asia. To the Hindus God is seen as something (rather than somebody) essentially nameless and formless. The many gods of Hindu

The Ganges, India's sacred river, begins its 1,560 mile (2,510 km) journey through India high in the Himalayas.

This Calcutta temple was built by Jainists, who refuse to inflict pain on other living creatures.

mythology are, in fact, considered different names applied to something which is really without a name. Thus, Brahma is the creator, Vishnu the preserver, and Siva the destroyer in a kind of Trinity. It is within the power of every individual to

A Hindu farmer and his family outside their home. Seven out of ten Indians are farmers.

reach, by a sort of personal deliverance, the divine goodness. After death, life begins again, the soul entering into another human or animal body. Accordingly, all living creatures are sacred, and it is a crime to kill even a cow or a snake.

Cows are considered sacred by the Hindus. They are permitted to roam freely through the streets of India.

Before praying, this Brahmin puts a ritual colour mark on his forehead.

This Sikh, with traditional beard and turban, is a member of India's presidential guard.

An Indian peasant. The average size of a peasant farm is 6.4 acres (2.63 hectares).

All meat-eating is thus forbidden to the followers of this religion. At least once in his life every believer should bathe in the purifying waters of the Ganges at Benares, which is the Holy City of the Hindus.

The second of the two principal religions of this area is Islam. Unlike the

This humble village near Delhi is typical of many Indian villages.

Hindus, the Moslems eat meat, with the exception of pork. That is a cause of antagonism between the followers of these two religions, especially the eating of beef, for cattle are particularly sacred to the Hindus. Another serious division is that the Moslems have no caste system. It was these deep divisions which led to the separation of the Moslems in the state of Pakistan when India became independent.

The famous warrior race of the Punjab, the Sikhs, have their own religion – Sikhism. Sikhism was founded in the fifteenth century by Nanak, who preached simplicity and equality and rejected idolatry and the Hindu caste system. He was followed by ten *gurus* (spiritual leaders or 'teachers'), the most famous of whom was Gobind Singh (1666–1708) who welded the sect into a nation of warriors. They took the name of Singh ('lion'). When British India was partitioned in 1947 the Punjab, and with it the Sikh people, was divided fairly equally between the countries of India and Pakistan.

Religious differences have been further aggravated by differences of language or dialect. Including minor ones, there are 200 of them. There are several Dravidian languages of some importance, but the most important of all are those derived from the Aryan or Indo-European stock. The chief of these are Hindustani and Bengali. But English, so long used in the administration of the country, has been accepted as the common language amongst educated Indians and Pakistanis, although the Indian government has recently made Hindi the official language.

The weight of the men as they run up and down the pole operates this water well. Many modern methods are now used, besides this primitive one.

An age-old method of ploughing. Children provide India with much of her labour and, although education is compulsory almost everywhere, enforced attendance is not practical.

Economies of India, Pakistan, Bangladesh and Sri Lanka

The principal countries of Southern Asia, India, Pakistan, Bangladesh and Sri Lanka, when combined together cover an area of over 1 million square miles (2½ million sq km), and have between them a population of over 660 million people. When independence was granted in 1947, the Moslem areas elected to separate, even though it meant forming a state in two separate parts, East Pakistan being nearly 1,000 miles (1,600 km) from West Pakistan. In 1971,

East Pakistan broke with West Pakistan, and was re-named the independent republic of Bangladesh. Pakistan now consists of Baluchistan, Sind, and almost the whole of the Punjab. The main city, Karachi, stands north-west of the Indus delta. Bangladesh contains most of Bengal and part of Assam. On separation, East and West Pakistan were very ill-balanced, since East Pakistan with one-sixth of the area of West Pakistan, had a slightly larger population.

Equal opportunity in higher education has opened many doors for Indian women.

The beautiful Taj Mahal at Agra.

Indian women harvesting wheat.

This Indian woman is a toxicologist, one who studies poisons and their antidotes.

Metal windmills, only recently used in Indian irrigation, dot the countryside near Delhi.

Pondicherry and the other small French possessions on the Indian coast were handed over to the Indian government in 1954. Portugal declined to do likewise, and Goa was seized by India in 1961.

Sri Lanka, formerly Ceylon, an island of 25,300 square miles (64,640 sq km), with a population of about 13 million, became independent in 1948. The government has invested in heavy industry, including chemicals and rubber; and in irrigation projects and power schemes such as the Mahaweli Ganga Dam. Nationalization of the large tea plantations is beginning.

By far the largest part of the population of Southern Asia live by farming – often on a very small scale. Families are large and grouped into villages containing a few hundred people. From an early age the children work in the fields beside their parents.

Farming methods are still generally very primitive. There is often little or no

machinery and a great shortage of fertilisers and manures. Carts, ploughs, weeders, etc. are drawn by bullocks, and they also provide the power to work the chain pumps for irrigation. To nourish the soil, leaf-mould is used, with household refuse, and even silt scraped up from the bottom of irrigation tanks. The soil, nevertheless, gets poorer and poorer, for the manure of the great herds of cattle, instead of going back on the land, is dried and used for household fuel.

Irrigation, which has been in use from ancient times, even in the rainy districts, enables more than one crop a year to be raised. The water is generally drawn up from wells, but in the southern provinces and Sri Lanka irrigation tanks form a familiar feature of the landscape. In the Punjab, the great alluvial plain swept out

A distribution point for power like this one in India supplies power for factories and homes.

Singhalese women pick tea. After picking the leaves must be dried before they are shipped.

by the five rivers that flow into the Indus, a whole network of canals was constructed by the British to water the vast dry patches between the rivers. Two dams, one constructed across the Indus at Sukkur, in northern Sind, and the Nagarjunsaga canal and dam project on the Krishna river have allowed a vast reclamation scheme.

Of the cereals grown, rice is by far the most important. It is found chiefly in Bengal and Assam, and in the coastal plains. With the first rains the peasants spread the grain, which is quickly buried in the wet soil. Each parcel of land has a low dyke to prevent the water running off. The water is not allowed to run off until the rice begins to ripen. After harvesting, the sheaves are beaten against packing cases to separate the grains. In its rough state, before polishing, rice is called paddy, hence the phrase 'paddy-fields'.

An elephant pulls a plough in Sri Lanka. Elephants are the tractors of Southern Asia.

New wells, like the one above, have been dug under the supervision of agricultural experts, as seen below.

In the drier areas of India, such as the interior of the Deccan, millet is the most important crop. Wheat is grown in the irrigated areas of the Punjab, and is the only cereal to be exported. Other food crops are chick-peas, groundnuts, and a rather poor quality sugar-cane. None of these is exported.

Tea is one of the great export crops of India and Sri Lanka. A great deal is grown in the Deccan, but particularly famous teas are those of Assam and Ceylon, as well as those of Darjeeling in the extreme north of Bengal. Hundreds of thousands of tons of tea are exported, the United Kingdom being the principal consumer.

Of the crops for industrial use, the chief are cotton and jute. Much of the cotton is grown on volcanic soil in the north-west of the Deccan, but Pakistan has a high production. Jute is grown over most of Bengal. Most jute and cotton is processed locally before export.

India is making great efforts with Five Year Plans to modernise the country and raise the standard of living of the Indian people. Her output of food grains in 1972–3 was 95 million metric tons, compared with 50 million tons in 1949–50. This increase was largely the result of the additional irrigation of nearly 16½ million acres (6½ million hectares). The irrigation of a further 51 million acres (20 million hectares) is taking place gradually and coming under cultivation.

Also, India has made rapid progress in developing her electrical and industrial capacity, as well as raising the welfare standards of her people. However, despite all India's efforts, the surface of the problem has hardly been scratched, as yet. The situation is aggravated by the rapidly increasing population in spite of more knowledge of birth control methods.

The division of India and Pakistan left India with very nearly all the existing industries and mineral resources, while Pakistan was, at the outset, an almost purely agricultural country. Since then, however, Pakistan has made considerable progress in building hydro-electric power stations and developing the textile, electrical, aluminium, vehicle, food-processing and chemical industries. Great efforts have also been made to increase food production by erecting barrages for irrigation, and by reclaiming salt affected land. In spite of this Pakistan still has to import some basic foods.

Large oil deposits are mined and refined in the Dum Duma area of upper Assam. Coal production has been increased to about 950,000 tons compared with 240,000 in 1948; and natural gas is also being exploited, although only on a comparatively small scale.

Iron and steel have been produced in India for many years. There are steel works in Jamshedpur in Bihar, and important reserves of coal and iron ore are nearby. There are also iron and steel works near Calcutta and in several other states. India also has deposits of manganese, copper and bauxite. Industry includes engineering and food proces-

Education has improved throughout Southern Asia, but many schools still work with inferior materials. However, recently television has been used for educational purposes in India.

sing, and the manufacture of cement, glass and chemicals, though textiles are the most important products. With industrial development, towns have grown. In India 20 per cent of the popu-

Hand-made clay bricks are still common building material over a large part of India.

Textiles are traditionally one of India's greatest industries.

lation live in towns, in Pakistan no more than 15 per cent. Calcutta, in West Bengal, is a great industrial conurbation with a population of over 7 million, and also a great port lying on a busy navigable river, the Hooghly. It is well supplied with railways, and is one of the busiest urban centres in the world. Its exports include jute and hessian, tea and oilseeds.

Bombay is on the west coast of India, on an island, but it is linked to the mainland by bridges. It has one of the finest harbours in the world and has a popula-

Calcutta is a city of great contrast between the rich and the very poor.

Bangladesh is a hot, damp lowland. Tropical plants such as coconut palms and jute do well here in this particular type of climate.

tion, with suburbs, of 6 million. Together with Calcutta and Cochin, it is being expanded for large shipbuilding projects. Bombay became a great cotton centre during the American Civil War, when England was unable to get cotton from the United States. It now has the biggest textile mills in India. As a port it benefited from the Suez Canal, but its importance in this respect has since declined.

Madras, on the east coast of India, is, with a population of 2.4 million, the largest town in southern India. Its industries produce textiles and machinery. Hyderabad, in the Indian province of that name, has a population of 1.7 mill-

ion, and is an important university and commercial town. Lastly Delhi, with 3.6 million inhabitants, is the capital of the Republic of India.

Islamabad is the capital of Pakistan which withdrew from the Commonwealth in 1972 but Karachi is the leading town. As a city and a port Karachi has grown rapidly, and now has a population of 3.5 million. Its enormous airport is of great importance, for through it pass the main routes from Europe to India, South-East Asia, the Far East, and Australia. Karachi has a pleasant dry climate and is much preferred by tourists to either Bombay or Calcutta. Its chief exports are wheat and cotton.

Lahore, in the Punjab, is the chief university town of Pakistan, and also a banking and commercial centre. It has a population of 2,148,000.

The most important town in Bangladesh is Dacca, and it serves as capital of the area. It has a population of over 1,302,000, including the suburbs, and it is the centre of the rice- and jute-growing area of the Ganges – Brahmaputra delta. Bangladesh has a Five Year Plan (1974–1979) to develop agriculture, industry, flood control, transport and family planning.

Colombo is the chief town and capital of Sri Lanka, with 562,160 inhabitants. Situated in the south-west of the island, it exports tea, rubber, coconut oil, and copra, its imports being sugar, cotton goods, fuels, and fertilisers.

Despite the progress it has made, this area suffers greatly from the blight of tropical diseases. The health of these countries is undermined by cholera and, still more, by malaria. The great povery of the mass of the people, and also to some extent the caste system of India, makes it very difficult to combat disease. The birth-rate is high, but so is mortality, especially infant mortality. These remarks apply to India and Pakistan much more than to Sri Lanka, which has a much lower death-rate. A great deal of progress has been made in both countries, however. In India, for example, the death-rate has been reduced by half during the last thirty years.

Nepal and Bhutan

North-east of India are two independent mountain states. The largest one, Nepal, has a population which totals 11.7 million.

Nepal is the usual starting point of international climbing expeditions into the Himalayas, and the home of the famous Ghurkas. Life in these two countries is concentrated in the valleys, where rice, maize, vegetables, and fruit are grown. The great valley of Nepal also produces sugar-cane and potatoes.

Despite modernisation, demonstrated by the Jamshedpur steel works, age-old customs still prevail.

This expedition, in search of the 'abominable snowman' of the Himalayas, camps at 15,000 ft (4,572 m).

The Sherpa tribe lives in the mountains. They are used to high altitudes and make good guides.

The capital of Nepal is Katmandu, and the population consists of the Newari people, related to the Tibetans, and the Gurkhas themselves, the ruling group whose language is derived from Sanskrit. A great deal of foreign currency comes into Nepal from the large number of Gurkha soldiers serving in the British and Indian armies. The first road from India to Katmandu was only completed in 1953, but the USA and India are now financing more road construction.

Bhutan is one of the most isolated countries in the world and is rarely visited by outsiders. It has an area of 18,000 square miles (46,600 sq km) and a population of 1,100,000. The capital and only important town is Thimphu.

Sikkim

The Himalayan state of Sikkim is now part of India. Formerly an independent kingdom, it has a population of only 208,670. The capital is Gangtok and its people, who are also related to the Tib-

etans, live by agriculture, in the valleys; by yak-breeding, and by making small but high value goods such as jewellery and radio assembly.

The source of the River Ganges in the Himalayas.

Fields of rice, Asia's chief food crop, stretch across the fertile lowlands of Thailand.

South-East Asia

Burma was split off from India in 1937 to become a separate British colony. Ten years later, the country became an independent federal republic with an area of 262,000 square miles (678,000 sq km), and about 28.9 million inhabitants who speak a language nearer to Chinese than to any Indian language. A high range, the Arakan Yoma, runs up the west coast, and its northerly extension, the Chin Hills, separates the country from India. In the east is a racial group, the Shans, about a million strong, who belong to the Thai race and speak Thai dialects, and are thus related to the Siamese. They occupy plateaus which belong to the vast mountain ranges of the Yunnan province of China, across which runs the Salween River.

Between the Arakan Yoma and the Eastern heights is the enormous basin of the Irrawaddy and its tributary, the Chindwin. A much smaller basin is that of the Sittang which runs parallel to the Irrawaddy. On the whole, the central area is fairly low, except for a range of hills, the Pegu Yoma, between the last two rivers.

95°

100°

Pangsau Pass

Putao

Shingbwiyang

INDIA

CHINA

Lonkin

Mogaung   Myitkyina

Indaw   Katha

Bhamo

Tropic of Cancer

Kalemyo   Mogok   Lashio

Hagiang   Caobang

Shwebo

Laokay   Backan   Langson

Gangaw

Maymyo

Muong Hou Neua

TONKIN

Vinhyen Dinhlap

Monywa   Mandalay

Mongnawng

Phongsaly   Dienbienphu   Sonla   Vanyen   Sontay   Haiduong

Sagaing   Kyaukse

Hoabinh   Hanoi   Haiphong

Pakokku   Myingyan   Taunggyi

Muong Sing

Namdinh   Ninhbinh

Meiktila   Yamethin

Chiang Khong

Paletwa

Kengtung

Chiangrai   Mekong R.   Muong Lane

BURMA   Mong Pan

Chiangrai

Luang Prabang   Thanhhoa   Cuarao

Akyab   Minbu   Magwe

Muang Fang

Xiengkhouang

Yenanma   Sale

Chiang Khan

Vinh   HAINAN

Kyaukpyu

Loikaw

Muang Nan

Nape   Hatinh

Thayetmyo   Prome   Paungde

Maehongson

ARAKAN YOMA   Myanaung   Papun   Lamphun   Lampang

Phrae   Loei   Vientiane   Udon   Nakhon   Thakhet   Ron   Donghoi

VIETNAM

Sandoway

L   A   O   S

Henzada   Pegu   Bilin   Uttaradit   Phanom   Quangtri

Danubyu   Insein

Tak   Phitsanulok   Sakonnakhon   Mukdahan   Savannakhet   Hue

Bassein   Rangoon   Thaton   Phichit   Phetchabun   Khonkaen   Tourane

Cape Negrais   Syriam   Moulmein   Roiet   Saravane   Faifo

Pyapon   Gulf of   Nakhon   THAILAND   Khong   Quangngai

Martaban   Sawan   Ubon   Sedone   Pakse   Kontum

Ye   Tha Hin   Nakhon   Khu Khan   Khong   Pleiku   Quinhon

Suphanburi   Ratchasima   Buriram   Cheo Reo   Songcau

Kanchanaburi   Ayutthaya   Prachinburi   Melouprey   Cape Varella

Tavoy   Nakhon   Saraburi   Sara Kaeo   Seam Reap   Stungtreng   Tubong

Pathom   Bangkok   Chonburi   Aranyaprathet   KompongKleang   Banmethuot

Palaw   Ratburi   Phetburi   Battambang   Kompong Thom   Honquan   Dalat

Mergui   Sattahip   Rayong   KAMPUCHEA   Kratie   Djiring

Tenasserim   Prachubkherikhan   Chanthaburi   Kompong   Kompong Cham   Bienhoa

Mergui   Trat   Chhnang   Pnompenh   SAIGON

Ko Chang   Tonle Sap   Takeo   Soairieng   Bencat   Cholon

Bang Saphan   Kut   Kampot   Mytho   Travinh

Archipelago   Chumphon   Ream   Longxuyen

Victoria Point   ISTHMUS   Phuquoc   Cantho   Bacieu

OF KRA   Ko Phangan

Surratthani   Ko Samui

Takua Pa

Phangnga   Nakhon Sithammarat

Phuket   Cha Mai

MALAY   Trang   Songkhla

Pattani

PENINSULA   Satun   Yala

Langkawi   Kota Bharu

Alor Star

George Town   Kuala Krai

Penang   Butterworth   Kuala Trengganu

Prai

Taiping   Ipoh   MALAYA

Kuala Lipis   Kemasik   NATUNA ISLANDS

Telok Anson   Kuantan   ANAMBAS ISLANDS

Jerantut   Pahang R.

Kuala Lumpur   Rompin   MALAYSIA

Port Swettenham   Endau   WEST

Seremban

Port Dickson   Kluang

Malacca

Bandan Maharani   Batu Pahat

SUMATRA   Kukup   Johore Bharu

SINGAPORE   BORNEO

Batam   Bintan

BAY OF BENGAL

Cape Negrais

Mouths of the Irrawaddy

ANDAMAN SEA

INDIAN OCEAN

Gulf of Siam

Strait of Malacca

Gulf of Tonkin

SOUTH CHINA SEA

Mouths of the Mekong

Inset (above): This map shows the relationship of South-East Asia to the Asian continent.

South East Asia

◉ **National Capitals**

100   200 miles

160   320 kilometres

© Copyright 1960 by Map Projects Inc.

The sun gleams off the brilliant gold-leaf-covered Buddhist temples in Rangoon, Burma.

Burma

Agriculture is the chief occupation of Burma. The central plain is rather dry, because the moist south-west monsoon is cut off by the Arakan Yoma. Crops needing little moisture are grown there, such as millet, sesame, and groundnuts. Where there is irrigation rice can be grown as well as cotton and sugar-cane. Large numbers of cattle are raised, many of which are used for haulage. In this area the peasants own their land. It is otherwise in the deltas, where they have to pay rent. There the abundant rain brought by the south-west monsoon makes rice-growing easy, and large quantities of it are exported. But though much money is made by this crop, little of it finds its way into the pockets of the peasants, who have had to borrow money from the bank, generally an Indian bank, in order to finance all their operations.

Burma these days has a policy of political neutrality and tends to be rather isolated.

The port of Rangoon, capital of Burma, stands on one of the mouths of the Irrawaddy, not far from the sea, and is very active as a port, particularly from May to December, when the rice is being exported. Another great export is teak, which comes from the tropical forests of the Pegu Yoma and from the whole region drained by the Chindwin. Elephants carry the trees down to the river, where they are floated down to Rangoon or shipped down on rafts.

Burma has mineral resources, but lit-

A passer-by drops some money into the begging-bowl of a Buddhist monk.

Teak logs, which must be dried by the sun before they can float downstream, are put in piles.

tle has been done so far to exploit them. The most important is oil, which is found in the central plain. Production had reached a considerable volume by 1939, but had to start again from scratch after the war. Between 1951 and 1975 it increased from 100,000 metric tons to over ten times that amount.

Burma produces gold and precious stones, such as rubies, sapphires, and jade. Her other mineral resources include tin, tungsten, copper, nickel, lead, and coal.

Thailand

Siam changed its name to Thailand in May, 1949. It is a country of some 200,000 square miles (514,000 sq km) with a population of almost 40 million. A range of low mountains runs down the centre of the country, dividing it into two basins. The western is the most populous, drained by the Menam and its tributaries. The eastern basin is drained by the Mun which flows towards Laos to join the Mekong on the frontier.

Teak logs float down a Thai river from the highlands to the coast, where they will be sold.

Rice paddies must be ploughed to stir up the mud before seeds are planted.

The principal crops are teak, rice, and rubber. Thailand also ranks fifth among the world's producers of tin.

Bangkok (population 3,967,000), the capital, is the chief port of Thailand and a port of entry for Laos. It lies on the east bank of the Menam about 20 miles (32 km) from the coast, and is built on

South-East Asia's chief beast of burden, the water buffalo, is a playmate for this Thai boy.

the banks of the innumerable canals and branches of the river, which earn it the nickname of the 'Venice of the East'. There are, in all, 300 Buddhist temples in Bangkok. In one of the most famous, the Temple of the Emerald Buddha, the statue of the Enlightened One sits on a throne of pure gold, and its ornaments of gold and precious stones are changed with the seasons, each time with great religious ceremony.

Kampuchea

Kampuchea (Cambodia) was formerly a French Protectorate, but became independent in 1955. It has an area of about 67,000 square miles (181,000 sq km), with a total population of 6.8 million.

The centre of the country consists of the great basin drained by the Mekong and its tributaries. The chief tributary is the Tonlé Sap, which broadens out into a great lake in the western half of the basin.

This crude water-scoop makes the task of hand irrigation somewhat easier.

A Vietnamese beats bundles of rice stalks against a frame to separate grain from straw.

In the dry season it has an area of about 1,000 square miles (2,600 sq km), while in June the water rises till the lake covers nearly three times that area, flooding all the neighbouring fields and forests, and encouraging the cultivation of rice. Mineral resources are confined to some precious stones and deposits of iron ore between the Tonlé Sap and the Mekong.

Phnom Penh, the capital, stands at the junction of the Mekong and the Tonlé Sap Rivers. It had a population of 1,800,000. Phnom Penh is a river port and a busy commercial centre. The river is navigable all through the year. The town is a great market for rice, maize, and dried fish and cotton.

Kampuchea became involved in the Vietnam War between 1970 and 1975, and subsequently in a civil war. This disrupted economy, towns and transport completely. Her present policy is to move people from the towns into the countryside. She is now isolated from the West.

Laos

Laos is a very mountainous country with deep valleys carved by the rivers. In the north, where the mountains are most rugged, the only fertile soil is close to the Mekong, as at Luang-Prabang and Vientiane where there is an integrated plan for agricultural and industrial expansion in the 1970s, by the new Communist government. The country's agriculture

This view of Bangkok shows how the traditional styles of the Far East are reflected in modern architecture.

The canals of Thailand are crowded with floating markets, from which sampan dwellers buy supplies.

depends entirely on the south-west monsoon which, between May and October, brings anything from 40 to 80 inches (1,000 to 2,000 mm) of rain to all areas.

Rice and maize are the two most important crops and fish provides an important part of the Laotian diet. The forests, though rich in teak, are little exploited: as are the deposits of tin and iron ore.

Most people live along the Mekong Valley, in small settlements. Vientiane is the administrative capital.

In 1975 the population was estimated to be 2,900,000. Two-thirds of these are Laotians who are racially akin to the Thais and the Shans of Burma and, like them, Buddhists. The remainder of the population consists of primitive tribes who live in the mountains. They clear a bit of the forest, grow crops for a few years, and then move on. An almost continuous state of war since 1953 has disrupted Laos's way of life, as it has in Kampuchea. It will take many years for these countries to recover.

Vietnam

Vietnam extends for over 1,000 miles (1,600 km) down the east coast of the Indo-Chinese peninsula. In the extreme north it is 320 miles (510 km) wide, but the rest is a relatively narrow strip. It is about 50 miles (80 km) wide for a considerable distance, broadening in the south to about double that width.

Most of Tonkin, in the north, is occupied by mountains, which are an extension of the southern Chinese ranges. The valley and delta of the Red River are teeming with human activity.

Vietnam has a typical monsoon climate, but the temperature varies considerably with the latitude. In the south it is always hot, while in the north there are marked warmer and cooler seasons. Rain falls over the whole country from May to October, except in central Vietnam, where it is a little later. It varies from about 60 inches (1,500 mm) in the south to 100 (2,500 mm) in the north. Fish abound in lakes, rivers, and even rice-fields, and contribute considerably to the

This mother and her son are typical of the handsome tribes from the mountains of Vietnam.

people's diet. Sea fishing also thrives.

The population is 44 million and is densest in Lower Tonkin which is one of the world's great rice-growing areas. Other crops are grown, however, including sugar-cane, maize, and tobacco.

After a war which has engulfed the last thirty years, Vietnam's economy and morale have become completely devastated. The factories, railways and roads need reconstruction and large areas of forests have been wiped out. Now Vietnam is governed by the communists, whose job it is to restore and revitalise the country.

Rice must be sown, transplanted, cultivated, and harvested by hand – a laborious process.

Central and Eastern Asia

Central and Eastern Asia comprise the great continental mass of China, the Korean peninsula, and the Japanese archipelago. It includes part of the Asian Highlands (Tibet and Mongolia), a number of plateaus and plains (Northern China and Manchuria), and regions of steep but not very high mountains (south China, Korea, Japan, and Formosa).

There is a certain uniformity derived from the climate which is dominated by the monsoons; the winter monsoon, which blows towards the Pacific and the summer monsoon, which blows landwards. There is also some cultural unity from the influence over the whole area of Chinese civilisation, together with the use of similar writing and, above all, from a general observance of Buddhism.

Apart from Mongolia, whose inhabitants are nomad herdsmen, the civilisation of these countries is predominantly agricultural. In consequence the mountains are almost completely empty. The whole population is crowded on to the plains, on which the bigger towns have become industrial centres. The total population of this area amounts to over 958 million people: one-quarter of the world's population.

Few countries in the world possess a written history so old, so continuous, and so authentic as the Chinese. Chinese civilisation is indeed one of the oldest in the world, and until last century China was regarded by the people of the West as a civilisation rather than a state: a collection of peoples, observing the same administrative traditions without any real national cohesion. That view is no longer possible. China is now very definitely a state. It is moreover the most populated state in the world, with about

Inset (below): This map shows the relationship of eastern Asia to the Asian continent.

95° 100° 105° 110° 115° 120° 125° 130° 135°

U. S. S. R.

Lake Baikal

nnu - Ola Mts.

Khirgis Nor

Uliassutai · Khangai
Mts.

Yusun Bulak · Bayan Khongor
Tsabkhan

MONGOLIAN PEOPLE'S REPUBLIC

Lake Khubsugul
Muren · Selenga R. · Altan
Bulak
Ider R. · Orkhon R.
Bulgan · Tsetserlik · Khadasan
Ulan Bator · Undur Khan
Dzun Modo · Kerulen R.
Burunurt
Arbai Khere
Mandal Gobi
Baishiktu
Sain Shanda
Dalan Dzadagad

GOBI (Desert)

U. S. S. R.

Moho

Ilkuri Mts. · Huma
Shihwei · Aigun · Lesser
Argun R. · Khingan Mts.
Manchouli · Hailar R. · Nunkiang · Pehan · Hailun · Tungkiang
Hailar · Tsitsihar · Suihwa · Ilan · Kiamusze
Solun · Hulan · HARBIN · Poli · Hulin
Choibalsan · MANCHURIA · Shwangcheng · Linkow
Taonan · Taoan · Fuyu · Mutankiang · Ningan
Changchun · Kirin · Tunhwa
Kailu · Tungliao · Nungan · Kungchuling · Szeping · Yenki
Linsi · Liao R. · Sifeng · Kaiyuan · Sungari Res. · Nanam · Najin
Kingpeng · Chihfeng · Faku · Sinmin · Tiehling Tunghwa · Kangye · Songjin · Unggi · Chongjin
Fusin · Tumen R. · NORTH KOREA

INNER MONGOLIA

Kweisui · Kalgan · Tienchen · Suanhwa · Chengteh · Miyün
Paotow · Linho · Yuyü · MUKDEN · Liaoyang · Anshan · Hamhung · Hungnam
Yellow R. · Tatung · Yinghsien · PEKING · T'ang-shan · Chinchow · Yingkow · Kaiping · Antung · SOUTH KOREA
Tengkow · Shohsien · Ningwu · Taihsien · Paoting · TIENTSIN · Liaotung Pen. · DAIREN · Pyongyang · Kaesong · Chunchon
Tingsin · ORDOS DESERT · Kolan · Tang R. · Tsanghsien · Port Arthur · Chinnampo · Haeju · SEOUL
Kiuchüan · Alashan · Yülin · Shihkiachwang · Tehchow · Hweimin · Hwangshien · Chefoo · Weihai · Ongjin · Inchon · Suwon · Wonju · Chungju · Samchok
Kaotai · Yinchuan Mts. · Lishih · Singtai Siatsing · Penglai · Yehsien · YELLOW SEA · Chongju · Chonan · Andong · Pohang
Changyeh · Wuwei · Suiteh · Fenyang · Tsochüan · Yitu · Kaotsing · Laiyang · Chungju · Taejon · Taegu
Chungwei · Yenan · Hwohsien · TAIYUAN · TSINGTAO · Kunsan · Namwon · Masan
Hwangyüan · Linfen · Anyang · Tsinan · Tzeyang · Kiachsien · Kwangju · Naju · PUSAN
Sining · Pingliang · Hotsin · Sinsiang · Tsining · Chucheng · Mokpo · Yosu
Lanchow · Hwanghsien · Tsinyang · Tzeyang · Lini · Tsingkow · Lienyün
Kweiteh · Lungsi · Fengsiang · Sanyüan · Tali · Loyang · Kaifeng · Süchow · Shuyang
Koko Nor · Tienshui · Tsinling Mts. · Tungkwan · Chengchow · Shangkiu · Suining · Hwaiyin
SIAN · Chowkiakow · Pohsien · Hungtze Lake · Yencheng
Nanyang · Pengpu · Kaoyu · Taichow · Jukao · Nantung
Pingwu · Nancheng · Yünhsien · Künhsien · Fowyang · Liuan · Hofei · Chinkiang · Soochow
Kienko · Ankang · Kwanghwa · Fancheng · Hwangchwan · NANKING · Wusih · SHANGHAI · EAST CHINA SEA
Langchung · Tahsien · Tzekwei · Siangyang · Chungsiang · Wuhu · Sungkiang
Kwanhsien · Santai · Kingmen · HANKOW · Anking · Kweichih · Ningkwo · Shaohing
Chengtu · Nanchung · Wanhsien · I-ch'ang · Wuchang · Hukow · Hangchow · Ningpo
Hochwan · Chunghsien · Shasi · Mienyang · Yoyang · Kiukiang · Kinhwa · Yühwan
Kangting · Luhsien · Hofeng · Changteh · Lisien · Fuchow · Chungan · Chühsien · Linhai
CHUNGKING · Yungshun · Yuyang · Iyang · Ningsiang · Lake Tungting · Nanchang · Taishun · Wenchow
Chungtien · Ipin · Yungsin · Kiencheng · Yuanling · Siangtan · Changsha · Kienyang · Chengho · Kienow · Juian
Yungning · Tsunyi · Chihkiang · Liling · Chu-chou · Nancheng · Foochow
Likiang · Tsuyung · Shihtsien · Lienhwa · Kian · Yungsin · Kwangchang · Ningtu · Shuikou · Futsing · Putien
Tali · Kütsing · Chenyuan · Sinning · Shaoyang · Hengyang · Linghsien · Shahsien · Jukin · Hweichang · Tsinkiang
Tengchung · Paoshan · Tsuyung · Anshun · Liping · Lingling · Kanchow · Namyung · Lungnan · Lungki · Amoy · Changpu · Keelung
Lungling · Kingtung · Kweiyang · Chüanhsien · Chenhsien · Linping · Tingnan · Hoyün · Meihsien · Ch'ao-an · Taichung · Taipei
Mienning · Chengkiang · Kweilin · Linhsien · Kükong · Tsingshih · Koyiu · CANTON · Swatow · Changhwa · TAIWAN
Kingku · Kienhsui · Ishan · Liuchow · Yingtak · Lungmoon · Wuchow · Tungkan · Namhoi · KOWLOON · Kitchioh · Tainan · Taitung
Lingyün · Wuchi Mts. · Nanning · Hokshan · Sunchong · Macao (Port.) · VICTORIA · Kaohsiung · Pintung
Tsungshan · Hoppo · Yeungkong · Mowming · Pescadores Is.
Pakhoi · Liuchow Pen. · Hainan Strait · Kiungshan
Ningerh · Mengtsz
Wuchi Mts. · Yülin · HAINAN

CHINA

AN SHAN (mountains)

AIDAM ression)

BAYAN KARA MTS.

AMNE MACHIN MTS.

Chamdo · Yalung R. · Kantse · Mekong R.

VIETNAM

LAOS

THAILAND

KAMPUCHEA

Yangtze R.

JAPAN

PACIFIC OCEAN

PHILIPPINE ISLANDS

SOUTH CHINA SEA

Gulf of Tonkin

Formosa Strait

Tropic of Cancer

JAP

SEA OF JAPAN

Eastern Asia

● National Capitals

0 100 200 300 400 miles
0 160 320 480 640 kilometres

© Copyright 1960 by Map Projects Inc.

The Potala, in Lhasa, is 400 ft (122 m) high and 1,200 ft (365 m) long. It was the most important monastery in Tibet.

800 million inhabitants determined to make their country, a land of enormous resources, one of the great economic powers of the world.

China is a single whole. Nevertheless, in an immense area of 3,760,000 square miles (9,738,350 sq km), we are forced to distinguish and consider separately: (1) the China of Central Asia, which is a great mass of mountains and plateaus, steppes, and cold, almost uninhabited deserts; and (2) the China of Eastern Asia which is real, living China.

Chinese Central Asia consists of Tibet, Sinkiang (Eastern Turkestan), and Mongolia. This is a region of mountains, plateaus, and deserts. It covers an enormous area but has a very small population.

In this area we find some of the highest mountains of Asia, the highest plateaus, and the most extensive deserts. The Tien Shan and Altai Mountains close the region on the north. Across it run the Kunlun Mountains which separate Tibet from Sinkiang. West is the plateau of the Pamirs. The Himalayas in the south divide Central Asia from India.

Two vast cold deserts, the Gobi and the Takla Makan, extend over thousands of square miles. Mountains and deserts form barriers which isolate this region from the rest of the continent. Central Asia is much too far from any ocean to receive the mild moist wind that brings rain.

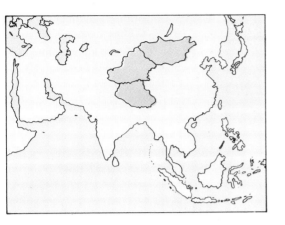

Tibet

The Chinese province of Tibet is the highest country in the world. Several of its summits are 20,000 feet (6,100 m) in height. The plateau of Tibet itself is more than 16,000 feet (4,900 m) above sea-level.

Few people can live at such a height and in so cold an atmosphere. The few who do are practically cut off from the rest of Asia.

Recently, however, the Chinese have built two great roads to Lhasa, the capital of Tibet. These have been extended towards the Indian frontier. Chinese efforts to modernize Tibet include the

An oasis in Sinkiang is a pleasant contrast to the surrounding mountainous country.

Asia's transition from old to new is seen in these Buddhist monks waiting to board a plane.

establishment of industry, irrigation projects, coalmining and the forming of agricultural communes.

Most of the Tibetans live in the southern part of the country, where soil can be irrigated. They scrape a living from their inhospitable land, using livestock: since leather, skins, wool, and felt provide clothing and shelter. Milk, butter, cheese, and meat are the main food. Dried dung provides them with fuel.

In a few special areas, Tibetans grow barley and wheat, by dry farming. The national dish is *tsamba*, a sort of porridge made of barley or wheat, with the addition of butter, and flavoured with tea. The pastures on the rolling plateaus and mountainsides enable them to rear sheep, cattle (yaks), and hardy ponies. Accustomed to the high altitude, the yaks draw the plough and serve as beasts of burden.

The religion of the people is Lamaism, which is a local form of Buddhism.

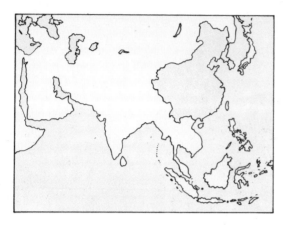

Sinkiang

Sinkiang or Eastern Turkestan is a high plateau surrounded by still higher mountains. As a result most of the area is a desert. Winters are bitterly cold, summers unbearably hot. No more than 6 inches (25 mm) of rain fall in a year. The melting snows of the mountains feed a few rivers that cross the desert.

One of these is the Tarim. Oases border the foothills of the mountains near the Tarim river. Wheat and some other crops can be grown. Enough grass grows near the oases to provide temporary grazing for the sheep and cattle of nomads who visit the oases to exchange wool, skins, meat, butter, and cheese for flour, leather, clothing, and tea.

Mongolia

Mongolia is another plateau country surrounded by high mountains, but the plateau is lower in this case: 3,000 (900 m) to 5,000 feet (1,500 m) high. Mongolia occupies part of the great Gobi desert, where explorers have discovered the relics of many prehistoric animals.

It was from here that Genghis Khan and his Mongol hordes advanced in the thirteenth century to conquer practically the whole of Asia. Today there are oil wells in the Eastern Gobi desert, but it is no longer extracted.

Towns in Outer Mongolia are small. This desolate country is inhabited primarily by nomads.

A Mongol tribesman leads a nomadic life. His yurt, or portable home, is made of wool felt.

A family group in Outer Mongolia. They are Buddhists and speak the Mongol tongue.

Most of the Mongolian plateau is covered with grasses. The nomad tribes wander from place to place with their sheep, goats, camels, and horses.

The whole life of the nomad herdsman is concentrated on his herd. He lives on meat, butter, milk, cheese. Sheep skins can be worn, and all skins turned into leather. Wool can be pressed into felt for boots, or woven into blankets. As we have seen already, dried dung provides fuel.

Horses, camels, and yaks are used for transport. They carry tea from China and *tsamba* from Tibet.

Traditionally the nomads despise permanent dwellers. When pastures give out, they pack up their tents and move elsewhere with their herds, families, and all they possess.

The Mongolian tent, or *yurt*, is round. The lower walls are vertical; above them the roof slopes gently upwards to a slightly rounded point. The *yurt* is made

Because they depend on their flocks, the life of many Mongols is a continual search for pastures.

Roads in remote parts of China are apt to be no more than winding footpaths.

A road worker outside Peking. There has been a tremendous drive forward to construct roads suitable for motor traffic in recent years.

of thick sheep's and goat's wool felt stretched on a flexible framework of laths. Although easily transportable, these tents are strong and capable of standing up to the worst blizzards.

In the winter it is often difficult for the herds to graze. Freezing blizzards form a thick surface of ice on top of the snow, preventing the animals from reaching the dry grass beneath. In recent years the Mongolian People's Republic has built thousands of shelters to protect the herds. But most of the tribes build corrals, like those used in America, to keep out the winter winds and wolves. The walls of the corrals are of bricks formed out of dried cow dung.

However, many herds winter out of doors, and the 13,000 wolf skins brought in each year give an idea of the number of wolves that prey on livestock, particularly sheep. An increasing amount of hay is now grown, building up the herds. Collectivisation of farms is in process, and Mongolia may one day become the great ranching country of Eastern Asia.

The government is trying to industrialise Mongolia, which has now two industrial centres and some power stations. There is a major coalmine at Ulan Bator. There is a shortage of labour so workers come from Eastern Europe and the USSR.

Caravan routes have crossed eastern Asia since the earliest times. They run east–west and north-east–south-west into India.

Turning to the railways, two lines link China with Soviet Russia: (1) the Trans-Mongolian, which is completed and runs from Peking to Ulan Ude, passing through Ulan Bator. (2) the line from Lanchow on the Hwang Ho to Kazakhstan through Urumchi and the Dzungarian Gates.

The Great Wall of China was built in the third century B.C. as a defence against Mongol invaders.

China

China, sometimes referred to as the Eighteen Provinces, extends from the plateau of Central Asia to the Pacific.

Northern China and south China are divided by the Tsinling mountains which are an eastward extension of the great Kunlun Mountains of Central Asia.

Although Peking is in the same latitude as Nepal, the climate of north China is severe: with cold, dry, windy winters and hot, rainy summers. In the west are the Taihang Mountains in Shansi, and, in the east, the immense plain of China and Manchuria. Almost

Rice is the main food crop grown in China. It is estimated that 140 million metric tons of rice are grown annually.

A ceremony to mark the opening of a new sports stadium in Peking.

everywhere the land consists of yellow loess to a depth of 1,000 feet (300 m). This loess is soil which has been blown in fine particles from the desert of Central Asia and is very fertile, excellent for the cultivation of wheat. It breaks away very easily, and silts up the rivers and estuaries. That is why the coast of China is flat and not indented. The peninsula of Shantung is the only one of note north of Shanghai. Under the loess are valuable mineral ores, besides which there are the coalfields of Shansi and Shantung, as well as the one at Fushun in Manchuria.

South China is much more hilly. In the west are the mountains of Szechwan and the plateaus of the Yunnan. In the east is a hilly country ending in a rocky, indented coast. Here the summers are hot and the winters mild. Rain falls throughout the year, but chiefly in summer under the influence of the monsoon. The vegetation is luxuriant and crops of the tropical type include rice and cotton. Mulberry trees, on which the silk industry depends, are common. It is often possible, particularly on the deltas, to grow two crops of rice a year.

The farmer who owns a water buffalo is lucky indeed. The animal can be used to help with the ploughing.

Heavy use of fertiliser, spread by hand, has kept the soil of southern China fertile for centuries.

The plain of Manchuria is drained by the Sungari, a tributary of the Amur. The great rivers of China are the Hwang Ho or Yellow River, in the north, the Yangtse Kiang, in the centre, and the Si-Kiang or Western River in the south.

The Hwang Ho is about 2,900 miles (4,670 km) long and drains a basin whose area is 28,000 square miles (72,500 sq km). Winding through the immense plains of yellow loess, it picks up great quantities of alluvium, hence its name, the Yellow River. It often overflows causing disastrous floods, during which it often changes its course.

The Yangtse with a length of about 3,400 miles (5,480 km) is the longest river in Eastern Asia and one of the greatest in the world. Though only about 500 miles (800 km) longer than the Hwang Ho, it drains a basin two-and-a-half times the size. It is navigable for 1,660 miles (2,670 km), and with its tributaries, contains over 10,000 miles (16,000 km) of navigable waters. It is thus the chief highway into central China, particularly into Szechwan, which is the most populated province with 70 million people. Nearly half of the total population of China lives in the Yangtse basin. Less irregular and less dangerous than the Hwang Ho, it is capable nevertheless of very serious floods. One, in 1931, flooded over 100,000 square miles (259,000 sq km) and drowned 3 million people.

Before leaving this area, another water highway should be mentioned. This is the Yun-Ho, or as it is generally known in Europe, the Grand Canal. It is a magnificent artificial river running from Hang-chow, south-west of Shanghai, first to the Yangtse, then to the Hwang Ho and then, beyond that river, to Tientsin, where it joins the Pai Ho, which links

The Thoughts of Chairman Mao are read by all Chinese. These happy young students come from Peking.

Many Chinese must do all their work by hand.

it with Tungchow in the neighbourhood of Peking.

The Si-Kiang is the most important river in the southern Provinces, with a length of over 1,000 miles (1,600 km). It is navigable to Canton, which is not far from the coast, and thereafter for over 100 miles (160 km) by smaller, shallow draft vessels.

The population of China is formed of Chinese proper or Hans, mingled with a considerable variety of races. In Central Asia, which is very thinly populated, the racial minorities – Mongols, Tibetans, etc. – prevail, while in the densely populated areas the population is largely Chinese. In some areas the density of population rises to as much as 1,500 per square mile (580 per sq km).

The population of China is already more than 800 million and is increasing at a rate of 10 million a year.

The chief agricultural areas of China are: (1) the loess plains (or yellow country) of Northern China. On these immense and monotonous stretches, broken only by the few trees round villages, wheat, maize, soya beans, potatoes, and groundnuts are grown, as well as a plant called kaoliang which is a sort of sorghum. (2) The Manchurian plains in the north-east are used for growing wheat, soya beans, kaoliang, tobacco, and sugar-beet. (3) The plains of the middle and lower Yangtse are of great fertility owing to irrigation. Here the farmers grow wheat and reap two harvests of rice a year; they grow tea, tobacco, oil-seeds, and cotton, the last being the most important crop of all. (4) The Red Basin (region of Chungking) where the crops are rice, colza, fruit, and vegetables, and where pigs are reared on a big scale. (5) The delta of the Si-Kiang, in southern China. The climate here is sub-tropical; the summer months are long and hot, and during them the monsoon brings torrential rains. There is no frost in winter. Tea is grown here, sweet potatoes, the mulberry trees necessary for silk production, and all sorts of sub-tropical fruit and vegetables. The principal crop however is rice. At least two crops a year can be obtained.

In fifty centuries of farming, the Chinese peasants have learnt how to put their land to good use. In particular they have learnt that, in food value, rice gives better yields per acre than any other crop.

The Chinese peasant, his wife, and his sons all work together in the rice fields. They sow the rice, flood the paddy fields, tend the plants, and pick the rice by hand. Here and there buffaloes may be seen at work, but for the most part every operation is performed by hand.

Farmers on a commune near Peking. China has made great strides in agriculture, with workers levelling whole hillsides for cultivation.

A Chinese farmer winnows grain. He is separating the good grain from the chaff.

Planting in a garden near Peking, children learn to work with hands as well as heads.

An interior view of a general shop typical of those found on Chinese communes.

The government has now introduced a major system of land reform under which the property of the landowners has been broken up into small lots, rarely more than three acres, and distributed amongst the peasantry. However, so enormous is the population that there is still insufficient production of food-stuffs. In times of floods or droughts there is a great threat of famine.

In an effort to increase production the government is trying to organise farming on a communal basis. A number of villages, which may be anything from thirty to eighty, are grouped together in a single community of anything from 20,000 to 70,000 people.

These communes, as they are called, began experimentally at first in the vast corn-land of Honan. From there the system spread until it was gradually introduced into all the provinces. At present all but one per cent of the peasantry are working in communes. The commune is an organisation with many functions, economic, administrative, social, educational, and even military. In return for pooling his land the peasant receives both food and clothing. The communes organise schools, canteens, public laundries, day nurseries, and medical centres.

Agricultural machinery is being emp-

loyed by some communes. As a result, the old-fashioned Chinese farming landscape, with its tiny fields, is rapidly disappearing.

An aerial view shows the years of work that have gone into this large open-cast coal mine.

These Chinese boys are pictured with oxen. But animals are not common on Chinese farms.

Sampans are widely used as permanent homes in the overcrowded river cities of China.

People of the Sampans

In south-eastern China there are millions of people who live all their lives and work on rivers and canals. No other region in the world has such a network of navigable waterways. In addition to the rivers, there are thousands of miles of

Some junks are used as ferries. Although they look awkward, they are very seaworthy.

canals; in fact in this part of China waterways take the place of roads.

Every village and every town is either on a river or on a canal. Many of the great towns of China, like Wuhan and Canton, are inland river towns, some of them deep in the interior. In many of them there is such a network of canals that boats are used instead of motor vehicles or trains for transportation.

The little ships used by the Chinese are called junks. Smaller boats of all sizes are called sampans. Neither junks nor sampans have changed appreciably through the centuries. Many of the sampans can only carry two or three people and a very small quantity of goods, while junks can carry substantial cargoes from one seaport to another.

Both junks and sampans are used to ferry people from place to place in towns like Canton. They also take people from the mainland to their work in Hong

Kong. Many more are used as homes for people who can find no other lodging.

Many junks are used for fishing on the open sea. They come back loaded with fish, shrimps, oysters, and edible seaweed.

Fishing is also done on the inland waterways. Some of the fishermen use cormorants, which they have trained to catch fish for them. By putting a straw noose round its neck, the fisherman prevents it swallowing its prey. He also holds a string tied to one of the bird's legs. The cormorant is an excellent diver, and as soon as it has caught a fish, the fisherman pulls on the noose to prevent it swallowing, and with the string hauls the bird, and the fish, on board.

Some people spend all their lives afloat. The boats may be secured to the river banks or to other boats that are

A sampan on a Chinese river is home to this family. They eat, sleep, and live on board.

lying alongside. Small children and the families' chickens are often tethered to prevent them from falling overboard. Often even vegetables are grown on board. In Canton more than a tenth of the population lives afloat.

Some boats on the Yangtze River near Shanghai are houseboats. Others are commercial vessels.

By using their greatest natural resource, manpower, the Chinese have progressed towards industrialisation. This dam will generate electricity in the Peking area.

The Industrialisation of China

The government of China is doing its utmost to transform an agricultural country into a great modern industrial power. China has set to work to build dams and hydro-electric power-stations, to construct railways and build factories. Emerging from its age-old lethargy, China is growing into a major force in the world economy, and is a major political power. Great dams have been constructed across the Hwang Ho and the Hwai Ho, which produce electricity and also conserve flood waters for use in the dry season.

Parallel with the constant harnessing of rivers to provide electricity is the continual development of coal-mining. Production of coal and lignite rose from 63 million metric tons in 1952 to over 400 million in just over ten years. Oil production has made rapid progress with reserves of 2,100 million metric tons. Production of iron and steel has also risen enormously: more than 35 million metric tons of pig-iron are now produced (3 million in 1954), and 27 million metric tons of steel (2½ million in 1954). Some of the richest iron ore fields in the world are at Wukan.

The north-eastern region (Manchuria) is one of the principal industrial centres of China. There are large deposits of coal, magnesite, and aluminium, processed by huge blast furnaces, steel mills, and rolling mills. Manufactures include machine tools, textiles, and chemicals.

New industrial regions are: on the coalfield of the province of Shansi, at Chungking in Szechwan, at Canton, in the south, and, in the north-west, at Lanchow.

For 1,000 miles (1,600 km) from its mouth the Yangtse is navigable by sea-going ships, and when the water-level is high in summer, ships of as much as 10,000 tons can steam up to the industrial centre of Wuhan. The canals and rivers of southern China are also navigable by junks and sampans, which manage to carry considerable quantities of goods.

Since 1949, however, it is in railway development that progress has been most striking. This is particularly so in north China, where they were most needed, since the Hwang Ho is not navigable.

The railways in this region join up with two lines to Soviet Russia. The first of these, the Trans-Mongolian, already runs from Peking across the Gobi desert to Ulan Bator, and then on to join the Trans-Siberian at Ulan Ude, and then to Moscow. The Trans-Mongolian reduces the journey by rail from Peking to Europe by nearly 2,000 miles (3,200 km). The second runs from Lanchow in a north-westerly direction, crosses Sinkiang and passes through the Dzungarian Gates to join the Turksib, the railway from Turkestan to Siberia. A branch from this line runs southward across the Tsinling mountains to the rich agricultural province of Szechwan.

The railways of Manchuria are the most well organised in China. They were constructed by the Russians, taken over by the Japanese and now converted to standard gauge by the Chinese. They link up with the railways of Korea, Siberia and the rest of China.

Roads are chiefly used for local traffic. But two arterial roads run to Lhasa. The major Chinese ports are Tientsin, Shanghai, Tsingtao and Canton. New ports are at Changchiang and Whampao.

Another long day's work begins in this steel mill in Anchang, Manchuria.

Oil tanks in the Yumen oilfields dot the Gobi desert, China's new industrial frontier.

Many women are labourers in Manchuria. Here we see one at work in a busy cable factory.

Most of the construction of the Ming Tombs dam has been done by men, rather than by machines.

Taiwan

The island of Taiwan lies 100 miles (1,600 km) off the south-east coast of China. It is now the last stronghold of what is called the Nationalist government of China. Before the Second World War, China was in the throes of a war with Japan, as well as being torn by years of civil war between the government on the one hand and the communists and various private war-lords on the other.

The civil war continued after the end of the Second World War and in 1949 the communists under Mao Tse-Tung succeeded in driving the Nationalists off the mainland. The Nationalist leader, Chiang Kai-Shek, who died in 1975, took his army to Taiwan, where they remained.

Taiwan is one of a chain of west Pacific volcanic islands which include Japan. It is about 235 miles (378 km) long and 90 miles (145 km) broad at its widest, its area being a little greater than that of Holland.

Less than one-quarter of the land is available for farming, as the bulk of it is occupied by a great mountain range

Because of its growing textile industry, more flax is being cultivated on Taiwan.

running the whole of its length. It has 48 peaks over 10,000 feet (3,000 m) in height. On the eastern side the mountains drop abruptly to the Pacific. The narrow plain along the west coast is rarely more than 25 miles (40 km) in width.

The climate of Taiwan varies with the seasonal winds. During the summer the south-west wind brings heavy rain to the south and to the coastal plain in the west, while the northern part of the island is clear and dry. From October to March the north-east wind brings heavy rains to the northern and eastern parts, while the south and west are dry.

Sometimes, in the late summer, viol-

Sugar cane is an important crop. Here it is harvested by a roadside in south-west Taiwan.

Children at a co-operative school in Taiwan follow their teacher in a medley of songs.

ent typhoons occur, causing terrible damage to homes, farms, and often entire villages. Torrents of rain flood the mountain streams, bringing down tons of stones, gravel, and sand, which are deposited on the fields.

About nine-tenths of the inhabitants of Taiwan are Chinese, but the original inhabitants were primitive, brown-skinned Malays. Until recent years some of these tribes still practised head-hunting. Now only about 200,000 of them are left. They live in the hills, having been crowded out of the fertile plains by the Chinese.

At present the population of Taiwan is about 15.5 million, many of them having fled from China with Chiang Kai-Shek. Taipei is the capital, and there are some other towns, but most of the population live in small farming villages surrounded by rice fields. Whether in town or village, the Chinese live as they did in China.

Fishing is important to the economy of Taiwan. This is a good catch off the coast at NanFanAo.

This village nestles at the foot of bare hills. De-forestation has ruined much of the land in Korea.

They do the same work and observe the same manners and customs. Rice is the chief crop and more than half the land farmed is devoted to it. Sugar-cane is another important crop, together with the tropical fruits, jute, and soya-beans.

There are many small factories on the island, making textiles, chemicals, pottery, steel and machinery. Food processing and cane sugar refining are important. There is a small amount of coal mining and oil production. The forests of Taiwan, which cover more than two-thirds of the island, are of considerable value, and three-quarters of the world's supply of camphor comes from here.

Korea

Korea is a peninsula jutting out from the coast of Manchuria towards the southernmost islands of Japan. It is separated from Japan by the Sea of Japan, from China by the Yellow Sea, and from Manchuria and Siberia by the Yalu and Tumes Rivers.

It is a very mountainous country. As a result a limited area is sufficiently flat and fertile to be used as arable land. The best farmland is along the coasts, though there are fertile valleys in the mountains.

North and South Korea differ considerably. The mountains in the north are

The chief crop of Taiwan is rice, grown in flooded fields.

Korean farmers carry huge loads of rice on their backs from the fields to the threshing floor.

higher and more rugged and are heavily forested. The climate is more severe, the winters being bitterly cold. North Korea is also more industrialised and has almost all of the mineral deposits of the peninsula. The Japanese, who governed Korea from 1895 to 1945, built many factories, railways, and hydro-electric power-stations there. South Korea is more agricultural. The climate is considerably warmer, the winters being quite mild. On the coastal plains rice is the chief crop. After the rice is harvested, the fields are drained and replanted with barley, cotton, wheat, or other crops. But the surrounding hills and mountains are almost devoid of vegetation. There is serious soil erosion.

South Korea is densely populated, the bulk of its 34 million inhabitants living in the farming villages along the crowded coastal plains.

Korean family life is mostly centred on the courtyards of the houses. Here the rice is dried and threshed; here the women make their *kimchi*. This is the national dish of Korea and is made of pickled radishes and spices.

Each courtyard has its vegetable garden and a few fruit trees. Rice is grown on

This old man wears the traditional black horsehair hat and white clothing of Korea.

the level ground outside the village. On the hillsides, the crops are wheat, barley, millet, rye, and vegetables.

Old people are greatly honoured in Korea. White clothes, common among all ages, are the rule with the elderly, who also affect tall, very black horsehair hats, and, very often, beards as well.

This photograph of Seoul was taken during the Korean war. Since then, extensive industrialisation has turned Seoul into a major manufacturing centre.

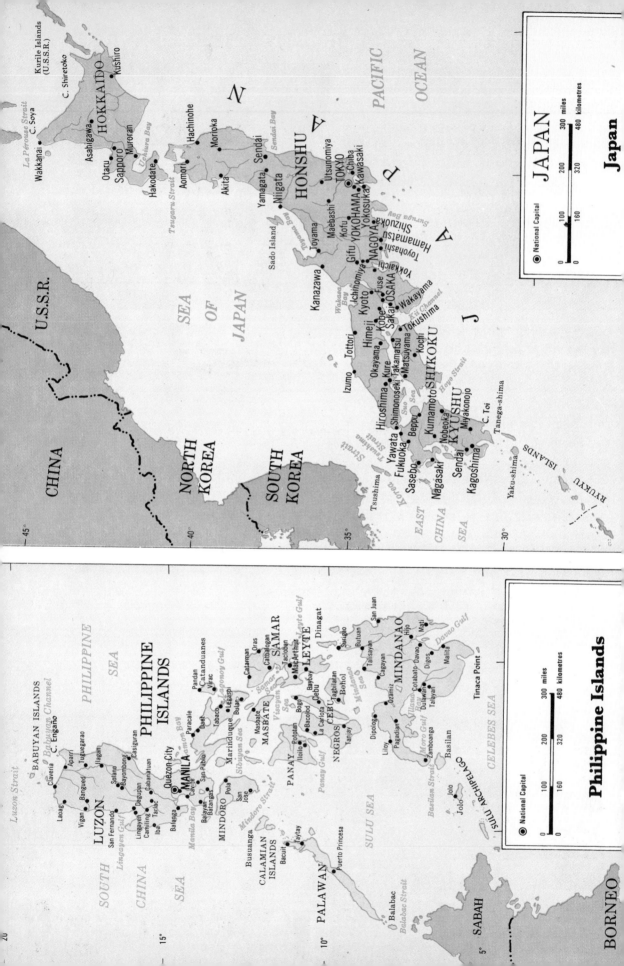

Japan

JAPAN

● National Capital

| 0 | 100 | 200 | 300 | miles |
| 0 | 160 | 320 | 480 | kilometres |

HOKKAIDO

Kurile Islands (U.S.S.R.)

C. Shiretoko

Kushiro

La Pérouse Strait

C. Soya

Wakkanai

Asahigawa

Otaru

Sapporo

Muroran

Uchiura Bay

Hakodate

Tsugaru Strait

Aomori

Hachinohe

Morioka

Akita

Yamagata

Sendai

Sendai Bay

SEA OF JAPAN

Sado Island

Niigata

Toyama

Kanazawa

HONSHU

Maebashi

Utsunomiya

Kofu

TOKYO

Chiba

YOKOHAMA

Kawasaki

Yokosuka

Yokkaichi

Gifu

NAGOYA

Toyohashi

Shizuoka

Hamamatsu

Suruga Bay

Ichinomiya

Fuse

Kyoto

Kobe

OSAKA

Sakai

Wakayama

Wakasa Bay

Kii Channel

Tokushima

Izumo

Tottori

Himeji

Okayama

Kure

Takamatsu

Matsuyama

Kochi

SHIKOKU

Hiroshima

Shimonoseki

Tsushima

Kitakyushu

Yawata

Fukuoka

Sasebo

Nagasaki

Kumamoto

Beppu

Nobeoka

Miyakonojo

KYUSHU

Sendai

Kagoshima

C. Toi

Tanega-shima

Yaku-shima

RYUKYU ISLANDS

EAST CHINA SEA

PACIFIC OCEAN

N

CHINA

U.S.S.R.

NORTH KOREA

SOUTH KOREA

Korea Strait

Tsushima Strait

45°

40°

35°

30°

Philippine Islands

● National Capital

| 0 | 100 | 200 | 300 | miles |
| 0 | 160 | 320 | 480 | kilometres |

Luzon Strait

BABUYAN ISLANDS

Babuyan Channel

C. Engaño

Claveria

Aparri

Tuguegarao

Laoag

Vigan

Bangued

Ilagan

Cassiguran

San Fernando

Solana

Bayombong

Dagupan

Cabanatuan

Lingayen Gulf

Camiling

Iba

Tarlac

LUZON

PHILIPPINE ISLANDS

PHILIPPINE SEA

Quezon City

MANILA

Cavite

Balanga

Batangas

Balayan

Manila Bay

San Pablo

Paracale

Daet

Tabaco

Legaspi

Catanduanes

Pandan

Virac

Lagonoy Gulf

Bulan

Marinduque

Pola

San Jose

MINDORO

Mindoro Strait

Busuanga

CALAMIAN ISLANDS

Bacuit

PALAWAN

Puerto Princesa

Balabac

Balabac Strait

SABAH

BORNEO

SULU SEA

Jolo

Jolo

SULU ARCHIPELAGO

Basilan

Basilan Strait

Zamboanga

Pagadian

Liloy

Dipolog

Ozamiz

Cagayan

MINDANAO

Iligan

Cotabato

Davao

Digos

Malita

Mati

Davao Gulf

Tinaca Point

CELEBES SEA

Moro Gulf

Cotabato

Bulawan

Talayan

Illana Bay

Mindanao Sea

Butuan

Surigao

Talisayan

San Juan

Dinagat

LEYTE

Tacloban

MacArthur

Catbalogan

SAMAR

Oras

Catarman

Leyte Gulf

Baybay

Maasin

CEBU

Cebu

Tagbilaran

BOHOL

NEGROS

Bacolod

La Carlota

Iloilo

PANAY

Janiuay

Tanjay

Pototan

Bogo

Masbate

MASBATE

Romblon

Sibuyan Sea

Visayan Sea

Samar Sea

Tablas

Cuyo

Calamian

Panay Gulf

SOUTH CHINA SEA

Lingayen Gulf

5°

10°

15°

20°

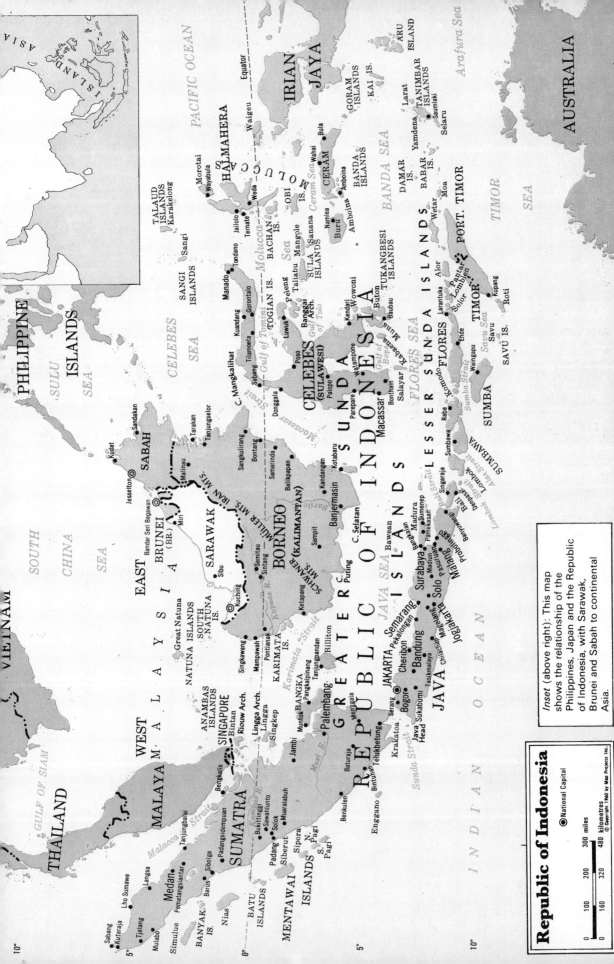

Republic of Indonesia

● National Capital

| 0 | 100 | 200 | 300 miles |
| 0 | 160 | 320 | 480 kilometres |

© Copyright 1960 by Map Projects Inc.

Inset (above right): This map shows the relationship of the Philippines, Japan and the Republic of Indonesia, with Sarawak, Brunei and Sabah to continental Asia.

Nagasaki, a leading Japanese port, was the first Japanese city which was opened to traders from Europe.

Island Asia

There are thousands of islands off the east and south-east coasts of Asia. Most of them are grouped in curved chains which are festooned from the continent. There are three main groups, each composed of several large islands and a number of smaller ones. They form the countries of Japan, the Philippines, Malaysia, and Indonesia.

Some of the islands can be seen on maps of Asia, but others are too small to be shown on any general map. And many islands which look close together on a map may be hundreds of miles apart.

These islands, which skirt the eastern edge of Asia, are the tops of great volcanic mountain ranges, which were thrown up many thousands of years ago.

On the seaward or Pacific side of these island mountain ranges is a series of ocean deeps or trenches. Some of the greatest ocean depths are found here. Near these islands depths have been recorded of over 5,000 fathoms (30,000 feet or 9,100 m).

The three island groups we are considering stretch in latitude from 45 degrees north to 10 degrees south of the Equator. This is a distance of more than 4,000 miles (6,400 km). But in spite of being in such very different latitudes the islands in these three groups have much in common.

Having what is called a maritime climate, they experience fewer extremes of temperature than do the inland areas of continents. They have plenty of rainfall, though the rainy season falls at different times. All three groups are affected by severe storms called typhoons, sometimes accompanied by tidal waves that cause considerable loss of life and destruction of property.

Being so mountainous, these islands have only a relatively small area of arable land. They are, moreover, densely populated. Accordingly, every manageable slope is cut into terraces so that the maximum amount of land may be cultivated. Though the people, and the crops they grow, differ from place to place, much the same primitive methods of farming are still used. Most of the work is done by hand. Most of the slopes that cannot be tilled are heavily forested. The timber grown is often of great economic value.

Being for the most part close together, and also close to large continental countries, these islands are well placed for trade.

Some very primitive tribes still live in the interior forests of New Guinea, Borneo, and the Philippines. But there are also people who have had a high level of culture and civilisation for thousands of years.

Most of these islands have, at one time or another, been colonies of European powers, who have left their imprint on them. As a result, besides Asiatic races found on them – Japanese, Chinese, Indians, Malayans, and Arabs – there are also people of Spanish, Portuguese, Dutch, British, and American descent.

Japan's total area amounts to only 142,000 square miles (372,500 sq km): only a little greater than that of Italy and Switzerland put together. The population however has risen to 110 million, which means an average density of 704 per square mile (300 per sq km). In the

Japanese farm workers, one wearing a thatched grass raincoat, cultivate hillside rice paddies.

Tidy rice-fields and trees are typical in mountainous central Honshu, Japan's largest island.

Japan's fishermen supply a major part of the nation's food.

Girls carry seaweed to be dried and processed. Seaweed is important in the Japanese diet.

past the over-population of Japan was a contributory cause of her drive to acquire additional territory; and since 1945 it has led her to redouble her efforts in the industrial field. It is only through exports that Japan can maintain her population.

Along the Japanese islands there runs a mountain range which sends out lateral branches. High peaks are separated by

comparatively low valleys, which lie at the height of the original uplands, above which the peaks have been thrust by volcanic action. Volcanic craters and cones are abundant. Fujiyama, the sacred mountain, which last erupted in 1709, is the highest in the country, being 12,395 feet (3,780 m) above sea-level. It is generally considered one of the most

The Japanese now lead the world in the export of cars and motor cycles.

The silk industry is an old one in Japan. Here newly woven cloth is washed in a stream.

beautiful mountains in the world. Japan also suffers repeated earthquakes, the worst of recent years being in 1923. The country has a remarkably indented coast. If the coastline could be stretched out, it would reach nearly half-way round the world.

Japan lies on about the same latitude as the Mediterranean. The climate is maritime. Rainfall is heavy, giving rise to luxuriant vegetation. 60 per cent of the land is covered by forest – oaks, maples, and beeches – in the north; sub-tropical forest in the south. The crops in the south include rice, tea, and cotton.

Owing to the mountains, only one-seventh of the area of the islands of Japan, amounting to 21,000 square miles (54,400 sq km), is capable of cultivation. To make up for this, the Japanese work with the utmost diligence to get the max-

Kimonoed girls pick tea from well-trimmed bushes in Shizuoka Prefecture, central Honshu.

imum yield from the land, employing every artifice, including the massive use of fertilisers. The very small size of the fields makes them suitable for this inten-

Shipbuilding is an important industry to an island nation. This yard is at Nagasaki.

Steel mills, like this one at Yawata and even more modern ones, have become common sights in present-day Japan.

Bundles of Manila hemp await shipment to the factory. Hemp is a major export of the Philippines.

Philippine mahogany is a beautifully grained wood which is in demand for fine furniture.

Primitive Igorot tribesmen of northern Luzon still grind their grain in crude mortars.

sive cultivation. In spite of all efforts, however, the country cannot produce enough food for its population. Rice, which forms the major part of Japanese diet, is naturally the chief crop. It occupies practically all the plains, pushing other crops up the hillside. The low dykes which separate the rice-fields are themselves planted with vegetables: particularly soya-beans, or sometimes with mulberry trees. The upper, non-irrigated fields are planted with a variety of crops so that both sowing and harvesting can be done progressively. With good organisation sometimes as many as four crops a year can be raised on a piece of land.

Steps have been taken to mechanise farming, in so far as it is possible. A good deal of ploughing, harrowing, and harvesting is now done by machinery. Sowing, transplanting, and harvesting of rice is still done by hand, but the threshing and husking are done by machinery. Until recently, rice had to be imported, but now there is a considerable surplus, due to change of diet and over production. The government is taking active steps to encourage a further diversification of crops.

Fishing is a most essential industry to the Japanese. It employs over 500,000 people, and the catch amounts to 10 million metric tons a year excluding whales. On the other hand, except for some dairy farming, there is very little livestock in Japan. Very little meat is eaten, barely 7 lb (3 kilos) per head per year. Japan is the world's greatest whale processing nation.

A third of the national income of Japan comes from her factories: 30 per cent of her population is employed in manufacturing, 24 per cent in commerce and 13 per cent in agriculture.

Industry in Japan exists on two levels. On the one hand there are a multitude of small factories and even smaller work-shops, supplemented by an appreciable amount of manufacture which is actually done at home in and around the big towns. Many part-time workers are engaged in this cottage industry, as it is called, particularly women and girls.

On the other hand there are the large organisations, the gigantic trusts, the *Zaibatsu:* grouping shipyards, steel-works, refineries, factories of every sort, railway companies, and big general stores.

Japanese industry suffers under the double handicap of being ill-provided with both sources of energy and raw materials. On the other hand she has a large supply of cheap, skilled labour.

Coal is poor both in quality and quantity. Only a third of it can be used for making coke. The output of oil from Honshu is small. Water-power is the only abundant source of energy, but even that is only available during the rainy season (the monsoon), so that hydro-electric power stations have to be duplicated by those burning coal or oil. However, copper and sulphur are fairly abundant and forests furnish all the cellulose necessary for the manufacture of plastic goods and synthetic fibres. Three gold veins are being exploited in north-east Japan.

Accordingly Japan has to buy many raw materials from the under-industrialised countries of Asia. To compensate for this expense Japanese industry produces a wide range of manufactures including textiles, chemicals, and a wide range of high value consumer goods, such as computers, radios, optical equipment, cameras and cars which are sold all over the world. Added to those are the products of heavy and processing industries. Japan leads the world in shipbuilding.

Terraced rice-paddies allow Balinese farmers to use even steep hillsides for food production.

The Philippines

The Philippines consist of more than 7,000 islands of varying size, forming a state that, in all, covers an area of 115,000 square miles (297,800 sq km). The two largest islands are Luzon, in the north, and Mindanao in the south. The capital is Quezon City, but the actual seat of government is in Manila, which, with a population of 1,500,000, is the only really large town in the archipelago. Both these towns are on Luzon which contains half the total population.

The islands are mountainous, and most of the mountains volcanic. Off the eastern shores, running north and south, is the deepest ocean trench in the world. At its deepest it is nearly 5,800 fathoms. The climate is tropical, moist and warm, becoming cooler in the mountains.

Just under half of the population of the Philippines are employed in agriculture, which provides two-fifths of the national income.

30 per cent of the land is cultivated, if we include fruit farming and the growing of coconuts. The development of trade with the United States has greatly encouraged commercial crops. In addition to Manila hemp, and copra and coir (the two products of the coconut), there are plantations of sugar-cane and tobacco. Main exports are copra and sugar.

These commercial crops take up 40 per cent of the arable land, with the result that home-grown food is not sufficient for the population, and a certain amount of rice has to be imported.

Industry, powered in part by hydro-electricity, is at present chiefly concerned with the processing of agricultural produce, such as sugar-refining, tinning pineapples, and the making of rope and cigarettes.

Dyak women doing their housework near a 'long house' in Indonesia.

After Malaysia the Philippines are the second biggest producer of iron ore in South-East Asia. The principal mines are in the north east of Mindanao and the south of Luzon. The Philippines come fourth amongst the countries of the world

Rice and cassava, grown in the coastal plains, are the principal food crops of Indonesia.

These cowboys of Jesselton, Sabah, are very colourful individuals.

in the production of chromium. There are also some gold mines.

In Manila there are some foundries and a certain amount of mechanical engineering.

Indonesia

The 3,000 islands of Indonesia compose the greatest archipelago in the world, and cover an area of more than half a million square miles (1.3 million sq km) with a total population of about 129 million. Running right across the Equator and enjoying an almost constant temperature, a little under 80°F (27°C), they have a luxuriant vegetation of palm trees, bamboos, lianas, and banana trees.

Java

Java is much the most important of the Indonesian islands. Though only one-tenth of the area of Indonesia, it has a population of 76 million, which is 58 per

cent of the total population. A population averaging over 1,200 to the square mile (460 to the sq km), in a country lying on the Equator, is remarkable, but there are various factors to explain it. The soil is extremely fertile, formed, as it is in many places, by volcanic ash, and irrigation schemes have not been difficult to introduce. To the traditional crop of rice, which the Javanese have for long been expert in growing, the Dutch added plantations of sugar-cane, coffee, tea, tobacco, and hevea, the tree which produces rubber. There is also oil in the eastern part of the island. Main towns are Jakarta, Surabaya, and Bandung.

Sumatra

Sumatra, lying to the north-west of Java, is a very much bigger island, but has only 20.8 million inhabitants. Chains of mountains run all along the south-west coast, some of the heights reaching

A fishing boat from a coastal village drops anchor off a tiny island in the Java Sea.

Latex from Malayan rubber plantations is shipped to all parts of the world.

Sheets of crude rubber – latex coagulated by adding acid – are dried on heavy racks.

10,000 feet (3,000 m), while on the other side of the island marshy plains, mangrove-covered, slope down towards the South China Sea. The population, living chiefly in the mountains, consists for the most part of Moslems, only the Bataks having been converted to Christianity. The big towns, however, are on the coastal plains, Medan and Palembang in the north-east and Padang on the south-west coast. Rice is the chief food crop, while rubber, coffee, tea, and tobacco are exported.

The small island of Bali has an area of 2,200 square miles (5,700 sq km) and a population of about 2 million. The peo-

This Malayan hut is built on stilts as a protection against floods and wild animals.

ple are the most expert rice-growers in the archipelago, and coffee and sugarcane are also grown. Unlike their Javanese neighbours, the Balinese have remained faithful to their Hindu faith.

These mountainous islands are volcanic. Altogether there are 100 active volcanoes.

On the foothills of the volcanic mountains are grown cinchona, tea, and coffee, as well as tobacco, oil-palms and heveas in Sumatra, coconut palms in New Guinea, and sugar-cane in Java. Indonesia comes second in the world's leading producers of rubber and quinine. But the plantations have never reached the degree of productivity of the intensively cultivated small-holdings, where the work is closer to the traditions of the people.

Coal is rare, but oil is abundant and a major source of revenue. Indonesia produced 71 million metric tons in 1974, which is about 80 per cent of the total production of Eastern Asia, leaving out China.

The chief oil-fields are in Sumatra, Java, and South Borneo.

Malaysia

Malaysia, with an area of 127,281 square miles (329,640 sq km), consists of Malaya, Sabah (previously called North Borneo), and Sarawak. Its total population is about 10.4 million. All the territories share the same characteristics of a hot, wet equatorial climate; a soil rich in mineral wealth; and a largely uncleared jungle.

Malaya produces more of the world's supply of rubber than any other country. In 1975, 1,300,000 metric tons of it were exported. Next in importance as an export is tin, of which Malaya produces nearly a third of the world's supply. The chief deposits are on the west coast of the peninsula under the gravel beds of rivers. The metal has to be separated from mud and sand and melted into ingots, which are then exported from Penang on the west coast, or Singapore. Rice, copra, palm oil, and pineapple are important crops and timber is a significant export. Industries are now fast growing-up around the towns and cities, notably near Kuala Lumpur, the federal capital.

Singapore

Separated from the mainland by the Strait of Johore is the island and town of Singapore. This independent island has a population of about 2.2 million.

Sabah

Sabah is about three-fifths the size of Malaya, but the population is only about 655,300. It is largely jungle-covered and undeveloped. However, it has the only railway in the Borneo territories, which runs from Jesselton to Weston on Brunei Bay.

A worker shaves off some of the bark from a rubber tree to permit the latex to seep out.

The Hong Fatt tin mine, more than 400 ft (120 m) deep, is one of Malaya's largest mines.

Many tribal Africans live in villages like this one in Zambia. The round huts have grass roofs.

This is Africa

The continent of Africa is washed by the waters of the Atlantic Ocean, the Indian Ocean, and the Red and Mediterranean Seas. From the extreme north in Tunisia to the Cape of Good Hope in the south, it stretches for 5,000 miles (8,000 km).

The continent, with 12 million square miles (31 million sq km), is the second largest of the world's seven continents, the largest being Asia. The land of Africa is nearly one-fifth of the world's total. It is so big that Western Europe, the United States, China, and India could be put into it.

Apart from the coastal regions, most of the continent was unknown until about 100 years ago. Many men had tried to penetrate into the interior, but the nature of the country made it difficult. Even the coastal parts were often inaccessible, for the smooth coastline offered few natural harbours, and ships found it difficult to get through the rough surf to approach the shore. Few of the rivers provide

waterways into the interior, for as a rule they reach the coast over waterfalls and rapids from a high plateau.

Inland, too, the way was blocked. In some places there were great expanses of sun-scorched desert, in others, dense jungle made travel equally difficult.

Yet some daring explorers were ready to brave all the dangers and difficulties. They crossed blazing deserts and treacherous swamps; they cut their way through the thickest jungles. And they brought back stories of strange people, unknown animals, mighty rivers, lakes, plains, and forbidding mountains. Only now, through fast transport, modern media, and increased tourism, are we really learning about Africa: appreciating its beauty, realizing its tremendous natural resources, and studying the customs of its 374 million people, a few of whom either visit, work or study in the Western world.

The greatest part of the continent

Africa

Scale 1 : 30 000 000

0 100 200 300 400 500 miles

0 160 320 480 640 800 kilometres

Depths		below sea level	Heights					
over 650	0–650		0–650	650–1650	1650–5000	over 5000	feet	
over 200	0–200		0–200	200–500	500–1500	over 1500	metres	

Heads of navigation —— Railways ▲▲▲ Canals ⚓ Wadi ▭ Desert

A young man of the Fezzan desert in Libya.

Kano, the ancient capital of northern Nigeria.

consists of a vast plateau which is lower in the north than in the south. In the extreme north-west are the Atlas Mountains, ranges of fold mountains that form part of the mountain system of southern Europe. At the narrowest part of the Strait of Gibraltar, where Africa approaches Europe, the continents are only 9 miles (14.5 km) apart. South of the Equator the plateau, which rises to a high ridge called the Drakensberg in the south-east, descends abruptly on all sides to narrow coastal plains.

Africa is a continent of great physical variety. The western half of Central Africa is covered by a vast tropical rain-forest. Rivers and narrow tracks are the only routes through the crowding trees and dense undergrowth. The branches of the taller trees intermingle to form a green canopy over all.

Rimmed around the edges of the tropical rain-forest is the savanna. This is made up mainly of grasslands with shrubs and scattered trees stretching for hundreds of miles between the jungles and the arid areas that lie to the north in the Sahara and south-west in the Kalahari and Namib deserts. Near the forest, the savanna has tall grasses, shrubs, and trees. As it approaches the

desert, it becomes treeless – the broad sweep of the plains of short grass being broken only here and there by stunted bushes. Most of the big game of Africa lives among the tall grass and long trees of the savanna: antelopes, zebras, giraffes, elephants, and lions.

North of the tropical jungles the savanna reaches into the Sudan. It stretches from the Atlantic, past the Upper Niger almost to the Red Sea and Ethiopia.

South of the savanna, in South Africa, is another area of grasslands known as the 'veld', a Dutch word meaning 'field'. The veld is bounded on the west by a very dry region known as the Kalahari Desert. The Kalahari is, however, a mere baby compared to the enormous Sahara which flanks the northern savanna.

The Sahara is the biggest desert in the world. From the Atlantic to the Red Sea it stretches for 3,000 miles (4,800 km). From north to south it is 1,000 miles (1,600 km) wide, and it separates North Africa from the rest of the continent. The Sahara occupies nearly a third of the entire continent.

Grassland covers a little more than two-fifths of the continent, forest a little less than one fifth. The remainder is desert. Within the broad areas of forest, savanna, desert, and coastal strips, there are many striking features. In East Africa, the land rises into highlands with extinct volcanoes towering above them. Even though they are almost directly on the Equator, Mount Kilimanjaro (more than 19,500 feet (5,900 m)) and Mount Kenya (17,000 feet (5,200 m)) are capped perpetually by a mantle of snow. Nearby is the East African Rift Valley, a deep valley running north and south, stretching for thousands of miles.

From a geological point of view Africa is considered unique amongst the continents because it consists of a single great shield of ancient rock. It is thought by some that the oldest rock of Africa was formed over 3,000 million years ago.

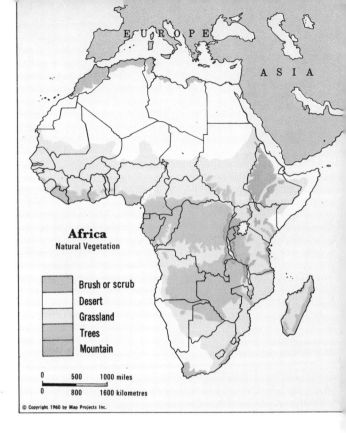

Africa
Natural Vegetation

Brush or scrub
Desert
Grassland
Trees
Mountain

| 0 | 500 | 1000 miles |
| 0 | 800 | 1600 kilometres |

© Copyright 1960 by Map Projects Inc.

Ethiopia, a land of rugged highlands and mountains, is surrounded by hot, dry lowlands. Because of its height, Ethiopia receives considerable rainfall, enough to support lush forests and meadows.

Rivers of Africa

Great rivers pour down from the heart of Africa. Five of them drain almost two-thirds of the continent. For hundreds of miles the rivers move sluggishly through marshlands or tropical forests fed by thousands of tributaries, large and small. Then as they begin their descent from the central plateaus the rivers gather speed. Some hurl themselves over immense waterfalls, others rush down in a series of short steep rapids. In either case navigation is impossible.

The longest river is the Nile – the longest not only of Africa, but of the whole world, if measured from its first source. From its head waters at Lake Victoria to its mouth in the Mediterranean, the Nile is over 4,000 miles (6,440 km) long. It is actually two rivers. The White Nile begins with the jungle rainwater draining into Lake Victoria, which lies at the junction of Uganda, Kenya, and Tanzania. It flows northward through the Sudan, and is joined at

Only a few stunted trees can live amid the sprawling sand-dunes of the Sahara desert. Yet water can make the desert bloom.

A contrast to the arid Sahara: the lush vegetation of the Nigerian jungle.

Khartoum by the Blue Nile. The Blue Nile rises in Lake Tana, high in the mountains of Ethiopia. The Nile continues northward, then turns sharply to the south-west to sweep in a great curve round the Nubian Desert. Then it drops sharply in a succession of rapids and flows through Egypt to the Mediterranean. The Lower Nile is as much as 10 miles (16 km) wide. Below Cairo it is broken up into many branches by the delta it has formed at its mouth.

The two Niles – the Blue and the White – flow into each other at Khartoum to form Africa's greatest river. Egypt's flourishing agriculture depends on the water of the Nile for irrigation.

Kilimanjaro, Africa's highest mountain, rears its snow-covered summit into the sky.

The next longest river is the Zaire. In the course of its 2,900 miles (4,700 km), it drains 1½ million square miles (3.8 million sq km) of Central Africa. In its descent from the central plateau, it passes over several series of rapids and two waterfalls. The Zaire is the only river in Africa to cross the Equator twice. In some places it is so wide that it splits into many arms. There are more than 400 islands in the river.

The third river is the Niger, 2,600 miles (4,200 km) long. For many years explorers sought to trace the course of this mysterious river which, they believed, flowed westward into the

Atlantic. Actually it rises in mountains 200 miles (300 km) from the Atlantic and starts to flow eastward. It then swings in a wide northerly loop into the Sahara Desert, where its flood-waters make it possible to grow rice and cotton in the area round Timbuktu. Then the Niger turns to the south, to the Gulf of Guinea, where its delta spreads across 200 miles (300 km) of marshy coast. The first white man to see the Niger was the Scottish explorer Mungo Park.

The Zambezi, about 2,200 miles (3,540 km) in length, forms the Zambia-Zimbabwe Rhodesia border and then crosses Mozambique to discharge into the Mozambique Channel, between Madagascar and Africa. Like the Zaire,

A rainbow arcs across clouds of spray from the thundering waters of Victoria Falls, where the Zambezi River plunges 347 ft (105 m) into a narrow, rocky gorge.

Mountain craters reveal the volcanic origin of the Canary islands, off Africa's north-west coast.

it drains a huge area of the Central plateau. Near the town of Livingstone, the Zambezi plunges over the Victoria Falls at a rate of 47 million gallons (213 million litres) of water every minute. Because of the booming sound it makes and the clouds of spray thrown upwards, the native tribes called the Victoria Falls the 'Smoke that Thunders'.

Leaving Central Africa, the chief river of the south is the Orange. It flows for 1,300 miles (2,100 km), almost completely crossing the Republic of South Africa, to discharge into the Atlantic some 400 miles (640 km) north of the

A lush oasis in Algeria.

Cape. It flows through parts of the Kalahari Desert, but this stretch is generally dry, and so the river is useless either for navigation or irrigation, except in isolated schemes. There are several diamond deposits near its mouth.

The waters of the Atlantic and Indian oceans meet at Africa's southern tip, the Cape of Good Hope, once called the Cape of Storms. Today many South African coastal areas are popular beach resorts.

A herd of zebras drinks at a South African waterhole. They keep a wary lookout for prowling lions.

The Animals of Africa

Africa has a richer variety of animal life than any other part of the world. Many of them are well-known: lions, elephants, gorillas, zebras, camels, giraffes, etc. But many are less familiar. The aardvark, for example, with its long ears, thick tail, sharp claws, and long snout is somewhere between an ant-eater and an armadillo. With its claws the aardvark tips open the tall mounds which are termite nests and scoops up thousands of the insects with its long sticky tongue.

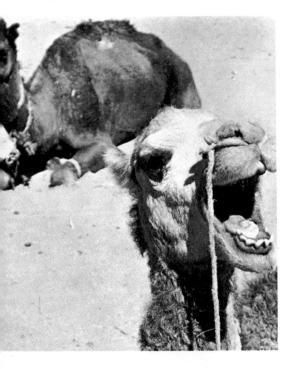

The evil-tempered camel snarls at its master, but it carries huge loads across the desert.

Giant anthills like the one shown provide food for the termite-eating aardvark.

Buffalo are among Africa's most feared animals because of their strength.

A lioness stalks warily through the bush. The African lion is known as the 'King of Beasts'.

Some animals live in particular areas. Zaire is the home of the gorilla. The lemur, related to the monkey, swings in the forests of Madagascar. The grey parrot, the variety that can learn to talk, lives mostly in West Africa. The jackass penguin, whose cry sounds like a donkey's bray, waddles about on the coasts of South Africa. An interesting desert animal is the fennec, a tiny fox that lives in the Sahara, hiding by day and hunting lizards at night. The biggest concentra-

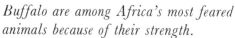

The spots on giraffes protect them from their natural enemies by acting as camouflage.

The speedy cheetah pauses to scan the plains for a possible victim for his next meal.

The hippopotamus feeds on plants and is always found in or near rivers and lakes.

tion of game is on the high open plains of East Africa. Here the visitor can sometimes see as many as 10,000 animals in a day. Even this figure is tiny compared with what it was a century or so ago. Today many species are threatened with extinction.

Among the most interesting features of Africa are the great National Parks and Game Reserves. Here animals are free to roam, and hunting is prohibited. Since they are never shot at, the animals have lost their fear of man, and a lion will often walk right up to a parked car, indifferent to the occupants within.

Although millions of wild animals are

A tick-bird perches on the back of an impala, a graceful antelope of the African savannas.

Although there are still flocks in the wild, ostriches are raised on farms for their feathers.

'Rhinoceros' is Greek for 'horn-nosed'. When a rhino twitches his ears, he is about to charge.

African waters teem with crocodiles. They can lie motionless for hours then move with lightning speed.

still at large in Africa, some experts estimate that nearly all the larger ones that have not sought the protection of the parks could be wiped out in twenty years by disease, by hunters, or simply the advance of civilisation. More and more ranches – even towns – are being developed where lions used to prowl. Thousands of square miles have been flooded by the building of new dams, as happened, for example, when the Kariba dam was built.

Some elephants having a bath. An elephant can eat 1,000 lbs (450 kg) of food a day.

The proud Tuareg live in the Sahara.

The Peoples of Africa

The peoples of Africa fall into five main groups:
(1) Arabs, living mostly in Egypt and North Africa.
(2) Hamites, who occupy Ethiopia and most of the Sahara.
(3) The 'true' Negroes who live in West Africa and the Sudan.
(4) Isolated aborigines: the Bushmen of the Kalahari Desert, the Hottentots of South-West Africa (Namibia), and the Pygmies of Zaire.
(5) The Bantus, Negro people who live in Central and Southern Africa.

To these must now be added some five million settlers of European stock, most of whom live either along the north coast of Africa or in the southern part. Inter-marriage has led to the creation of a still more complicated racial pattern.

About 90 million (mainly in the north and east) are Moslems. About 30 million

A Libyan boy cradles his pet, a baby gazelle, in his arms. This tiny antelope lives in the desert.

Nigeria. The armour worn by the Emir of Kano's guard once belonged to the Crusaders.

Barefoot boys pass in front of the Coptic cathedral in Addis Ababa, Ethiopia's capital.

Berbers, the chief native race of North Africa, are noted for their skill as horsemen. These men are armed with antique brass-bound muskets.

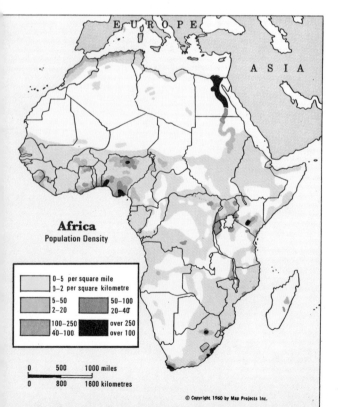

Africa
Population Density

| 0–5 per square mile |
| 0–2 per square kilometre |

| 5–50 | 50–100 |
| 2–20 | 20–40 |

| 100–250 | over 250 |
| 40–100 | over 100 |

| 0 | 500 | 1000 miles |
| 0 | 800 | 1600 kilometres |

© Copyright 1960 by Map Projects Inc.

have been converted to Christianity. That leaves well over 100 million who are either Africans worshipping tribal gods, or Indians, who are Hindus.

Within the population of about 374 million there are many different colours

It may hurt a bit, but these youngsters are proud of the anti-tuberculosis vaccinations.

A water seller fills a drinking cup. Water sellers are very important people in the dry regions of North Africa.

Mud houses are typical of northern Ghana.

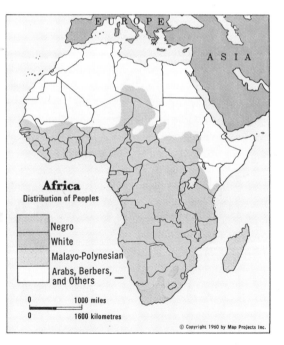

Africa
Distribution of Peoples

- Negro
- White
- Malayo-Polynesian
- Arabs, Berbers, and Others

0   1000 miles
0   1600 kilometres

© Copyright 1960 by Map Projects Inc.

and races, and there are innumerable tribal groups. At least sixteen separate major languages are spoken, within each of which are many varieties of dialect and pronunciation.

Today, anthropologists, who study the

Villagers in the Sudan build their circular huts round a central clearing.

evolution of the human race, believe that the earliest men developed in Africa. Bones of ape-like creatures with some human characteristics have been found in different parts of East Africa, and it may be they are the long-sought 'missing links' of our evolutionary history.

Except for the area along the Mediterranean coast, very little was known of Africa until about 200 years ago, but we know now that important civilisations flourished in the heart of the continent 1,000 years ago, having spread, according to one theory, from the fertile regions of north-east Africa.

About the year 3,000 BC the Sahara dried out into the desert that it is today, forming an almost impassable barrier between the Mediterranean area and the interior of the continent. But some people did manage to cross it, either in search of new land or under the pressure of the conquerors from Europe or Asia, and they were the ancestors of many of the African tribes of today.

Egyptian steelworkers watch the tapping of the furnace.

Watusi tribesmen are the world's tallest people, some men reaching a height of 7 feet (2.1 m).

A boatman crosses the Uélé River in Zaire.

Two warriors of the famed Masai tribe.

Two Pygmy children.

A woman of a Bushman tribe tends her children.

A Ndebele girl grinds corn.

Zulu women display their beadwork.

A Hottentot child in front of his hut.

Wachagga women carry bananas to market.

A Kikuyu market in Kenya.

The largest concentration of people of European descent in Africa is centred on the South.

Nairobi, the capital of Kenya, is a fine city with a magnificent climate. It is famous as the Safari centre of Africa.

These maps show the average temperature and rainfall of Africa. You will see that the temperature of a place does not necessarily correspond to its distance from the Equator. You will also notice that south of the Equator the seasons are reversed. Midsummer is in January, and midwinter comes in July.

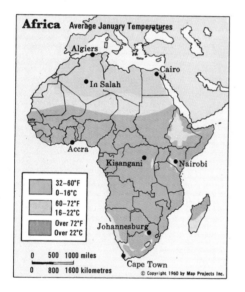

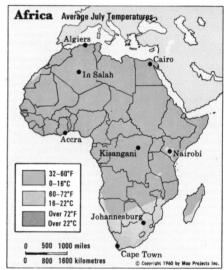

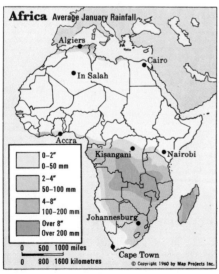

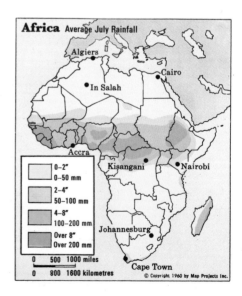

Climate and Products

Three-quarters of Africa – about 9 million square miles (23 million sq km) – lies within the Tropics. Except in a few mountainous parts the climate of this huge area varies from warm to hot, and the only real seasons are the wet and dry seasons.

Looking at the maps on the opposite page we see that the main climate zones correspond to a considerable degree to what has already been said about the different areas of vegetation. Along the Equator, the centre of the tropical forests, the weather is always hot and the rainfall heavy. Temperatures range from 70° (21°C) to 90°F (32°C) and there is rain daily, even in the driest periods. As the land rises towards the east, both temperature and rainfall become less. In July the average temperature in Addis Ababa, 8,000 feet (2,440 m) above sea

Unloading a cargo of sugar cane and grain from a Nile sailing vessel.

level, is 17°F (10°C) lower than it is at Freetown, which is at about the same latitude but in the lowlands of the West Coast. The highest mountains, like Kilimanjaro, are snow-capped all the year round. Rainfall gradually decreases as we move from the tropical forests to the savanna of the north or south, where there are definite dry and wet seasons of varying lengths, the dry season lengthening as the desert is approached. Cool weather alternates with warm. In the dry season, because of the high temperatures, the savannas dry up. Some trees lose their leaves, and the ground becomes too dry for arable farming.

The highest temperatures in Africa are not found on the Equator but in the great deserts. The highest temperature ever recorded in the world was 136°F (58°C) in the Libyan Sahara. (This, of course, was the *shade* temperature. In the sun the temperature would have been very much higher. And in the desert there is virtually no shade.) It is said that the surface of the ground is sometimes as hot as 170°F (77°C). Such temperatures are hot enough to cause the rocks of the desert to crack. On the other hand, the temperature may fall as much as 60°F (34°C) at night, and in the northern regions frost is quite common in the winter months. The desert climate is very dry, and so there is little vegetation. In some places there is practically no rainfall, and what little there is comes as swift violent storms that can cause local floods. Conditions in the southern deserts, though similar to those in the Sahara, are less extreme.

The northern and southern coastal districts of Africa have a Mediterranean type of climate, with hot, dry summers and cool, rainy winters. Because of this

Buyers and sellers bargain for red peppers at the open-air market in Dakar, Senegal.

rainfall, most crops are raised in the winter. Summer crops depend entirely on irrigation.

Over 85 per cent of the people of Africa live off the land and its products. Most of them farm, tilling their small plots of land in the traditional manner. Some keep cattle, and a few of the most primi-

tive tribes depend for their food on game and wild plants.

Those who farm in Africa have many problems. The most important are those created by the unreliable supply of water. In the broad savanna lands, where so many people live, the rainfall varies widely from place to place and

A lone herdsman grazes his cattle on the fertile plains at the foot of Mt Meru in Tanzania.

Africans thresh and winnow grain near Lesotho's high Maloti Mountains.

from year to year. Sometimes the rainfall is not enough to keep the crops alive, and thousands of people go hungry. In other years the rain comes too early or too late. When it does come, it comes in abrupt, heavy downpours, either causing flooding or soil erosion.

The heat is another serious problem. In much of Europe, Asia, and North America 25 inches (635 mm) of rain a year will support farming. But the moisture in the soil is dried up very quickly in hot climates. So a much heavier rainfall or a system of regular irrigation is necessary if farming is to succeed.

The common method of farming on the savanna is to clear a small piece of land by burning off the wild growth. The soil is then broken up and the ash worked in as a fertiliser. Crops are grown on it for a few years, after which the farmer abandons it, moving on to another patch. The abandoned field is soon covered by natural growth which binds the soil and gradually restores its fertility. However, if all the nutrients have been worked out of the soil, nothing will grow, and it quickly turns to desert. There is very little agricultural machinery in Africa. While tractors and similar implements greatly raise production, in many places oxen are a far more valuable asset, for not only do they help with the work, but they create manure for the land as well.

Most Africans live mainly on cereals and starches. They do not get enough meat to eat, which means they suffer from lack of protein. Many tribes depend on wild game for their meat supply. Over large areas of Africa it is impossible to raise livestock because of the tsetse fly, which transmits a deadly disease called *nagana* in animals, and 'sleeping sickness' in human beings. Even those tribes

249

Tribesmen from regions south of the Sahara come to the cotton market at Ndjamena, Chad Republic.

which have large herds of cattle do not get enough meat, because they regard their cattle as wealth and will not kill them. Little fish is eaten in Africa except in the immediate neighbourhood of lakes or rivers. Fish spoils quickly in hot climates unless it is dried.

Until new crops were introduced by Europeans, the Africans grew only millet (a kind of coarse cereal) and some rice. Groundnuts, cassava, maize, tobacco, potatoes, coconuts, cocoa beans, and bananas were introduced from America. Citrus fruits came from Portugal. Wheat and barley also came from Europe. The date palm was introduced by the Arabs, who also brought the clove trees to Zanzibar in the nineteenth century.

In the coastal areas bordering the Mediterranean, the fertile valleys are good for farming. Cereals such as wheat and barley, and fruits like figs, grapes, and olives, grow very well in this area.

Nearer to the Sahara farms give way to

Fronds of the date palm are a familiar North African sight. The tree usually signals an oasis.

A Liberian slices into the tough bark of a rubber tree, preparing to tap the valuable liquid latex.

Native cattle grazing on the high pastures of the Jos Plateau in Nigeria.

Workers with machetes cut sisal leaves and pile them on flat-beds for transport to the coast.

the tents of the nomads, who drive their flocks of sheep from pasture to pasture, from waterhole to waterhole. Crops can only be grown at oases.

On the open savanna, millet and maize are grown, as well as tobacco and cotton. Rice grows near rivers. In the drier areas some of the tribes breed horses and cattle. Large-scale spraying with chemicals is eliminating the tsetse fly, thus making millions of acres of land available for stock-breeding.

In the healthy uplands of Kenya there are many coffee plantations and here, and in other parts of East Africa, cattle breeding is an important pursuit. The main crops of West Africa are palm-oil, groundnuts, and cocoa beans.

The continent has also great stores of mineral wealth, many of which are still unexploited. South Africa is famous for its enormous deposits of diamonds and gold, and there are immense copper mines in Zambia and also in Zaire. Africa has also important deposits of tin, iron, chromium, manganese, cobalt, uranium, and bauxite. South Africa and Nigeria are the only countries with large coal deposits, but oil and natural gas have been found in the Sahara and Libya.

A native farmer in Sierra Leone prepares to harvest the last of the year's cacao crop.

The Exploration of Africa

We owe our knowledge of Africa to the efforts and courage of many men – sailors and soldiers, adventurers, traders, and missionaries – of whom these are the most important:

GIL EANNES (Portuguese) in 1434 sailed past Cape Bojador on the north-west coast of Africa, and showed the way to later navigators. Previously it had been thought the sea beyond Cape Bojador was filled with monsters, and that in any case strong currents would drive ships back.

BARTHOLOMEU DIAS (Portuguese) in 1487 was driven by strong winds round the Cape of Good Hope, and passed Algoa Bay beyond Port Elizabeth.

VASCO DA GAMA (Portuguese) sailed round the Cape of Good Hope and along the east coast of Africa and reached India in 1498.

JAMES BRUCE (Scottish) travelled through Ethiopia in 1770–2, tracing the course of the Blue Nile.

MUNGO PARK (Scottish) travelled up the Gambia River in 1795, and then crossed the savanna to reach the Niger. On his second trip in 1805 he explored over 1,000 miles (1,600 km) of the Niger before being killed in an attack by natives at the Bussa Rapids.

HUGH CLAPPERTON (English) crossed the desert from Tripoli to Lake Chad in 1821 and explored the centre of the Sudan. In 1825 he started north from the Guinea coast, and after two years' travelling through the jungle, reached the Niger at Bussa. He died at Sokoto.

RICHARD LANDER (English) descended the Niger from Bussa all the way in 1830–1, proving it did not flow either into the Nile or the Zaire, as many had thought.

RENÉ CAILLIÉ (French) crossed the Sahara disguised as an Arab, in 1827, reaching Timbuktu.

HEINRICH BARTH (German) made a map of the Sudan and part of the Sahara between 1850 and 1855. He was the sole survivor of a British expedition, and he carried on alone for months.

DAVID LIVINGSTONE (Scottish missionary) spent most of his life in Africa. Between 1849 and his death in 1873 he explored the Kalahari Desert, the Zambezi River, Lake Nyasa, the Shiré River, and the upper course of the Zaire. He discovered the Victoria Falls in 1855.

HENRY M. STANLEY (English–American) made a famous trip to rescue Livingstone in 1871. In 1874–7 Stanley followed the Zaire down to its mouth, opening up the region for other travellers to follow him.

PIERRE SAVORGNAN DE BRAZZA (French) explored the area round the Lower Zaire, 1875–80.

Africa Exploration

Diogo Cão (Port.) 1482
Bartholomeu Dias (Port.) 1487
Vasco da Gama (Port.) 1498
James Bruce (Scot.) 1770–72
Mungo Park (Scot.) 1795–96; 1805
Hugh Clapperton (Eng.) 1821; 1825–27
Richard Lander (Eng.) 1830–31
René Caillie (Fr.) 1827–28
Heinrich Barth (Ger.) 1850–55
David Livingstone (Scot.) 1849–73
Henry M. Stanley (Eng.-Amer.) 1871; 1874–77

© Copyright 1960 by Map Projects Inc.

Cities Old and New

The cities of Africa span thousands of years of history: the first cities were those of ancient Egypt – Alexandria, Thebes, Memphis. Then came seafarers from Phoenicia, Greece, and Rome, crossing the Mediterranean to found such North African outposts as Carthage and Tingis (which is now called Tangier). For centuries North Africa was a Roman Province.

Even hundreds of years after the Arabs conquered North Africa the only cities were those on the coast and a few almost legendary towns that served as trading posts in the western Sahara. Of these Timbuktu and Kano (Nigeria), whose 1,000-year-old walls still stand, are two of the best known.

But today Africa can boast dozens of major cities. Some are not as large or as thickly populated as those of Europe and America, but they are often just as busy and just as modern. Some of the most exciting new architecture in the world is to be found in the newly independent

The city of Kano, in northern Nigeria, has been a trade centre for 1,000 years.

Dakar, capital of the Senegalese Republic, has many modern districts. It is a major African port.

The world's largest mosque is in Cairo. This city has long been a centre of Islam.

states of Africa, where old cities are being expanded. These cities present a striking contrast between the old and the new Africa. Each one has its modern quarter. Fine office buildings, luxurious hotels, smart shops, and blocks of flats line the

Cars and modern buildings in the centre of Addis Ababa, capital of Ethiopia.

broad streets. There are fine restaurants and cafés, and modern hospitals and government buildings.

But only a mile or two away many Africans live as they have lived for hundreds of years. In the cities of North Africa, the *casbah*, or native quarter, is still a crowded place of narrow, winding streets and heavily shuttered houses. Merchants still sell their goods from open stalls in the market-place or *bazaar*.

Not all of the new Africa is modern office buildings and luxurious hotels. There is much poverty and misery. Natives coming from tribal reserves often find it difficult to adjust to life in industrialised cities, and many of them must live in slums in the hearts of big cities, or in shanty towns on the outskirts.

Much of North Africa's trade is carried on in open-air market places like this one in Marrakesh, Morocco.

The modern city of Salisbury, capital and largest city of Zimbabwe Rhodesia, is in the Savanna.

The city of Cape Town, South Africa, is spread out at the foot of Table Mountain.

The colourful ceramics market of the ancient city of Kano, Nigeria.

Veiled women in the narrow streets of Tangier only 40 miles (64 km) from Gibraltar.

Arched gateways and medieval battlements guard the ancient entrances to Tunis's Moslem quarter.

Johannesburg, Africa's fifth largest city, is surrounded by the huge mounds of debris from its gold mines.

Communications

There are striking contrasts in the way people travel about in Africa. Communications are either of the most modern or most primitive kinds. Vast areas of Africa are crossed by neither roads nor railways, so travellers in areas where there are no rivers must either walk or go by air.

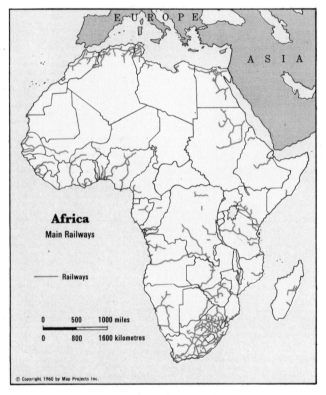

Africa
Main Railways

Railways

0   500   1000 miles
0   800   1600 kilometres

© Copyright 1960 by Map Projects Inc.

Fast efficient transport is difficult to run economically in Africa, for three reasons. One is the great distances involved, another is the problem of building roads or railways across deserts or through dense jungles. The third is the shortage of skilled labour and materials.

The chief railway lines are in South Africa, North Africa, and Egypt. But perhaps the most important ones are the smaller railways that link the navigable stretches of Africa's rivers. The rivers are Africa's greatest highways, both for goods and passengers. But most of the big rivers are broken by waterfalls or rapids, so railways have had to be built to bypass them.

Sturdy river steamers ply the Nile, the Niger, the Zaire, and other waterways.

Many hundreds of miles of roads are now being constructed in Africa, but most of them are far from being adequate modern highways. Very few are surfaced, and in wet weather many are impassable. Far from being arterial roads, most of them merely lead to the nearest river port or railway station. Cars are increasing but most of the traffic consists of buses and lorries. Under these circumstances air travel naturally assumes great importance. It has succeeded, not merely in saving some people's time, but in opening up many remote areas. But the aeroplane has its limitations. It is very expensive to run

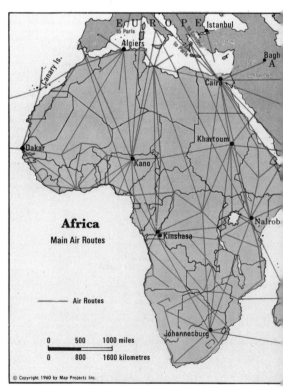

Africa
Main Air Routes

Air Routes

0   500   1000 miles
0   800   1600 kilometres

© Copyright 1960 by Map Projects Inc.

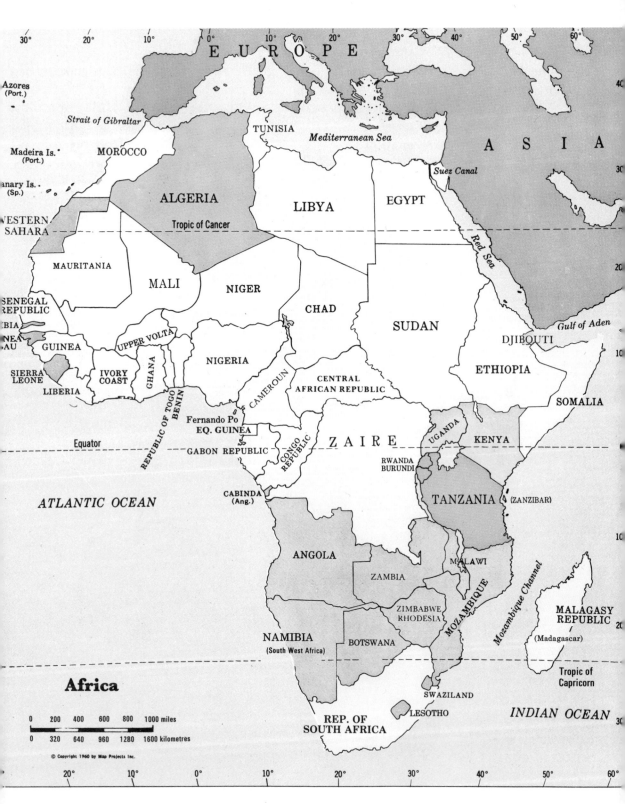

Africa

| 0 | 200 | 400 | 600 | 800 | 1000 miles |
| 0 | 320 | 640 | 960 | 1280 | 1600 kilometres |

© Copyright 1960 by Map Projects Inc.

so that the only goods that can make use of it are those that are light, compact, and valuable, and, as for passengers, few can afford to pay the fare. As a result, air travel has made little impact on the vast majority of Africans.

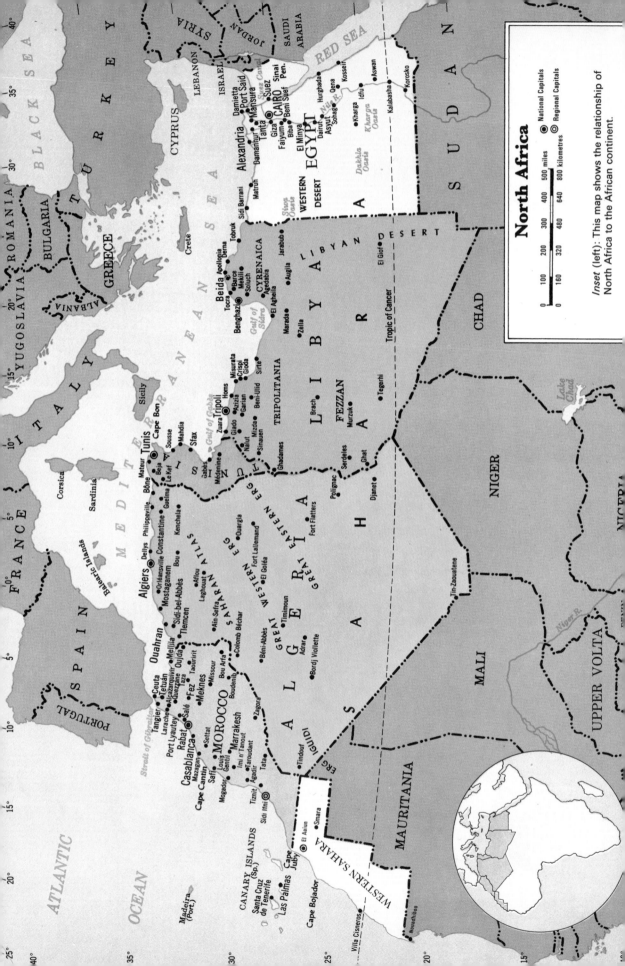

North Africa

Inset (left): This map shows the relationship of North Africa to the African continent.

National Capitals
Regional Capitals

An ancient Berber fortress-village nestling in a valley in the Atlas Mountains.

North Africa

North Africa is rather like an island. It is separated from other lands by the Atlantic and the Mediterranean, and from the rest of Africa by the Sahara Desert. The Arabs call it by the name *Djezira-el-Magreb*, or the Western Isle.

North Africa has a long and fascinating history. The oldest inhabitants were the Berbers, hence the term 'Barbary'. But many other people have since intruded into the Berbers' country: Phoenicians, Greeks, Romans, Vandals, and finally Arabs. And although it later came under the rule of the Turks, French, and Spaniards, North Africa has remained mainly Arabic in language, in religion, and in culture to this day.

Excluding Egypt, North Africa is composed of five countries: Morocco, Western Sahara, Tunisia, Algeria, and Libya. The first three are narrow strips of land fringing the coast, the last two extend from the coast deep into the desert. Egypt will be considered sepa-rately because it belongs geographically to the basin of the Nile.

Much of North Africa consists of plateaus and mountain ranges. Some of the mountains are covered with snow in winter. Where winter rainfall is abundant, the farms and vineyards yield good crops and the mountains are forested; but, as one moves southward from the coast, the basins between the mountains become drier; forests give way to wiry grasses or scrubs. Finally the desert takes over completely, relieved only by the occasional oases.

Morocco

The Kingdom of Morocco, with an area of 166,000 square miles (458,730 sq km), is approximately four-fifths of the size of France. Almost all of its population of about 16.3 million are Moslems. The capital is Rabat, but the main commercial town is Casablanca. Marrakesh and

North Africa is rich in historic remains. This is the famous Roman theatre at Leptis Magna.

Fez are ancient and picturesque cities.

When Morocco gained independence in 1956, Spain gave up her protectorate of Spanish Morocco. Ifni gained independence in 1968. The only possessions that Spain still has within the Moroccan borders are a number of towns on the Mediterranean coast which include Ceuta and Mililla.

In the *casbahs* (the native quarters) of the large towns, and throughout the old walled cities of Morocco, the women are always veiled and the men wear flowing robes and cloaks, and always keep their heads covered. The shops and market-places have exotic foods, rich silks, jewels, swords, and beautiful leather work. Five times a day the muezzin calls the Faithful to prayer from the minarets.

The national dish of Morocco is *couscous*, which is made from semolina. It plays much the same part in a North African meal as rice does in an Indian one. Just as rice is eaten with all sorts of curries, so *couscous* is eaten with all sorts of meat and vegetables.

The fertile fields of Morocco yield a harvest of wheat, barley, and vegetables. There are many vineyards in Morocco, and some wine is made, though only for Europeans, as all intoxicating drinks are forbidden to Moslems. More olives are being grown, and other crops include figs, almonds, and citrus fruits.

Where the land is drier, arable farming gives place to stock-breeding. Cattle are kept, as well as sheep and goats, and horses and camels. Raw wool forms an important export, as do cork and timber from Morocco's forests – especially from the moist slopes of the Atlas mountains. There is good fishing off the coast. Sardine-fishing, combined with canning factories, is quite an important industry in Morocco.

The mineral resources of Morocco are of great note, and many railways have been built to help their development. Morocco has some manganese and a certain amount of iron ore, lead, coal, and oil. However, much the most important mineral consists of the great deposits of phosphates from which fertilisers are made. Morocco is the world's largest exporter of phosphates which make up nearly a quarter of her total exports.

Western Sahara

The Western Sahara lies south-west of Morocco. It is a desolate area, but with phosphate deposits. Because of the high value of these and their proximity to Morocco, in 1975 the Moroccans launched a massive trek into Western Sahara to demonstrate their wish for the territory. It is now divided between them and Mauritania.

Algeria

Considerably larger than Libya, Algeria is the biggest North African country and the most important after Egypt. Nevertheless of its 878,000 square miles (2,300,000 sq km), more than nine-tenths lying south of the Atlas mountains is desert.

Consequently the bulk of Algeria's 14.6 million people live in the small remaining tenth, in the north. This area, the Fell, is fertile farming land. The coastal plains, valleys, and terraced lower slopes of the hills grow enormous crops of wheat and barley. The vineyards yield abundant quantities of wine. Olives, tobacco, fruit, vegetables, and dates are also grown in large quantities.

The Sidi Kacem refinery in Morocco refines oil from the important fields in the Sahara.

A Moroccan girl harvests wheat with a sickle, the method of Biblical times.

The plateaus that stretch southwards to the desert are drier and less fertile, and chiefly provide grazing land for sheep and goats.

Algeria's principal natural resources are oil, iron, natural gas, and phosphates. These resources, except for oil, are largely unexploited: though 3 million metric tons of iron ore are exported every year, mostly to Britain. The oilfields of the Sahara are of great importance to Algeria's economy. However there is little industry based on oil so few people are employed in it. Many pipelines carry it across the desert to the ports for export. In 1974 oil production was 50 million metric tons, placing her twelfth among world producers.

Tunisia

The Republic of Tunisia, lying to the north-east of Algeria, is the smallest of the North African states, with an area of

An open square in Fez, Morocco, holds scores of huge wooden vats where leather goods are dyed.

48,300 square miles (125,096 sq km). Most of the population of just over 5.3 million are Moslems. They live either by

Camels are more than 'ships of the desert'. A Libyan farmer yokes one to his primitive plough to farm his land.

An Algerian orange grove. Fruit is an important Algerian export.

farming the rich coastal plains, through the mining of Tunisia's natural resources, or by working in the new industries of steel, petrol refining and cellulose.

About half the cultivated land produces cereals. The chief agricultural exports are olive oil, wine, and dates.

Tunisia's mineral output is important – exports include phosphates, iron ore, lead, and zinc. Tunisia was well-known to the ancient world. The ruins of Carthage are near the present capital, Tunis.

Libya

Libya is a very big country, having an area of nearly 680,000 square miles (1,759,540 sq km). Yet the population is only a little over 2.3 million. Of these over a third live in the chief towns, and of the remainder many are Bedouin nomads driving their sheep and goats from oasis to oasis.

Libya has three distinct regions: Tripolitania, Cyrenaica, and the Fezzan. Tripolitania lies in the west. Its capital, Tripoli, is a clean and modern town, looking on to the Mediterranean.

Cyrenaica is eastern Libya. Its capital is Benghazi. Benghazi and Tripoli are the joint capitals of Libya, and almost a third of the total population live there.

Ghadames is the most important town of the Fezzan, the desert area in the south. Part of the town is built underground to escape the heat of the desert.

Although Libya has always been regarded as one of the most beautiful countries in Africa – with many famous Greek, Roman, and Byzantine remains – until recently it was also one of the poorest. This was largely due to Libya's dependence on agriculture.

However, the discovery of oil and natural gas in great abundance in 1958 has altered the situation and has enabled vast improvements to be made. Output was 77 million metric tons in 1974, making Libya eighth in world oil production. The Libyan government is making great efforts to increase the production of cereals, olives, dates, citrus fruit, vegetables, and forest products. The communications system and the capacity of the ports – particularly Benghazi – are being rapidly expanded, and the new town built at Beida. A Ten Year Plan which began in 1973 co-ordinates all this and encourages new industry to prosper alongside the traditional silver, embroidery, leather and carpet crafts.

The three great Pyramids near Cairo rise from the desert sands. The cultivated areas are irrigated by the Nile.

Egypt, Land of the Nile

The greatest oasis in the Sahara, one that is 700 miles (1,100 km) long, is the valley of the Nile. Flowing through the length of Egypt, it is the lifeline of the nation. Its waters, flowing from sources deep in the rain-forests of Central Africa and the mountains of Ethiopia, are the life-blood of Egypt.

Except along the Mediterranean coast it scarcely ever rains in Egypt. At Cairo about an inch (25 mm) of rain falls in a year. Over nine-tenths of the country is desert. All farming depends on the Nile, but in the past the Nile has been a most wasteful river. Every August and September for thousands of years the Nile overflowed its banks, irrigating the parched soil. Yet so large was the volume of the flood-water that much of it was wasted, and when the waters drained off they carried away much of the topsoil. Finally when the floods were fully drained away, the land was short of water again.

Irrigation and water storage are thus of the utmost importance. Many canals have been dug to lead the flood-waters into basins, which are flat fields enclosed by low embankments. Various water-lifting devices are used to raise the waters of the Nile up to the higher fields. About 100 years ago the government began to build dams along the river at strategic points. These dams succeeded in increas-

The Archimedean screw, a spiral lifting device, raises water from irrigation canals to the fields. Many modern barrages have now been completed.

An Egyptian woman helps her husband harvest vegetables. The Nile is behind them.

ing the size of the harvest, but they did nothing to store water for use during the long dry period. The Aswan Dam was the first to create a reservoir to hold back a body of water which could be used throughout the year. The High Dam at Aswan is changing the pattern of the flow of the Nile – and of the life of Egypt – for ever. The reservoir created by this dam now extends 124 miles (200 km) into the Sudan, and is of basic importance both for irrigation and the production of electricity to support the growing demands of Egyptian industry.

Although towns such as Cairo are modernised, many of the people in the provinces of Egypt still live in very primitive conditions. However, the Egyptian government is making great efforts to bring modern education, medical care, and farming methods to the backward areas of Egypt. The chief crops are cotton and rice in Lower Egypt, that is to say, round the delta of the Nile, and sugarcane in Upper Egypt. Miscellaneous food crops are grown on the small plots belonging to the peasants.

Shallow-draft dahabiyas ply the Nile, their lateen-rigged sails set to catch the slightest breeze.

Hieroglyphics on the mighty Karnak Temple pillars record the exploits of the Pharaohs.

Against the backdrop of a colourful desert sunset, Bedouins lead their camels to the night's camp.

The Faiyum is a basin in the western desert of Egypt. It lies below sea-level and as it is connected to the Nile by a channel it has become a major oasis. In this region the peasants grow all kinds of citrus and other fruits, together with grapes and olives.

The population of Egypt, now over 36 million, is growing so fast that the increased crops produced by the control of the waters of the Nile are still not enough to support the country. Egypt is therefore turning to industry. Many looms have been started for the weaving of Egyptian cotton. Other industries include metal-working, sugar-refining, petrol-refining, and the manufacture of glass, leather goods, and fertilisers.

The chief port of the country is Alexandria, on the Nile delta, a port whose history goes back 2,300 years. The delta itself is an immense triangle of sand, through which flow the seven branches of the river.

The pyramids of Egypt rank among the wonders of the world. They were built as tombs for the ancient Pharaohs; one of them, the great pyramid of Cheops, is built of 2½ million separate blocks of stone, and is estimated to weigh nearly 5 million metric tons. The Egyptians of today, however, are more concerned with building factories, and ports

An isolated village sits in the gravel desert that surrounds the Egyptian city of Thebes.

for the future welfare of the economy.

Before the construction of the Suez Canal there was no direct link between the Mediterranean and the Red Sea.

The work was started in 1859, and it was not until 1869 that the canal was finally opened. In 1870, 500 vessels went through. By 1913, yearly transits had increased to over 5,000, and by 1955 to nearly three times that number.

Of the total length of 101 miles (160 km), 56 miles (90 km) consist of lakes. The remainder was dug out by hand above water level and by mechanical dredgers below. The difference in water level at the two ends does not exceed 4 feet (1·2 metres), so no locks are needed. The Suez Canal is the world's greatest man-made waterway. In 1967 it was closed because of the Arab-Israeli war. It was re-opened to international traffic in 1975, but Israel is restricted to non-strategic traffic.

Egypt is hoping to rebuild Port Said, Suez, and the canal zone with the intention of turning it into a tax free industrial zone. The hostilities with Israel have upset the Egyptian economy and caused some movement of population away from this zone.

Giant sand dunes cover the 'Great Erg' region of the Sahara. Dunes are formed by the wind.

At a more flourishing Saharan oasis than the one above, springs yield enough water for irrigation canals.

The Desert Lands

Sahara is an Arabic word meaning 'emptiness'. No better word could be chosen, for the Sahara Desert is 3½ million square miles (9 million sq km) of 'emptiness'. This immense area of sand and rock stretches from the Atlantic Ocean to

Dwellers of this date-palm oasis raise precious water from their well with a primitive sweep.

the Red Sea and cuts off northern Africa from the bulk of the continent.

The word desert always brings a vision of sand, but in fact only a small part of the Sahara consists of sand dunes. Like all dunes, they are constantly shifting under the action of the wind. This section, called the Great Erg, is the most feared of all. Most of the Sahara is made up of rocky plateaus and vast flat plains of loose stones and pebbles.

In the middle of the Sahara are huge mountain chains, chief amongst which are the Ahaggar Mountains occupying an area comparable to that of the Alps, but their peaks do not rise much higher than 8,000 feet (2,400 m). They were created by volcanic eruptions millions of years ago. Scientists at one time thought that the Sahara was the bed of an ancient

A camel train winds across the trackless Sahara. Caravan guides can memorize the routes.

A caravan pitches its tents near a 'ksar' – an oasis village once fortified against Tuareg marauders.

ocean that had dried up. But nowadays they believe it was formed by the weathering of the mountains. The sharp change between the heat of the day and the cold of the night, added to the action of the constant winds and occasional violent rain-storms or sand-storms, tend to crack and break up rocks into smaller and smaller pieces, which are finally reduced to grains of sand. This process is still going on. Many thousands of years from now, given the same climatic conditions, the present-day mountains in the Sahara will have been reduced to sand. During the weathering processes, salts contained in the rocks are not washed away, and salty areas are formed.

The 'emptiness' of the Sahara must not be taken too literally, for the desert is not utterly bare. Much of the rocky part is thinly covered by a scraggy growth of coarse grass or stunted bushes. In certain cases the underground water is near enough to the surface for many desert plants to sink their long roots into it. These are the oases of the Sahara. In some, there is enough water for wells to

Women of the Tuareg tribe spend much of their spare time dressing each other's hair.

Tea-drinking is a ritual among the Tuareg.

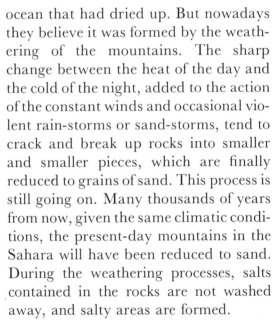

271

An Egyptian tractor crew works beside an irrigation canal in Egypt's Liberation Province, a major land-reform and reclamation project.

a trickle of water to those whose many springs give rise to towns with populations of several thousands. A typical oasis grows dates, citrus fruits, and vegetables.

Sometimes, instead of digging downward to make a well, people dig horizontally into the side of a hill to make what is called a *foggara*. If the channel strikes water under the hill, it will flow outward into the oasis without having to be pumped.

Travellers across the desert move from oasis to oasis. Fifty years ago the Sahara could only be crossed by camel, 'the ship of the desert'. Camels have adapted themselves by nature to cope with the problems of the desert. The nourishment

be dug, and even for land to be cultivated. There are in fact oases of all degrees, from tiny clumps of bushes and

The export of sheep and goats is a big trade in Tunisia. The quality is very high.

Lorries are now used more frequently to transport goods and people acrosss the Sahara.

and liquid stored in the fatty tissues of their bodies, particularly in their humps, enables them to go without food or water for several days. Therefore, for crossing the great areas of shifting sand dunes, the camel has no rival.

There may be over a hundred camels in an Arab caravan, whose leaders are expert navigators who know every landmark on their route.

Nowadays it is also possible, though difficult and sometimes dangerous, to cross the Sahara in a car. Drivers must notify the authorities of their departure and their route. If they do not reach their destination within twenty-four hours of the expected time, a rescue team is sent to search for them. The major oases in the roads are from 200–300 miles (320–480 km) apart, and breakdowns can be fatal. Anyone stranded in the Sahara without water in summer is unlikely to live much more than a day.

The inhabitants of the desert, nearly all of whom are Moslems, are of mixed Berber and Arab stock. There are those who live permanently at the oases and the nomads who wander from one oasis to another. Of the nomads the Tuareg are of Berber origin, while the Bedouin are Arabs. There are also those who now work in the oilfields of the desert.

In the south-eastern part of the Sahara live the Tibbus, a word which means 'the rock people', for their home is in the rocky Tibesti Mountains near the Sudan. They are of partly Negro stock.

The most interesting of the peoples of the Sahara are the Tuareg. Their origin is obscure, but they are thought by some to be descendants of Berbers who fled to the Sahara before the advance of the many waves of conquerors who poured into North Africa. They are still a proud and independent people. They are nomads, wandering over the desert with their goats, sheep, and camels.

Whereas in the rest of the Arab world the women are veiled, amongst the Tuareg it is the faces of the women that are uncovered while those of the men are veiled. One explanation that has been offered is that the Tuareg wanted to distinguish themselves from other Arabs. More probably the veil is simply a good means of protection from the desert sun.

Because of long dry periods, water is precious. Algerian slopes are carefully irrigated and contour ploughed.

Five Desert-Margin States

Sudan

The Sudan is the largest country in the whole of Africa, covering an area of nearly a million square miles (2.6 million sq km). It is almost entirely an agricultural and pastoral country, with no

The Djezireh region between the White and the Blue Nile is an important cotton growing area.

very important mineral resources. There is considerable variation in the climatic conditions: desert and semi-desert in the north, humid in the south.

In the central and northern zones water-shortage is a great problem. The Sennar dam on the Blue Nile has made possible the irrigation of the fertile *djezireh* zone between the Blue and White Nile, and the spread of cotton plantations.

Another dam is projected on the Blue Nile at Roseires. The lake formed by the Aswan dam which extends some 124 miles (200 km) into the Sudan helps to irrigate this parched region.

Cotton accounts for three-quarters of the Sudan's total exports, the next most important being gum arabic – of which the Sudan produces the bulk of the world's supply.

The principal towns are Khartoum, the capital, which has, together with Khartoum North, a population of over 337,000; and Omdurman with 231,000.

Natural gas from Hassi R'Mel in the Sahara is exported in liquid form. These flare-stacks are known locally as 'Les Torches'.

The old port of Fuakin has lost its importance to Port Sudan, which handles three-quarters of the country's overseas trade.

Chad Republic

The Chad Republic can be divided into two parts: the desert in the north and the savanna regions in the south. There are no known mineral deposits so the economy rests on the produce of the south. Cotton and groundnuts are grown as cash crops, but livestock is more important. About 500,000 out of the total population of 3.9 million are nomadic Arabs.

Niger

Niger is a huge, thinly populated country, mainly taken up by the Sahara desert. Deposits of iron ore, tin at Air,

Maintenance work in progress along the banks of the Suez Canal.

200 miles (320 km) north of Agades, and salt and uranium are being mined. The south is the most important region for agriculture: here the greater rainfall (about 25 inches (635 mm) a year) and the Niger river enable the inhabitants to rear large flocks of sheep, goats, and cattle. The chief food crop is millet, and groundnuts are grown for export.

The capital is Niamey, a route centre and one of two termini on The Trans-Sahara motor route. Most trade is with Nigeria, but there is an increasing amount with Benin. As an area of 'big game' its tourism is increasing.

The Tuareg are one of the last nomadic peoples of the Sahara desert. Here a Tuareg child is playing with a beautiful kite at an oasis in the Sahara.

There are regular steamer services on the Niger.

Mali

Mali is a vast landlocked country sparsely populated. Large areas are desert or semi-desert, but some areas, in the south in the Niger valley, are extremely fertile. Chief crops are rice, cotton, and groundnuts, but away from the flood plains the rearing of cattle, sheep, and goats is more important. Of the towns, Bamako, the capital, is the most important, being on the end of the railway to Dakar (Senegal), which is Mali's chief link with the outside world. Timbuktu has declined in importance as a caravan and route centre.

Mauritania

Mauritania forms the bridge between North and West Africa. Agriculturally it is a poor country, but there is a considerable cattle population, dates are grown, and the fishing industry is important and capable of considerable expansion. However, Mauritania's principal resources are the large deposits of high-grade iron ore at Fort Gouraud, accounting for 90 per cent of her exports, and the considerable deposits of copper near Akjoujt.

The chief towns are Port Etienne, a fishing centre and port which is expanding with the growth of the mining industry; and Fort Gouraud round which the industry will be centred.

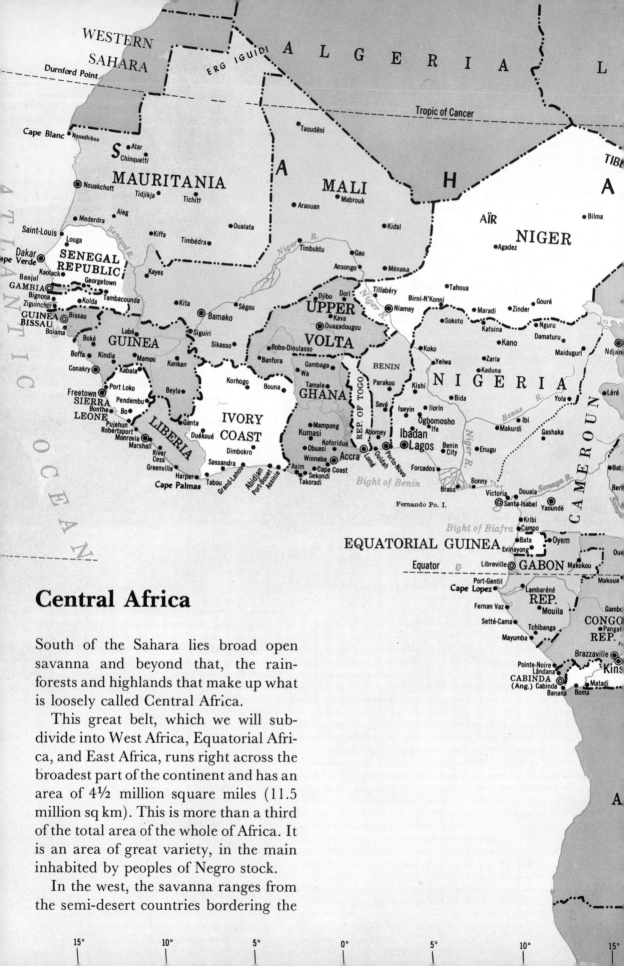

Central Africa

South of the Sahara lies broad open savanna and beyond that, the rain-forests and highlands that make up what is loosely called Central Africa.

This great belt, which we will sub-divide into West Africa, Equatorial Africa, and East Africa, runs right across the broadest part of the continent and has an area of 4½ million square miles (11.5 million sq km). This is more than a third of the total area of the whole of Africa. It is an area of great variety, in the main inhabited by peoples of Negro stock.

In the west, the savanna ranges from the semi-desert countries bordering the

EGYPT

RED SEA

GULF OF ADEN

Cape
Guardafui

• Largeau

R

A

• Wadi Halfa
• Selima
• Muhammad Ghul
• Delgo
Port Sudan
• Dongola   • Kareima   Berber   • Suakin
• Debba   • Atbara   • Aqiq
• Shendi
Massawa
Omdurman
Khartoum   • Kassala   Keren
Wad Medani   • Asmara
• Gedaref   Umm Hajar   Mersa
Fatma
ERITREA
Makale

CHAD

SUDAN

• Abéché   • Geneina   • El Fasher   El Obeid
• Nyala   • Nahud   • Kosti   Roseires
Am-Timan   • Muglad   • Talodi
N'Délé   • Malakal
• Gore
• Gondar
Lake
Tana
Debra
Markos   • Belfodio
Addis Ababa
ETHIOPIA
Saio
Jimma
• Soddu
DJIBOUTI
◉ Djibouti
Dikhil
• Bulhar   Karin
• Berbera   Buran
• Hargeisa   • Gardo
Bender Beila
Bohotieh
• El Hamurre
Harar   • Diredawa

Bender
Kassim

• Fort-Crampel
ngoa   • Grimari   • Yalinga
AI AFRICAN REPUBLIC
Bomu R.
• Kouango
zongo   • Ango
• Yambio
Gogrial
• Wau   • Tonj
• Akobo
Nasir
• Maji
• Alga
• Ginir
• Negelli
Gorrahei
• Wardere
Shebeli R.
• Dabaro

SOMALIA

• Hararrdera
• Meregh

• Businga
Uele R.
• Monga
• Buta
• Paulis
• Mongalla
Juba   • Torit
• Mega
• Mandera
• Dolo
Isha
Baidoa
• Itala
◉ Mogadishu
Merca
• Lisala   • Bumba
Zaire R.   • Kisangani
• Irumu
Kitgum
• Masindi   Soroti
Lake
Turkana
Lodwar
• Marsabit
Wajir
Juba R.
• Afmadu   Brava
• Gelib

• Monkoto
Lomela R.
Stanley
Falls
• Kirundu
Lake
Edward
UGANDA
Fort Portal
Entebbe   Kampala
Kisumu   • Nakuru   • Muddo Gashi
KENYA
• Naivasha
Nairobi ◉   • Bura

Mbandaka
• Lomela
Kabale
Lake
Kivu
Lake
Victoria
Ngong
• Witu
Lamu

ZAIRE
Kindu
RWANDA
BURUNDI ◉
Jumbura
Rutana
• Fizi
Kigali ◉
• Mwanza
• Arusha
• Moshi
• Malindi
• Takaungu
Mombasa
INDIAN

Kikwit
• Luebo
• Kabalo
Zaire R.
• Ujiji
Lake
Tanganyika
• Tabora
• Kondoa
Pemba
(ZANZIBAR)
• Zanzibar

sai R.
• Kapanga
Lake
Upemba
• Manono
Moba
Karema
Dodoma
• Mpwapwa
◉ Dar es Salaam
OCEAN

• Sandoa
• Lubudi
• Pweto
Lake
Mweru
• Kasanga
TANZANIA
Iringa
• Chunya
• Mbeya
• Mohoro
• Kilwa

• Dilolo-Gare   • Kolwezi
• Jadotville
Lake
Malawi
• Mwaya
• Manda
• Lindi
• Masasi   Cape Delgado
Lubumbashi
• Sakania
MALAWI
• Tunduru   • Newala

LA

ZAMBIA

ZIMBABWE
RHODESIA

20°   25°   30°   35°

Central Africa

| 0 | 100 | 200 | 300 | 400 | 500 miles | ◉ National Capitals |
| 0 | 160 | 320 | 480 | 640 | 800 kilometres | ◉ Regional Capitals |

Inset (above): This map shows the relationship of
Central Africa to the African continent.

© Copyright 1960 by Map Projects Inc.

The dense growth of head-high grasses with scattered bushes and trees is typical of savanna landscapes.

Sahara to the coastal forests. In some coastal areas impenetrable mangrove swamps extend for many miles. In the east the grasslands of the Sudan rise to the mountainous regions of Ethiopia and to the high plateau of East Africa, with its great peaks like Mount Kilimanjaro, Mount Kenya, and Ruwenzori, and the plains which are the home of big game.

Between these western and eastern regions lie the wet, humid jungles of the central equatorial plateau, and the immense basin of the Zaire.

Central Africa is traditionally the land of tribal chiefs and witch-doctors, of the tsetse fly and the malaria-carrying mosquito. Yet, even here, modern cities are springing up alongside the jungle villages of mud and thatch. Though still fairly undeveloped it is an area of great natural resources, and great potential wealth.

The Central African savanna consists of a belt of rolling uplands about 700 miles (1,100 km) in breadth, covered

Brazzaville, the capital of the Congo Republic, boasts a large, modern airport.

with grassland, scattered trees, and shrubs. Part of it is used for arable farming or stock-breeding. The plains in the east, covered with tall grasses, are the big game country.

Cattle-breeding is carried on for the most part in the northern section of this belt, where the short grass makes good grazing land for the herds. Of the African tribes who go in for cattle-breeding the Masai of East Africa, a tall, proud tribe of warriors, are the most famous.

Cattle-breeding is often restricted by the tsetse fly. Thousands of head of cattle are killed by it. However, in recent years some progress has been made in clearing regions by the use of chemical sprays. This, and the banning of movement of infected cattle into the newly cleared areas has improved the situation.

A woman of the Samburu tribe and her children guarding native flocks on the Kenya plains.

There are 592 miles (950 km) of railway track open in Ghana today. The main line links Takoradi to Accra.

West Africa

Perhaps the most interesting part of Africa today is West Africa. In the rush of progress the old and the new provide striking contrasts. Huts with corrugated iron roofs stand next to modern office buildings, and African taxi-drivers, dressed in picturesque native robes, steer their cabs through the traffic.

West Africa stretches from Cape Verde on the Atlantic to the mountains of Cameroun in the east, and from the edge of the Sahara in the north to the swampy coast of the Gulf of Guinea. Its chief rivers are the Niger, the Volta, and the Senegal.

By and large, West Africans are happy and friendly people. The men are tall and good-looking. The women dress in gaily coloured cotton clothes.

There are few good natural harbours along the coast of West Africa. The coast is unindented and the water off-shore

Local produce on sale in a new, covered, concrete market-place in Abidjan, Ivory Coast.

shallow. Consequently ocean-going vessels have to unload by lighter – the most famous example being the huge canoe-like boats formerly used by the boatmen of Accra. The best ports on the west coast are Freetown (Sierra Leone), Lagos (Nigeria), and Takoradi (Ghana).

Senegal

Senegal, formerly the oldest of the French African colonies, is distinguished in being the intellectual centre of French-speaking Africa. In the past its economy has been almost completely dependent on goundnuts, but efforts are being made to reduce the country's dependence on this crop, by developing industries, of which the most important are textiles, phosphates, salt and oil refining. In addition to these, estimated reserves of 980 million metric tons of iron ore have been found at La Faleme, and it is thought that Senegal could become one of Africa's major iron producers. Dakar, the capital, is the largest town and one of the chief ports of Africa. Its industries include the extraction and refining of groundnut oil and the manufacture of soap, cement, and textiles. There are railway workshops and ship-repairing yards. Dakar airport is the largest in West Africa. 12 per cent of Senegal's total population of 3.9 million live in and around Dakar.

Gambia

Gambia is a long, narrow strip of territory bordering the lower and middle reaches of the Gambia river for just over 200 miles (320 km) inland. The width of Gambia is about 20 miles (32 km) near the coast and about 12 miles (20 km) further inland.

Gambia is one of the poorest countries in Africa; 95 per cent of her exports consist of groundnuts, and there seems little chance of extending agriculture, except for local consumption.

The old slave steps on King Jimmy's Wharf in Freetown, the capital of Sierra Leone.

The harbour at Lagos. Lagos is one of the most important ports on the west coast of Africa.

Guinea

Guinea is a rapidly developing country with considerable agricultural resources and mineral deposits. Diamonds and, most important, iron ore and bauxite are being exploited, and there is a growing use of the country's hydro-electric potential. Guinea has trade and military connections with the USSR.

Citizens of Accra queue up for water when the dry season cuts the normal supply.

Sierra Leone

Sierra Leone is one of the smallest of West African states – its area is only 27,925 square miles (73,326 sq km). On the other hand its population is 3.1 million (70 per square mile or 41 per sq km), which is dense by African standards.

Most of the population is engaged in subsistence farming, but Sierra Leone

Huge 'dunce's-cap' thatched huts in a typical Liberian village.

Workmen in Senegal pile up a huge mound of peanuts for shipment. Peanuts are Senegal's chief crop.

exports palm kernels, oil, cocoa, coffee and ginger and is the leading world producer of piassava, used for brooms and hard brushes. However, Sierra Leone's principal export is diamonds, and she also has extensive deposits of very rich iron ore at Marampa and, to a lesser extent, bauxite and chromite – all accounting for 79 per cent of her exports.

The capital is Freetown, with one of the finest harbours in Africa. It is very important not only to Sierra Leone but to the economy of the whole of the west coast of the continent.

Fishermen's painted canoes are a colourful sight on the beach in Ghana.

Liberia

Liberia is the oldest independent state in West Africa, having been chosen in 1820 as a home for freed American slaves. Liberia has the world's largest merchant fleet. The chief cash crops are rubber and coffee. However, minerals are of growing importance to the Liberian economy. Gold and diamonds are exported, but – most important – there are rich deposits of iron ore north of the capital, Monrovia, and near the border with the Ivory Coast.

The modern Supreme Court buildings in Ghana are good examples of modern architecture.

Logs of valuable tropical wood float in a Ghanaian harbour awaiting transport to lumber mills.

Modern machinery stockpiles iron ore on the loading docks of Liberia.

Ivory Coast

The Ivory Coast, with a population of more than five million, is one of the most thriving territories of West Africa, with an economy based upon an increasingly commercialised agriculture. Coffee and cocoa are easily the two most important products. In fact the Ivory Coast is the third largest world producer of coffee. Timber and bananas are also exported.

A cacao grower inspects the pods on one of his trees to see whether they are ready to harvest.

For many years the development of the territory was hindered by the very dense rain-forests of the southern third of the country, and the difficult coastline: cliffs along the western half of the coast, sand-bars and lagoons along the east. However, roads are now opening up the forests, and the Vridi Canal pierces the sand-bar opposite Abidjan, the chief port and capital. The canal and new roads have greatly improved communications.

Ceremonial robes, worn for a state occasion, in Ghana.

An African clothed in ritual robes moves down a jungle path to a shrine in Ife, Nigeria.

Upper Volta

Unlike many countries of West Africa, the Republic of Upper Volta is both agriculturally unproductive and without mineral resources. Large areas in the west are infertile, extensive areas in the east unhealthy. The remaining areas are densely populated and poor. The only exports of any size are cattle and man-power, which go to Ghana and the Ivory Coast. A new dam project is transforming a barren plain near Zhorgo for rice and sugar growing. There are similar plans for other parts of the country.

Dense rain-forest borders the Ogooué River in Cameroun, scene of Dr Schweitzer's work.

Ghana

Ghana is one of the richest countries in Central Africa, with large mineral resources. These include gold (before independence Ghana was known as the Gold Coast), diamonds, manganese, and bauxite. The chief export is cocoa, and a third of the world's supply comes from Ghana. A disease called 'swollen root' is a great menace to the industry, and at one time threatened to wipe it out. It has now been brought under control, but because of this threat, farmers are trying to diversify exports by planting coffee, coconuts, and oil palms in place of cocoa plantations. A dam constructed across the Volta near Ajena is important for irrigation and as a source of hydro-electric power. This power has enabled a bauxite-smelting industry to be set up nearby.

Accra is the capital (population 848,825) and formerly an important

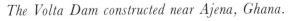

The Volta Dam constructed near Ajena, Ghana.

The River Ouémé flows into the Bight of Benin at Porto Novo.

port, which is now outmoded. The chief ports today are Takoradi and Tema, a new site which is of particular importance with the completion of the Volta project.

Fishermen drying their nets in a lagoon on the coast of Benin.

Nigeria

The Federal Republic of Nigeria, with a population of more than 58 million, has the largest population and highest population density in Africa.

The Niger and its principal tributary, the Benue, divide the country into three parts. In the north are the monotonous 'High Plains of Hausaland', in the southwest the lower plateau of the Yoruba country, while south-eastern Nigeria is a land of vales and escarpments.

Nigeria is primarily an agricultural country. Oil-palm products come from the north-east and the southern rainforest belt. Cocoa grows in the southwest, centred on Ibadan; some plantation rubber grows near Benin; and the area around Kano, market town for the north and focus for caravan routes to the

Lagos is the federal capital of Nigeria, and its leading port.

Sahara, is important for millet, ground-nuts, and cotton.

Nigeria has substantial oil reserves and, while 70 per cent of the working population is employed in agriculture, earnings from the export of crude petroleum are providing the basis of economic growth. There are also deposits of coal, tin and columbite. The coal is of importance as no other large reserves are known in West Africa. Nigeria is the world's leading producer of columbite, used to make special steels for jet engines.

The Niger dam, at Kainji, was completed in 1969, and now provides power in the rapid drive for industrialisation.

Lagos is the Federal capital and leading port. Much export traffic, including coal, passes through Port Harcourt, and the largest city is Ibadan.

Nigeria's chief exports are palm produce, groundnuts and oil, cocoa, cotton, and rubber.

These brightly dressed women are pounding yams. Yams are part of the staple diet of West Africa.

Benin and Togo

Benin and Togo, lying between Nigeria and Ghana, are amongst the smallest and poorest territories in West Africa. Nevertheless, Benin, though largely dependent on French economic aid, is an important producer of oil-palm produce, cocoa, and coffee; and the wealth of Togo has been increased by the discovery

A group of men drive animals laden with sacks of grain down a flooded African road.

289

and exploitation of phosphates, bauxite and iron ore near Lomé, the capital.

The capital of Benin is Porto Novo, but the largest town is Cotonou, the chief port and leading commercial centre of the country. The two cities are situated on either side of the Ouémé delta.

This village is more typical of Zaire than modern cities like Kinshasa and Lubumbashi.

Equatorial Africa

The dominant feature of Equatorial Africa is the rain-forest. Nourished by a hot climate and an abundant rainfall throughout the year, broad-leaved ever-green trees rise to amazing heights. This region is not entirely covered by forests. The height of the land varies greatly along the equatorial belt. There are mangrove swamps and mountains near the coast of Cameroun. And in the east of the Zaire basin the land rises to high open forests, where the dry and rainy seasons alternate, and the trees shed their leaves accordingly.

Zaire

The heart of the rain-forest is Zaire, once known as the Belgian Congo. Over 24.3 million people, divided into more than 200 tribes, live in its 905,564 square miles (2,345,400 sq km). Most of them are concentrated in a few areas, where condi-

A steamer on the Zaire chugs up river between jungle-lined banks, carrying assorted cargo.

tions are relatively healthy and most suitable for raising crops. The rain-forest is the haunt of gorillas and chimpanzees. It is also the home of the Zaire peacock and the rare okapi, a relative of the giraffe, but no bigger than a mule, which has become adapted to forest life.

Together with its tributaries, the Zaire River dominates everything. It is the chief artery of communications and transport, and navigable for 8,500 miles (13,700 km). River steamers ply the Zaire and its tributaries.

Like all the major African rivers, the Zaire falls steeply towards the sea from a central plateau. Accordingly its navigable stretches are interrupted by rapids and waterfalls. All the heavy waterborne traffic has to be carried past these obstacles by a series of short, but extremely important, railways. For instance, just below Kinshasa, the capital of Zaire, the river passes through a series of violent rapids. So goods are unloaded and sent by rail to Matadi, the chief port, where they are reloaded. Another port, Ango-Ango, is used by tankers, and a pipeline connects it with Kinshasa, where fuel oil is needed for the Zaire river-steamers. Economically the most important area of Zaire is Shaba, the south-eastern area of the Zaire Basin. Shaba is one of the greatest mineral-bearing areas in the world, particularly for copper. It is also rich in tin and zinc, has more cobalt than any area in the world, and is one of the chief sources of uranium. Other minerals include: manganese, tungsten, and coal. Kinshasa is a very modern city, and so too is Lubumbashi, the principal town of the Shaba region. Zaire is developing rapidly. She sends many students to study overseas and has her own university for 16,000 students.

The modern city of Kinshasa, Zaire.

A child from Zaire helps with the chores.

Cameroun Republic

The Cameroun Republic falls into two very different regions; tropical rain-forests in the south, dry savanna in the north.

In the tropical north there is a large agricultural population. The chief crops are millet, groundnuts, and cotton, while cattle rearing is also very important.

In the equatorial south, coffee, cocoa, bananas, tobacco, palm kernels, and wild rubber are produced.

It is thought that there are large deposits of bauxite in Cameroun, and the

Cone-shaped huts from the village of Patoko, in the Cameroun.

aluminium industry is already well established, using imported aluminium and the hydro-electric power generated by a modern dam at Edea.

A vegetable market in Doukoula, Cameroun.

The most important outlet of Cameroun is Douala, on the Sanaga estuary. Douala exports coffee, bananas, cacao, palm oil and hardwoods.

Gabon, Congo Republic, Central African Republic

To the north and west of the Congo basin is a cluster of independent states formed from what was formerly French Equatorial Africa. These are Gabon, the Congo Republic, and the Central African Republic. They are all economically poor and undeveloped countries. Of the three Gabon is the most advanced, though even here most of the leading agricultural products are 'wild' rather than cultivated. Most agriculture is subsistence level. Lack of transport, though roads are developing, is a great handicap, especially for the Central African Republic, where millet, maize, cotton, sisal, and tobacco are grown on the savanna lands. This region is capable of great development as a cattle-breeding area.

The Congo Republic has small quantities of copper, diamonds, gold, and zinc, and enormous deposits of potash salts. Manganese, uranium concentrates and natural gas are exported from Gabon. Large deposits of iron ore were found in 1971.

Industries include plywood and petrol products from Gabon.

Brazzaville in the Congo Republic, on the opposite bank of the river Zaire to Kinshasa, is the most important town, and the rail link with Ponte-Noire is important for the mining and agriculture of both the Congo and Gabon.

Rwanda and Burundi

Rwanda and Burundi have dense populations and a healthy climate. Cattle-rearing and farming take place. Coffee is important, but Rwanda's chief asset is manpower, which goes to Shaba, Zaire.

A Pygmy from the Central African Republic. Ceremoniously dressed, he is playing a drum accompanying the dancing of his fellow villagers.

The Eastern Highlands

Ethiopia

As we move eastward the savanna ends abruptly at a mountain barrier that

forms the highlands of Ethiopia, a rugged land with a long history that goes back thousands of years. Legend has it that Ethiopia was once ruled by the Queen of Sheba.

293

Rich farmlands lie part fallow, part cultivated at the foothills of the mountains of Ethiopia.

Beeswax is exported from Ethiopia. The beeswax is checked as it hardens in moulds.

Ethiopia's volcanic mountains rise to 15,000 ft (4,600 m). On the higher levels cattle, sheep, and goats are kept, while, on the lower slopes, a variety of crops is grown, including grain, sugar-cane. cotton, coffee, dates, figs, and citrus fruits. The produce of the drier plains consists of gum arabic, beeswax, and frankincense and myrrh.

Djibouti

Djibouti, formerly known as Afars and Issas, is a barren desert region on the Gulf of Aden. It became independent from France in 1977. Its single port and town, Djibouti, handles 60 per cent of Ethiopia's trade.

Somali Republic

South of Ethiopia is the Somali Republic which is becoming important in African politics. It is mainly a pastoral country with a few known mineral reserves.

Still further east, the land drops swiftly to the Red Sea and the Indian Ocean. Most of the coastal lands are desert. South of Ethiopia, the East African Plateau rises sharply from the coast. It is separated from the Central African Plateau by the Great African Rift Valley,

Ploughing in Ethiopia. Oxen are a valuable asset to African farmers.

which contains a string of long, narrow, deep lakes. The plateau is a region of high plains and mountains that used to be known as British East Africa. Now the various territories are independent members of the Commonwealth.

Kenya

Much of this region, especially Kenya, is 5,000 feet (1,500 m) or more above sea-level, which makes for a comfortable climate, even though Kenya's highlands run right across the Equator. Temperatures range from about 80°F (27°C) during the day to as little as 35°F (2°C) at night. Three-quarters of Kenya gets less than 30 inches (760 mm) of rain a year, and most of the central and northern areas between the coastal plain and the highlands are arid. Livestock are very important where it is not too dry.

Kenya's chief commercial crops are coffee, tea, sisal, wattle extract, pyrethrum, and cotton, the most productive areas being north and west of Nairobi. Other crops, including fruit and vegetables, and even wheat and barley, are grown, especially round Nairobi.

Nairobi is the chief town, with a population of more than 520,000. Its importance has increased greatly with the opening up of the Kenya Highlands, especially the rich coffee and sisal areas tapped by the Fort Hall railway. Nairobi also has a very important international airport. Mombasa is the only port of Kenya, and the new modern harbour at Kilindini probably makes it the best harbour on the whole east coast of Africa. It handles a considerable amount of the rail traffic from Uganda and north-east Tanzania as well as that of Kenya.

Industry is increasing; at present it is mainly food processing. Soda-ash and a

Nairobi, the capital of Kenya. This thriving city has an international airport which plays an important part in the communications of East Africa.

small quantity of gold are also produced. Minerals are numerous but in small quantities.

Nairobi is the great centre for safari. There are six national parks and six game reserves in Kenya. One of them, the Tsavo reserve, is 8,000 square miles (20,800 sq km) in area and is kept specially for elephants. South of Nairobi, on the other side of the Tanzania frontier, is another area rich in animal life – the famous Serengeti plains.

Tanzania

Tanzania is larger than Kenya and Uganda put together. Much of it is dry, arid country. Large areas are covered by scrub and grassland. Farming is poor, except in the regions surrounding Mount Kilimanjaro, which is reasonably well watered. The rain falls on the sides of the mountain and feeds the streams and lakes of the surrounding country, giving

Thousands of animals gather at a waterhole in the Serengeti Plains, an area famous for its game.

enough water for farming. The main crop was sisal, which thrives on poor, dry soil. Since 1967, however, diversification has been practised, with more land being planted with cotton. Coffee and oil seeds are also grown successfully, and cashew nuts and maize have been introduced recently. Livestock is also an important part of the economy.

Tanzania has recently become an important producer of minerals, especially diamonds, lead, and gold. Tanzania is now one of the world's leading diamond producers. Other minerals exported include salt, mica, tin, and small quantities of silver and copper. Large coal deposits also exist. Hydroelectric schemes have been built at Tanga and Kidatu.

Dar es Salaam is the capital and chief port of Tanzania.

About 22½ miles (36 km) off the coast lies the island of Zanzibar, the other part of Tanzania. Formerly a British protectorate, it has elected to join Tanzania, an independent state within the British Commonwealth.

Zanzibar used to be a busy centre for Arab slave-traders. Now Zanzibar, together with its sister island of Pemba, exports a large part of the world's total supply of cloves and copra. They also produce chillies, tuna, and sardines.

Broad-sailed Arab dhows are a common sight in Zanzibar harbour.

Moshi Mosque in Tanzania is a religious centre for Moslems. In the background is Mt Kilimanjaro.

A Moslem in Tanzania weaves a straw sleeping mat. Mats like these are popular with tourists.

The narrow, winding streets and Arab-style houses of Zanzibar resemble those of North Africa.

tobacco, tea, coffee, and sugar are also grown. Copper is its chief mineral export.

Lake Victoria is a huge, shallow body of water lying between Kenya, Uganda, and Tanzania. It occupies a depression in the plateau and is the largest lake in Africa. Of the other lakes which lie in a chain along the Great Rift Valley the most important are Lake Turkana, Lake Mabutu, Lake Edward, Lake Kivu, Lake Tanganyika, and Lake Malawi. Of these, Lake Tanganyika and Lake Malawi are much the biggest.

Although Lake Victoria is the second largest body of fresh water in the world, its greatest depth is only 250 feet (76 m). Its waters are infested with crocodiles, hippopotami, and a mollusc which harbours the pernicious flat-worm bilharzia. The lake is important as the source of the White Nile. The dam at Owen Falls helps to control the flow of water in the Nile, as well as providing Uganda with electricity. Eventually this dam may help to provide cheap hydro-electric power for a large area of the Zaire Basin as well.

Fish from Uganda's 13,695 square miles (35,470 sq km) of lake water are an important source of food.

Tea is a major product of Uganda. Trees are planted to provide shade for the tea shrubs.

Uganda

Uganda, a relatively small country with no outlet to the sea, is an intermediate territory between the northern savanna and Equatorial Africa. In the north, the swamps merge with those of the Sudan. In the south-west, it borders the Zaire rain-forest. Uganda is fertile and prosperous. The main crop is cotton, but

The rocky coastline and jutting headlands of Pringle Bay, South Africa.

Southern Africa

The relatively narrow southern part of the continent differs greatly from the northern and central sections. As we have already seen, the belt of savanna is not so broad as the northern savanna. It forms an intermediate area between the Zaire rain-forest and the deserts of Namibia and Botswana, which are small compared to the Sahara.

At the southern tip of the continent we are no longer in the tropics. The Republic of South Africa lies almost entirely south of the Tropic of Capricorn. Here, as in South America, the seasons are reversed compared with those in Europe, and Christmas, for example, falls in the middle of summer.

The healthy climate of this area soon attracted white settlers, and colonies were founded long ago by the Portuguese, the Dutch, and the British.

This southern part of the continent is a region of considerable variety. Zambia and Zimbabwe Rhodesia are mining countries. South Africa has rich arable and grazing land wherever there is a supply of water. On the coast are industrial towns and seaside resorts.

Horse and rider pause to view the majesty of 630 ft (192 m) Maletsunyane Falls, in Lesotho.

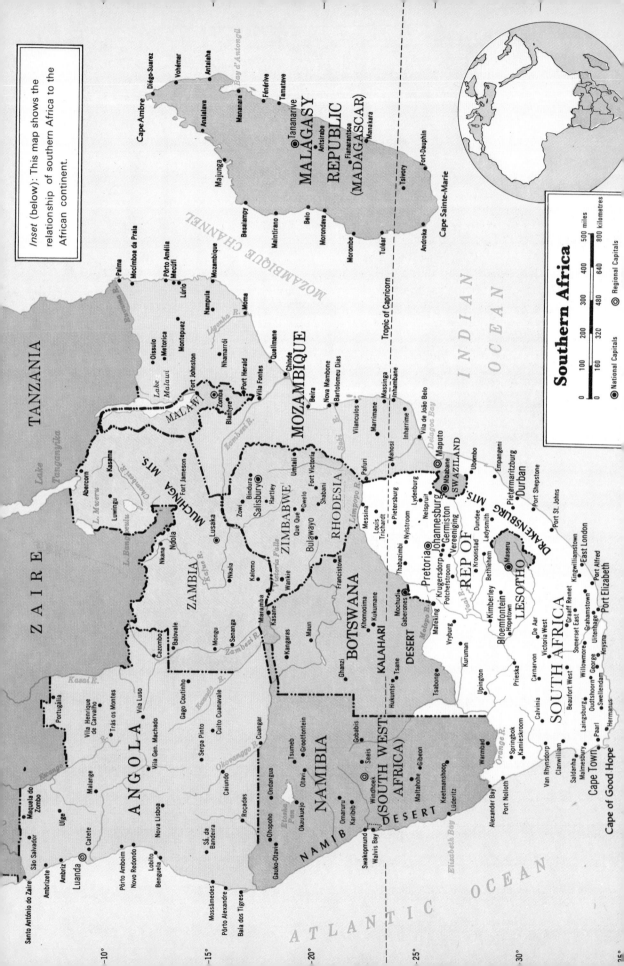

Inset (below): This map shows the relationship of southern Africa to the African continent.

Southern Africa

● National Capitals   ◎ Regional Capitals

| miles | 0 | 100 | 200 | 300 | 400 | 500 |
| kilometres | 0 | 160 | 320 | 480 | 640 | 800 |

ATLANTIC OCEAN

INDIAN OCEAN

MOZAMBIQUE CHANNEL

Bay d'Antongil

MALAGASY REPUBLIC (MADAGASCAR)

Diégo-Suarez
Vohémar
Antalaha
Cape Ambre
Analalava
Mananara
Fénérive
Tamatave
Majunga
Tananarive
Antsirabe
Fianarantsoa
Manakara
Besalampy
Belo
Morondava
Maintirano
Fort-Dauphin
Cape Sainte-Marie
Moromba
Tuléar
Tsivory
Androka

TANZANIA

ZAIRE

ANGOLA

Santo Antônio do Zaire
São Salvador
Ambrizete
Ambriz
Pôrto Redondo
Novo Redondo
Mossâmedes
Pôrto Alexandre
Baia dos Tigres
Lobito
Benguela
Luanda
Catete
Maquela do Zombo
Ulge
Portugália
Vila Henrique de Carvalho
Trás os Montes
Malange
Nova Lisboa
Sá. da Bandeira
Serpa Pinto
Gago Coutinho
Cuito Cuanavale
Vila Luso
Vila Gen. Machado
Caiundo
Rôcadas
Ohopoho
Okahuejo

Kasai R.
Kwango R.
Kwanza R.
Kunene R.
Okovanggo R.

Abercorn
Kasama
Luwingu
Ndola
Nkana
Nkala
Kalomo
Lusaka
Mongu
Senanga
Kangaras
Maun
Ghanzi
Cazombo
Balovale
Zambezi R.
Kafue R.

MUCHINGA MTS.
Fort Jameson

Lake Tanganyika
L. Mweru
L. Bangweulu
Chambezi R.

ZAMBIA

MALAWI
Lake Malawi
Fort Johnston
Zomba
Blantyre

Palma
Mocímboa da Praia
Pôrto Amélia
Mecifi
Lúrio
Moma
Nampula
Montepuez
Oissulo
Metorica
Nhamarroi
Vila Fontes
Port Herald
Chinde
Quelimane
Nova Mambone
Bartolomeu Dias
Beira
Zambezi R.
Rovuma R.
Ligonha R.

MOZAMBIQUE

Vilanculos
Marrimane
Messinga
Inhambane
Vila de João Belo
Delagoa Bay
Maputo
Mahosi
Pafuri

ZIMBABWE
RHODESIA
Salisbury
Bindura
Hartley
Zowi
Que Que
Gwelo
Shabani
Fort Victoria
Umtali
Bulawayo
Wankie
Francistown

Victoria Falls
Kasane
Maramba
Kazungula

BOTSWANA
KALAHARI DESERT
Khomodima
Kukumane
Isane
Hukuntsi
Tsabong
Ghanzi
Gaberones
Mochudie

NAMIBIA (SOUTH WEST AFRICA)
Windhoek
Gobabis
Seeis
Maltahohe
Gibeon
Keetmanshoop
Lüderitz
Tsumeb
Grootfontein
Otavi
Otjiwarongo
Omaruru
Karibib
Swakopmund
Walvis Bay
Gauko-Otavi
Ondangua
Etosha Pan

NAMIB DESERT

Tropic of Capricorn

SWAZILAND
Mbabane
Ubombo
Empangeni

Messina
Louis Trichardt
Pietersburg
Nylstroom
Lydenburg
Nelspruit
Thabazimbi
Pretoria
Johannesburg
Germiston
Vereeniging
Krugersdorp
Potchefstroom
Kroonstad
Vryburg
Kuruman
Upington

REP. OF SOUTH AFRICA

Dundee
Ladysmith
Bethlehem
Vryheid
Empangeni
Pietermaritzburg
Durban
Port Shepstone
Port St. Johns
East London
Port Alfred
Port Elizabeth
Grahamstown
King William's Town
Uitenhage
George
Knysna
Oudtshoorn
Swellendam
Willowmore
Somerset East
Graaff Reinet
Beaufort West
De Aar
Bloemfontein
Hopetown
Kimberley
Prieska
Carnarvon
Victoria West
Laingsburg
Calvinia
Van Rhynsdorp
Clanwilliam
Springbok
Kamieskroon
Alexander Bay
Port Nolloth
Warmbad
Saldanha
Malmesbury
Paarl
Cape Town
Hermanus
Cape of Good Hope
Elizabeth Bay

LESOTHO
Maseru

DRAKENSBURG MTS.
Orange R.
Vaal R.
Limpopo R.
Sabi R.
Molopo R.

GLOBE INSET

The Malagasy Republic (Madagascar)

The streets of Tananarive, Madagascar, are full of busy traffic — some of it very quaint and picturesque.

Madagascar (the Malagasy Republic) is one of the world's largest islands. It is nearly 1,000 miles (1,600 km) long, and has an area of 229,233 square miles (594,180 sq km), which is nearly four times the size of England and Wales. It lies some 250 miles (400 km) off the nearest point of the east coast of Africa, from which it is separated by the Mozambique Channel. The eastern half of the island consists of a high mountainous region 3,000 to 5,000 feet (900 to 1,500 m) above sea-level.

The people of Madagascar, the Malagasy, originally came from Southeast Asia, and Africa. The Asiatic and Negro groups intermarried and today the inhabitants are, for the most part, a mixture of the two races. The language is similar to that spoken by the early settlers of the Pacific islands. The capital of the island is Tananarive, in the central highlands, about 100 miles (160 km) from the coast.

At the cattle-farm centre of Ponte de Fiana, Madagascar's humped cattle are bred for hides.

In the central mountains of Madagascar, Tananarive, the capital city, clings to the sloping hillside.

The chief export crops are coffee, vanilla, and sugar-cane but rice, maize, and vegetables are grown for local consumption. The cattle of the island are the zebus, which are humped and bony creatures reared more for their hides than for either milk or meat. The animals and vegetation of Madagascar are distinct from those of the African mainland. Madagascar has sometimes been called the Red Isle, because of its red soils. The island has many industries, including oil refining, paper, vehicle assembly, light metals, and plastic goods.

South Africa exports large quantities of fruit. This pineapple field is in Natal Province.

Republic of South Africa

The Republic of South Africa covers more than 472,000 square miles (1,221,000 sq km), an area slightly larger than France, Spain, Portugal, and the Low Countries put together. It is the most powerful state of Southern Africa.

The population is about 21.5 million, of whom about 15 million are Bantu. About 2 million, called the Cape Coloured, are of mixed blood, and over half a million are Asiatic, leaving less than one-fifth of the population of pure white descent. The Asiatic section of the population are mainly Indians living in Natal. Of the four provinces, the people of the Cape and Natal are predominantly of British descent, while the people of the Orange Free State and the Transvaal are predominantly Afrikaners, people of Dutch descent.

The landscape of Transvaal – flowering trees, rocky crags, level grasslands.

The 'Union of South Africa', as it used to be called until May 1961, was formed after the Boer War, fought at the turn of the century, by joining together what had previously been separate Dutch and British colonies. Transvaal and the Orange Free State had been Dutch, and Natal and Cape Colony had been British. After the defeat of the Boers these colonies were united. At the same time the Union was made self-governing. The colonials of Dutch extraction are called Afrikaners, and the language they speak is called Afrikaans. It is derived from Dutch, and has been influenced by other European languages.

A Zulu youth wanders the grass-covered hillsides of Natal Province with his donkeys.

Rickshas in Durban. These Zulus are dressed in colourful tribal costumes.

South Africa consists of a high central plateau, bounded by mountains in the east and dry lands towards the west. Hills and valleys alternate, coming down in great 'steps' towards the coast.

Most of the country gets little rainfall, though when the rain does come it is often so heavy that it washes away the soil. The few rivers are generally either flooded or dry. In some areas dams have been built to create reservoirs for irrigation; elsewhere there are deep wells.

The Cape and Natal form the coastal regions of South Africa. They are the most fertile regions, and their scenery is the most picturesque. The coastal provinces were the first areas to be settled by Europeans. The Portuguese landed there as long ago as 1482. When it was realised that whoever controlled the Cape of Good Hope was master of the sea route to India, both the Dutch and the English began to colonise the Cape. The only African tribes there at that time were primitive Bushmen and Hottentots.

In the interior of Cape Province river valleys curve through mountains carpeted, in spring, with wild flowers. Orchards and vineyards climb the slopes of the valleys.

Fishing, picnicking, and painting are popular activities at the South African resort of Knysna.

Nearly a million people live in Durban, South Africa's chief port.

On the coast, modern towns have sprung up behind broad, curving beaches. The capital of the province is Cape Town, which sits at the foot of the flat-topped Table Mountain.

Wheat is the chief crop in the Cape, but fruit, especially oranges and apples, is grown everywhere. And Cape vineyards make excellent wine, much of which is exported.

Natal is often called the garden province of South Africa. It receives a considerable quantity of rainfall, and grows citrus fruits, bananas, pineapples, and papaws. But the chief crop is sugar-cane. The most important town in Natal is Durban, which is South Africa's chief port. Exports from Durban include large quantities of coal, as well as gold and other minerals from the interior of the country. Durban is also South Africa's most popular holiday resort.

Behind the mountains that separate the east coast of South Africa from the central plateau is the *veld* – rolling grassland something like the savanna – lying largely in the Transvaal and the Orange Free State. These two former colonies, now provinces, were created by what is

Negroes labour in the vineyard tending grapevines. South Africa produces excellent red and white wines.

An Indian woman of Natal poses with her children. Most Natal Indians are shopkeepers or gardeners.

Rolling fields of the Transkei are used for grain crops and cattle breeding.

African women working in the fields of a South African soya bean plantation.

known as the Great Trek, which is one of the milestones of South African history. It began in 1836, when the pressure of British colonists in the coastal regions began forcing the Dutch farmers (the Boers) into the interior. The word Boer, at one time widely used for all Afrikaners, really means farmer.

The Boers hitched sixteen oxen to their huge covered wagons, and set out across the grassy plains. They faced thirst and starvation, attacks by hostile Zulus and other warrior tribes. They were tired and sick, but they plodded on. They crossed the Orange River and founded the Orange Free State; they crossed the Vaal and founded the Transvaal.

Depending on the altitude and the amount of rainfall, the veld is now used for arable farming or for grazing cattle.

A typical farm in the Orange Free State is a very lonely place. Immense flocks of Merino sheep, famous for their silky wool, graze on the veld. In the lower veld of the Transvaal grazing gives way to arable farming.

The Orange River is the focus of an enormous irrigation project. Nearly all parts of South Africa need irrigation to meet the agricultural demands of their population. The scheme began in 1966 and will take 30 years to complete. It includes 12 dams for irrigation, 20 hydro-electric stations and a network of canals.

Maize, called mealies locally, is a staple part of the African diet.

Cattle graze on the treeless plains of the High Veld, over 6,000 ft (1,800 m) above sea level.

Government buildings in Pretoria, South Africa's capital, frame the statue of the Boer hero Louis Botha.

Ndebele tribesmen, who live in villages near Pretoria, are famed for their magnificent decorative work.

The chief crops are maize, wheat, and citrus fruit. About a third of the Transvaal is covered by the treeless, grassy, High Veld. But most of it is Bushveld, with scattered shrubs dotting the flat lands that lie between range after range of low hills. The farms of the Transvaal produce cotton, tobacco, and groundnuts. Orchards and cattle ranches also add to the produce of the region; wool, hides, and skins are important exports.

The Transvaal is the centre of the mining industry of South Africa. Besides the world-famous Johannesburg gold mines, there are coal, diamonds, asbestos, platinum, chromium, manganese, and copper. Iron-ore from the important deposits north-west of Pretoria is fed into the enormous blast furnaces and steel mills at Pretoria, and near Vereeniging on the Vaal. West of Port Elizabeth, the first important natural gas field is in production.

Pretoria, the capital of the Transvaal, is the seat of government. The legislature is in Cape Town. The most important city of South Africa is Johannesburg.

The Kruger National Park is the most famous of all the African game reserves. About half the size of Switzerland, it is the greatest sanctuary of wild life in the world, where one can see lions, leopards, elephants, giraffes, zebras, crocodiles, baboons, and many other animals.

The dry lands in the western half of South Africa are very limited in their usefulness. One such area, known as the Upper Karroo, occupies much of northern Cape Province and western Orange Free State. It stands on the plateau at a height of 3,000 to 4,000 feet (900 to 1,200 m). Rainfall is uncertain, coming in short violent showers, and makes agriculture very difficult. Where there is a farm, a wind pump will probably be

Dual-language road signs in Afrikaans and English in a Johannesburg street.

seen bringing water to the surface.

Vegetation consists mostly of stunted shrubs, but the plants provide food for large flocks of Merino sheep and goats. Wool is one of the country's chief exports. The same area is famous for its Karakul sheep. These animals are bred for the beautiful tightly-curled skins of the young lambs, known as 'Persian Lamb'.

Further south and at lower levels, like steps down from the high plateau to the coast, are the Great Karroo and the Little Karroo. In these areas, too, sheep farming is the chief occupation.

The Mines of South Africa

South Africa is a store-house of mineral wealth. The gold produced amounts to 77 per cent of all the gold mined in the non-communist world. Its diamond mines yield fabulous jewels.

The discovery of gold in the Transvaal was the making of Johannesburg, the fifth largest town of Africa. Only founded in 1886, its population is now 1.6 million. About two-fifths are white. These include the mineowners, and form virtually all the financial, commercial, and professional community. The African majority work mainly as mine workers, factory workers, and domestic servants.

Johannesburg stands on the Witwatersrand, a plateau 6,000 feet (1,800 m) above sea-level, beneath which the vein of gold-bearing ore stretches for about 100 miles (160 km). Mineshafts and tunnels run thousands of feet deep beneath the town. On its outskirts are great slag-heaps of waste material from the mining operations. Johannesburg is the biggest of the towns of Southern Africa that have arisen with European colonisation. It comprises, on

Johannesburg's fabulous gold mines, with their huge dumps of debris, create a striking backdrop for the city.

Johannesburg lies at the centre of the gold mining area. Waste from these mines lies in the foreground.

the one hand, a thriving, busy modern town such as might easily be standing in Europe or America, and, on the other, the African 'locations' on the very outskirts of the city where the living conditions of the Africans provide a marked contrast to the affluent white suburban areas.

In addition to the African labourers living on the numerous locations, hundreds of thousands of mine workers live in compounds built by the mine owners outside Johannesburg. These workers are Bantus, many of whom have come from neighbouring countries. Whole townships have been built for the African employees of the mines and factories, who, because of South Africa's policy of apartheid, live separately from the white population.

Long before gold was found, diamonds were being mined in South Africa. The

A compound: built to house Africans hired to labour in the Johannesburg gold mines.

This unexciting rock is rich gold ore.

great centre was the mining town of Kimberley. The mine nearby is called the Big Hole. It is three-quarters of a mile (1.2 km) wide and nearly a third of a mile (.5 km) deep – one of the largest man-made holes on earth. Millions of pounds worth of diamonds have been mined from it. Diamonds are measured in carats. A carat is two-tenths of a gramme. The value of a diamond depends on its weight, its colour (a bluish-white being the best), and on the skill with which it has been cut. The biggest diamond ever found was the Cullinan, which came, not from the Big Hole, but from a mine near Pretoria. It was the size of a man's fist. There are also diamond fields near the mouth of the Orange River. In this area anyone may spot a diamond lying in the sandy desert or on the beaches. But the area is closely guarded, and even visitors are searched when they leave the area.

When first exploiting her mineral wealth, South Africa had to import all her mining and transportation equip-

ment and most ores were exported in their raw, or crude, state. As the value of these ores as exports went up, and local sources of power and iron ores were discovered, and as a large workforce which could be paid minimal wages began to materialise from African tribes, South Africa began to invest in more and more local industry, until now manufacturing of every kind is the biggest employer of the urban population.

The mining area of Southern Africa extends northwards into Zimbabwe Rhodesia, Zambia and Malawi. Zimbabwe Rhodesia has one of the few high quality coal deposits in Africa. Asbestos, gold and chromite are also mined. Mining is an important industry in Zambia as well. Huge quantities of copper ore are mined, smelted and refined there with some zinc, lead and cobalt.

A fortune in gems is held in these hands. The value of the diamond depends on its weight, its colour, and the skill with which it has been cut.

Water slowly fills one of the first great diamond mines to be worked at Kimberley.

Mine workers forget daily toil in the excitement of tribal dances. Teams compete before packed stands.

The Kariba dam in Zimbabwe Rhodesia. Lake Kariba is the world's largest man-made lake.

Zimbabwe Rhodesia

Much of Zambia and Zimbabwe Rhodesia is savanna. On the grassy plateau of Zimbabwe Rhodesia a great deal of cattle-ranching is done. The most important crops are maize and tobacco. The coalfields at Wankie produced 4 million metric tons a year, but this is not nearly enough to meet the needs of an area that is rapidly becoming industrialised. In Salisbury, the capital, and Bulawayo, there are many manufacturing industries. But at present the whole of her economy and transport system is disrupted due to her Unilateral Declaration of Independence of 1965. She has a population of over 6 million of which 273,000 are white.

The border with Zambia is formed largely by the Zambezi River. The town of Livingstone, named after the famous explorer is right on the border at Victoria Falls which are about a mile (1.6 km) wide.

This is typical housing for Africans in Angola.

A huge steam shovel looks like a toy as it digs ore from an open-cast copper mine in Zambia.

Zambia

The mines of the copper belt of Zambia produce even more metal than the neighbouring Shaba region of Zaire. Thus Zambia has a good foundation on which to build her growing industries. She also has plentiful supplies of hydro-electricity, with nine power stations and a new Kariba North project which is in the middle of being constructed. The reservoirs are beginning to be effective in irrigating the vast amount of undeveloped land which exists in this territory.

The new Tan-Zam railway gives land-locked Zambia access to Dar es Salaam.

Malawi

Malawi is a long strip of territory running along the western shore of Lake Malawi. Formerly a British Protectorate, most of the people of independent Malawi are Negroes. 78 per cent of Malawi's export is from agricultural produce. Tea and tobacco are raised in the highlands, and cotton on the Lower Shire Valley. The first stage of the Tedzani Project is now completed, and this, together with other hydro-electric schemes, is providing power for Malawi's industrial development. Malawi, like her neighbours, is landlocked. She has access to Beira and the deep water port of Nacala.

Maputo is a leading African port.

Newly Developing Countries of Southern Africa

To the east and west of Zambia, Zimbabwe Rhodesia and Malawi, are the two former Portuguese territories: on the east, Mozambique, on the west, Angola. In 1975 they became independent. Both have limited economies but have programmes for development under their new governments.

Angola

Angola has a population of 5.6 million in an area of 481,353 square miles (1,246,700 sq km). In the savanna, cattle-breeding is carried on and a variety of crops are grown, including coffee and groundnuts, sugar-cane, and maize. There are valuable diamonds in Angola and iron ore is mined.

Since independence, Angola has been involved in civil war at times and this has upset her economy and prospects for development.

Mozambique

Mozambique has a population of over 8.2 million in an area of just under 300,000 square miles (785,000 sq km). The chief crops here are sugar-cane, cotton, sisal, and coconut products – copra, from which coconut oil is produced, and fibre for rope-making, etc. The most flourishing parts of the country are the capital, Maputo, and Beira, which are two of the chief ports of Africa. From them many of the exports of Zambia and South Africa are shipped.

A common sight on the southern African veld are the windmills which pump water for farmers.

Groups of fenced huts make up the village of Kanye, Botswana, on the edge of the vast, dry Kalahari Desert.

Namibia

Namibia, with a population of about 823,145, is a dry plateau falling abruptly to the sea. Much of it is desert, for part of the Kalahari Desert extends into it. It is a United Nations trust territory administered by South Africa and will achieve full independence in 1978. Scattered on the desolate countryside are ranches on which cattle, sheep, and goats are bred. A few metals (tin, lead, copper, and zinc) are worked in the northern area of the country, and there are important coastal diamond fields.

Botswana

In this part of Africa three areas were, in the past, set aside as native reserves. The largest of these is Botswana, which lies between Zimbabwe Rhodesia, Namibia, and South Africa. In this area,

African women pound cassava roots in huge tubs to make a pasty meal which is their main food.

more than twice the size of the United Kingdom, there are only about 750,000 people, nearly all of them Bantu tribes-

317

In Botswana, African families wait patiently in long lines for X-ray examinations.

Youngsters gather around the pump in a Botswana village. Behind them is a clinic.

men. The southern part of Botswana is occupied by the Kalahari Desert, whose few inhabitants are Bushmen, one of the world's oldest races.

The northern part of Botswana consists of swamps. Large nickel and copper deposits have been found here. Orapa, near the Kgalagadi desert, has the second largest diamond bearing pipe in the world. Production began in 1971 and diamonds are now Botswana's biggest export. The new nickel-copper complex at Selebi-Pi-kwe is now in production and there is an open cast coalmine at Serowe.

Lesotho and Swaziland

The two other areas are enclaves, that is, they lie like islands surrounded by a foreign country. Lesotho lies within the frontiers of the Republic of South Africa, and Swaziland between South Africa and Mozambique. Until their recent independence both of them were administered by Britain. They are more

Southern African tribesmen regard their long-horned cattle as a sign of wealth.

thickly populated than Botswana, but the land is poor. The tribes live in *kraals*, or villages, and follow the traditional ways of tribal life. They rear cattle and live near their herds in small round huts. In spite of the freedom they enjoy and the generally bad living conditions on the Rand, many of the younger men in the reserves drift towards the mining areas of South Africa or seek work in the towns.

Soil conservation projects and improved cropping methods are vital to the economies of these countries; and rotational grazing is being practised in the highlands.

Swaziland has a large iron-ore output from Mbanane. A railway links this mine with Goba in Mozambique, for export of the ore. Coal, asbestos, and kaolin are also mined.

The scenery of South Africa combines rugged mountains and fertile valleys.

Forests cover the lower slopes of the Rocky Mountains. Still higher are barren or snow-covered peaks. This mountain wall stretches from the south-western United States northwards across Canada into Alaska.

This is North America

North America is the northern half of the New World. It consists of Canada, the United States, and Mexico. In the course of this century, the United States has become one of the two greatest powers in the world. Canada too has made enormous strides, and her status today is utterly different from what it was in 1900, when she was still a British Crown Colony. Compared with the countries of Europe, both these states are continental in their dimensions, Canada alone being as large as the whole of Europe. If we are accustomed to compact states that can be crossed from end to end in a matter of hours, it is difficult even to imagine the spaciousness of the countries that make up the land mass of North America.

Compared to the complicated outline of Europe, the map of North America shows us a solid block, extending from the icy Arctic Ocean to the warm sea of the Tropics. An appreciable amount of Alaska and northern Canada lies within the Arctic Circle.

New York and Los Angeles, on opposite sides of the continent, are 2,500 miles (4,000 km) apart, whereas the distance from the west coast of Ireland to St John's, Newfoundland, is less than 2,000 miles (3,200 km). As for North America's natural resources, they too are on the same scale. Technologically, Americans are in the first rank. Financially, the United States is the richest country in the world. With such assets, it is only natural that the United States should be a leading world power.

North America

Scale 1 : 30 000 000

| 0 | 100 | 200 | 300 | 400 | 500 | metres |
| 0 | 160 | 320 | 480 | 640 | 800 | kilometres |

Depths		below sea level	Heights			
feet over 650	0–650		0–650	650–1650	1650–5000	over 5000 feet
metres over 200	0–200		0–200	200–500	500–1500	over 1500 metres

Railways   Canals   Heads of navigation   Desert

Selected labels visible on map:

U.S.S.R. · ARCTIC OCEAN · North Pole · GREENLAND (Denmark) · ICELAND · Reykjavik · Faeroe Is. (Den.) · Jan Mayen (Norway) · Arctic Circle

Bering Strait · Wrangel I. · Chukchi Sea · Beaufort Sea · Point Barrow · Banks I. · Victoria I. · Baffin Bay · Baffin Is. · Devon I. · Davis Strait · Angmagssalik

ALASKA · Alaska Range · Fairbanks · Anchorage · Yukon · Dawson · Whitehorse · Gulf of Alaska · Kodiak I. · Alexander Arch. · Queen Charlotte Is.

Great Bear Lake · Great Slave Lake · Yellowknife · Coppermine · Fort Radium · North West Territories · Port Radium · Hudson Strait · Labrador (Nfld.) · Hebron · Goose Bay · Gander

CANADA · British Columbia · Alberta · Saskatchewan · Manitoba · Ontario · Quebec · Lake Athabaska · Reindeer Lake · Lake Winnipeg · Churchill · Port Nelson · Hudson Bay · Knob Lake

Vancouver I. · Vancouver · Calgary · Edmonton · Regina · Winnipeg · Fort William · Lake Superior · Sudbury · Ottawa · MONTREAL · Quebec · New Brunswick · Prince Edward I. · Nova Scotia · Halifax · Cape Breton I.

ROCKY MOUNTAINS · Mt. Robson · Mt. Columbia · Seattle · Mt. Rainier · Portland · Columbia River · Mt. Hood · Mt. Shasta · Coast Ranges · Sierra Nevada

Oakland · San Francisco · Great Salt Lake · Salt Lake City · Great Basin · Yellowstone Park · Black Hills · Badlands · St. Paul · Minneapolis · Milwaukee · CHICAGO · DETROIT · Cleveland · Pittsburgh · Buffalo · Lake Erie · Lake Ontario · Lake Michigan · Lake Huron

UNITED STATES · Denver · Pikes Peak · Mt. Whitney · Mt. Elbert · LOS ANGELES · Santa Fe · Colorado Plateau · El Paso · Kansas City · Ozark Mts. · St. Louis · Omaha · Cincinnati · Washington D.C. · PHILADELPHIA · NEW YORK · Long Island · Boston · C. Cod · Chesapeake Bay · C. Hatteras · Allegheny Mts. · Appalachian Mts. · Mt. Mitchell · Atlanta · Birmingham · Charleston · Savannah · Jacksonville · Dallas · Red River · Houston · San Antonio · Galveston · New Orleans · Florida · Gulf Stream

ATLANTIC OCEAN · PACIFIC OCEAN · Tropic of Cancer · Baja California · Gulf of California · Monterrey · Mazatlán · Tampico · Gulf of Campeche · Guadalajara · MEXICO CITY · Vera Cruz · Popocatepetl · Nevado de Colima · Acapulco · Gulf of Tehuantepec · Sierra Madre · Clarion I. · Socorro I. · Revilla Gigedo Is. · Guadalupe I. (Mex.) · Cocos I. (Costa Rica)

Gulf of Mexico · Yucatan · Mérida · Havana · CUBA · Santiago de Cuba · Bahama Is. · Great Antilles · Haiti · Hispaniola · Dominican Republic · JAMAICA · Caribbean Sea · Port au Prince

BELIZE · Belize · Guatemala · GUATEMALA · HONDURAS · Tegucigalpa · EL SALVADOR · San Salvador · NICARAGUA · Managua · Lake Nicaragua · COSTA RICA · San José · PANAMA · Colón · Panama · Gulf of Darien · Barranquilla · Medellín · Bogotá · Cali · Pasto · ECUADOR · COLOMBIA · VENEZUELA · Equator

Physical Features

The mountains and plains of North America are in keeping with the rest, simple and vast. The detail, of course, varies greatly. The Atlantic coast, for instance, changes from the rocky cliffs of Maine to the gently shelving sandy beaches of Florida. Sometimes there are great estuaries like those which serve the ports of New York and Philadelphia, or, greatest of all, that of the St Lawrence in Canada. Inland from a broad coastal plain the mountains begin. The Appalachians consist of a number of parallel ranges extending from the Gulf of St Lawrence in the north to western Alabama in the south. The highest peak, in North Carolina, is less than 7,000 feet (2,140 m) in height. They were high enough, in early colonial days, to halt penetration into the country. The presence of coal and oil has, in Pennsylvania, transformed them into an industrial zone.

On the western side, stretching from Alaska to New Mexico, are the vast ranges of the Rocky Mountains, whose snowy peaks remind us of the Alps. This great mountain system consists, for the most part, of two great chains, one running down the Pacific coast, the other more or less parallel to it some hundreds of miles inland, between which there are many plateaus and river valleys. With all their rainfall, snow, and glaciers, these mountains offer an immense reserve of water-power, which can be converted into electricity. More important still is the vast mineral wealth lying beneath.

Between the Rockies and the Appalachians the whole centre of the country consists of huge plains drained by the great river system of the Mississippi and its tributaries.

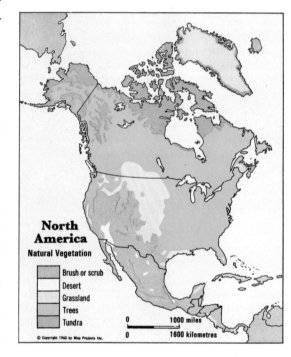

North America

Natural Vegetation

- Brush or scrub
- Desert
- Grassland
- Trees
- Tundra

0   1000 miles

0   1600 kilometres

© Copyright 1960 by Map Projects Inc.

Northern North America is covered by thousands of square kilometres of marshy Arctic tundra.

Farm buildings, fields, and highways on the level prairies of the North American Mid-West form neat chequered patterns when seen from the air.

Beautiful natural rock formations in Monument Valley, Arizona.

Climate

The two temperature charts show which areas of North America are the warmest and the coldest. The southernmost band, going right across the continent, is the hottest, being the closest to the Equator. Further north the differences between the temperatures of January and July are greater. In the middle zone, temperatures are similar to those in Central Europe, with four clear-cut seasons and with abrupt periods of heat and cold. In the south, the winters are short, and the temperature in January generally mild. To the north, the winters are long and cold, and spring and autumn are very short.

It is, above all, in Canada that the winters are the longest and the coldest, with snow lying for many months. Summer is short. In the west the climate is somewhat exceptional owing to the presence of the Rocky Mountains. The mountains in the north are covered with snow. The days may be warm, but the

This map shows the average January temperatures in North America. It is extremely cold in the far north of Canada, while the south of the continent is hot, being near the Equator.

This map shows the average July temperatures in North America. In Canada, the summers are short and cool, while in the south the summers are long and hot.

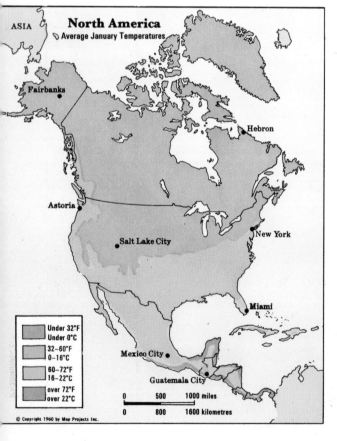

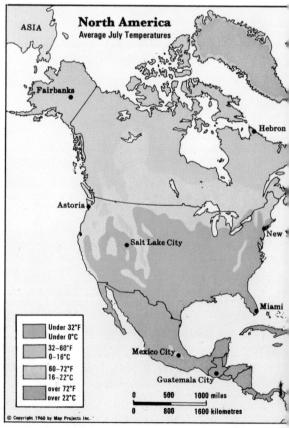

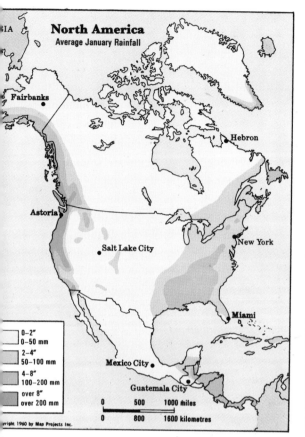

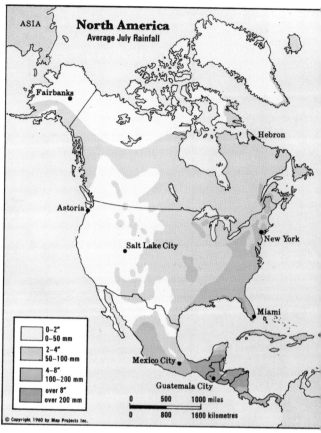

This map shows the average January rainfall in North America. The abundant rainfall on the west coast is caused by the Rocky Mountains, while the eastern area comes within reach of winds from the Atlantic and the Gulf of Mexico.

This map shows the average July rainfall in North America. You will notice that there is a vast dry area on the eastern side of the Rocky Mountains, stretching from Canada to Mexico.

nights are always cold. The mountains in the south have a temperate climate, mild enough to have favoured the Aztec civilisation of Mexico. Moreover, sea breezes bring warmth to the land, so that in winter there is a relatively mild belt stretching all along the coast almost to Alaska, in which the average temperature is above freezing point.

The amount and distribution of rainfall also affects the climate. A glance at the appropriate map will show that the Pacific coast of Alaska, Canada, and the United States has abundant rainfall, again due to the presence of the Rockies.

On the eastern side of the Rocky Mountains is a vast dry area extending from Canada to Mexico. It is far from any sea, so has little opportunity of capturing moisture from the air. Further east, in the south-eastern United States, we find a climate increasing in humidity, for this area comes within reach of air masses from the Atlantic and the Gulf of Mexico. The north-eastern States also receive ample rainfall.

Grand Falls, Arizona. These spectacular falls flow once a year when the snow melts in the White Mountains.

A typical red barn in Pennsylvania.

A girl barrel-racing at a rodeo in Arizona.

Shell fishermen landing their catch at Nassau.

The Peoples of North America

North America has a population of 321 million which, on the average, amounts to about 28 per square mile (11 per sq km). Thus, compared to Europe, which has 224 per square mile (85 per sq km) or Asia, with 163 per square mile (64 per sq km), it is a thinly populated continent.

Of course, the population is not spread evenly over all the land area. It is concentrated in towns, and thinly spread in the rural areas. The towns themselves are sometimes far apart, sometimes close

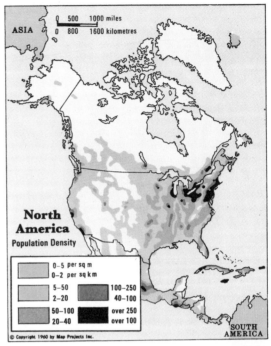

A view from the Empire State building across the Manhattan skyline to the Chrysler building, one of the most graceful skyscrapers in New York.

These Sioux Indians represent the 350,000 Indians that live in the United States today. Many more Indians live in Canada, Mexico, Central America, and the Caribbean islands, as well as in South America.

together, and in some parts of the continent there is not so much as a village for many miles. The population is also very varied, being composed of many different races, Eskimos, American ('Red') Indians, white immigrants from Europe, and Negro descendants of slaves imported from Africa.

The first inhabitants were American Indians, believed to have come from Asia across the Bering Straits. Present-day research is trying to date their arrival accurately. When the first European explorers discovered the New World, there were some 5 million Indians in North America. The bulk of them lived on the high plateaus of Mexico and Central America. There were less than a million, scattered in different tribes, in what is now the United States and Canada.

Four-fifths of Mexico's people are at least part Indian. Over a quarter are pure Indian.

Over nine-tenths of Haiti's people are Negroes. The official language of Haiti is French.

Perhaps the largest of the waves of immigrants from Europe came from Ireland as a result of the Irish Potato Famine of 1846. A great many others, particularly from Germany and Scandinavia, came during the American Civil War, and in the 1870s, when the great American wheat-lands were opened up.

Besides the immigrants we have been speaking of, who were all Europeans, others of a different sort had been entering the country. In the Southern states, and in the West Indies, Negroes from Africa had been brought over as slaves. They were essential on the large plantations of tobacco and cotton. As a result, today one-tenth of the population of the United States is Negro. At the beginning of the century yet another racial influx began with the immigration of Chinese and Japanese into the States along the Pacific Coast. Besides these distinctive races, there are, amongst the European immigrants and their descendants, national groups like the Irish and the

Over 650 people per sq mile (250 per sq km) crowd Puerto Rico. Yet more than half of the people are farmers.

Poles, who retain their individual character. Nevertheless, the American way of life does a great deal to bind all these various elements into a united whole.

Guatemala has Central America's largest population. Many are descendants of the ancient Mayas, perhaps the most remarkable of the ancient Central American civilizations.

North America

Hawaii

Communications

The three maps on this page give a picture of the lines of communication in North America. In the thickly settled areas in the East there is a dense network of roads, railways, and air services.

In the relatively empty areas of Canada, Mexico, and Central America, neither passengers nor freight are sufficient to make building many railways worthwhile, particularly with the rough country involved.

In North America there are about 4 million miles (6.4 million km) of main roads and 130 million motor vehicles. Special 'super highways' have been built to accommodate these enormous numbers. But even so the problem of traffic control is still unsolved. In the United States alone, 42 million truckloads of goods per year are carried by rail. Internal air services cover 8,000 million miles (13,000 million km) a year, carrying over 50 million passengers.

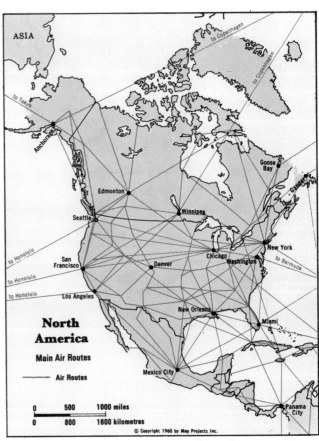

North America

Main Air Routes

Air Routes

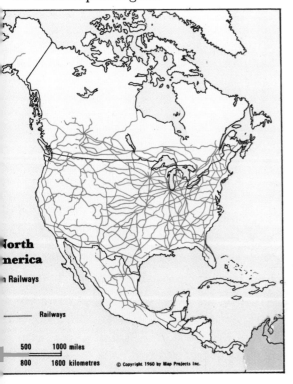

North America

Railways

Railways

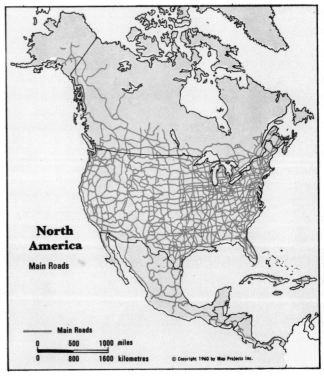

North America

Main Roads

Main Roads

Leading Towns and Cities

If North America has huge mountain ranges and vast plains it has also a large number of great cities, including one of the greatest in the world. Of about 150 cities in the world whose metropolitan areas have populations in excess of a million, North America possesses forty.

These towns have grown up within the last hundred years, keeping pace with the development of industry and the construction of railways. Previously the large towns had all been on the coast or on the rivers, but, with the coming of railways, they grew wherever mines were found or industry developed.

Boston, one of the chief cities of the U.S.A.

The Capitol in Washington D.C., is the seat of the federal government of the United States.

New Orleans is famous for the beautiful wrought iron work that adorns its old buildings.

Pittsburgh, in the state of Pennsylvania, is an important steel-producing centre.

The towns have grown most thickly in the north-east of the United States, between Boston and Baltimore – an area which includes New York and Philadelphia. Another area is on the Great Lakes (Chicago, Detroit, etc.), and yet another stretches from Pittsburg, down the Ohio River basin, and on to St Louis on the Mississippi. In Canada the thickest area is from Quebec on the St Lawrence to Toronto on Lake Ontario. All these areas together occupy only a small but important portion of North America, which is very often referred to as the 'American Manufacturing Belt'.

The American Manufacturing Belt is the greatest industrial workshop of the

United States and Canada. It contains more than 400 manufacturing towns. Fifty of these are along the Atlantic seaboard of the southern Great Lakes. Well over 200 of them are on navigable rivers. Some are on canals. All but seventy of them can be reached by water, and those owe their growth to the presence of railways.

Philadelphia is a city rich in history. The Declaration of Independence, written by Thomas Jefferson, and signed by representatives of the Thirteen Colonies, was signed in 1776, in Independence Hall, which also houses the Liberty Bell.

Catalina Island, California. California is the fastest growing state in the U.S.A.

New York is the greatest urban centre in the world. Together with its suburbs it now has a population of over 17 million. It is also the greatest port in the country, and, as a financial centre, its wealth and its influence are formidable. Yet it is not the capital of the United States, nor even the capital of New York State, that role being the small town of Albany.

The capital of the United States is Washington. When the country gained its independence, there was some jealousy between the various States as to which capital should be chosen as the seat of government. To avoid friction, it was finally decided to set aside a separate district on which a national capital should be built. This is called the District of Columbia, and the capital is officially called Washington D.C. – the initials being rather important since there are several Washingtons in the country. Washington lies on the banks of the Potomac. Its most famous buildings are the Capitol, seat of Congress, the White House, the President's residence, and the Supreme Court, the highest court in the land.

Probably the oldest North American city, Mexico City is the capital of Mexico and one of the world's largest towns. Its wide avenues pass Aztec ruins, old Spanish churches, and ultra-modern buildings, each architectural style reflecting the history of the city.

The Golden Gate Bridge spans San Francisco Bay. San Francisco has a fine natural harbour.

The courtyard of a 1,000 columns at Chichen-Itza, one of the centres of the Mayan civilisation.

In Montreal, Canada's largest city, the French language is being increasingly used.

Canada

Canada has a slightly larger area than the United States, and only two countries are larger: the USSR and China. Canada spreads over nearly half of North America, yet it has only one-fifteenth of the population. Vast areas in the north are uninhabited.

Ottawa, with 603,510 inhabitants, is the capital of Canada, but Montreal, with a population of 2,750,000, is the largest city and the economic centre of the country. It lies on the St Lawrence, and is the country's chief port. Toronto, with a slightly smaller population, is another great commercial and banking centre. It also has a textile industry.

On three sides, Canada is bordered by the sea: by the Atlantic, the Pacific, and the Arctic Oceans. On the south she has a frontier some 3,000 miles (4,830 km) long with the United States. And it shows how close these two countries are that this frontier should be totally undefended.

Cod drying in the sun is still a common sight in the Atlantic Provinces of Canada. But today great quantities of fish are quick-frozen, tinned, and shipped to all parts of the world.

Industries of Canada

Fishing was one of Canada's first industries. Fishermen from Europe are believed to have caught large quantities of fish off the coast of Newfoundland before any explorer sighted the mainland of North America. That is not altogether surprising since the shallow waters they fished in, called the Grand Banks, were both stormy and foggy. The Grand Banks still form an important fishing ground. From New Brunswick to the tip of Labrador is an indented coastline totalling some 5,000 miles (8,000 km), with many sheltered harbours and with great schools of cod, herring, halibut, mackerel, and haddock, making this coast one of the world's great fishing grounds.

Canada's Pacific coast is also famous for its fisheries. Deep fjords and a shallow ledge, 50 to 100 miles (80 to 160 km) off-shore, are excellent feeding ground for fish, and British Columbia today ranks close to the Atlantic Provinces in the value of its hauls.

The salmon is the king of fish on the Pacific Coast. The sock-eye salmon is particularly valued by the tinning industry, though other kinds of salmon are often larger.

There are few countries in the world which possess so great a wealth in the form of forests as Canada.

The saw-mills are at work incessantly. British Columbia stands first in the lumber trade, Quebec and Ontario coming second and third. Between them, these three Provinces account for four-fifths of Canada's timber.

Much of the Pacific area is covered by forests, producing softwoods (firs, pines, etc.) and, in particular, the giant Douglas fir, which provides some of the finest timber of North America. Although in rather northerly latitudes the area has, as we have seen, a mild climate; owing to the temperate moist winds from the Pacific, the rainfall is heavy. All these factors favour the rapid growth of trees.

Much of the wood, particularly from eastern Canada, is turned into pulp,

Salmon have made the North Pacific coast one of the North America's most important fishing regions.

Logs come tumbling down swift Canadian streams on their way to the saw-mills. About 46 per cent of the land is forested.

Lumber being assembled for transportation down river to the pulp-mills. Paper-making is a very important industry.

Canada

Here are the log-sorting ponds and the great saw-mills of Victoria, British Columbia. Wood is used in the pulp and paper industries.

which is the chief raw material for paper-making. Canada's first pulp-mill was built about 100 years ago, but the industry has grown rapidly. Today pulp and paper-mills are the biggest single employer.

This has become an important industry, and its rapid development is due, not only to the abundant supply of wood, but also to the ready supply of water-power which keeps the mills running.

Furs were one of Canada's earliest products. Trappers explored much of the Canadian wilderness. A few trappers are still working the snow-blanketed northern forests, but today most of Canada's

fur comes from fur farms. Fur farming started on Prince Edward Island in the Gulf of St Lawrence: fox, mink, chinchilla, and marten being reared in captivity. It was so successful that the example was soon followed in other Provinces. Nearly 10 million pounds sterling worth of furs come from Canada each year.

If trapping brought a handful of Canadians into the wild country of the north, gold brought thousands. It has been found right across the country, from Newfoundland in the east, to the Yukon far in the north-west. Many of the early camps were so inaccessible that they could only be reached by boat or by long difficult treks overland. When the gold was exhausted the camps were abandoned. If a strike turned out to be really big, the rough camp was replaced by a proper town. Much the same thing is happening today.

Canada is the third biggest producer of gold in the world, after South Africa and the USSR. Most of it is mined in an area sometimes called 'The Valley of Gold' which stretches from central Ontario eastward into Quebec. Despite the large quantity mined, it is believed that reserves have barely been touched.

Prospectors hunting for gold sometimes find other minerals. Occasionally deposits of great value are found in this way, or even quite by accident. About seventy-five years ago, rocks were being blasted near Sudbury in Ontario, where a railway was being built. In the process, huge deposits of copper and nickel were revealed. The mines are still working today. In fact, three-fifths of the world's

The Yellow Knife Mine, on the Great Slave Lake, produces a large share of Canada's gold.

Steep Rock Mine, north-west of Lake Superior, is one of Canada's richest sources of iron ore.

This mine at Beaverlodge, Saskatchewan, is producing one of Canada's important mineral resources – uranium.

supply of nickel comes from there, and the reserves will last for 100 years.

At Sudbury, copper, platinum, and nickel are mined. With every pound of nickel, two pounds of copper are extracted; about two-fifths of the world's supply of platinum also comes from Sudbury.

The world's growing industries need more and more raw materials, and a constant search for minerals is today being carried out in northern Canada. Modern prospectors, however, are not the lonely adventurers of the past. They are trained geologists, and their surveys are done by air. Aircraft have done more than anything else to open up northern Canada, and many other parts of the world. They can carry geologists and their equipment

to the most isolated places, keep them supplied in all weathers, and furnish air photographs which speed up the work of survey enormously.

An important part of their work is the search for pitchblende. It is from pitchblende that radium and uranium are extracted. It was first discovered at the eastern end of Great Bear Lake, far to the north. A mining town, Port Radium, has grown up on the site, which is only 28 miles (45 km) from the Arctic Circle.

Further discoveries of pitchblende have recently been made, and another town called Uranium City, has grown up on the northern shore of Lake Athabaska, in Central Canada. Uranium City has grown to a town of several thousand within the space of a few years.

No mineral is more important than iron however. An enormous deposit of iron-ore is now being mined from Lac Jeannine to the lonely Ungava area, on the border of Quebec and Labrador.

How to get this 'far away' iron-ore to the steel-mills was quite a problem. Eventually a railway was built 360 miles (580 km) in length from the mines to Sept Isles, a port at the mouth of the St Lawrence, where the ore is loaded on to ships.

Canada has enormous supplies of coal which, unfortunately, is situated in the wrong places. The industries that need it are in the St Lawrence lowlands and round the Great Lakes, but three-fifths of the coal comes from Alberta and British Columbia on the other side of the country. Most of the rest comes from the Atlantic Provinces. As a result, the industrial areas import a good deal of coal from the United States. Canada is rich in oil and natural gas. A few years ago a gigantic field of oil was found near Edmonton, in Alberta, and oil now ranks first in value among Canada's mineral resources, with copper second. Canada produced 79 million metric tons of oil in 1974.

Canada is rapidly becoming one of the great industrial nations of the world. Her industry is centred on the Great Lakes and St Lawrence lowland. Raw materials from every quarter converge here to supply the factories.

Mineral ore, wood-pulp, furs, and timber come from the mines and forests of Ontario and Quebec. From the Prairie Provinces come wheat, meat, and oil. And from the Atlantic Provinces come coal, wood and food products. Saskatchewan is rapidly developing into a major manufacturing area. She has the world's largest supplies of potash and is the only Western source of helium.

Much of the energy consumed in the factories is derived from water-power. It is converted into electricity, of which

This aluminium plant at Kitimat is one of the largest in the world.

In this plant at Sarnia, Ontario, synthetic rubber is manufactured from available raw materials.

Canada uses an enormous quantity. In particular, a great quantity of power is provided by the Niagara Falls.

Canada's industrial plain extends from Windsor (just opposite Detroit), between Lake Erie and Lake Huron, to Quebec. It includes Toronto and Montreal. This area is served by a network of roads and railways, which make transport easy, as well as the great St Lawrence Seaway.

First among the industries come woodpulp and paper-making. Few areas in the world are better suited for it. Forests lie on the one side, and the great markets of the United States on the other. Water-power provides 65 per cent of the electricity, and new sources are being tapped in Labrador.

Water-power is also used in the rapidly growing aluminium industry in both the St Lawrence River valley and in British Columbia. The manufacture of plastics, textiles, and chemicals, all require great quantities of water and electricity.

The production of iron and steel has for long taken a leading place in Canadian industry. Hamilton, in Ontario, is sometimes called the Pittsburgh of Canada, Pittsburgh being the greatest American iron and steel centre.

Canada is a great commercial nation, and imports and exports play a great part in her economy. Before the last war, the United Kingdom was the greatest buyer of Canadian goods, but today, it is the United States which plays the key role in the Canadian territory.

Agriculture

Farming has a very important place in Canada's economy, although far more people are now employed in the manufacturing industries. There are two great agricultural areas. In the east, there are the lowlands round the St Lawrence and the Great Lakes. Further west are the prairies of Manitoba, Saskatchewan, and Alberta. Both these areas are in the south. Further north, the summer is too short for crops to grow and

These Hereford cattle are part of a vast herd on a ranch in Alberta.

ripen. Thus only a very small part of the land is suitable for farming.

The lowlands of the Great Lakes and St Lawrence are sometimes called Canada's Heartland. It is less than a tenth of the country. Yet it houses more than two-thirds of the population and contains four-fifths of the country's factories. It produces half of Canada's agricultural produce. In this it is helped by the fact that the ground is not hilly and thus is easily ploughed, and also by the summers being warmer than in any other region. Moreover the St Lawrence Seaway has opened the whole area to the Atlantic and thus to the countries overseas. The Canadian Heartland is really the Canadian part of a farming area that includes the north-eastern part of the United States. It is sometimes known as the 'hay and dairy region'. Much of the land on the Canadian side is stony. It none the less makes excellent pastures and is ideal for growing hay and oats, as winter fodder.

The other area is part of the great stretch of plains that reaches from the Gulf of Mexico to the Arctic Ocean. The Canadian portion consists of Manitoba, Saskatchewan, and Alberta, which are known as the Prairie Provinces.

The country here has been farmed ever since the first settlers arrived. The soil is rich, but the winters long, making the growing season short. Drought is often experienced. Under these conditions only a few cereals can be grown.

First among them is spring wheat. It is grown on more than three-quarters of the area. It is the farmer's favourite crop, for it demands little rain, and ripens rapidly. Moreover this Canadian 'hard' wheat has a ready market in Europe for bread and biscuit making.

Some parts of the Prairie Provinces are

A farmer in Alberta harvests wheat, the leading crop of Alberta, Saskatchewan, and Manitoba.

too dry even for wheat. Here are the ranches. Canada's ranches are enormous and the herds on them often consist of several thousand head of cattle.

Special crops grow in some areas. In the Annapolis-Cornwallis Valley for instance, in Nova Scotia, apples are grown that are known the world over. Grapes and peaches of the finest quality come from the Niagara Peninsula in Ontario. Potatoes are grown in New Brunswick and Prince Edward Island.

The rugged land of British Columbia is for the most part unsuited for anything but forestry. In a few districts however, fruit and vegetables and bulbs are grown, and dairy-farming flourishes round the larger towns. Most of the farming is done near the mouth of the Fraser River and in the southern part of Vancouver Island. These areas get abundant rainfall, and the growing season is longer.

Inset (above): This map shows the relationship of the United States to the North American continent.

United States

0	100	200	300 miles
0	160	320	480 kilometres

◎ National Capital   ● State Capitals

© Copyright 1960 by Map Projects Inc.

Under the shadow of the majestic Rocky Mountains, a herd of fine beef cattle grazes in a high meadow in Wyoming. Note the winding pattern of the stream that carries away water from melting snow.

The USA

With a favourable climate, a fertile soil, and vast mineral and fuel resources, the 212 million people of the United States have for long enjoyed a very high standard of living. Their 'pioneering spirit' gave them the initiative, and their very well-endowed land the incentive, to develop their country to its full. The country has only 6 per cent of the world's land area and less than 7 per cent of the world's population. Yet the people of the United States consume nearly half of all that the world produces.

The United States consumes 140 million metric tons of iron ore each year.

The North-East

New York's crowded harbour serves the world's busiest port. It handles cargoes of all kinds, especially containers.

Industry is largely concentrated in the north-eastern States of the USA. The output of the factories varies from heavy locomotives to precision instruments, from the finest silk to the roughest canvas, from paper and pens to aircraft and nuclear-driven submarines. In fact, in this area literally everything that can be made is made.

Of the manufacturing towns in this area, New York and Pittsburgh have already been mentioned. Philadelphia is the fourth largest town in the country. Its industry includes the manufacture of carpets and rugs, and a wide range of textiles and clothing. Baltimore is one of the most important Atlantic ports. Its population of nearly 4.8 million is

Pittsburgh, Pennsylvania. Pennsylvania is the leading producer of iron and steel in the U.S.A.

Colourful fishing boats crowd the docks at New Bedford, Mass., once the world's greatest whaling port.

Forests of the North-East and Canada provide the raw materials for this paper mill in Maine.

Unusually fertile soils plus careful farming methods have made south-eastern Pennsylvania one of the United States' most prosperous agricultural regions. Farmers have tilled this soil for 250 years.

engaged in a number of industries, including canning and preserving.

Boston with a total urban population of 3.3 million is a historic town with a high standing in the world of culture. Its industries include printing and publishing, sugar refining, and clothing manufacture.

Fishing has always been an important industry in the north-east. Towns like Boston and Portland began as little fishing villages.

With modern times, fishing has changed. Sail has given way to steam or to the diesel engine. Nets that were once hauled in by hand are now hauled in by winches. The typical modern fishing vessel is the steam or motor trawler, which drags her nets along the bottom of the sea.

To assist navigation, vessels are fitted with echo-sounders. This instrument, the forerunner of radar, transmits sound

waves which bounce off the bottom of the sea and return. The instrument gives the depth of the water by measuring the time the echo has taken. The same method is also used to locate shoals of fish.

Much of New England's soil is rough and stony. Compared with the rest of America the growing season is short. Accordingly, many farmers go in for dairy-farming. Thus green meadows, hayfields, hayricks, and cow-sheds contribute much to the New England landscape.

Further south, farming is more mixed. On a long, narrow strip of land, running down to the Atlantic Coast from Long Island to Maryland, huge fields of vegetables dot the landscape. The soil here is light and easy to cultivate. There is plenty of rain and the growing season lasts a good six months. This 'truck farming' is like market gardening on a much larger scale.

The Middle West

No other farming area of the world equals the Middle West either in production or in the prosperity of its farmers, who often specialise in one crop only. The Middle West is an enormous area, and the farms themselves are big and highly mechanised. They produce nine-tenths of the soya beans grown in the country, three-fifths of the wheat, four-fifths of the maize, three-fifths of all livestock, and seven-eighths of the pigs.

Maize is grown in the southern part, often called the 'corn belt', which includes western Ohio, Indiana, Illinois, Iowa, Missouri, Nebraska, and Kansas.

Maize is the 'pioneer' American crop. American farmers learnt its cultivation from the Indians. As the pioneers moved westward, they took their maize-growing with them. In the Middle West they found an ideal climate for it. Maize likes the heat both by day and night; it also likes rain. In hot, rainy weather, the plant will sometimes grow an inch (25 mm) or more in a day. Most farmers feed their maize to pigs and cattle, as that is a more profitable way of using it. Though maize is the largest individual crop, it is grown on less than half the land. On the remainder a variety of crops is grown, including soya beans, oats, wheat, and hay.

This Mid-Western scene shows how contour farming follows the contours of the land, to avoid soil erosion.

The total number of farms in Wisconsin has declined over the last forty years, but the farms have become larger and more productive.

In Illinois, broad fields of maize provide farmers with their most valuable cash crop.

In the northern part, the long, cold winters, and cool, moist summers are unfavourable for the growing of maize, but are ideal for dairy-farming.

The western parts of the Middle West are drier. From the Dakotas southward is wheat country. The farms here are posi-tively enormous, and one can drive for kilometres and see nothing but endless fields of wheat, waving in the breeze.

The Middle West has everything necessary to make it into a great man-ufacturing area. There are abundant deposits of coal, natural gas and oil,

The steel industry's demand for iron ore created this large mine in Minnesota's Mesabi range.

Grain is stored in huge elevators at flour mills in Minneapolis, Minnesota.

An oil refinery in Minneapolis, Minnesota.

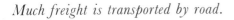

Much freight is transported by road.

iron-ore, timber, and all kinds of raw materials. There is a large labour force: Chicago, with a population of over 6.9 million, being the region's biggest city.

For a long time the processing of food-stuffs ranked first amongst Mid-Western industries. But recently metal production and the manufacture of machinery and motor-cars have taken the leading place.

Once, practically all slaughtering and meat-packing was done on the farms where the livestock was reared. Now, with fast transport and refrigeration available, animals are taken to great packing stations in the larger towns.

Many metric tons of wheat are delivered by rail to the mills in Minneapolis, Kansas City, St Louis, and Wichita. Buffalo, on Lake Erie, is another great milling centre. It is cheaper to transport goods by water than by rail, so every year huge grain ships deliver their cargoes of wheat to the Buffalo mills.

Cheap water-borne transport also favours the growth of an important iron and steel industry along the shores of the Lower Great Lakes. Ships have been specially designed to carry iron ore from the mines of Minnesota, Wisconsin, and northern Michigan to the blast furnaces and steel mills of towns such as Gary, which lies on Lake Michigan, a little to the south-east of Chicago. Coal and limestone (also essential for the production of iron and steel) come from mines and quarries in the neighbourhood. Sea-borne ships can sail 2,347 miles (3,770 km) from the Gulf of St Lawrence on the Atlantic to the extreme western end of Lake Superior, using the St Lawrence Seaway. Shiploads of iron-ore can therefore come direct from the rich deposits newly opened up in Labrador, or from any part of the world.

More than half the motor vehicles manufactured in the United States are made in the Middle West, and the great centre of this industry is Detroit.

The South

The South is, for the most part, a land of hot summers, and mild winters. Rainfall is abundant.

For a long time this vast agricultural area specialised in three main crops: cotton, tobacco, and maize. Cotton and tobacco were grown for the market, maize for subsistence and animal-feed.

These crops did the soil a lot of harm. All three are grown in rows, and the land between the rows has to be hoed. As a result, there is not enough vegetation left

Mild winters and abundant sunshine and rainfall make Florida a great citrus-growing state.

Tobacco, one of the traditional crops of the south, is dried before further processing.

Texas, famous for cowpunchers and cattle, still leads the United States in livestock production.

to protect the soil during heavy rains. The rains in the South are very heavy indeed. During summer thunderstorms, the rain streams off the land carrying good soil with it. In some places great gullies have been formed, and the land has had to be abandoned.

Big changes are taking place, for farmers are now making a great effort to conserve and improve their soil. Fertilisers are being widely used, and fields are being ploughed *along* rather than *across* the contours so that they hold back the rain. This is called contour farming. New crops are being produced, including groundnuts and soya beans. But the greatest change in Southern farming has been the development of cattle-breeding. Discarded cotton lands have become ranches which, in some cases, are larger even than those of the West. The mild Southern winter makes it possible for cattle to graze all the year round. Today, the South is becoming cowboy country.

Mechanical cotton-pickers have replaced the traditional hand labour of the cotton fields of the South.

Closeness to raw materials, abundant and cheap fuel supplies, and a good location on the Gulf Coast ... all these combine to make Houston, Texas, a centre of the chemical industry.

One of the many granite quarries in Georgia. The south is rich in mineral deposits.

The South, though essentially an agricultural region, is becoming increasingly industrialised. Sulphur and salt are found in great domes along the coast of the Gulf of Mexico, in Louisiana and Texas. All the United States' sulphur comes from this course, which amounts to nearly 70 per cent of the world's total production. Sulphur and salt form the basis for a growing chemical industry.

Phosphates, too, are of great importance, and Florida and Tennessee supply most of the nation's needs.

Bauxite is found in many areas of the South, but 90 per cent of the amount extracted comes from central Arkansas.

There are also great deposits of iron ore, but these have only been exploited in a few places – such as Birmingham, Alabama. One bed of ore near Birmingham stretches for over 25 miles (40 km). With coal and iron ore close at hand, Birmingham has naturally become an important producer of iron and steel.

The South has supplies of every source

The Telstar communications satellite enables television to span the world. Cape Canaveral Florida, is the centre of United States' space research. From here rockets have been launched to the moon, Mars, and near Venus and Saturn.

Refining petroleum is one of the leading industries in the South. Huge oil-refineries dotting the landscape are a common sight. However, the U.S.A. does import large amounts of oil as her demands are so large.

of energy: coal, oil, natural gas, and water-power. Large unestimated quantities of oil lie beneath the swamps and plains of the South. Southern coal-fields provide two-fifths of the total production of the United States. The Southern Appalachians is one of the areas of the United States in which water-power has been most exploited.

More than half the land in the South is covered with forests. Two-fifths of the country's timber, more than half the wood-pulp, and one-third of the paper made comes from this region.

Florida is a southern State with a difference. Its climate is sub-tropical, and its landscape is a mixture of mangrove swamps, rich fruit farms and beautiful beaches. It attracts 24 million tourists a year and is a favourite place for wealthy Americans to retire to.

Sulphur from nearby Gulf Coast mines is loaded on to a ship in Galveston harbour.

Western United States

| 0 | 100 | 200 | 300 miles | ◎ State Capitals |

| 0 | 160 | 320 | 480 kilometres |

Inset (left): This map shows the relationship of the western United States to the North American continent.

© Copyright 1960 by Map Projects Inc.

Ripening oranges cover the neatly spaced trees of this Californian orange grove.

In the spring, sheep are driven high into Western mountains to seek fresh, green pastures.

The West

There are few places in the world where the land is put to such a variety of uses as the West, due to its range of climatic conditions with latitude and altitude changes.

There are vast areas of desert. But there are some places where enough rain falls to allow scrub to grow and thus make ranching possible. In some areas the vegetation is so thin that it takes 120 acres (48.5 hectares) to support a single head of cattle. Thus ranches tend to be enormous, some being of over half a million acres (200,000 hectares).

The driest land is used for sheep, for they can browse on plants which cattle will not eat, and can be moved into the mountains in summer time.

In contrast to the great Western ranch is the small irrigated farm produc-ing fine crops of vegetables, and melons.

The three coastal States of the West: California, Oregon, and Washington, are thriving agriculturally. But there is a great difference in the kind of crops produced in central and southern California and in the northern farmlands.

Today four-fifths of California's farm-lands are used for grazing or to grow cereals. However, the crops of the remaining fifth are the most valuable: cotton, vegetables, fruit, especially grapes, and dairy-farming.

California is now second only to Texas as a cotton-producing state, and grows half the country's fruit and vegetables.

The more northern states of Oregon and Washington have a coastal belt with a maritime climate – mild winters, relatively cool summers, and abundant rainfall. It is ideal country for dairy-farming, and, indeed, over four-fifths of the land is

Cattle branding is a busy time on Western ranches. Brands help to distinguish cattle from different herds.

Huge aircraft factories in California and Washington produce modern jet aeroplanes.

used for grazing or to grow hay or other fodder crops. Both Washington and Oregon are also important fruit-growing states, the former being the leading state for apples and hops. They are also rich in timber.

In the western mountain states the most important industry is mining. More than half the labour force is employed in it. When mining began here over 100 years ago the miners were only interested in gold and silver, and had little use for the copper, lead, and zinc they found with the precious metals. But today they are more important in the western states than gold and silver. The Green River valley of Wyoming and Utah has very extensive deposits of oil, in oil shales.

The population of the West Coast is growing fast. By 1970 California had become the most populous state.

The chief industrial area is around Los Angeles. Only New York, Chicago, Detroit, and Philadelphia have a larger industrial population than Los Angeles. Seventy years ago it was a country town. Then oil was discovered, and today California is the third most important oil producing state in the USA after Texas and Louisiana. Then the cinema industry developed – centred on the suburb of Hollywood, bringing much glamour and wealth.

However, it was during the Second World War that Los Angeles became a really great manufacturing town. The building of aircraft became the chief industry, but there were many others, including missile engineering, cars, tyre manufacture, foodstuffs, and machinery. Now over 8 million people live in the Los Angeles-Long Beach conurbation.

Another great industrial area on the West Coast is San Francisco Bay. A fine harbour and well-equipped port have attracted many industries. Food-processing and oil refining have long been carried out there, and now electronics is becoming an important industry.

The third industrial area is in the north-west. Seattle and Tacoma are both inland ports engaged in the lumber trade. Aerospace projects are the chief industry of Seattle where shipbuilding, too, is carried on.

Portland, Oregon, is also an inland port. Its manufactures include wood-products, foundry and machine-shop products, and tinned foods.

Hawaii

Granted statehood in 1959, the Hawaiian islands have a population of 846,900. The capital is Honolulu, sugar and pineapples the staple industry, and tourism the vital factor in the economy.

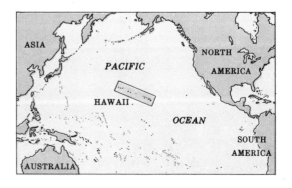

It is easy to see why beaches, on the island of Kauai, Hawaii, are popular for holidays. Tourism is an outstanding factor in Hawaii's economy.

Alaska

Alaska was bought by the United States from Russia in 1867. The price was seven million dollars, but even at that modest price, many people thought the Russians had got the best of the bargain.

Today we know better. There are large reserves of oil in the Swanson River and Cook Inlet fields and even larger deposits in the Arctic Coast region. Many countries have bought shares in Alaska's oil reserves. The movement of oil is mainly by pipelines, with one major feat of engineering under the bleak tundra landscape to the northern field.

Alaska's fishing industry is very important, and she has enormous reserves of timber. There are two large paper mills in the state, which has 330,000 inhabitants.

Alaska's importance has grown with aviation. More people own and fly aircraft than in any other state. Alaska is by far the largest state in the Union, but it has very few roads and still fewer railways. Towns are far apart. Accordingly those who have to travel are practically forced to fly.

Where prospectors once panned for gold, today large dredges scoop up gold-bearing gravel from the Yukon River basin near Fairbanks.

Snow-capped Mount Popocatapetl rises nearly 18,000 ft. (5,500 m) above sea level. It is Mexico's second-highest mountain. A volcano, it emits vast clouds of smoke, at times.

Mexico, Land of Contrasts

Mexico has, within its frontiers, examples of almost all types of physical feature. At least two-thirds of the country is mountainous, and the slopes are so steep that people when they travel do not think of east and west, or north and south, but only of up or down.

The remaining third of Mexico is low. There are narrow valleys, broad basins, swampy coasts, and an extensive limestone plain with underground rivers.

In the south, the rainfall is heavy, and part of this region consists of tropical rain-forests. In the north, on the other hand, there are deserts.

The immense interior tableland rises to over 8,000 feet (2,400 m), but in the lowlands, however, the heat is intense.

Parts of the land are practically uninhabited. On the central plateaus it is quite otherwise. Mexico City is an over-populated area. It is the third largest city in North America, after New York, and Los Angeles.

In 1519, the first European landed on the coast of Mexico. He was the Spaniard Hernando Cortes. Cortes fought his way to the capital of the ruling Indians, the Aztecs. Before the Aztecs, Mexico had been ruled by the Toltecs, and before

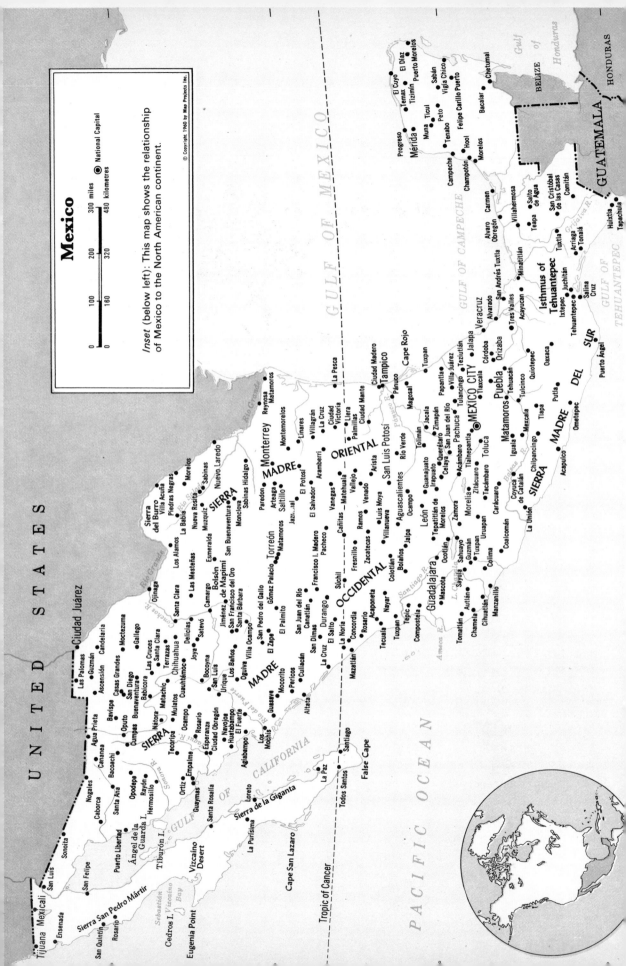

Mexico

● National Capital

0	100	200	300 miles
0	160	320	480 kilometres

© Copyright 1960 by Map Projects Inc.

Inset (below left): This map shows the relationship of Mexico to the North American continent.

UNITED STATES

GULF OF MEXICO

GUATEMALA

HONDURAS

BELIZE

Gulf of Honduras

GULF OF CAMPECHE

GULF OF TEHUANTEPEC

PACIFIC OCEAN

GULF OF CALIFORNIA

Tropic of Cancer

Tijuana
Mexicali
Ensenada
San Quintín
Rosario
Sonoita
San Felipe
San Luis
Sierra San Pedro Mártir
Cedros I.
Vizcaíno Desert
Sebastián Vizcaíno Bay
Eugenia Point
Cape San Lazaro
La Purísima
Sierra de la Giganta
Loreto
Santa Rosalía
Ángel de la Guarda I.
Tiburón I.
Cape San Lazaro
Todos Santos
False Cape
La Paz
Santiago

Nogales
Caborca
Santa Ana
Agua Prieta
Cananea
Bacoachi
Bavispe
Oputo
Cumpas
Babícora
Opodepe
Rayón
Hermosillo
Guaymas
Ortiz
Empalme
Tecoripa
Esperanza
Ciudad Obregón
Navojoa
Huatabampo
Agiabampo
Los Mochis

Ciudad Juárez
Las Palomas
Ascensión
Guzmán
Candelaria
Casas Grandes
San Diego
Buenaventura
Las Cruces
Santa Clara
Chihuahua
Cuauhtémoc
Matachic
Mulatos
Nátora
Ocampo
Rosario
San Luis
Bocoyna
Joya
Urique
Los Baños
Oguiva
Villa Ocampo
El Fuerte

Sierra del Burro
Villa Acuña
Piedras Negras
La Babia
Nueva Rosita
Sabinas
Múzquiz
Monclova
San Buenaventura
Esmeralda
Las Mesteñas
Bolsón de Mapimí
San Francisco del Oro
Santa Bárbara
Jiménez
Camargo
Satevó
Delicias
Terrazas
Santa Clara
Los Alamos
Ojinaga

Morelos
Villa Acuña
Sabinas Hidalgo
Nuevo Laredo
Reynosa
Matamoros
Montemorelos
Monterrey
Linares
Villagrán
Villa Juárez
La Pesca

SIERRA MADRE OCCIDENTAL
SIERRA MADRE ORIENTAL
SIERRA MADRE DEL SUR

Paredón
Arteaga
Saltillo
El Potosí
El Salvador
Jaz...nal
Vanegas
Cañitas
Matehuala
Vallejo
Venado
Arista
San Luis Potosí
Río Verde
Ramos
Luis Moya
Ocampo
Aguascalientes
Villanueva
Jalpa
Guanajuato
León
Tepatitlán de Morelos
Ocotlán
Sahuayo
Tuxpan
Guzmán
Colima
Manzanillo
Coalcomán

Francisco I. Madero
Pacheco
San Pedro del Gallo
San Juan del Río
Canatlán
Durango
El Salto
La Noria
Concordia
Rosario
Acaponeta
Tecuala
Nayar
Tepic
Compostela
Mascota
Autlán
Chamela
Cihuatlán
Tomatlán

Torreón
Matamoros
Gómez Palacio
El Zape
El Palmito
San Dimas
La Cruz
Altata
Mazatlán
Culiacán
Mocorito
Pericos
Guasave

Súchil
Fresnillo
Zacatecas
Bolaños
Colotlán
Sayula
Guadalajara
Zamora
Morelia
Uruapan
Tacámbaro
Zitácuaro
La Unión

Palmillas
Llera
Ciudad Victoria
Ciudad Mante
La Cruz
Tula
Ciudad Madero
Tampico
Pánuco
Cape Rojo
Tuxpan
Papantla
Tulancingo
Teziutlán
Pachuca
Celaya
San Juan del Río
Acámbaro
Querétaro
Zimapán
Jacala
Tolimán

Magosal
Villa Juárez
Villa Juárez
Tlahepantla
Toluca
Coyuca de Catalán
Carácuaro
Tacámbaro
Zitácuaro
Ixtapa
Acapulco
Chilpancingo
Iguala
Mexcala
Tlapa
Putla
Ometepec
Puerto Ángel

MEXICO CITY
Tlaxcala
Puebla
Tehuacán
Matamoros
Tulcingo
Quiotepec
Oaxaca

Papantla
Villa Juárez
Jalapa
Veracruz
Córdoba
Orizaba
Tres Valles
Alvarado
Acayucan
Minatitlán
San Andrés Tuxtla
Álvaro Obregón
Carmen
Villahermosa
Teapa
Salto de Agua
San Cristóbal de las Casas
Comitán
Tuxtla
Arriaga
Tonalá
Huixtla
Tapachula

Isthmus of Tehuantepec
Ixtepec
Juchitán
Tehuantepec
Salina Cruz

El Cuyo
El Díaz
Temax
Tizimín
Puerto Morelos
Vigía Chico
Progreso
Mérida
Muna
Ticul
Tenabo
Peto
Hool
Campeche
Champotón
Morelos
Bacalar
Chetumal
Felipe Carillo Puerto
Sabán

Río Grande
Río Salado
Conchos R.
Río del Fuerte
Santiago R.
Balsas R.
Pánuco R.
Grijalva R.
Ameca R.
L. Chapala

This ancient pyramid is one of many found in the Central Valley of Mexico, where a large part of Mexico's population lives today.

them, by the Mayas, whose remains go back to the fourth century. Both the Mayas and the Toltecs were highly civilised, but the Aztecs, who overran the country in the twelfth century, were a brutal, warlike people, most of whose civilisation was acquired from their defeated enemies.

The Aztec capital was far from being an Indian village. On the contrary, it was a genuine town with beautiful palaces, splendid temples, and many enormous pyramids. The Aztecs knew how to weave, and they were good craftsmen in gold, silver and copper.

The beautiful things they made and their fine towns are, however, only one side of the picture. On the other are the altars of their gods, drenched with the blood of human sacrifices. In the years before the Spanish arrived, 20,000 victims a year, some of them children, were sacrificed to win the favour of the rain god alone. The priesthood was enormous. Cortes found over 5,000 priests in Mexico City.

Aztec, Toltec, and Maya remains can still be seen in Mexico today. The fine pyramids are as highly considered as those of Egypt. Many of the people in Mexico today are directly descended from those ancient tribes.

In 1525, the great silver vein of Guanajuato was discovered, and for 400 years the mine poured out an endless stream of silver, amounting to between one- and two-fifths of the entire supply of the world. Hundreds of millions of pounds' worth of silver has come from Guanajuato. Today Mexico still produces nearly a quarter of the world's silver supply. Minerals in great variety are found in Mexico. Besides gold and silver, there is copper, iron, lead, zinc, mercury, graphite, manganese, coal, oil, and many others. Nearly all the mines are foreign owned. Oil was first discovered in 1901 near Tampico, and a few years later one of the greatest 'gushers' ever known was struck. It produced over 60,000 barrels of oil a day. It flowed so fast from the well that earth reservoirs had to be hurriedly

Much of the world's supply of silver comes from mines like this one in the Mexican highlands.

Mexican oil is refined at modern plants like this one at Salamanca, high above sea level.

built to hold it back. Today Mexico has several huge oil refineries, but still has to export crude oil and import refined products – principally petrol, of course.

Mexico is becoming an industrial country. Hitherto most manufacturing has been done by craftsmen at home or in very small workshops. Leather goods, basketwork, pottery, silver work – all done by hand – still constitute an important part of industry. But changes are taking place.

Cotton mills have been constructed in the textile centres of Puebla and Orizaba, south-east of Mexico City. Monterrey, the established iron and steel centre of the country, has recently added new blast furnaces. Many United States manufacturers have set up branch establishments in Mexico, particularly in Mexico City. These factories are producing machinery, drugs, radios, chemicals and a wide range of other products.

Mexico still imports many manufactured goods, but she is rapidly becoming more self-supporting. Nearly three-quarters of her imports come from the United States, which in turn takes well over half of Mexico's exports.

The bulk of the Mexican population is not urban, but lives in villages little different from those of the Indians before them and many of them are very poor. In Indian times all the land belonged to the tribe. When the Spaniards conquered Mexico the King of Spain divided the country among the *Conquistadores* – and in this way a few thousand Spaniards soon owned practically all the farmland of Mexico.

These large estates became known as *haciendas*, that being the Spanish term for a large farm worked by tenants or labourers instead of by the owner.

Most of the villages used to be part of haciendas. But a few years ago the Mexican government began to buy large haciendas, and allotted the land to the men who had been working it, so that they could farm it for themselves.

The diet of the peasants is more or less summed up by the two words *tortillas* and *frijoles*, the first being maize pancakes, the second broad beans. Much the biggest part is played by maize, which was grown long before the Spaniards arrived in the country, and still takes up half of Mexico's arable land.

Though taking second place, broad beans are none the less important. They contain a lot of protein, and can thus take the place of meat, which most peasants are too poor to buy except on rare occasions.

Arable farming land is limited by the fact that much of the country is too high and too rough for ploughing. In fact arable land amounts to no more than one-twentieth of the total area of the whole country.

Cattle are reared in the dry country in the north. The ranches are big, some of them enormous. They are so dry that many of the cattle are taken to other parts of Mexico to be fattened before slaughtering. The leanest cattle of all are

An adobe brick-maker plies his ancient craft at Valle de Guadalupe in central Mexico.

A Tarahumara Indian girl grinds maize into flour with her metate and rubbing stone.

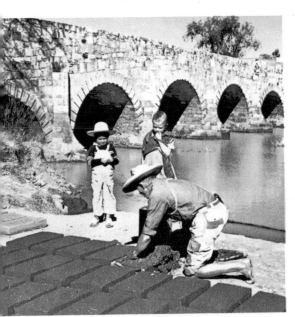

371

Traditional ways of life change slowly in Mexican villages like this one.

occur here and there in the vast stretches of desert. These patches are irrigated by government projects which also include soil conservation techniques.

Mexico's largest irrigation project is in the Laguna district near the town of Torreon. More than half the arable land here is used for growing cotton, which has now become one of the country's leading exports.

On the cool, high central plateaus, wheat and maize are grown. The slopes of the mountains produce coffee, while the hot coastal plain produces bananas, sugar-cane, and coconuts. At each height a different crop is grown, since the height determines the temperature.

sold as they are, merely for their hides and for the making of tallow.

As in the United States, green patches

From the Yucatan Peninsula come

Mexican women do their washing at the communal laundry, while a farmer hoes his maize in the background. Corn is Mexico's chief food crop.

This irrigation project at Culiacán, in western Mexico, provides water for a booming farming region.

two important products. One is raised on plantations in the drier north, while the other is gathered in the tropical rain forest in the south. The plantation crop is a species of agave which produces a fibre called henequen, used in the manufac-

Fishermen of Lake Patzcuaro are famous for their butterfly-shaped nets. Many Indians live in villages unchanged from those of their ancestors.

ture of twine. Mexico produces half of the world's henequen, but now faces competition with sisal, and synthetic fibres. The other product of Yucatan is *chicle* which is the milky juice of a tree called *sapodilla*. Chicle is used to make chewing gum.

Mexico City

Mexico City is the capital of a Federal Republic which became an independent state about 150 years ago, before which it had been for 300 years under Spanish rule. In 1900 the population was just under 300,000. By 1975 it had grown to over 8.6 million together with another 1.7 million in the valley of Mexico. The city possesses a great cathedral built on the site of a former Aztec temple. The national palace is built where the palaces of Cortes and Montezuma once stood.

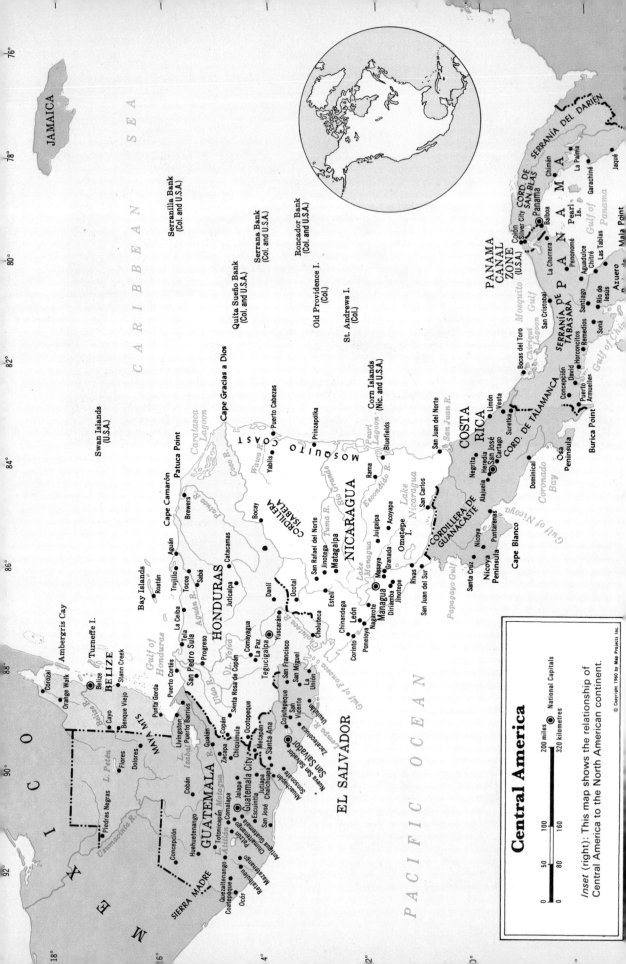

Central America

| | 0 | 50 | 100 | 200 miles | ● National Capitals |
| 0 | 80 | 160 | 320 kilometres | |

Inset (right): This map shows the relationship of Central America to the North American continent.

© Copyright 1960 by Map Projects Inc.

JAMAICA

CARIBBEAN SEA

Serranilla Bank (Col. and U.S.A.)

Serrana Bank (Col. and U.S.A.)

Roncador Bank (Col. and U.S.A.)

Quita Sueño Bank (Col. and U.S.A.)

Old Providence I. (Col.)

St. Andrews I. (Col.)

Swan Islands (U.S.A.)

Cape Gracias a Dios

Patuca Point

Cape Camarón

Carataska Lagoon

Corn Islands (Nic. and U.S.A.)

Prinzapolka

Pearl Lagoon

Bluefields

Rama

San Juan del Norte

SERRANÍA DEL DARIÉN

SERRANÍA DE SAN BLAS

CORD. DE

Chimán

La Palma

Garachiné

Gulf of Panama

Mala Point

Jaqué

PANAMA

PANAMA CANAL ZONE (U.S.A.)

Colón

Panamá

Silver City

Balboa

San Cristobal

Pearl Is.

La Chorrera

Penonomé

Aguadulce

Chitré

Las Tablas

Santiago

Río de Jesús

Soná

Azuero

SERRANÍA DE TABASARA

Bocas del Toro

Mosquito Gulf

Chiriquí Lagoon

Remedios

Horconcitos

Puerto Armuelles

David

Concepción

Burica Point

CORD. DE TALAMANCA

Oká

COSTA RICA

Limón

Vesta

Suretka

San José

Cartago

Heredia

Alajuela

Negrita

Dominical

Coronado Bay

Osa Peninsula

CORDILLERA DE GUANACASTE

Santa Cruz

Nicoya

Nicoya Peninsula

Puntarenas

Gulf of Nicoya

Cape Blanco

Papagayo Gulf

San Carlos

San Juan del Sur

Rivas

Lake Nicaragua

Ometepe I.

Jugalpa

Acoyapa

Juigalpa

Boaco

Bocay

Waspuk R.

Wawa R.

Coco R.

Yablis

Yabis

Puerto Cabezas

MOSQUITO COAST

CORDILLERA ISABELIA

NICARAGUA

Lake Managua

Managua

Masaya

Granada

Diriamba

Jinotepe

León

Chinandega

Corinto

Poneloya

Nagarote

Matagalpa

Jinotega

San Rafael del Norte

Estelí

Ocotal

Danlí

Chontales

Tuma R.

Río Grande

Bocomósido R.

Coco R.

Ulúa R.

HONDURAS

Tegucigalpa

Yuscarán

San Francisco

Comayagua

La Paz

Juticalpa

Catacamas

Sabá

Tocoa

Trujillo

Roatán

Bay Islands

La Ceiba

Tela

Progreso

Puerto Cortés

San Pedro Sula

Santa Rosa de Copán

Copán

Gualán

Zacapa

Chiquimula

Gracias

L. Yojoa

Aguán

Aguán R.

Brewers

Patuca R.

Choloma

Choluteca

San Miguel

La Unión

Cojutepeque

San Vicente

Zacatecoluca

Usulután

EL SALVADOR

San Salvador

Nueva San Salvador

Santa Ana

Metapán

Ahuachapán

Sonsonate

Chalchuapa

San José

Escuintla

Jutiapa

Jalapa

Cuilapa

GUATEMALA

Guatemala City

Antigua Guatemala

Chimaltenango

L. Atitlán

Totonicapán

Sololá

Quezaltenango

Retalhuleu

Mazatenango

Coatepeque

Ocós

SIERRA MADRE

Huehuetenango

Comalapa

Cobán

L. Petén

Flores

Dolores

Piedras Negras

Concepción

Usumacinta R.

MAYA MTS.

Livingston

Puerto Barrios

L. Izabal

Cayo

Benque Viejo

Punta Gorda

Stann Creek

BELIZE

Belize

Turneffe I.

Ambergris Cay

Orange Walk

Corozal

Gulf of Honduras

Motagua R.

Belize R.

MEXICO

PACIFIC OCEAN

Gulf of Fonseca

Gulf of Tehuantepec

Lempa R.

76°

78°

80°

82°

84°

86°

88°

90°

92°

18°

16°

14°

12°

10°

8°

Ruins of the ancient Maya civilisation are found in both Mexico and Guatemala.

Central America

Central America is a narrow bridge of land joining North America to South America. Though over 500 miles (800 km) in width at its broadest point, it is relatively narrow compared with the enormous masses of land which it joins. It consists of Belize, Guatemala, Honduras, Salvador, Nicaragua, Costa Rica, and Panama. All are independent states, except Belize which is self-governing within the Commonwealth. In 1821 Central America joined Mexico in becoming independent. For a while all except Panama became part of Mexico. However, by 1842 the map of Central America was as we see it today.

The history of Belize is somewhat different from that of the others. Almost

Lake Atitlan, completely surrounded by volcanoes, is in the highlands of Guatemala.

These women are taking great loads of flowers to a village market in Honduras.

Careful picking of only the ripe berries makes Central American coffee especially valuable.

continuously, since the seventeenth century, British settlers, originally composed of buccaneers, had established themselves on the shores of the Gulf of Honduras. Nominally under the Spanish king, they were in fact largely independent, and were constantly attacking their neighbours. It was only in the nineteenth century, however, that Great Britain formally laid claim to the colony, and it was not till 1862 that her sovereignty was completely recognised.

The population of Central America is largely Indian in descent. Guatemala is the most Indian of the states. There, three-fifths of the population is descended from the Mayas.

Some of the people of Central America have maintained their ancient traditions. They live in small villages, and each village has its own manners and customs, and even its own style of clothing.

In these tropical countries, the plains are so hot that no one lives there if they can avoid it. Nearly all the big towns and most of the roads, railways, airports, and even farms are found high above sea-level. In some of the countries only a

quarter of the population lives on the plains. In the highlands, coffee is the chief crop. It was first planted in Costa Rica more than 150 years ago. Today it is grown in all the Central American countries. Most of it is grown between 2,000 (610 m) and 4,500 feet (1,370 m) above sea-level.

Great care is lavished on the coffee shrub. Sometimes trees are planted under the shade of taller trees, as shade-ripened coffee has a delicate flavour.

Care is also needed for the harvesting, as only the ripe, dark red berries are picked. The coffee pickers return to the same tree again and again, each time picking only the ripe berries. The work is slow and laborious, but the coffee has a very fine reputation.

The soil is rich and deep, and contains volcanic ash, which is particularly favourable for coffee growing. The climate too, is perfect. The hills on which

Bananas are exported from the port of Tela. Bananas are Honduras's chief export product and major foreign currency earner.

An odd mixture of Christian and Pagan ritual at Chichicastenango, Guatemala.

Spraying operations are carried on regularly to prevent the spread of banana diseases.

coffee is planted are high enough to give a moderate temperature, without the danger of frost. Moreover, fifty to sixty inches (1,250 to 1,500 mm) of rain fall in the year, and there is always a dry season for harvesting.

The coastal plains are devoted to the growing of bananas – the hot, wet climate is ideal for their cultivation.

Banana growing is a big undertaking. First the forest has to be cleared and the roots of the trees pulled up out of the soil. Then engineers have to construct a system of drains to prevent the low land being flooded. Rails have to be laid throughout the plantation and down to the sea ports. Towns also have to be built for the plantation workers.

Indians gather around a pottery seller in a Guatemalan village market.

The Panama Canal

The idea of a canal across the Isthmus of Panama to link the Atlantic and Pacific was first projected by the Spaniards in the sixteenth century.

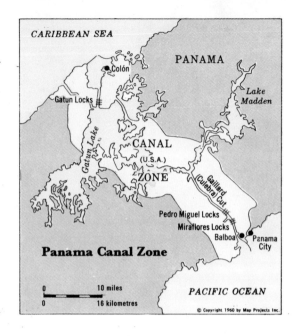

The importance of a canal linking the Atlantic and Pacific Oceans is that it reduces the voyage of a ship sailing, for example, from New York to San Francisco, by more than half. In 1879 a French Panama Canal Company was formed, with Ferdinand de Lesseps (of Suez Canal fame) as president. Work was actually started, but the company got into greater and greater difficulties, and the United States took over the task, bringing in a population which is 44,000 today. The canal took thirteen years to build, and cost 367 million dollars.

The construction of the Panama Canal was one of the greatest engineering enterprises of modern times. It was much more difficult than the Suez Canal, owing to the relatively high land.

It takes a ship about eight hours to pass through the Canal. In 1974 there were 14,033 transits of ocean-going merchant vessels through the Canal, and the tolls paid totalled nearly 119 million dollars. About one quarter of these were ships sailing under the American flag, linking the Atlantic, Gulf and Pacific coasts of the United States and the east and west coasts of South America.

Over 14,000 ocean-going vessels passed through the Panama Canal in 1974. The famous Minaflores Locks lower ships from the Gailland Cut to the Pacific Ocean.

St Lucia is a beautiful tropical island in the Caribbean, and a member of the British Commonwealth. Its fertile valleys and narrow coastal plains are mainly used in growing sugar-cane, the island's chief product.

The Caribbean Islands

The east coast of Central America is washed by the Caribbean Sea. This sea is girdled by a line of islands running in a great curve to near the eastern end of the coast of Venezuela. Some are called the West Indies, a reminder that Columbus was looking for a westward route to India when he discovered America. These islands are the tops of mountain ranges rising above the sea. Cuba, the biggest, is larger than Portugal; Jamaica is about twice the size of Lancashire. Many are much smaller, and there are thousands of tiny islands, too small for anyone to live on. But more than fifty of them are populated. In the north the islands run in two main lines. The Bahamas form the outer line. Within them are the larger islands of the Greater Antilles: Cuba, Hispaniola, Puerto Rico, and Jamaica. East of Puerto Rico, the Virgin Islands begin the long chain of the Lesser Antilles. Finally there is another group of islands off the coast of Venezuela, the largest being Curaçao.

Cuba is a communist country with close ties with the USSR. Puerto Rico is closely linked with the United States. Hispaniola is shared by Haiti and the Dominican Republic; Martinique and Guadeloupe are French; Jamaica, Barbados and Trinidad and Tobago are in the Commonwealth, and most of the other islands are associated with Britain.

These islands have a maritime climate, and the moist Trade Winds blow

Asphalt is a principal export of Trinidad.

in from the Atlantic. Accordingly, the windward slopes of the mountains have plenty of wet weather, while the lee slopes are often quite dry. San Juan, for instance, on the northern coast of Puerto Rico, receives over 60 inches (1,500 mm) of rain in a year, while Ponce on the southern coast receives only 36 (900). Some of the highest islands receive a very heavy rainfall indeed. One weather reporting station on the windward side of the Blue Mountains in Jamaica records an annual rainfall of 222 inches (5,560 mm). At the same time in Kingston, on the other side of the mountains, only thirty miles (48 km) away, the average rainfall is 29 inches (735 mm).

On the windward or weather side of the islands, the sea is inclined to be rough, which made them dangerous for shipping in the old days of sail. There were safer anchorages on the lee side. That is why almost all the big towns are found on the western or southern coasts.

The mild tropical climate favours the growth of a great variety of crops. Much the most important is the sugar-cane. Planting the cane is done in the early spring, but it does not have to be repeated each year, for new plants grow

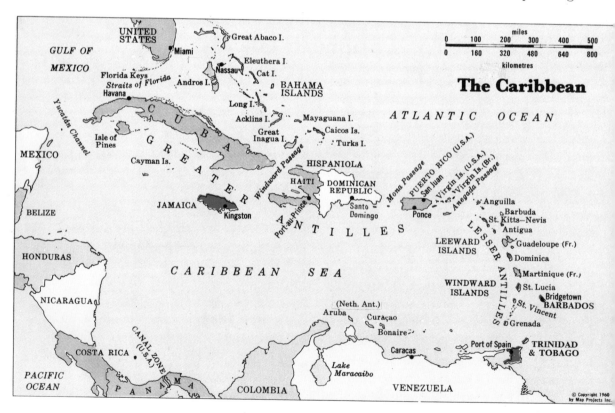

Huge fields of sugar-cane occupy Puerto Rico's fertile valleys.

from the stalks of the old ones. In some places planting machines are used, but in most cases the work, both of planting and tending the sugar-cane, is done by hand. For tending the plants in summer and autumn little labour is needed, and seasonal unemployment is the great curse of the sugar-growing industry. But from the harvest onwards, from December to June, every available hand is hard at work. The cane is cut by hand, then driven to the mill in ox-wagons, lorries, or railway trucks. At the mill, it is cut into pieces, crushed by huge rollers, and then, finally, the juice is boiled until hard crystals of sugar are formed.

Although sugar-cane is by far the most important crop of the lowlands, many other crops are grown: pineapples, grapefruit, bananas, etc., most of which are exported.

As a rule, in the mountains the slopes are too steep and the soil too thin for farming. Here and there, however, particularly in western Cuba, Haiti, Puerto Rico, and eastern Jamaica, special highland crops – such as coffee and tobacco – are grown. The mountains are thinly populated, and the other crops are grown merely for subsistence.

Many Puerto Rican farmers use tiny hillside patches like this one to produce tobacco.

Cuba

Cuba has an area of 44,206 square miles (114,524 sq km) and a population of 9.17 million. Havana is the capital.

The Cuban economy is planned by the government. Industry, agriculture and

Some of the hard work of cutting sugar-cane is still done by hand in Cuba.

mineral resources are nationalised. Cuba is a member of Comecon and most of her exports go to Eastern Europe and the USSR. 50 per cent of her imports come from Russia.

Industrial development has been fairly slow with the focus remaining on the manufacturing of local primary produce; for example there are 152 sugar refining mills in the country, and the tobacco industry is also important.

Sugar accounts for 80 per cent of exports. Indeed, Cuba is the world's second largest producer. Tobacco, fish, and nickel are also important exports.

Cuba's reserves of nickel and iron ore are very large. Other minerals include copper, gold, silver, and oil.

Most of Cuba's farmland is state owned, in co-operatives and 'people's farms'. Sugar estates, with their own railways connected to the main lines, are widespread; tobacco for cigars is grown in the Vuelta–Abajo district; coffee in Oriente province; and henequen is cultivated. Three unusual fibre crops are grown: *kenaf*, which is replacing the functions of jute; *yarey*, and *majagua* which is used in the tobacco industry. Tropical fruits are grown and recently rice has been cultivated on a highly mechanised basis. Cuba's extensive hardwood forests are being exploited.

Cuba's land area and her population are very small. Her natural resources and agricultural potentials are not enormous, but politically Cuba is very important in the world today.

Jamaica

Jamaica has a total population approaching two million, of whom 377,000 live in the capital, Kingston. The country is very mountainous: the highest peak, in the Blue Mountains, being 7,388 feet (2,251 m). Once sugar-growing and rum-making were almost Jamaica's only industries. In the nineteenth century fruit growing, particularly bananas, took the lead, but in recent years bananas have suffered heavily from banana disease. Sugar-growing has again taken the leading place in agriculture, but coffee is also of prime importance, and the tourist trade is now another source of revenue.

Jamaica has now a wide range of manufacturing industries, including oil refining, agricultural machinery and cement. Jamaica is the world's second leading exporter of bauxite. Her deposits are worked by American and Canadian firms.

Trinidad and Tobago

Trinidad, less than half the size of Jamaica, has a population of 1,048,400, the greater part of which is of African descent. About a fifth of the population is of East Indian origin, while the remainder is of English, French, Spanish, and Portuguese descent. The capital is Port of Spain, with a population of 97,000, which is well situated in the lee of the north-west corner of the island. Trinidad is much less mountainous than Jamaica, its heights barely reaching 3,000 feet (900 m). As a result rather more than half the island is capable of being cultivated. The exports are sugar, rum, cocoa, grapefruit, and coconuts. Besides these Trinidad has rich oil wells for which three oil refineries have been built. Deposits of asphalt are worked, and the exports of these two commodities exceed all other products.

Trinidad is joined politically with Tobago, a smaller island to the north-east. Together they form an independent member state of the Commonwealth.

Barbados

Barbados, the most easterly of the islands, has a population of about 250,000, about 88,809 of whom live in the capital, Bridgetown. Except for one part, the island is of coral formation, and it is almost entirely surrounded by coral reefs, which make the coast dangerous. The island has only one harbour. It is relatively flat and for the most part covered with a thin layer of very fertile soil, composed largely of volcanic ash blown from the Soufrière, the volcano of St Vincent 100 miles (1,600 km) away. Barbados became independent within the Commonwealth in 1966.

West Indies Associated States

In 1962 Jamaica and Trinidad opted out of the West Indies Federation and the West Indies Associated States was established with the remaining islands. These islands now include the Leeward Islands of Antigua, St Kitts-Nevis-Anguilla,

These women, in the highlands of Grenada, are preparing coffee berries for drying. The berries must be carefully dried to ensure a good flavour.

which are self-governing within the Commonwealth; Montserrat and the Virgin Islands which are British; and the Windward Islands of St Vincent, the Grenadines, St Lucia and Dominica, which are also self-governing within the Commonwealth, and Grenada which became independent in 1974.

These islands are all of volcanic origin, and they belong, with Jamaica, Montserrat, the Bahamas, Belize, and Guyana, to the Caribbean Free Trade Area (CARIFTA).

Commonwealth of the Bahamas

The Bahamas became independent from Britain in 1973, though they are still in the Commonwealth. They consist of a chain of 700 coral islands whose total area adds up to only a little less than that of Jamaica. Their total population is a little over 170,000 of which over 50,000 live in the capital, Nassau. The Bahamas live chiefly on the tourist trade, particularly from the United States.

Bermuda

The Bermudas are a group of about 150 islands, which, however, are generally called by the singular name Bermuda.

All the islands are connected by bridges or causeways. The entire length of the chain is 22 miles (35 km) and the total area is 21 square miles (53 sq km). The population is 53,000, about one third of whom are white. Only about a quarter of the total area is suitable land for farming, but it is fully used for market gardening and bulb growing. The climate is pleasant and very healthy. Winter temperatures vary from around 60° (16°) to 70°F (21°C). The scenery is very attractive and this, together with the pleasant climate, attracts many tourists.

The Andes are new mountains, still sharp and very high. The chain runs all the way down the west coast of South America.

South America

National Capitals

Scale 1:30000000

| 0 | 100 | 200 | 300 | 400 | 500 | miles |
| 0 | 160 | 320 | 480 | 640 | 800 | kilometres |

Depths		below sea level	Heights			
feet over 650	0–650		0–650	650–1650	1650–5000	over 5000 feet
tres over 200	0–200		0–200	200–500	500–1500	over 1500 metres

Railways ⏚⏚ Canals ⚓ Heads of navigation 〰 Swamps and marshes ▦ Desert

This is South America

South America is almost completely surrounded by water. Only the Isthmus of Panama, linking it to North America, prevents it being an island. It is almost 7 million square miles (18 million sq km) in area, about one-eighth of the total land surface of the world, yet its total population is no more than about 190 million, or less than one-twentieth of the total world population. It is not always realised that South America lies not south, but south-east of North America.

The eleven republics of South America are Argentina, Bolivia, Brazil, Chile, Colombia, Ecuador, Paraguay, Peru, Uruguay, Guyana and Venezuela. Guiana is an overseas territory of France and Surinam is independent.

A great mountain system, the Andes, extends along the entire western edge of the continent.

The Andes constitute the longest continuous mountain system in the world, extending for 4,400 miles (7,100 km) from the Caribbean Sea in the north to Tierra del Fuego in the south. They are the highest mountains in the world except for the Himalayas. Several of the peaks are over 21,000 feet (6,400 m) high, and the highest, Mount Aconcagua, reaches a height of 22,835 feet (6,960 m). At their widest point, in Bolivia, the Andes are 400 miles (640 km) wide; but in most places the width is no more than 150 miles (240 km). In the northern part the mountains divide into two ranges with deep valleys and wide plateaus, sometimes 10,000 feet (3,000 m) high.

The other two mountainous areas are the Pacaraima and Guiana Highlands in the north, and the Brazilian Plateau and Coast Ranges in the eastern bulge of the continent, especially inland from Rio de Janeiro. A few of them rise as high as 9,000 feet (2,740 m), but they have no sharp crested peaks like the Andes.

The Guiana Highlands extend from Venezuela into Guyana, Surinam, and northern Brazil. They are almost unoccupied as they are very rugged and inaccessible. The Brazilian Highlands, commencing 400 miles (640 km) south of the Amazon River, cover a much larger area. They are highest along the coast at the Tropic of Capricorn. There the coast is rugged with natural harbours. This eastern portion has rich soil and a good deal of forest. It is the most populated part of Brazil. The western portion is savanna grassland – the Mato Grosso.

The west coast of South America is forbidding, being mostly composed of gaunt rocky cliffs, rising straight up from the sea. A belt of barren desert runs along

Chile's Atacama Desert is one of the driest places on earth.

the coast for 1,000 miles (1,600 km) from southern Ecuador to northern Chile. The coastline is so straight that harbours are few except in the north and south.

East of the Andes, in the south, is a high plateau called Patagonia, which stretches all the way to the east coast. Several rivers run through it. In many of the valleys there are lakes formed by the glaciers of the Ice Age. Except round rivers and lakes, Patagonia is barren.

South America has three great rivers, the Orinoco, the Amazon, and the Paraná-Paraguay system. The Orinoco rises in the Southern Guiana Highlands, flows in a great semi-circle north-west, north, and east, and empties into the Atlantic through a wide delta south of Trinidad. Some of its tributaries rise in the Andes. It is 1,800 miles (2,900 km) long and is navigable for more than half its length.

The Amazon is the second longest river in the world, draining with its tributaries at least half the continent. Its hot steamy plain varies in width from 20 (32 km) to 800 miles (1,290 km).

The Amazon and its tributaries have well over 5,600 miles (9,000 km) of water navigable by shallow-draft boats, and ocean-going ships can steam up as far as Manaus, nearly 1,000 miles (1,600 km) from the coast. Vessels drawing 14 feet (4.2 m) can go up-river as far as Iquitos, in Peru, over 2,300 miles (3,700 km) from the coast. The Amazon brings down so much water to the sea that the latter is fresh for 40 miles (64 km) around the mouth, and it carries so much alluvium that the Atlantic is muddy for 200 miles (320 km).

The Paraná and Paraguay rivers drain the southern part of the Brazilian Highlands and the Central Andes. Their basins form South America's third great

Dense, almost impenetrable jungle lines the banks of the River Amazon in Brazil.

plain. The northern part of the Paraná-Paraguay plain is an almost empty area of wooded grassland called the Gran Chaco. It is an almost flat plain, sloping gradually from the foot of the Andes to the Paraguay River. In the south is a vast fertile plain called the Humid Pampas.

The Paraná River empties into a gigantic estuary called the Rio de la Plata, or River Plate, which is 170 miles (270 km) long and 140 miles (230 km) broad at the mouth.

South America is one of the last 'frontiers' of the world. Sparsely populated and underdeveloped, its potential as a source of raw materials and food is prodigious. It is now developing rapidly, but with political unrest and instability in many states.

South America

Average January Temperatures

Under 32°F
Under 0°C
32–60°F
0–16°C
60–72°F
16–22°C
over 72°F
over 22°C

© Copyright 1960 by Map Projects Inc.

South America

Average July Temperatures

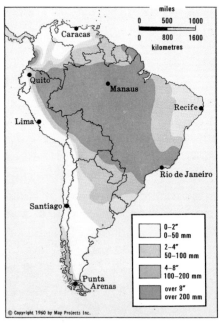

0–2″
0–50 mm
2–4″
50–100 mm
4–8″
100–200 mm
over 8″
over 200 mm

© Copyright 1960 by Map Projects Inc.

South America

Average January Rainfall

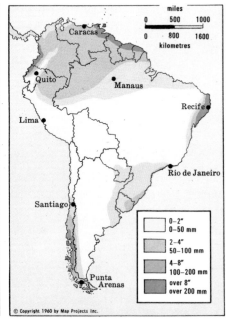

0–2″
0–50 mm
2–4″
50–100 mm
4–8″
100–200 mm
over 8″
over 200 mm

© Copyright 1960 by Map Projects Inc.

South America

Average July Rainfall

Climate and Vegetation

Most of South America lies south of the Equator, which means that the seasons are reversed compared with Europe. All of South America lies within the tropics except Uruguay, most of Argentina, Chile, a small portion of southern Brazil, and half of Paraguay.

In the equatorial region, the average temperature is over 70°F (21°C), but such a temperature, constantly maintained, and with a high degree of humidity, is difficult for northerners to bear. In the mountains the climate is much less extreme. At Quito, for instance, which is right on the Equator but at an altitude of nearly 10,000 feet (3,000 m), the average temperature is only 55°F (13°C), winter and summer alike. One of the worst climates is at Manaus, on the Amazon, where the average temperature is just over 80°F (27°C) all the year, and it rains for 240 days in the year. In other regions rain is seasonal, falling mostly in summer and irregularly at other times. Indeed, in north-east Brazil and on the north coast of Venezuela, droughts occur. On the Pacific side, the coasts of Peru and northern Chile are cold and cloudy, being swept by the Peruvian current of cold water from the south.

Plant life in South America is divided into several broad zones, corresponding to the climate and land forms. In the hot rainy areas of the Amazon basin is the tropical rain-forest. The trees here are tall and straight. They are always green, and they grow so close together that their tops interlace to form a dense canopy. The forest floor gets too little light for undergrowth to grow, but along the streams where the light gets through, the undergrowth is so thick that a man can hardly make his way through it.

North and south of the tropical rain-forest, where the weather is hot but the rainfall irregular, plants must be able to live through a dry season. This region is the savanna where vegetation consists of tall grasses with scattered bushes and shrubs or, occasionally, where the land is moister, open woodland. Grasses may grow to heights of 12 feet (3.6 m). Along the streams grow taller trees. In the dry season, many trees and shrubs lose their leaves and the grass becomes dry and brown.

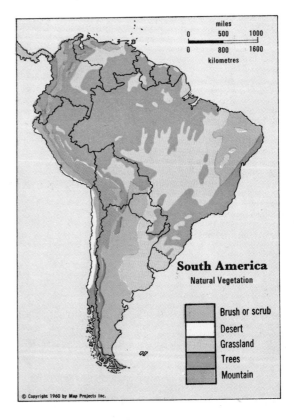

South America
Natural Vegetation

- Brush or scrub
- Desert
- Grassland
- Trees
- Mountain

© Copyright 1960 by Map Projects Inc.

The Andes form a very complex zone. In the north, the vegetation is similar to that of the lowlands nearby, that is to say, rain-forests in the wet areas, and savanna in the dry areas. Further south, where it is cooler and drier, conifers and deciduous trees (those which shed

389

Some passes in Bolivia's towering mountains are higher than the peaks of the Rocky Mountains. reaching heights of 13,000 ft (3,962 m).

Lake Titicaca is over 12,000 ft (3,657 m) above sea level. The Aymara Indians make their rafts of woven reeds.

their leaves) replace the broad-leaved evergreens of the rain-forest.

Above the tree-line, the slopes and plateaus are covered with short grass and shrubs. The vegetation becomes sparser as it approaches the snow-line, where it stops abruptly.

South of the Tropic of Capricorn the continent becomes drier. Much of the land is covered with a similar sort of grass to the prairies of North America. In the cold, dry region of Patagonia, the grass gives way to desert. The cool, rainy region in the south-west is covered with a dense forest of mixed conifers and deciduous trees.

This young Aymara boy wears the typical hat and cape worn by Bolivians in the region of Lake Titicaca.

The hat and coin-spangled belt are special fiesta decorations of the Araucanians of Chile.

The Peoples of South America

South America has a population of about 190 million, an average of 25 per square mile (9 per sq km). That is a very scanty population compared to that of Europe, which has 210 per square mile (54 per sq km). As in other parts of the world, it is unequally distributed.

It is thought that the first people to come to South America came from Asia. They may well have come from Siberia over the Bering Strait into Alaska, and gradually moved down through North and finally into South America. Columbus called them Indians because, when he landed on one of the Bahamas, he thought he had reached India. When Magellan, sailing far to the south, found the passage through to the Pacific which bears his name, the search for the route to India stopped and the conquest of

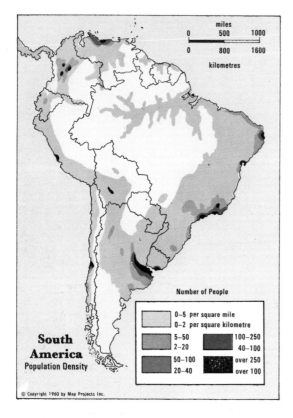

South America
Population Density

miles
0 500 1000
0 800 1600
kilometres

Number of People

0–5 per square mile	
0–2 per square kilometre	
5–50	100–250
2–20	40–100
50–100	over 250
20–40	over 100

© Copyright 1960 by Map Projects Inc.

South America began in earnest. It was the Spaniards who started. They landed on the north coast, and worked their way far into the interior. They overran Peru, Ecuador, Colombia, and much of Chile. Driving still further south, they established colonies by the Rio de la Plata and later in Paraguay in the interior.

While the Spaniards advanced from the north-west, the Portuguese took possession of the east coast. Within a short time they had occupied the whole Brazilian coast. Spain and Portugal between them were by this time firmly established on the continent.

However, the American War of Independence and then the French Revolution stirred up ideas of freedom amongst the people of South America. One by one they rose against their rulers and after a succession of wars, the map looked much as it does today.

When the first white explorers arrived, Indians were scattered widely over the continent. Three-quarters of them were in the northern Andes near the west coast. Farming was much easier there than in the tropical lowlands, where the soil was generally poor and crops were ravaged by insects.

These Indians included two very advanced civilisations. The largest was the Inca Empire which included the Quechuas and Aymaras of Ecuador, Bolivia, and Peru, and a few Araucanians in northern Chile. A smaller group

This young boy is one of the many people who work on coffee plantations in Brazil.

An Arawak Indian mother travels with her three children in a flat-bottomed wooden canoe.

consisted of the Chibchas of Colombia.

The first white explorers were men from Spain and Portugal, where there was very little prejudice about marrying people of another race. Many of them married Indian women. Their children were called *mestizo*, which meant of mixed blood. Today by far the largest part of the population of South America is Indian or part Indian. In Colombia, Venezuela, and Chile two-thirds of the people are mestizos. In Paraguay almost the entire population is mestizo. There is no country where there are not some mestizos.

A Quechua of Ecuador plays a wooden flute. Most of the Inca peoples were Quechuas.

The Latacunga market in Ecuador is in an ancient Inca town, once destroyed by an earthquake.

This little Colombian girl, dressed in her Sunday best, is on her way home from church.

Some Indians, however, did not mix with whites. In Ecuador, Bolivia, and Peru more than half the people are of pure Indian stock. But these Indians live almost entirely in the mountains.

The adventurous, hard-riding cowboys of South America are called gauchos.

When the Portuguese began settling on the east coast of Brazil, they found only a few Indians, and these were not willing to work on the plantations. Accordingly, the Portuguese brought African slaves. Of the population of Brazil today more than 5 million are of Negro origin. Most of them live either on the east coast or in the west central part of Brazil near the goldfields. Along the remainder of the coast and along some of the rivers the people are mixed Portuguese, Indians, and Negroes.

There were no settlers on the land south of the Rio de la Plata until the nineteenth century. When European settlers did come, the Indians had already been driven out. As a result the people of Argentina are almost entirely white.

In this great mixture of peoples there are a few groups whose way of life has hardly changed. Such are the Bush Negroes of the Guiana jungles. They are descended from runaway slaves of the seventeenth century. In Guyana there are large numbers of East Indians who were brought over at the same time as those who went to Trinidad. They are Hindus and have retained Asian customs.

Some colonies of European emigrants have clung jealously to their identity and refused to intermingle with others, and there are Indians at the southern tip of the continent who live exactly as their ancestors did in the Stone Age.

Only a third of the population lives in towns. Those who do, live very much like the town-dwellers of Europe or North America, except that the contrast between rich and poor is much more sharply drawn. The appalling housing conditions of the poor are thrown sharply into relief when compared to the handsome buildings which house the better-off.

Magnificent modern buildings in Sao Paulo, Brazil. An impromptu market is taking place.

The Towns of South America

The towns of South America, though not so old as those of Europe and Asia, have far more history than the towns of North America. A number of them, like Quito, Bogota, and Cuzco were Indian capitals long before the Spaniards arrived. Many others were founded in the sixteenth and seventeenth centuries by the Spanish and Portuguese conquistadors.

In the warmer regions, the Spanish preferred to build their towns high up, where the climate was more agreeable. Such places were, however, generally less accessible, and the majority of towns were built in valleys, where they could be reached by boat and where there was land on which to grow crops for the population. Today the largest towns are those that can be reached by water.

Some towns were built for mine workers, others as residential towns for wealthy landowners. Manufactures started late in South America, and factories tended to spring up where there was already a population to man them. Few specifically industrial towns have been built.

Though many of the old towns have beautiful buildings, South America is better known for its advanced modern architecture and town planning. Brasilia, the capital of Brazil, has some of the most modern architecture in the world.

Towns have grown rapidly in recent years with the development of industry and the provision of better communications; and to them comes a steady stream

The Plaza de Mayo in Buenos Aires, the capital and chief sea-port of Argentina.

of people from the villages, anxious to escape the monotony and privations of life on the land.

Buenos Aires, the capital of the Argentine, with a population of 8.7 million, is the largest city in South America. It is a great industrial town and a flourishing port, being the outlet for the massive export of Argentine beef and grain. With its surroundings it houses one-fifth of the population of the country.

São Paulo is Brazil's largest town and one of the fastest-growing cities in the world. It is also the centre of the country's richest agricultural area, which is also the great coffee-growing area. It possesses a wide range of industries. It is built on high ground, some 40 miles (64 km) from its port, Santos.

Rio de Janeiro, a town of 4.3 million inhabitants, was the capital of Brazil until 1960, when this function was taken over by the newly built capital, Brasilia, in the centre of the country. Founded by

A spectacular view looking across Rio de Janeiro to the mountains beyond.

Modern South American cities are alive with activity. These two views of Sao Paulo show the hustle and bustle of city life.

the Portuguese in 1567, Rio stands on a deep landlocked bay. Though it has some industry, its chief concern is shipping. Its beautiful setting and beaches make it a popular holiday resort.

Montevideo, the capital of Uruguay, is the centre of a flourishing agricultural region and is also an important port. It has a pleasant climate and serves as a resort for the wealthy classes of both Brazil and Argentina.

La Paz, in the Andes, is the highest

Montevideo, Uruguay, is so pleasant that tourists come to it from Brazil and Argentina.

The Spanish founded La Paz in a deep canyon sunk in a high wind-swept plateau.

Quito, the capital of Ecuador, is another mountain town. It is built on the side of an extinct volcano. Its temperature is unusually steady, the monthly average hardly ever changing.

Santiago, capital of Chile, stands on a broad plain at the foot of the Andes. Founded in 1541, it has been repeatedly destroyed by either Indian attacks, earthquakes or floods, but it has now grown to be the fourth largest city, with 3.7 million inhabitants, in South America. Nearly a quarter of the population of Chile lives in or around Santiago, which enjoys a pleasant climate, and is the commercial and industrial centre of the country.

capital in the world, sited nearly 12,000 feet (3,700 m) above sea-level. It is built at the bottom of a deep gorge which provides shelter from the cold winds of the bleak plateau, or Altiplano. Remote as it is, La Paz is nevertheless the industrial centre of Bolivia. It was founded in 1548, and is now an important communications centre.

Lima, the capital of Peru, was founded by Pizarro, the Spanish conquistador, in 1535. For more than 300 years it was the largest and the wealthiest city of South America. Its university, founded in 1551, is the oldest on the continent.

Bogota, the capital of Colombia, has little industry but is a famous cultural centre. It was founded by the Spaniards

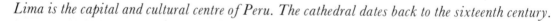

Lima is the capital and cultural centre of Peru. The cathedral dates back to the sixteenth century.

River houses built on stilts in Salvador da Bahia.

in 1538, the town being built on the site of a former Indian capital. There are several universities, the oldest dating from 1572, with students from many countries.

Caracas, the capital of Venezuela, stands 6 miles (9.6 km) from the coast of the Caribbean at an altitude of 3,000 feet (900 m). Owing to its elevation, it has a pleasant climate. Founded in 1567, it has been largely rebuilt in recent years and is famous for its modern architecture. It is the centre of a flourishing agricultural region, and is developing industrially.

Much of Caracas has been rebuilt recently. Prosperity from oil has made this possible.

South America

80° 70° 60° 50° 40°

TRINIDAD & TOBAGO

VENEZUELA

GUYANA

COLOMBIA

SURINAM

GUIANA

| 0 | 200 | 400 | 600 | 800 | 1000 miles |
| 0 | 320 | 640 | 960 | 1280 | 1600 kilometres |

© Copyright 1960 by Map Projects Inc.

Equator

10°

ECUADOR

Cape São
Roque

B R A Z I L

−10°

PERU

BOLIVIA

−20°

PARAGUAY

Tropic of Capricorn

30°

PACIFIC

ATLANTIC OCEAN

−30°

CHILE

OCEAN

URUGUAY

ARGENTINA

90°

−40°

−50°

Strait of Magellan

(Br.)
FALKLAND
ISLANDS

100°

TIERRA
DEL
FUEGO

Cape Horn

South America

Main Railways

—— Main Railways

| miles |
| 0 | 500 | 1000 |
| 0 | 800 | 1600 |
| kilometres |

© Copyright 1960 by Map Projects Inc.

Communications

South America depends heavily on sea transport, but aircraft are being used more and more, and for passengers and postal services they provide a very efficient form of transport, but not for heavy, or bulky, goods.

In mountainous regions the cost of building railways is so great that freight charges are very high. In Venezuela, for instance, 217 bridges had to be built, and eighty-six tunnels cut, to construct a railway only 200 miles (320 km) long.

Proper roads are being constructed and improved; the Pan American Highway being the most important. Where such roads exist, a lorry can carry goods at one-twentieth of the cost of mule transport. But roads, too, are expensive to build, particularly those built inland from the west coast. In the whole length of Chile, which stretches for 2,740 miles (4,410 km), there are only half a dozen roads over the mountains.

Naturally flat countries like Argentina and Uruguay have long stretches of railway lines. The Argentine pampas have a network of lines converging on the main ports, but very few good roads, because the dusty soil blows about in the dry season and turns into a sea of mud as soon as it rains. Uruguay has good roads and railways, for it has supplies of gravel.

In the north and north-east, rivers form the chief means of transport. The Guianas have hardly any railways or good all-weather roads. Most rivers, however, are only navigable for a limited distance, in fact up to the first waterfall or rapids. One river is so narrow that ships are unable to turn in it, and, having reached their destination, have then to be towed stern-first downstream. Brazil has no roads or railways at all except in the coastal belt. Elsewhere all transport is by water. The Amazon playing an important part in this system.

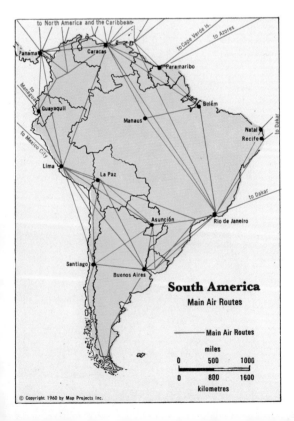

South America
Main Air Routes

— Main Air Routes

miles
0   500   1000

0   800   1600
kilometres

© Copyright 1960 by Map Projects Inc.

South America
Main Roads

— Main Roads

miles
0   500   1000

0   800   1600
kilometres

© Copyright 1960 by Map Projects Inc.

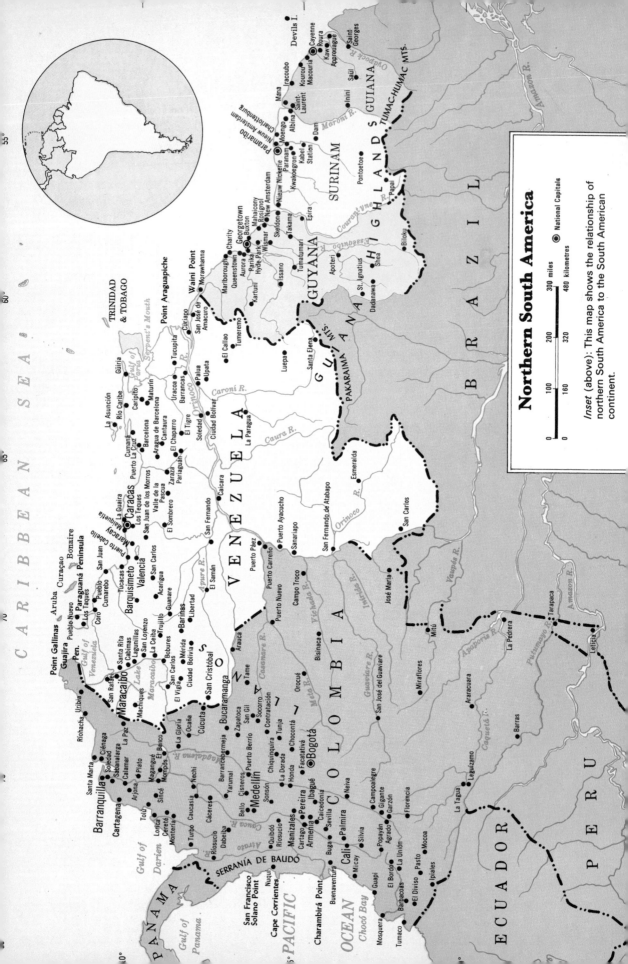

Northern South America

Inset (above): This map shows the relationship of
northern South America to the South American
continent.

● National Capitals

| 0 | 100 | 200 | 300 miles |
| 0 | 160 | 320 | 480 kilometres |

CARIBBEAN SEA

PACIFIC OCEAN

Gulf of Panama

Gulf of Darien

PANAMA

San Francisco
Solano Point

Cape Corrientes

Charambirá Point

SERRANÍA DE BAUDÓ

Chocó Bay

ECUADOR

PERU

BRAZIL

COLOMBIA

VENEZUELA

GUYANA

SURINAM

FRENCH GUIANA

TRINIDAD & TOBAGO

TUMACHUMAC MTS.

GUIANA HIGHLANDS

PAKARAIMA MTS.

GUIANA MTS.

Point Gallinas

Guajira Pen.

Paraguaná Peninsula

Point Araguapiche

Waini Point

Gulf of Venezuela

Lake Maracaibo

Point of Paria

Serpent's Mouth

Aruba Curaçao Bonaire

Riohacha
Uribia
Santa Marta
Barranquilla
Cartagena
Soledad
Sabanalarga
Ciénaga
Calamar
La Paz
San Rafael
Santa Rita
Cabimas
Lagunillas
La Ceiba
Machiques
El Vigía
San Carlos
Mérida
Bobures
Trujillo
San Lorenzo
Valera
Guanare
Barinas
Libertad
El Samán
Arauca
Tame
Casanare R.
Orocué
Puerto Carreño
Puerto Páez
Puerto Nuevo
Campo Troco
Bisinaca
Meta R.
Vichada R.
Guaviare R.
Inírida R.
Mitú
Apaporis R.
La Pedrera
Tarapaca
Leticia
Putumayo R.
Amazon R.
Vaupés R.
José María
San Fernando de Atabapo
Esmeralda
San Carlos
Orinoco R.
Sanariapo
Puerto Ayacucho
Caura R.
Apure R.
San Fernando
Calabozo
Caicara
El Sombrero
Zaraza
Valle de la Pascua
San Juan de los Morros
Caracas
Los Teques
La Guaira
Maiquetía
Maracay
Valencia
Barquisimeto
Tucacas
San Felipe
Acarigua
Guanare
San Carlos
Coro
Pueblo Nuevo
Los Taques
San Juan
Puerto Cabello
Cumarebo

Maracaibo
Cúcuta
San Cristóbal
Ciudad Bolivia
Ocaña
La Gloria
El Banco
Bucaramanga
San Gil
Socorro
Zapatoca
Contratación
Barrancabermeja
Puerto Berrío
Chiquinquirá
Tunja
La Dorada
Honda
Facatativá
Bogotá
Chocontá
Gigante
Campoalegre
Garzón
Florencia
Neiva
Ibagué
Caicedonia
Sevilla
Armenia
Pereira
Manizales
Cartago
Buga
Palmira
Cali
Buenaventura
Micay
Guapi
Popayán
Silvia
Agrado
La Unión
El Bordo
Pasto
Mocoa
Ipiales
El Diviso
Barbacoas
Tumaco
Mosquera

Medellín
Bello
Sonsón
Cisneros
Riosucio
Quibdó
Nuquí
Dabeiba
Cáceres
Caucasia
Nechí
Yarumal
Zaragoza
Mompós
Magangué
El Banco
Plato
Aipona
Cereté
Montería
Sincé
Tolú
Turbo
Lorica
Riosucio
Atrato R.
Cauca R.
Magdalena R.

La Asunción
Río Caribe
Güiria
Carúpano
Cumaná
Maturín
Caripito
Cantaura
Aragua de Barcelona
Barcelona
El Chaparro
Pariaguán
El Tigre
Soledad
Ciudad Bolívar
Barrancas
Tucupita
Curiapo
San José de Amacuro
Uracoa
Palua
Upata
El Callao
Tumeremo
Santa Elena
Luepa
Dadanawa
Shea
St. Ignatius
Apoteri
Tumatumari
Issano
Kurtini
Kartuni
Hyde Park
Parika
Buxton
Georgetown
Aurora
Mahaicony
Wismar
New Amsterdam
Mariborough
Queenstown
Charity
Morawhanna
Biloku
Papai
Kabel
Station
Kwakoegron
Paranam
Nieuw Nickerie
Skeldon
Wageningen
Essequibo R.
Corantyne R.
Berbice R.
Courantyne R.

Paramaribo
Nieuw Amsterdam
Charlottenburg
Albina
Moengo
Saint-Laurent
Mana
Iracoubo
Kourou
Macouria
Cayenne
Roura
Approuague
Saint-Georges
Saül
Inini
Devils I.
Kaw
Pontoetoe
Oyapock R.
Maroni R.
Amazon R.

In villages like this, Surinam's 'Negroes' carry on the way of life of their African ancestors.

Guiana, Guyana, Surinam

These three countries are densely forested regions. The Spanish and Portuguese conquerors disliked forests and made no serious attempt to settle there. When settlers came from Northern Europe, the Spanish and Portuguese did not take the trouble to drive them out.

In the seventeenth century Surinam (formerly Dutch Guiana) belonged to the British, who, however, exchanged it for the Dutch colonies on the Hudson River, which, as a matter of fact, they had already taken over. The Dutch were convinced that Surinam was the more valuable.

Guiana (formerly French Guiana) is the smallest of the three with an area of 35,000 square miles (91,000 sq km).

Surinam covers 63,037 square miles (163,265 sq km) and independent Guyana (formerly British Guiana) 83,000 square miles (215,000 sq km).

More than half the inhabitants of Surinam and Guyana are East Indians. Most of the remainder are Negroes with a certain number of mixed origin and a few American Indians such as Arawaks, Caribs, etc. The population of Guiana is mostly Negro.

In the whole of Guiana, nine-tenths of the population live in one-hundredth part of the country, the mountains being too rugged for settlement. The population of Guiana is only 49,200 and over half lives in Cayenne, which is the capital and the only town of any consequence. Surinam is much more densely populated with about 400,000 inhabitants. More than a third of them live in the capital, Paramaribo. The population of

Canal barges take sugar-cane to the refinery in the marshy lowlands of Guyana.

Freighters carry bauxite from Guyana and Surinam to aluminium refineries in North America.

Guyana is nearly 740,000. Most people live and work on the sugar plantations on the coast in the neighbourhood of Georgetown, the capital, and the only other town of size, New Amsterdam.

By far the most valuable resource of Surinam is bauxite, the principal ore in aluminium. There are five aluminium refineries and Surinam is, in fact, one of the world's leading bauxite producers. This mineral is also produced in large quantities in Guyana. Mining for gold and diamonds is carried out in Guyana, and a little gold is found in Guiana.

Plywood is made in Surinam. The Dutch government is now surveying the forests with a view to controlling and conserving the timber resources of the country. Timber is a valuable product of Guyana, too. There are many lumber mills on the coast, which prepare it for shipping.

The largest export from Guyana is raw sugar and its products, rum and molasses. The chief crop in Surinam is rice, but fruit and various other crops are grown along the coast. In Guiana the people only grow enough for their own subsistence. The only food product exported is shrimps, which are sent to the United States.

Buxton village in Guyana is a typical Asian Indian village. These women are Hindus.

This farmer in Surinam threshes his rice by letting cattle trample the grain from the chaff.

The city of Medellin, in a high mountain valley, is a busy market and manufacturing city in Colombia.

Venezuela and Colombia

The early Spaniards, exploring the region round Lake Maracaibo, found Indian villages built on piles in the shallow water. It was this discovery which prompted the name of Little Venice or Venezuela. Colombia was named after Christopher Columbus. The people in these two countries live in the mountains. In Venezuela the greater part live in the Venezuelan Highlands, a continuation of the eastern chain of the Andes. The Guiana Highlands, on the other hand, which occupy the southern half of the country, are practically uninhabited. In Colombia most of the people live in narrow mountain valleys. The great lowland of the Orinoco, south-east of the Andes, which constitutes two-thirds of the country, is almost uninhabited.

The Venezuelan coastal range rises abruptly from the narrow coastal plain. The latter is very hot and dry, but the mountains are cool and have plenty of rain. Almost all the activity and half the total population of the country is concentrated here. In one of the valleys of this range is Lake Valencia and the town of the same name. In another is Caracas, the capital of the country, standing about 3,000 feet (900 m) above sea-level and with a climate like perpetual spring. It has a population of over 2.2 million.

Bogota, the capital of Colombia, is also a mountain town, being in the eastern chain of the Andes. It is a very inaccessible capital, but flourishes as a home of art and learning.

Two-thirds of the people of Colombia work on the land, more of which is being used as the roads improve. More than four-fifths of the country's exports are agricultural. In Venezuela, on the other hand, only half the people are on the land. Oil and other minerals make up more than 95 per cent of the exports, although the government has called for diversification.

Oil production is quite a recent development in Venezuela, which is now the world's fifth largest producer. It is extracted in the region round Lake Maracaibo.

Since Lake Maracaibo was too shallow for shipping, a refinery and a loading port capable of taking ocean-going ships was built on the western side of the Paraguana Peninsula. A pipe-line runs from the wells to the refinery. The lake

Iron ore from Cerro Bolivar is loaded aboard ocean-going freighters at Puerto Ordaz, on the Orinoco River. From here it is shipped to steel mills in Pennsylvania and Alabama.

This brightly lit Venezuelan oil refinery works a busy round-the-clock schedule.

Shallow Lake Maracaibo's great oil field is tapped by oil derricks standing far out from shore.

has been dredged, however, and since 1956 ships have been able to get in to load oil, coffee, and other products.

The mountains north-east of the lake were, until recently, a dry, desolate, and almost uninhabited area. Now it has been provided with roads, and a huge oil refinery and petro-chemical complex has been built. In fact, a vast industrial centre is being planned which will bring prosperity to the region. Oil and natural gas have also been found on the Orinoco plains. The oil is piped to the coast for shipping, and the gas supplies the towns.

Oil wells exist also in Colombia near the Venezuelan frontier and in the Magdalena valley. A pipe-line runs from the wells to the coast.

Until the second half of the nineteenth century no one except a few explorers had ever been into the heavily forested mountain area of south-east Venezuela, which is part of the Guianà Highlands. Then rich veins of gold were discovered at El Callao, and Sosa Mendez. Today gold is exported with manganese, nickel, coal, and phosphates.

Rich deposits of iron ore were discovered in the mountains, and two private companies are working mines near the Caroni River. A state-owned steel industry has also been established near Puerto Ordaz, and as a result heavy industry is being developed.

In Colombia a steel mill has recently been built north-east of Bogota, where nearly all the raw materials for steel manufacture are available. There are emerald mines in the same area near Bogota, but they only work intermittently. Another important mining region of Colombia is the thinly settled Atrato Valley in the north-west of the country, near the Panamanian frontier. Here gold and platinum are found. Colombia has long been one of the leading platinum producing countries, and now the Atrato Valley gold mines promise to be the richest in South America.

In Colombia, commerce and industry are chiefly concentrated in the isolated region of Antioquia in the central chain of the Andes. The towns of this region are built in the narrow valleys carved by the rivers. Travel is so difficult over the steep mountains that the region was formerly almost completely cut off from the rest of the country. The leading industry is weaving, which is centred on the town of Medellin. About half the industrial workers are employed in textile mills. Other manufactures include drugs, chemicals, and electrical appliances.

The biggest agricultural area of Venezuela is the Valley of Valencia and its surrounding slopes. Here cotton is grown

The mine at Paz del Rio supplies iron ore for Colombia's newly developed steel industry.

The trampling hoofs of horses thresh wheat spread in a circle of stones in the Venezuelan Andes.

for the textile factories of Valencia and Caracas; here food is grown for the towns and dairy produce raised.

Coffee and cacao (cocoa beans) are grown on plantations. Colombian coffee is of outstanding quality. It is the second largest producer and leads in mild coffee exports. There are large coffee plantations along parts of the Magdalena Valley, where it can grow on slopes unsuitable for most other uses. Coffee is one of the chief earners of foreign currency.

Large numbers of cattle are raised in Venezuela and Colombia. Sometimes they graze in the hot lowlands, but they do better in the cooler climate of the mountain pastures. The plains of the Orinoco Valley are far from ideal cattle ranges. The grasses are low in food value; in the dry season, they are too hard to be eaten, and in the wet season, there are extensive floods.

Communications

Communications have always been a big problem in Venezuela and Colombia. In Colombia especially, the high mountains divide the population into isolated groups, which are only now beginning to be able to make contact with each other.

In Venezuela the building of roads and railways was found to be so expensive that most goods were still being carried by pack-mules until a few years ago. One of the first roads practicable in all weathers was that built from La Guaira on the coast to Caracas in the mountains, six miles away. To cover this distance the road had to wind upwards for 23 miles (37 km) to get over a mountain pass 3,400 feet (1,040 m) high. Since then a much shorter road has been built, going through the mountains with the aid of bridges and tunnels instead of over them.

In the mountain district of Colombia, the river Magdalena has for long provided the main highway to the sea. In its long course, it passes through many of the most productive areas of the country, but it is not always a good highway. For one thing it is subject to drought in the dry season. For another thing, there are impassable areas, particularly at Honda. In such areas, goods are unshipped and carried overland between one navigable section of the river and the next. Despite these problems, the river is navigable for 900 miles (1,450 km), and steamers ascend to La Dorada, 592 miles (952 km) from the mouth at Barranquilla. The port of Cartagena, which has the best harbour on the north coast of South America, is linked by canals with the Magdalena and also by an all-weather road with the town of Medellin.

When coffee berries turn cherry-red they are ready for picking. Coffee beans are their seeds.

Colombia was the first country of the Western Hemisphere to have a commercial air service, and it is still a leading country in the sphere of air travel.

Venezuela has preferred to concentrate on building arterial roads practicable in all weathers. It now has a large network of them, and road transport has developed enormously.

Colombian workers spread coffee beans in the sun to dry. Before roasting the beans are a pale colour.

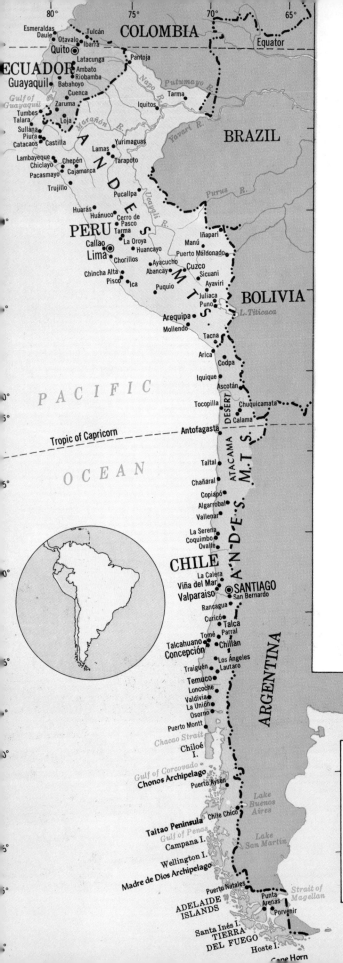

Three Countries of the Andes — Ecuador, Peru and Chile

The countries of the Andes have small populations, but, as so much of their area is forested and mountainous, the habitable parts are relatively crowded. Many of the 6 million people of Ecuador and the 14 million people of Peru live in tight clusters in the valleys between high mountain peaks. Most of the rest live on the parts of the coast that do not suffer from being either too wet or too dry.

Nine-tenths of the 10 million people of Chile live in the central third of the country. Nothing can be grown in the northern desert and the south is too wet and stormy. Most of the people are mestizo (mixed race).

In Ecuador and Peru, four-fifths of the people are pure Indians (Amerindians). Most of them are descended from the Indians who inhabited the country at the time of the Incas.

The Incas were skilful engineers. They paved their roads and built bridges across gorges. They dug out terraces on mountain slopes to prevent the soil being washed away. They made irrigation ditches for dry areas. They had no carts

Countries of the Andes

```
0    100   200   300   400   500 miles
|----|----|----|----|----|
0   160   320   480   640   800 kilometres
```
◉ National Capitals

Inset (left): This map shows the relationship of Ecuador, Peru and Chile to the South American continent.

The volcanoes in Ecuador tower over the valley

as they did not understand the use of a wheel, yet they were capable of moving ten-ton blocks of stone for long distances to use for building. These blocks are so closely fitted together that is impossible to insert the blade of a knife between them. Buildings so constructed have withstood earthquakes that have caused modern buildings to crumble.

The Incas designed beautiful pottery and cloth, and made exquisite objects of gold and silver. Although they had no writing they managed to keep accounts using a system of knots. Their calculations followed a decimal system, and they knew a great deal about the stars.

The Araucanian Indians who inhabited Chile were nomadic hunters and fishers, but they did a certain amount of farming as they moved from place to place. The northern Araucanians were conquered by the Incas, but the southern tribes, who lived in the forests, knew how to defend themselves so well among the trees that they were never conquered. The hardiest and bravest Spanish soldiers were sent to conquer these Indians, and many of them married Araucanian women. It is from these mixed marriages that the mestizos, found today in central Chile, are descended. About two-thirds of the Chileans are mestizos.

The Indian farmers of Ecuador and Peru live mostly in high mountain valleys and are very poor.

So mountainous are these areas that it is practically impossible to transport any

A stream cuts its way through the Andes in Peru, providing irrigation for valley farms.

In primitive parts of Peru, potatoes are planted much as they were in the days of the Incas.

produce, so the peasants grow just what they need for their own use.

Crops change progressively with the altitude. Potatoes can be grown up to 14,000 feet (4,200 m), where the climate is suitable. Below them barley is grown and, below the barley, wheat. Below 11,000 feet (3,300 m) the peasants grow maize and lucerne, which is a clover-like plant grown for fodder. Cotton and sugar-cane are grown in lower valleys.

Only the cattle are taken to market, for they can generally be driven there down the mountain tracks. They lose so much weight on the trip, however, that they have to be fattened again before being sold.

Many of the Indians are tenant farmers. These are descendants of the original population whom the Spaniards turned into slaves. They work under large landowners descended from the conquistadors. They have been emancipated from slavery but they are still very badly off.

Other Indians work their own land or they farm co-operatively in groups, much as they did during the Inca Empire. They know hardly anything of modern farming methods. In some cases, instead of ploughs drawn by oxen, they use small foot ploughs or even hoes. Corn is winnowed by tossing it up in the wind, or threshed under foot by animals on a threshing floor.

There are a few commercial farms in the mountains of Peru. The produce is not sent down to the coast, but sold to mining towns nearby.

Cattle can graze on areas too high even for potatoes. But some slopes, especially in Peru, are too high for cattle and are used for grazing sheep, alpacas, llamas, and vicunas. Shepherds keep flocks at heights sometimes of as much as 17,000 feet (5,100 m).

On the coastal plain of Ecuador, the population is chiefly mestizo and Negro. On their small farms they grow bananas, coffee, and rice. Negroes were the first to

Macchu Picchu was a lost city, built before the time of the Incas. It has only recently been rediscovered.

A herd of llamas and sheep passes by ancient Incan irrigation terraces cut into the mountain slopes.

This open cast copper mine at Chuquicamata, Chile, is one of the largest in the world.

In a Peruvian mountain valley 15,000 ft (4,572 m) up, this mine produces tin, gold, silver, lead and zinc.

grow bananas in this area. Now they are the country's biggest export crop. Shipping them is difficult and expensive, however, so that banana-growing is not very profitable. They are carried by mules or porters, loaded on to lorries, and driven to river-boats or barges. On the coast they have to be transferred from the one set of boats into banana boats lying at anchor, as in the ports the water is too shallow for them to come alongside.

The most fertile region in Ecuador is the plain north-east of Guayaquil. The climate is hot and moist, and the soil is rich. Coffee and rice are grown here. But fresh land is cleared for each crop, instead of fertilising the land and using it again and again. This wasteful method of using the soil is gradually spoiling much of the land and landscape of South America.

It is hard to believe that the strip of desert on the west coast of Peru could be any use for farming. However, along the coast are forty oases stretching like green stripes across the dry land. Mountain streams cross the desert to the coast, and their water is used to irrigate the land. In this cool, dry, cloudy region, cotton, sugar-cane and rice are grown. And in the middle section there are also vineyards and vegetable farms to supply the towns.

The cool coastal climate along the Peruvian coast is caused by the cold ocean current (the Humboldt current) that sweeps up the shore from the south. This water abounds in fish, which are eaten by the millions of sea birds which nest on the off-shore islands. The birds' droppings form guano, the valuable fertiliser, which is one of Peru's exports. Peru is also an important fishing country and supplies 45 per cent of the world's fish meal for fodder.

The landowners of central Chile are much closer to their land, and to their tenants, than most of the other South American landowners. They live on their haciendas instead of enjoying the comforts and pleasures of a town. Many of them have as much Indian blood in their veins as their tenants.

The owner raises cattle and grows fodder for them. And he also plants wheat. Chile and Argentina are the only countries in South America where more wheat is grown than maize. On small farms fruit and olives are often grown instead of grain. Chile does not grow enough food to feed her population, and has to import two-thirds of her needs every year.

Grapes grow particularly well in the central valley. Almost every farm and hacienda has vineyards, some of them very large. The raisins and wine made from Chilean grapes are famous. They are sold to North America and Europe as well as to South American countries.

The hacienda system is changing in Chile. Many of the large estates are being divided and sold to small farmers. Some people have pushed southward to clear areas of the forest on which to make farms. They were led by small groups of Germans, who have opened up the country, building good roads and strong permanent homes. Enormous numbers of trees have to be cut down to make a farm. Most of the wood is used for fuel.

Four-fifths of the population of Ecuador live and work on the land. The country is not devoid of mineral wealth, however. There is gold near Esmeraldas, though the Spaniards did not find it. There is an oil field west of Guayaquil on the Santa Elena peninsula, and near the river Putumayo. Copper, iron, lead and coal are found in the mountains and the empty country to the east.

An oil refinery at Talara, Peru, processes oil from several fields in the north of Peru.

Ores mined nearby are processed in these smelters at Cerro de Pasco. The work is done by skilled Indians.

The people of Peru are also chiefly occupied with agriculture, though somewhat less than their neighbour is.

Minerals account for 40 per cent of Peru's exports. Copper and iron ore are produced near the coast, but the chief mining towns of Peru are high in the mountains. In the seventeenth century an enormous deposit of silver ore was found near Cerro de Pasco. This silver mine was worked for hundreds of years. The silver was smelted and made into rough bars. These were carried down a mountain track from a height of nearly 15,000 feet (4,500 m) to Lima, 200 miles (320 km) away.

Eventually the deposit began to be exhausted. Mining had practically ceased when, in the early years of this century, a mining company took over the area hoping to find other minerals. An amazing railway was built up the mountains from Lima, going over innumerable bridges and along rocky ledges cut out of the mountainside, winding through spiral tunnels and zig-zagging up the slopes. It was a very expensive undertaking, but it has been proved worth while, for it has served a double purpose, taking equipment to the mines and bringing down the ores.

Many valuable minerals have been found in the mines round Cerro de Pasco. There are deposits of gold, lead, zinc, bismuth, diamonds, titanium, iron ore, vanadium, and new veins of silver have been discovered. Copper, however, is the most important metal in Peru and one of the chief exports.

Coal, of excellent quality, has been found near Cerro de Pasco and at Alta Chicama. This is an important discovery, because South America has so little. The supply is estimated to be considerable, and Peru is likely to become the leading producer in South America. There are oil wells on the coast and also on the continental shelf in the extreme north.

417

Most of the exports from Chile's fertile Middle Valley go through the port of Valparaiso.

Much of Chile's mineral wealth lies below the Atacama Desert. In colonial times this desert was used as a highway, but otherwise no one went near it.

The first minerals to be worked were silver and copper. But the prospectors who located these metals also found deposits of sodium nitrate in the dried up lake beds of the desert. For a time the demand for nitrates as fertilisers and for the manufacture of explosives created a nitrate boom which made Chile prosperous. But this came to an end when a way was found to extract nitrogen from the air. Now the Atacama supplies only one-tenth of the world's nitrates. Iodine is a by-product.

At present the largest mineral export of the country is copper. Chile has 40 per cent of the world supply. Most of it comes from three mines high in the Andes, two in the Atacama region and the third south of Santiago. Chile also has some coal, and iron ore has taken over from nitrates as the second largest export. Oil output is small, but increasing. A nationally owned steel works has been built near Concepción. Sulphur too is found in the Andes, but it is too difficult to exploit it successfully to become very profitable. The deposits are found inside the craters of extremely high volcanoes. A little sulphur is extracted, but the high altitude makes mining difficult. Accordingly Chile's exports of sulphur are small. Gold, silver, and other metals are also produced.

Ecuador has very little industry of any kind. Panama hats are made in several places, and cloth and leather goods are produced in the capital, Quito.

There is considerably more industry in Peru and it is the fastest growing sector of the economy. The capital, Lima, has long been the centre of government, social life, and commerce, and now with Callao it has 70 per cent of the industrial activity of the country. It has many small factories, engaged in such things as food-processing and weaving and the manufacture of soap, leather goods, vehicle assembly, and electrical goods.

In Chile about 65 per cent of the total population live in towns, which are growing fast. Santiago, the capital, is a sprawling mass of new buildings and factories which dwarf the town.

Valparaiso, the port of Santiago, was built on the coast at the foot of a steep incline. As the city grew it crept up the slope. In the modern town there are many parts to which people travel not by bus but by lift. Two other towns which are rapidly becoming industrialised are Concepción and Valdivia. The lure of the factory is bringing many people from the country into the town.

The industries of central Chile use raw materials from many parts of the country. Grapes come from local vineyards. Wool is brought down mountain tracks from the upper reaches of the Andes, and hides are similarly brought down to the tanneries. Corn is made into flour and beer. In Valdivia there are furniture factories using wood from local forests, a steel industry, textiles, and wood pulp.

The Far South

Tierra del Fuego, which means the Land of Fire, is an island at the extreme tip of South America.

The extreme south is a region of snow-covered mountains and glaciers, of storms and pounding seas.

The town of Ushuaia, on Tierra del Fuego, is the most southerly town in the world. A more important town is Punta Arenas, on the northern side of the Magellan Strait.

Punta Arenas is the only important centre of this region. It stands on the only part of Chile that lies east of the Andes. This region is sheltered from wind and rain by the mountains. To the north of the town is good sheep-rearing country, and as many as 3 million sheep are kept and reared there.

During the Second World War oil was discovered on Tierra del Fuego, and there are now a hundred wells in an area that was uninhabited a generation ago.

Ushuaia in Argentine Tierra del Fuego is the southernmost permanent town in the world.

Cattle are brought to this part of the Argentine pampa to be fattened before they are sold.

Argentina

Next to Brazil, Argentina is the biggest country in South America. It has a million square miles (2.8 million sq km) and 23 million people, that is to say nearly a

A group of Argentine gauchos prepares to cook the evening meal over a fire on the pampa.

sixth of the total area of South America and almost a sixth of the total population. Unlike most South Americans, the Argentines are accustomed to prosperity. Most of the people can read and write. Only a quarter of them work on the land.

Over 90 per cent of the population is of European origin. There are hardly any Negroes, and most of the mestizo population is along the borders of other countries.

The western frontier of Argentina is for the most part in the Andes. It is very dry in the north, but further south there are oases in the foothills near the Sierra de Cordoba.

Tucuman was once a fortress at the southern end of the great Inca road from Cuzco in the Andes. Later it became a centre at which travellers fitted themselves out for journeys to the east or the west. Now it is the centre of the Argentine sugar plantations. Protected by the mountains, the region enjoys a warm climate with abundant rain; it never freezes. A little further on, the climate is either too dry or too cold.

South of Tucuman are the oases of the dry belt. Each river that comes down from the mountains is used to irrigate a strip of land. Many Italians live in the settlements round these oases. The largest are San Juan, Mendoza, and San Rafael. Their most lucrative crop is grapes.

An important oil field has been found in north-west Argentina, and uranium has been discovered in the Andean foothills. There are bauxite deposits at San Isidro.

The Entre Rios province, which lies between the Paraná and Uruguay rivers, is rolling, green, well-wooded country. Where the Paraná and Iquazú rivers drop over the edge of the Paraná Plateau there are magnificent waterfalls.

The northern part of Entre Rios is cattle country. The southern part is one of Argentina's biggest sheep, sunflower, and flax districts. Maté, cultivated in the far north, is a shrub of the holly family, used for making a sort of tea very popular in Argentina, Uruguay, and Brazil. There are few people on the maté plantations except at harvest when people pour in from as far as Brazil and Paraguay to pick the leaves.

The Gran Chaco is an enormous lowlying area shared by Argentina, Bolivia, and Paraguay. The Argentinian part is covered with scrub and grass. In the east the rivers overflow their banks in summer covering vast areas with water. The Pilcomayo River which forms part of the frontier between Argentina and Paraguay changes its course so often at the time of flood that the frontier is constantly shifting. Cotton is planted on some of the shifting floodlands after the water has drained off.

People come from far away to harvest maté leaves, from which a popular beverage is made.

The scrub forests of the Chaco contain millions of quebracho trees, which yield tannin for tanning leather. Their wood, which is very hard, is used for railway sleepers. The mills which extract the tannin require a great deal of water and have to be built on rivers.

Heavy quebracho logs are loaded on to carriers by primitive methods, then hauled by oxen.

BOLIVIA
PARAGUAY

Inset (below): This map shows the relationship of the southern countries east of the Andes to the South American continent.

Tropic of Capricorn

La Quiaca
Aguaray
Tartagal
Orán
Embarcación
Tilcara
Ledesma
Jujuy
Salta
General Güemes
Las Lomitas

San José de Metán
Monte Quemado
Pirané
Formosa
Puerto Iguazú

Antofagasta

Tafí Viejo
Tucumán
Resistencia
Corrientes
Posadas

Bella Vista
Monteros
Concepción
La Banda
Santiago del Estero
Añatuya
Bella Vista
Santo Tomé

Catamarca

Chilecito
La Rioja
Reconquista
Goya
Mercedes
Curuzú-Cuatiá
Paso de los Libres

Jáchal
Deán Funes
San José de Feliciano
Monte Caseros
Artigas

Cruz del Eje
Rafaela
La Paz
Rivera

Córdoba
San Francisco
Concordia
Salto

San Juan
Alta Gracia
Santa Fe
Paraná
Concepción del Uruguay
Tacuarembó
Melo

Retamito
Villa Dolores
Villa María
Diamante
Paysandú
Mirim Lake

Mendoza
San Luis
Bell Ville
Casilda
Rosario
Gualeguaychú
Fray Bentos
Treinta y Tres

San Martín
Río Cuarto
San Nicolás
Zárate
Durazno

Mercedes
Venado Tuerto
Pergamino
Tigre
BUENOS AIRES
Minas

San Rafael
Laboulaye
Rufino
Mercedes
Avellaneda
Rocha

Chivilcoy
Lomas de Zamora
La Plata
Montevideo

Pico
Bragado
Chascomús

Malargüe
Trenque Lauquén

Santa Rosa
Saladillo
Dolores

PAMPAS
Azul
Tandil
Ayacucho

Coronel Suárez
Juárez

El Huecú
Coronel Pringles
Mar del Plata

Zapala
Tres Arroyos
Lobería
Necochea

Neuquén
Bahía Blanca

Colorado R.
Bahía Blanca

Coronel Pringles

San Antonio Oeste
Carmen de Patagones
Viedma

San Matías Gulf

Puerto Pirámides

Esquel
Trelew
Rawson
Las Plumas
Paso de los Indios
Chubut R.
Chico R.

Sarmiento
Comodoro Rivadavia
Gulf of San Jorge

Deseado R.
Caleta Olivia
Fitz Roy

Tamel Aike
San Julián

L. Viedma
Río Chico
Santa Cruz R.
L. Argentino
Bahía Grande

Gallegos R.
Río Gallegos
Strait of Magellan

Río Grande

TIERRA DEL FUEGO

Ushuaia

Cape Horn

PACIFIC OCEAN

CHILE

ANDES MOUNTAINS

ARGENTINA

PATAGONIA

CHACO

Bermejo R.
Pilcomayo R.
Paraná R.
Uruguay R.
Río Salado
Río Dulce
Río Salado
Río Negro
Río de la Plata
Negro R.
Colorado R.

BRAZIL

URUGUAY

ATLANTIC OCEAN

FALKLAND ISLANDS (Br.)
West Falkland I.
East Falkland I.
Stanley
Falkland Sound

Southern South America

0	100	200	300 miles
0	160	320	480 kilometres

◉ National Capitals

© Copyright 1960 by Map Pro

Cotton is also grown in this region, mostly by squatters, who clear the land or move in after the wood-cutters have cleared it.

The dry southern part of Argentina is called Patagonia. Only one per cent of the population live there. There are constant gales, which whip up waves on the lakes at the foot of the Andes. Spectacular mountains are covered with glaciers. Practically the only habitable places in Patagonia are the gorges that cross the dry plateau.

The sheep ranches are enormous. They cover thousands of square miles, and usually have their headquarters in a gorge where there is a supply of water. Sheep are also raised on Tierra del Fuego.

The pampas are the south-eastern

These cattle are bred from prime English stock brought into Argentina in the nineteenth century.

part of the great Argentine plains. The Dry Pampa where rainfall is scanty is to the west and south. The Humid Pampa is to the east. The Humid Pampa is a boundless plain, which was covered with rustling grass when the early explorers

On a sheep ranch in dry, wind-swept Patagonia, water is pumped by a windmill.

Teams of mules, guided by their riders, pull the ploughs on an Argentine sugar-cane plantation.

Cattle ranges in Argentina's dry north-west depend on streams from the Andes for irrigation.

came. The winters are mild and the summers are hot. The rainfall is plentiful. The growing season is longer in the north than in the south and west.

This entire area, except for a few hills, is covered with deep fertile soil. It is made of dust blown from the dry west and south and silt carried down by the rivers. The Argentinian cattle ranchers improved the quality of their beef by breeding from British cattle. These were not as hardy as the native breed, and special food had to be grown for them. Labour for arable farming came from Italy, Spain, and many other countries. Some of the tenants planted their own wheat, and eventually wheat became a very important crop.

It is difficult to maintain good roads on the Pampa. Where there is no grass, the fine soil blows away in the dry season and turns to deep mud as soon as it rains. But building railways, on such level ground, is a very simple matter. Railways fan out from all the Pampa ports into the agricultural areas, covering far more ground than the arterial roads.

The Humid Pampa today is divided into four agricultural regions. In the east

cattle are reared for beef, and sheep for wool and mutton. Butter too has become an important product. The western and southern parts are entirely devoted to wheat, lucerne, and cattle. This is the area that borders on the Dry Pampa. In the north the maize region round Rosario is thickly settled by Italians. All round Buenos Aires there is a region of vegetable and fruit farming. Some of the market gardens reach right into the edges of the city.

Newly sheared sheep are gathered near the headquarters of a Patagonian sheep ranch.

Buenos Aires attracted the early colonists because its harbour had deep enough water for their ships. With the development of the Humid Pampa, it has become the biggest town in Latin America. The port, however, is not deep enough for modern ships without constant dredging. In 1935 an entirely new port was built directly north of the old one.

Argentina heads the South American countries in the matter of trade. It has small amounts of oil, coal, and steel. But it ships almost all the wheat, linseed, and maize, most of the meat, and more than half the wool, hides, and other grains that leave the continent. No other country in the world exports so much fresh meat.

Uruguay

This, the smallest of the South American republics, has an area of only 72,000 square miles (186,470 sq km) and a population of over 3 million. But Uruguay makes full use of her land; no part of it is unoccupied. The capital is Montevideo, with a population of just over a million. The Uruguayans are mostly white, being of Spanish and Italian descent. There are a few whites from other European countries, and a certain number of Negroes. Near the frontiers are some mestizos.

The country of Uruguay is an intermediate region, sloping down from the Brazilian plateaus to the Humid Pampa of the Argentine. A strip of low land runs

The modern skyline of Buenos Aires illustrates how much this city has grown in recent years, to become the largest city in Latin America. The population of Argentina is mainly European in origin, the immigrants coming principally from Italy and Spain.

Hides are unloaded at a Buenos Aires tannery. The bales hold wool for textile factories.

pampas, but grassy slopes and wooded valleys. There are no extremes of temperature, and rainfall is adequate throughout the year.

British traders were the first to realise the value of the grassland of Argentina and Uruguay. In 1840 they introduced a good breed of sheep for wool, and within ten years there were about 2 million sheep being reared in Uruguay.

Until the middle of the nineteenth century the millions of cattle reared on the unfenced pastures of Uruguay were used only for tallow, hides, and salt beef. Eventually meat processing plants were built and, at the same time, barbed-wire fences were put up to separate cattle, so as to make scientific breeding possible. Refrigeration made it possible to ship meat to other countries. British breeds replaced the native Uruguayan cattle.

Today Uruguay has more livestock in proportion to its population than any other country in the world except New Zealand. Animals and animal produce

down the Atlantic coast and along the Rio de la Plata, but most of the country is hilly. There are no great plains like the

Cattle graze beside a stream on the vast stretches of Argentina's western pampas.

These Uruguayan gauchos herd horses. Much land in Uruguay is used for horse and cattle raising.

These sheep are in an open field, but Uruguay builds fenced runways for them in settled areas.

This hydro-electric station supplies much of Montevideo's power.

This Uruguayan market-gardener raises vegetables and potatoes for the city markets.

account for 70 per cent of exports. About four-fifths of the land is used for grazing; the remaining fifth, in the south, being used for raising crops, including rice, sugarbeet, grapes, and fruit trees.

The railways in the country were British built. There is a state-owned civil airline to the interior. Roads surfaced with gravel have recently been built and much of the country's transportation is now motorised.

Montevideo is the political, commercial and industrial centre of the country. Its industry is of recent growth, but there are many factories, most of which use local material. Electricity is derived from two power-dams on the Rio Negro and from a power-station in the town which uses imported coal. Montevideo is the base of a fishing fleet, a popular holiday resort, and a port for the river traffic from the interior.

It is unusual for a country in which almost half the workers are on the land to be prosperous, but this is the case in Uruguay, where food is cheap and there is a welfare state rather like the one in Britain.

Brazil, the Giant of South America

Brazil contains almost half the population of South America. The United States of Brazil is larger than the United States of America excluding Alaska. If we exclude Venezuela and the Guianas, Brazil is as large as all the other South American countries put together. It is composed of twenty-two States, a Federal District, and four Territories. Brazil is the only independent country of South America where the official language is not Spanish but Portuguese. The bulk of the inhabitants of Brazil are concentrated on or near the coast.

Brazil has more land capable of being farmed than any other country of its size, and agriculture accounts for 75 per cent of its income. It has the finest natural harbour and the longest navigable river in the world. The resources of its forests are endless, and it has great stores of iron ore and manganese. It has not attracted more settlers because its wealth is almost inaccessible and difficult to exploit.

The coast consists for the most part of steep cliffs. They are especially steep behind the two largest towns, São Paulo and Rio de Janeiro. Most of the rivers rise in the highlands behind the coast, but instead of running towards the sea they wander off for hundreds of miles, to join either the Parana River in the south or the Amazon in the north. They are therefore useless as a means of transport from the coast.

The Amazon, the longest navigable river in the world, wanders endlessly through the immense forests of the interior whose trees are of great value. It might provide a highway for this timber, but unfortunately the wealth of the forests is very scattered indeed, and there are too few people living there to collect it. Only when the Amazon region is fully developed will the river prove its true worth as an inland waterway.

Tropical Recife is a port named after the coral reef which shelters its spacious harbour.

In Brazil's most southerly state, Rio Grande do Sul, most people live in valleys and lowlands.

The Amazon

The Amazon country of Brazil is a vast area of forests and rivers. Upstream, the Amazon plain is 800 miles (1,300 km) wide. It narrows as it passes between the Brazilian and Guiana Highlands, then broadens again to occupy the greater part of the north coast of Brazil. In spite of the enormous amount of silt brought down each year, the river has never succeeded in forming a delta. That is because of a phenomenon known as a tidal bore, which is a wave of water five to twelve feet high, which advances upstream with a roar at a speed of from ten .to fifteen miles an hour. Fourteen great rivers discharge into the Amazon, and a multitude of secondary rivers which in any other part of the world would themselves be called great rivers.

When the Amazon overflows its banks, as it does regularly, it floods large areas on either side of the river. Some of the silt brought down by the Amazon is deposited on the flooded surface. This makes the soil very rich, but the land is flooded so often that farmers can make very little use of it.

Most people think that the climate of the tropical Amazon must be unbearably hot. Actually the temperature itself is not unduly high. But the air is laden with moisture, and even ordinary summer heat becomes very difficult to bear. There is no dry season here, only one that is less wet. Both in summer and winter there are sudden sharp showers, and then, with equal suddenness, the sky is clear and without clouds again.

The nights, however, are almost always brilliant and clear.

There are thousands of different sorts of trees in the forest of the Amazon Basin, but they grow quite haphazardly. Rarely can one find a number of the same sort of trees growing together. The value of some of the trees is very high indeed. But, as has already been pointed out, they are so widely scattered that it is not profitable to attempt to exploit them on a large scale.

What the forest chiefly lacks is population. There are very few areas in the world of its size which are so thinly populated. Compare it, for example, with Alaska, which is considered a very thinly populated area, with one person to about

The Amazon jungle, often so dense that travel through it is impossible, engulfs the edge of the river.

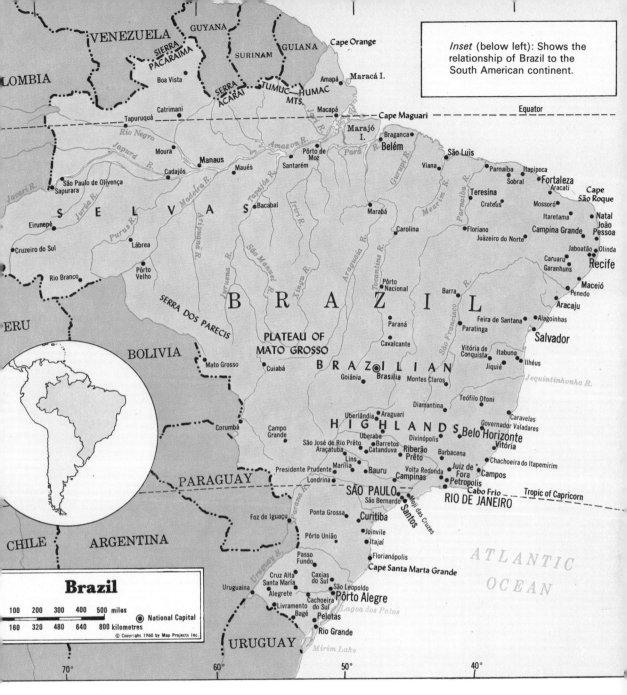

every 2½ square miles (6.5 sq km). In the Amazon basin there is one person to about every square mile (2½ sq km). Half of these live near the coast, however, so that further up the river there must often be no more than one person to every 2 or 3 square miles (5 or 7.7 sq km). Ever since the Amazon was explored attempts have been made to exploit its riches. But those who have tried have always encountered one great stumbling block: the inability of the area to support a work force.

The isolated groups of Indians that live in the forest fear the white man and avoid him. Their fears are not altogether unfounded, for the early explorers brought disease, and sold the Indians into slavery.

Even today contact with civilisation

The way of life of Amazon Indians, such as these, is now threatened by modern civilisation.

This huge opera house at Manaus was built during the Amazon rubber boom.

often seems to wither the spirit of the Indians so that many tribes have died out. Diseases like measles and influenza, to which the Indians have no natural resistance, still take a heavy toll. The more remote tribes are fiercely independent, and a few are still untouched by civilisation. This cannot be regretted since it has proved so mixed a blessing to many Indian tribes.

Rubber gatherers in the Amazon jungle smoke the latex in huts until it can be formed into a ball.

Amazon Forests

Rubber trees have the largest place in the story of the Amazon forests. When the world began to be in need of rubber, around the middle of the nineteenth century, Brazil possessed most of the rubber trees in the world. People rushed to buy land along the Amazon, then set out on a frantic search for hands to work for them. Indians from the eastern side of the Andes, where law did not run, were seized and enslaved. And workers came from the dry areas in the east at the rate of 20,000 a year.

Most of the towns along the Amazon were originally bases for the rubber traffic. The biggest boom towns were Belém and Manaus.

The Brazilian rubber boom came to an end when an Englishman smuggled some seeds out of the country, and rubber plantations were started in Malaya and Sumatra. The trees on the Asian plantations yielded three to six times as much rubber as those growing wild in the Amazon forests. And workers could gather three times as much when the trees were all in one place. Within thirty years Malaya and Sumatra were producing most of the world's rubber, whereas business in Brazil had declined rapidly.

This country produces most of the Brazil nuts in the world. But the nuts are gathered from wild trees, not cultivated ones. There are farms which produce cotton, while the main food crops are manioc, maize, rice, and beans.

A new development is the growing of black pepper and jute by Japanese immigrants near Santarem. At a small factory, the jute is made into the bags in which coffee and sugar are shipped. And jute is also used for rope making. One of the most important things about the jute plantations is that for the first time the rich Brazilian flood-plains are being put to regular use.

North-eastern Brazil falls into two distinct regions climatically. Along the coast is an area that has regular rainfall. The western part alternates between long droughts and disastrous floods, in addition to which the soil is too poor for anything to grow but stunted trees and brush.

Most of eastern Brazil is mountainous, though there are a few low-lying areas along the coast. The São Francisco River rises in the Brazilian highlands, in the state of Minas Gerais, flows northward for a considerable distance, then curves eastwards to discharge itself on the east coast. It is not much used as a waterway, nor does it do much in the way of irrigation, but its power-stations supply a large part of the country's electricity.

Freighters are able to travel far up the Amazon, even to the foothills of the Andes.

Agriculture and Industry in Brazil

The early colonists soon realised that sugar-cane would grow well in the north-east. They cleared the forests around Salvador and Recife, and brought in Negro slaves to work on the plantations. These spread rapidly until all suitable land had been used up.

At the same time Portugal offered enormous grants for cattle-breeding. Cattlemen became as rich as sugar planters.

The tobacco fields of Bahia state are mostly worked by descendants of freed Negro slaves. Every inch of land is used for production, but the farms are tiny and the farmers are poor. This is the only region, apart from one other in the south, in which fertilisers are used regularly. Much of the tobacco crop is made into cigars in small local factories.

Most of the land, however, in this part of Brazil is used for the grazing of cattle and goats. The cattle are put on the better land, while the goats succeed in finding food in the poor, dry areas. In these areas, the main product is goat skins. For cattle, on the other hand, trees have to be cleared and grass planted.

Efforts have been made to control floods and to conserve water for the dry periods. In the past they have usually failed, however, because of bad planning. Dykes built along rivers have crumbled under the pressure of a flood. Reservoirs have been built where there was no suitable land to irrigate.

Some useful produce grows wild in this area: cord is made from tree cotton, hammocks of caroé fibre. Carnauba wax, of which Brazil is the chief source, is used for polishes and cosmetics and the babaçu palm gives a valuable oil. Cacao beans are grown on large plantations along the coast near Bahia. Workers come from the interior for the harvest.

New roads have been built in the north-east, an area of soil erosion and poverty and the people are now beginning to depend on the exchange of goods instead of trying to be self-sufficient in their agriculture.

South-eastern Brazil consists of the states of São Paulo, Minas Gerais, Espirito Santo, Rio de Janeiro and Guanabara. Behind them in the interior is the vast, sparsely inhabited area that forms the states of Mato Grosso and Goiás.

The state of Minas Gerais consists for the most part of large estates *(fazendas)* on which stock-breeding and dairy-farming are carried out.

The early settlements in Minas Gerais were built along roads. Colonial roads were built over the mountains, where the

People from all along the river come to sell their goods on market day in Belém.

Many homes in Manaus are small floating houses built on rafts. A dugout canoe serves as transportation, though motor boats are becoming more widespread and more people are living in permanent land-homes.

forest was thinnest. Later, railways were built on level ground, when possible. People moved towárds the railways, and many of the early settlements were abandoned. Now new arterial roads are replacing the railways.

Minas Gerais is rich in minerals. Iron and many other important metals are present, as well as precious stones. Gold and diamonds were discovered at the beginning of the eighteenth century.

The Government is now developing what is thought to be one of the richest reserves of iron ore in the world (35,000 million tons) and it has become one of the country's leading exports. A large-scale steel plant at Volta Redonda produces pig iron and steel, but coal for smelting is imported from the USA.

Rio de Janeiro is a magnificent city, built on the shores of a natural harbour. The town was originally built as a shipping port for the gold from Minas Gerais.

With a high wall of rock behind it, it was well placed for defence against Indians and Spaniards. Today it is the commercial capital of the whole country.

A harbour-side market in Salvador, Brazil.

Brasilia, the capital of Brazil, features some of the most exciting architecture to be found anywhere in the world.

The land of eastern Brazil is not all divided up into fazendas. In the Paraiba Valley which receives fertile deposits from occasional floods, modern farms have been started. In this area many farmers who had previously worked the old land-shifting cultivation method are now using more modern methods.

The State of São Paulo was first settled by adventurers who came seeking their fortunes. When the gold of Minas Gerais was found, people from all over Brazil poured into the east. The surface gold was eventually exhausted at a time when coffee became popular in Britain and North America. Accordingly, large

After the coffee beans are harvested, they must be spread in the sun to dry. Some of the 'Fazendas' have over 100,000 coffee trees.

Coffee beans must be carefully roasted so as not to spoil their flavour and aroma.

numbers moved off to the land round São Paulo city to plant coffee trees. Before long Brazil was supplying three-quarters of the world's coffee. By 1920 the country's coffee production had risen enormously. In fact it had reached a point at which Brazil was growing twice as much as the needs of the whole world.

Coffee growers began to lose money, but then a new boom started with the urgent demand for cotton. Young coffee trees were hastily pulled up to make room for cotton. Many coffee growers switched over entirely to cotton, and new plantations were started by new growers.

During the last war cotton could not be sold to Japan or Europe, and many cotton planters switched once more, this time to oranges, since Brazil is second only to the US in orange exports. Oranges may be destined to supplant cotton altogether. Already, so little cotton is being grown that local textile manufacturers are beginning to be afraid they will soon have to import it.

There are now many progressive modern farms in the state of São Paulo. The government has encouraged immigrants from Japan and Europe, and people have also come from other parts of Brazil. The farms of the Parana settlers are on the São Paulo border. Although they are actually in the state of Paraná, the roads and railways connect with São Paulo, so they look on that as their centre.

These farms have been very successful. Exhausted land has been renewed. Virgin forest is being preserved. Mixed crops are grown, instead of single crops. Fertilisers and modern machinery are used. Where the land slopes, it is terraced so that the soil will not wash off. Roads and railways are carefully organised to connect the farmers with the markets at which they must sell their produce.

But the São Paulo coffee planters still work on the fazenda system. The tenant clears the forest and plants the coffee shrub for the owner. In return he may plant his own crops between the rows until the trees begin to bear, after about five years. Then he moves on. The owner

As a result of falls like this, the state of São Paulo, utilising hydro-electric power stations, produces three-fifths of Brazil's electricity.

harvests the coffee until the crop declines, then he too moves on and starts again, on fresh land. It is a wasteful procedure.

São Paulo is the richest state in Brazil. With a population of 16.3 million it produces nearly half the coffee, more than half the cotton, and a quarter of the sugar produced by the whole country. The city of São Paulo is the largest manufacturing town in Latin America, with 50 per cent of the textile mills of Brazil and car assembly plants. The hydro-electric power-stations of the state produce three-fifths of the country's power.

We find a very different picture when we turn from this productive area to the vast highland country of Mato Grosso and Goias. Though forming more than one-fifth of the area of Brazil, these two states have only about 3 per cent of the country's population. There are a few successful farms within reach of roads, but much of the area has reverted to cattle grazing, because farmers had no means of getting their produce to any potential market.

The mining region near Corumba produces iron and manganese, and has brought sufficient prosperity to the town for an airport to have been constructed.

Central Brazil

The physical centre of Brazil lies in that vast, almost empty area, and on this spot the new capital, Brasilia, has been built. Brasilia did not grow haphazardly, but was completely planned in advance.

It was designed to house half a million government workers and those who provide them with goods and services, and it was inaugurated in April 1960. In choosing this spot for the capital the government hoped that settlers would be attracted to clear the surrounding forests and grow food for the townsfolk.

This is not the first time such an attempt has been made to open up the interior of the country. The state of Minas Gerais built a similar new capital, Belo Horizonte, but after fifty years there are still hardly any farms round this beautiful town, and all the food still has to be brought in from other areas.

Southern Brazil

Southern Brazil consists of three states, Paraná, Santa Catarina, and Rio Grande Do Sul. Plains follow the coast, except where it is flanked by the Great Escarpment. The first two states are plateaus with a few high mountains. Further to the south and west are lowlands bordering on northern Argentina and Uruguay.

The Paraná Plateau is one of the largest lava plateaus in the world. Deep gorges have been cut by the rivers that cross it. At the heads of these gorges are spectacular waterfalls with a drop of several hundred feet.

Most of the area has plentiful rainfall throughout the year. In the north are thick forests of tropical trees. In the south trees become thinner and the land is covered with grass. The cool highlands are covered with dense pine forests. The minerals of this area are mainly copper and iron, but there are also some low-grade coal deposits.

The southern Brazilians are of European, but not Portuguese descent. They are of German, Swiss, Austrian, Italian, and in Paraná, of Polish and Russian origin. These settlers were not like most of the others in Brazil. They did not expect to make a quick and easy fortune, but settled down to establish permanent homes and villages.

The first settlements in the south sponsored by the Brazilian government were often badly placed so that the farmers could not reach any market.

The new wheat growing settlements in the state of Paraná are better planned. Each settlement is located so as to have access to one of the old-established roads, and these settlements have prospered from the start.

Southern Brazil grows large quantities of rice. Here, a machine does the hard work of threshing.

Volta Redonda is a giant modern steel manufacturing centre near Rio de Janeiro.

The large estates survive chiefly in the open plains where gauchos roam with cattle and sheep, and in the Jacui River valley where people of Portuguese descent grow rice for large landowners. In the cattle country, the main products are hides, wool, and salt beef. The beef is processed in many large factories situated in Pelotas.

In the forests of western Paraná, maté (Paraguayan tea) is grown. Porto Alegre is an important road and rail centre and has numerous factories.

On the open prairies of Brazil's far south are great livestock ranches similar to those of Argentina.

439

Countries of the Interior

Bolivia

Bolivia is quite a large country having an area twice that of France. But most of its population of over 5 million live in an area only half that of Holland. Bolivia is completely landlocked but has port facilities in several countries.

Although practically all of the country's income is derived from mining, only about 4 per cent of the people are miners. Most of the people live either in the mountains or on the Altiplano, a high, bleak plateau between the eastern and western ranges of the Andes. To prevent overpopulation the government is gradually moving families to the tropical areas.

The Altiplano is over 12,000 feet (3,700 m) above sea-level. La Paz, the seat of the Bolivian Government, is

Lake Titicaca is one of the few dependable sources of water for farming in the Bolivian highlands.

situated at the bottom of a gorge 1,400 feet (430 m) deep in the Altiplano.

In the area round Lake Titicaca, there is sufficient rain to grow crops without irrigation. The lake is very large, being 120 miles (190 km) long, and is in some places over 100 fathoms deep (600 feet or 180 m). Here the Aymaras, an Indian people, grow potatoes and grain and keep herds of llamas.

The main farming regions of Bolivia are the warm, well-watered valleys of the eastern chain of the Andes. The people here are mostly mestizos or Europeans. Where the valleys are narrow, farms cling to the streams for miles. Various grains are grown, and fruit does well on the lower slopes. Farm produce is sold to the mining towns in the mountains. Sucre, the legal capital of Bolivia, is located in one of these basins. There are few settlers in the Yungas, the rainy, forest-covered eastern slopes of the Andes. There is some gold mining, and a few planters grow cacao beans, sugar, and coca bushes, whose leaves contain the drug cocaine. Some wild rubber is gathered in the forests, and cattle are grazed on the wet savanna.

The south-eastern part of Bolivia is relatively dry. Its vegetation is stunted forest and grassland. Oil was discovered in 1920, and, with it, this isolated region became important. Pipelines have been laid to refineries at Cochabamba and Sucre, and to Arica, the Chilean seaport. A natural gas pipeline extends into Argentina. There is an arterial road between Santa Cruz, the chief town of the Chaco, and Cochabamba.

The mountains of Bolivia are rich in metal. The copper mine at Corocoro has been worked since Inca times. It is one of

The South American Interior

0   100   200 miles
0   160   320 kilometres

◉ National Capitals

Inset: This map shows the relation
ship of Bolivia and Paraguay to
the South American continent.

© Copyright 1960 by Map Projects Inc.

the two sources of pure copper in the
whole Western Hemisphere.

Another mining centre is Potosi,
which stands nearly 14,000 feet
(4,300 m) above sea-level. The town was
founded in 1547, two years after the first
discovery of silver in the mountain which
towers above it.

Steep slopes and rocky soils of the Bolivian Andes make farming difficult and crop yields low.

This Bolivian miner of Potosi must wear heavy clothing against the cold of the 14,000 ft (4,267 m) height.

Mines at Oruro and Uncia are now more important. Though their ores are not as rich as those of Potosi, they are easier to work. Tin is the chief product of those mines, but other metals include lead, zinc, and gold. Important uranium deposits have been found south-east of La Paz.

Bolivia's most serious problem is that she depends on one product, tin, for 68 per cent of her income. If the price of tin falls, the result is very serious. Bolivia is the world's second largest tin producer, after Malaysia.

There are very few industries in Bolivia though new investment laws are providing industrial incentive.

Paraguay

Paraguay is less than half the size of Bolivia. The eastern third is a plateau, between 1,000 (300 m) and 2,000 feet (600 m) high. The rest is a level plain.

In the north the Paraguay River, flowing southwards from the frontier with Brazil, first crosses the country, and then, having joined the Pilcomayo near the capital, Asuncion, it forms for a while the frontier with Argentina. The river is bordered by great swamps. West of it is the Gran Chaco. East of it are forests of tall trees, some of them evergreens.

Paraguay could well become a rich agricultural country like Uruguay. The climate is moderate, and there is enough rain for farming. The soil is rich.

Most of the population (mainly mestizo) live in the hills between the plateau and the east bank of the Paraguay River. In this area the land is high enough to escape flooding and the farmers are near the country's chief waterway. Asuncion, the capital, stands at a spot where the high ground comes up to the river.

The country's chief commercial crop is cotton. Other crops are wheat, soybean, rice and manioc. Sugar, tobacco and coffee are increasing in importance.

Quebracho, which grows along the western bank of the Paraguay River and

A street market in Asuncion, the capital of Paraguay.

The imposing Presidential Palace in Asuncion overlooks the Paraguay River.

Cotton is one of Paraguay's most valuable exports, and cotton production is becoming increasingly important.

is used in tanning, is exported. Maté is either grown as a crop or gathered wild. The eastern forests yield valuable timber.

Another export is orange-flower or petitgrain oil, which is used in perfumes.

Paraguay produces seven-tenths of the world's supply of this oil.

Small deposits of iron, copper, and manganese have been very little exploited. Industry is limited to manufacturing local produce.

Plentiful rain supports lush tropical vegetation on the high, volcanic Pacific island of Tahiti.

This is Oceania

The Pacific Ocean covers about a third of the world's surface. It is larger than any other ocean and larger than all the continents put together.

At its widest, from Panama to the Malay peninsula, the distance across the Pacific is about 12,500 miles (20,100 km). This is half the distance round the earth.

In this vast expanse of water, the land area is relatively small. The only great land-mass is the island of Australia, and that is a little less than the size of Europe, and less than one-twentieth of the area of the Pacific.

Complex chains of underwater mountains stretch south-east from Asia. The tops of some of them form the islands of Indonesia, New Guinea, and the Solomons. The New Hebrides and New Caledonia are also part of these chains, which appear above sea-level again as New Zealand.

Further to the north and east are other mountains. Most of them are submerged beneath the surface of the Pacific, but here and there are a few peaks rising above sea-level. These peaks form small and widely scattered islands.

In so vast a region there is naturally a

great variety of landscape. In Australia alone, the country varies from desert to tropical forest.

So great is the variety in the Pacific that geographers distinguish seven types of islands, each type having its own characteristic landscape, soil, climate, and vegetation.

Treeless atolls are low coral islands. They have poor soil and little drinking water. There are plenty of sea-birds and fish around them, yet the natives avoid them, preferring islands with trees. But the treeless atolls make good landing grounds for aircraft and some of them are used as military air bases. The Canton and Johnson Islands are both groups of treeless atolls.

Dry-forest atolls are also low coral islands. Because of their salty air and brackish water few plants grow on them; those that do are especially adapted to these conditions and generally form a dry scrub forest.

Few people live on the dry-forest atolls. As on the treeless atolls there is often a shortage of drinking water, and it is hard to grow crops in the salty soil.

Most of the Marshall and Tuvalu Islands, and many of the Tuamotu and northern Cook Islands are dry-forest atolls.

Moist atolls are the beautiful coral islands so often shown in films. They receive plenty of rain, and trees grow abundantly. Coconut palms and breadfruit trees are everywhere. Excellent crops can be grown, producing food in plenty. Typical of the moist atolls are the Gilbert and Tokelau Islands.

Coral is made by a very small organism called a coral polyp, which lives in warm sea water. Coral polyps are very simple animals of the same family as the jelly fish. They absorb the carbonate of lime that is dissolved in sea water and with it form stony walls round their bodies. When the polyps die, the limestone walls (the coral) remain, and a new generation of coral polyps builds on the skeletons of the old. In that way, in the course of time, great thicknesses of coral are formed.

Coral often forms on the tops of submerged mountains just beneath the surface of the sea. In time the coral reaches

Scrub vegetation and bare, eroded hills are characteristic of the drier regions in the heart of the continent of Australia.

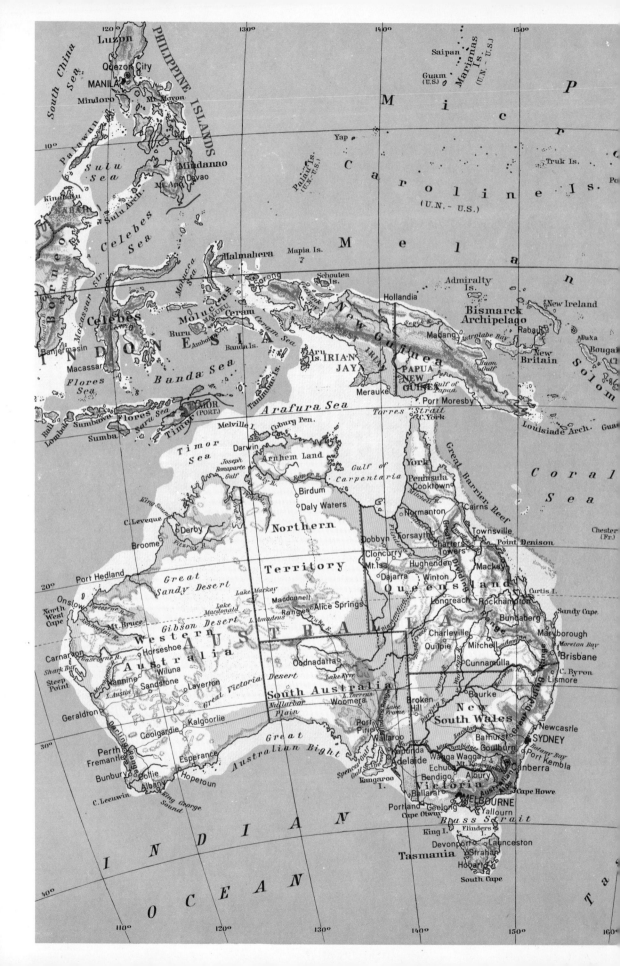

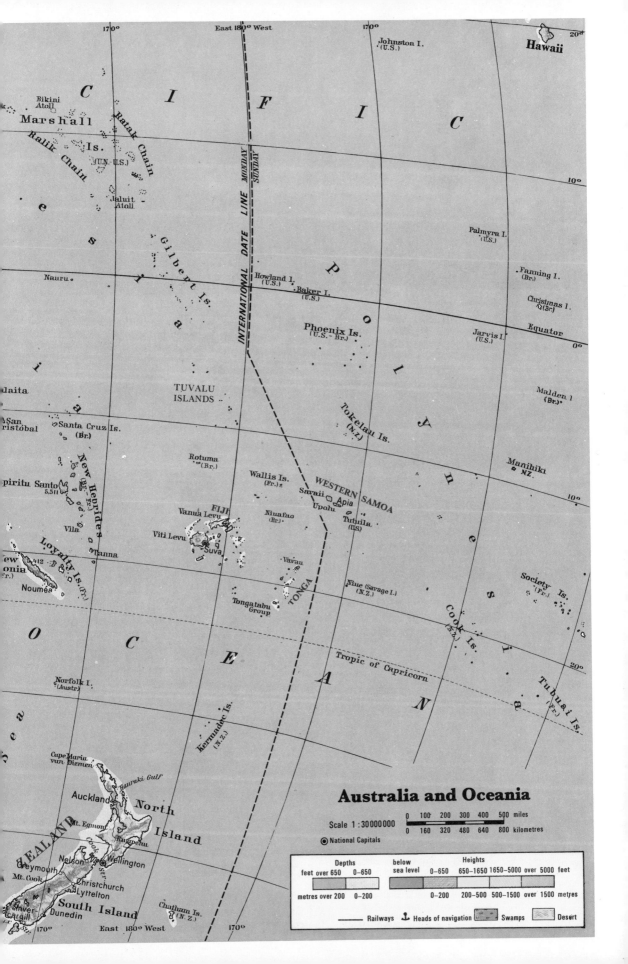

C I F I C

20°

Hawaii

Johnston I.
(U.S.)

Bikini
Atoll

Marshall

Ratak Chain

Ralik Chain

Is.
(U.N.-U.S.)

Jaluit
Atoll

10°

P O L Y

Palmyra I.
(U.S.)

Fanning I.
(Br.)

Nauru

Gilbert Is.

INTERNATIONAL DATE LINE   MONDAY   SUNDAY

Howland I.
(U.S.)

Baker I.
(U.S.)

Phoenix Is.
(U.S.-Br.)

Christmas I.
(Br.)

Equator

Jarvis I.
(U.S.)

0°

alaita

TUVALU
ISLANDS

Tokelau Is.
(N.Z.)

Malden I
(Br.)

San
ristóbal

Santa Cruz Is.
(Br.)

Rotuma
(Br.)

Wallis Is.
(Fr.)

WESTERN SAMOA

Manihiki
N.Z.

10°

piritu Santo
5,511

New Hebrides
(Br.-Fr.)

Savaii   Apia
Upolu

FIJI

Vanua Levu

Niuafao
(Br.)

Tutuila
(U.S)

Vila

Viti Levu

Suva

Vavau

Society Is.
(Fr.)

ew
onia
r.)

Loyalty Is. (Fr.)

Tanna

Tonga

Niue (Savage I.)
(N.Z.)

Cook Is.
(N.Z.)

Noumea

412

Tongatabu
Group

O   C   E   A   N

Tropic of Capricorn

20°

Tubuai Is.
(Fr.)

Norfolk I.
(Austr)

Kermadec Is.
(N.Z.)

Sea

Cape Maria
van Diemen

Hauraki Gulf

Auckland   North

Australia and Oceania

Scale 1:30000000

| 0 | 100 | 200 | 300 | 400 | 500 | miles |

| 0 | 160 | 320 | 480 | 640 | 800 | kilometres |

◉ National Capitals

ZEALAND

Mt. Egmont

Island

Ruapehu

Cook Str.

Nelson   Wellington

Greymouth

Mt. Cook

Christchurch
Lyttelton

Invercargill

South Island

Dunedin

Chatham Is.
(N.Z.)

170°   East 180° West   170°

	Depths		below		Heights		
feet over 650	0–650		sea level	0–650	650–1650	1650–5000	over 5000 feet
metres over 200	0–200			0–200	200–500	500–1500	over 1500 metres

—— Railways   ⚓ Heads of navigation   Swamps   Desert

Streams of molten lava flow into the ocean as Hawaii's great volcano, Mauna Loa, erupts. The Pacific Ocean has long been a centre of volcanic activity, and many of the islands are of volcanic origin.

the surface, and is battered by the waves. Gradually the coral is ground into 'sand', while the living coral keeps on growing round the edge. Eventually the typical coral reef is formed with sandy soil in the middle.

Raised coral islands are composed of layer upon layer of old coral. Some have been raised 200 feet (60 m) and more above sea-level. The coral of which they are composed forms limestone rocks. Limestone dissolves easily, so there are many caves and sinkholes. Because limestone soaks up water rapidly these islands are often quite dry. Some, like Nauru Island and Ocean Island, have

This coral island is part of Australia's Great Barrier Reef. Stretching for 1,250 miles (2,011 km) along Australia's north-eastern coast, this reef is the world's largest single coral deposit.

rich deposits of phosphates.

Unweathered volcanic islands have little vegetation. When rock is weathered it gradually breaks up, forming soil. These islands have little soil, except for what has accumulated in the bottoms of valleys, where the islanders grow their coconut palms and other crops. The Northern Marianas are examples of unweathered volcanic islands.

Weathered volcanic islands often rise hundreds of feet above sea-level. These islands have different soils and climates, providing a variety of plants. In them the natives can grow almost everything they need to live on. Only commercial minerals are lacking. The Hawaiian, Society, and Samoan Islands are good examples of weathered volcanic islands.

Continental islands contain rocks that were formed under conditions of great heat and pressure, which occur only on the continents or along their borders. These rocks are often very old, and because of their age the islands have an even greater variety of plants and soils than is possessed by the weathered volcanic islands.

The spectacular fiords of New Zealand's South Island were formed by the action of glaciers.

These continental islands have therefore a great variety of landscape. They have high mountains, dense forests, and broad areas of swamp. On them human life has developed in many different ways. Continental islands have the great advantage of possessing mineral resources. Some of the most important islands in the Pacific ocean are New Zealand, New Guinea, New Caledonia, Guadalcanal, New Britain, and New Ireland.

Aerial view of an atoll showing the surrounding coral reef.

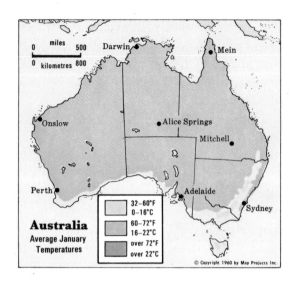

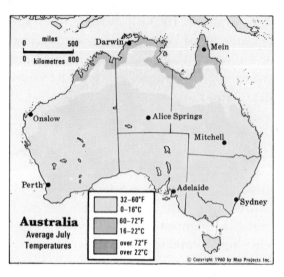

This map shows the average January temperatures in Australia. While the tropical areas in the north are warm all the year round, summer temperatures in the south are nearly as hot. Some of the highest temperatures known have been recorded in the deserts of central Australia.

This map shows the average July temperatures in Australia. Australian winters are generally mild throughout the country, except on the high plateau and in mountain regions.

Climate

The great variety of climate found in the Pacific depends primarily on the distance from the Equator, but it is also to some extent dependent on height above sea-level. Ocean currents also play their part.

The weather on islands on, or near, the Equator varies very little. Heavy and daily rain is the rule, and there is very little difference in temperature between the warmest and coldest months.

The higher the island the more rainfall it gets. Air is forced to rise to pass over the mountains. It cools as it rises, and, since cold air cannot hold as much moisture as warm air, some of the moisture is released in the form of rain. Low-lying islands are relatively dry.

Great tropical storms, called typhoons, occur from time to time in the Pacific. They cause great damage. Trees are stripped of their branches and often uprooted; roofs are ripped off and whole buildings destroyed. Everyone has to stay under cover for protection. Even the largest ships have to heave-to to ride out the worst of these storms. When typhoons are particularly ferocious the wind may reach 150 miles (240 km) an hour and can whip-up great tidal waves which sometimes sweep completely over any low-lying islands in their path.

The maps on these pages give some facts about the climate of Australia. As it is south of the Equator its seasons are the reverse of our own in the Northern

Hemisphere. In November, December, January, and February, when it is winter in the north, Australians are bathing and lying on the beaches. Their winter is from June to August.

Australia lies between the latitudes of 10° and 40° south. The tropical northern parts of the country are warm all the year round. The parts farther south are very nearly as hot in summer, but cooler in winter, though winters are generally mild throughout the country except on the high plateau and in the mountain regions.

Tropical Australia gets its rain from the summer monsoon. Rainfall is heavy near the coast, but diminishes rapidly in the more inland areas. During the cool season, which lasts from May to October, it is very dry.

The interior of the country is very dry, and so is much of Western Australia. Most of these areas consist of desert. The Great Sandy Desert and the Great Victoria Desert are amongst the largest deserts in the world.

South-western Australia and the coast of South Australia have mild rainy winters. The summers are hot and dry.

South-eastern Australia receives a fair amount of rain throughout the year, which has helped to make this a more densely settled region than any other part. Here, the winters vary from cool to mild, and the summers are less hot than elsewhere.

Lying to the south is the island of Tasmania. Its climate, like that of New Zealand, is far enough south to be immune from heat and drought, and for conditions to be mild and moist like the west coast of Europe.

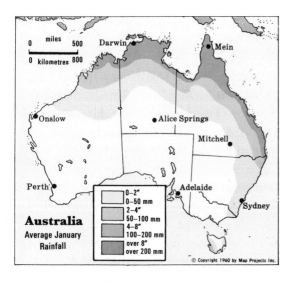

This map shows the average January rainfall in Australia. Australian summers are hot and dry, except for the tropical areas in the north which get their rain from the summer monsoon. However, this rainfall diminishes rapidly in more inland areas.

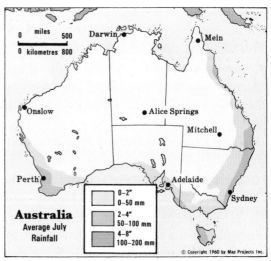

This map shows the average July rainfall in Australia. Winter rains fall around the coasts of south and eastern Australia, but the interior of the continent is very dry, with vast deserts in central Australia.

The Koala is a marsupial native to Australia. It lives mainly on eucalyptus leaves.

An emu inspects its eggs. This large flightless bird of Australia is related to the ostrich.

Animals of the Pacific

In the remote past Australia and its islands were joined to Asia. But the land which linked them has been covered by the waters of the Pacific for millions of years. During this time, a great variety of plants and animals have developed in the Pacific area.

Many islands have native plants that are found in no other places in the world. Such plants are said to be *endemic*. In New Zealand, almost seven-tenths of the flowering plants are endemic. In New Caledonia, which boasts 2,500 species of flowering plants, four-fifths are found nowhere else in the world.

Islands that are isolated generally have only a few species of plants or animals, but those which are close to continents have many. The islands of Oceania (excluding Australia) have no native mammals at all apart from bats, and bats, of course, can travel great distances by flying. Cattle, deer, goats, pigs, rabbits, and rats are not native at all; all have been introduced by man.

Australia has been separated from other countries for so long that many of its animals are endemic. These animals have no close relatives in the world.

Two-thirds of the native mammals of Australia are marsupials, which are animals that carry their young in pouches – like kangaroos and opossums. Australia's famous 'teddy bear', the Koala, is also a marsupial.

The only mammals to lay eggs come from Australia and its neighbouring islands; one of them is the duck-billed platypus found in Australia and Tasmania. The other is the echidna, or spiny ant-eater, found in Australia, Tasmania, and New Guinea.

A baby wallaby peers out of its mother's pouch. The wallaby is a smaller relative of Australia's kangaroo.

The duck-billed platypus is one of Australia's most unusual mammals. Like the echidna, which is also known as the spiny-anteater, the duck-billed platypus lays eggs.

Sharp teeth and a vicious temper gave the Tasmanian Devil its name. About the size of a badger, it sometimes kills sheep.

The bearlike Australian wombat is a marsupial like the kangaroo. It is 2 to 3 ft (0.6 to 0.9 m) long, lives in a burrow, and feeds on plants.

Australian aborigines cook a meal of boiled fish.
A boomerang lies on the ground nearby.

A group of New Guinea tribesmen, dressed for a
ceremonial dance.

The Peoples of the Pacific

The first white men who sailed across the Pacific mistakenly called the dark-skinned islanders Indians. That name did not last long. As more and more islands were discovered, the explorers found a great variety of native populations. In the western islands they had copper-coloured skin and straight black hair, and were expert boatmen. In the islands further to the east, the explorers found brown-skinned or black-skinned natives with curly or frizzy hair.

Who were these island people? Where had they come from? And how had they managed to sail thousands of miles across the ocean?

To understand their extraordinary voyages we must see them as the result of gradual progress. The island of Sumatra is, at its closest, about the same distance from the Malay peninsula as Calais is from Dover. It needed no great adventurous spirit or technical skill for primitive people to cross the Malacca Straits. Once on the island of Sumatra, they could pass from island to island across

still more narrow straits. In fact they could have travelled some 3,000 miles (4,800 km) from the mainland of Asia without undertaking a single voyage of any great length. By that time they must have become skilful seafarers with some elementary understanding of navigation. It must also be realised that those who left an island did so as a rule under pressure from some stronger and more warlike tribe. The Kon-Tiki expedition also proved that it was possible for some part of the population of the Pacific islands to have come from central South America on great balsa-wood rafts blown by the Trade Winds. This would account for some of the racial variation of the islands' inhabitants.

The islands of Indonesia have been occupied by man from the earliest times. Further east, the smaller the islands became the more widely were they scattered. The Polynesian Islands, in the middle of the Pacific Ocean, were the last of these islands to be occupied.

This movement from island to island

must have been spread over thousands of years. The people concerned must have come from different sources, for they seem to have differed greatly in appearance, language, and customs. As a result the people of the Pacific Islands fall into different groups. Scientists have divided them into four main groups, each of which is confined to one part of the island world.

The Australian aborigines ('original inhabitants') occupied this island continent long before its discovery by white men. Many aborigines have adopted civilisation – partially at least – but some have kept their primitive ways. These live in small groups, grow no crops and live by hunting and off wild-growing edible plants. Their chief weapon is the

Indian women on Fiji wear their traditional saris. Indians have become farmers and merchants there.

Swimming is a popular sport in Australia, since most of the people live on or near the coasts, because most of the interior is desert. Here, Sunday bathers enjoy the surf at Bondi Beach in Sydney – one of the world's most famous beaches.

In sailing canoes like this one, the ancestors of the present islanders sailed all over the Pacific. The outrigger keeps the canoe from capsizing in heavy seas.

boomerang which, skilfully thrown, will come back to the thrower if it misses.

The aborigines are constantly on the move, always in search of food. They can move easily because they have no homes and very few possessions of any sort.

The next group we come to are the people living in the islands of Melanesia. The people of the islands of Melanesia ('black islands') have dark skins and frizzy hair. These islands lie in several groups north-east of Australia. They are the Bismarck Archipelago, the Solomon Islands, the New Hebrides, the Fiji Islands, and New Caledonia. There are also a number of smaller islands. Melanesians use their canoes for both fishing and trading. They are firm believers in magic, and magicians are often the richest and the most important people amongst them.

The third Pacific Island group is called Micronesia, which means the 'small islands'. The islets of the Caroline, Mariana, and Marshall groups form the bulk of Micronesia.

The Micronesians are skilful sailors. Their canoes are fitted with outriggers, which prevent them capsizing, so that they can be used for ocean voyages. Their triangular sails enable them to go about (to shift from one tack to another) very easily. The canoes of Micronesia are fastest of all the Pacific native craft.

A Fijian builds a hut with a wooden frame and reed-matting walls.

A Polynesian family on Samoa watching dancers at a celebration. Polynesians are fond of singing and dancing, which they have developed to a fine art.

Last of the island groups comes Polynesia, the word meaning 'many islands'. Polynesia covers an enormous area from Hawaii, in the north, to New Zealand in the south, and to Easter Island, which lies some 2,000 miles (3,210 km) off the coast of Chile.

Of all the native people in the Pacific Islands, the Polynesians were from the first the most popular with the explorers. They are indeed a handsome and friendly people. They live by farming and fishing, but they do not have to work hard on their lovely islands, for the land is productive and food is plentiful.

In some places a mixture of races may be found. In New Guinea, for instance, though the bulk of the inhabitants are Melanesians, there are some Polynesian tribes. Other tribes are related to the Negritos of the Philippines and to kindred tribes in the Malay archipelago. Fijians are of mixed Polynesian and Melanesian stock.

In more recent times many newcomers have arrived in the Pacific. In the Fiji

New Zealand Maori children: descendants of fierce Polynesian warriors.

Islands, for example, there are more Indians than native Fijians. Chinese traders have settled on many islands, and white people have come from nearly every country in Europe. The bulk of these live in Australia and New Zealand. The majority are of British origin, but Australia, which is still fairly thinly populated, is at present allowing limited immigration from other countries.

A view across Sydney, looking towards the harbour bridge with the opera house in the background.

Countries and Cities of the Pacific

Many countries have had a hand in ruling the islands of the Pacific. Today some are still controlled by the United States, Great Britain, and France, but some are administered by Australia and New Zealand, who also claim nearly half of Antarctica.

Australia and New Zealand are fully independent members of the British Commonwealth. Until this century the Australian continent was divided into five British colonies, with the island of Tasmania as a sixth. In January 1901, these six colonies were federated to become the six states of the Commonwealth of Australia. You may be sur-

prised to hear of the *six* states of Australia when the map of Australia is divided into seven sections. This is because the largely uninhabited Northern Territory is not a state. It is governed by an administrative and legislative council and allowed to send one member to the House of Representatives. Although he could take part in debates, he has only had full voting rights since 1968.

Australians are predominantly townsfolk. Less than a third of the population lives in the country. The towns, moreover, are growing all the time as people move away from the country or arrive as immigrants from Europe.

Mechanical farm equipment makes it possible for fewer people to grow Australia's crops. At the same time industry is continually growing, and industry is usually concentrated in large towns because there is a constant supply of labour and a market for the produce.

Half the people of Australia live in the six capitals of the states of the Commonwealth, and a third of the total population lives in the cities of Sydney and Melbourne alone.

Of the great cities of the Southern Hemisphere, Sydney and Melbourne in

St Patrick's Roman Catholic Cathedral, Melbourne. Melbourne is the second largest city in Australia.

Canberra is the seat of the Australian government. This view shows the Cook fountain and the National Library.

Australia rank fifth and sixth, after Buenos Aires, São Paulo, Santiago and Rio de Janeiro. They both have populations of more than 2.5 million.

Wellington, the capital, is the second largest town in New Zealand.

Sheep graze on this wooded hillside overlooking Auckland, New Zealand's chief town and port.

Sydney has one of the world's finest natural harbours. Both Sydney and Melbourne have all the equipment of first-class commercial ports. Both of them have industries producing goods for local consumption. Their principal exports are wool, meat, hides, and wheat.

However, the capital of Australia is neither the great city of Melbourne nor Sydney. The capital is Canberra, beautifully situated on high ground within a circle of wooded hills. When it was selected in 1909 it was little more than a hamlet, but the population has risen to well over 185,000 and the town is still developing.

New Zealand has few large towns. Nevertheless the four largest of them, Wellington, Auckland, Christchurch, and Hamilton, contain more than half of the population. Auckland is the largest and it is the country's leading seaport. The first Europeans to settle in the country founded Auckland in 1841. Wellington, the capital, is the second largest town and an important seaport.

There are few real towns in the Pacific Islands, and not one of them could be called big. The largest is Suva, the capital of the Fiji Islands, which is on the island of Viti Levu, the largest of the group. It has a fine sheltered harbour, and most ships crossing the Pacific call there. Passenger ships call for fresh provisions and other supplies, while cargo ships load with sugar and copra. The population is only 96,000, but there is a medical school where doctors and nurses are trained.

The only real town in the whole of Eastern Polynesia is Papeete on the French island of Tahiti, yet its population is about 22,000. Most of the large business houses in Papeete are operated by Europeans, but there are many Chinese shopkeepers in the town. Nearly a fifth of the population of Papeete is of Chinese descent.

Suva, capital of the Fiji Islands, is a regular port of call for shipping lines and also a centre of island trading.

Tahiti's lush green mountains rise behind the harbour of Papeete, the capital of France's Pacific island territories. The exports are copra, vanilla, phosphates, and mother-of-pearl.

Australia,
the Island Continent

Until recently, Australia was one of the least known parts of the world. This is not altogether surprising considering its remoteness and the fact that it is little more than 360 years since Australia was discovered. The first European settlement in Australia was not made until 1788. Excluding the primitive aborigines, Australia is the most recently inhabited continent in the world. Physically, though, it may well be the oldest of all of the continents. Rocks have been discovered in the north-west of the island which are believed to have been above water for 1,600 million years. The aboriginal population, too, is an old one. Some of these Stone Age people are believed to have been living in Tasmania as long as 30,000 years ago.

Australia is the lowest of all the continents. The average elevation is less than 1,000 feet (300 m), and only one-seventeenth of the entire continent is over 2,000 feet (600 m).

The highest peak, Mount Kosciusko, is only 7,328 feet (2,233 m) above sea-level. The principal highland areas are the Great Dividing Range in the east and the vast plateau of Western Australia.

The first European settlements were made on the east coast. A few miles

Cattle and sheep graze on the well-watered uplands of New South Wales and Victoria.

A desolate, dry plateau – about 1,500,000 sq miles (3,885,000 sq km) – covers the western half of Australia.

Heron Island, part of the spectacular Great Barrier Reef, is a very popular Australian tourist resort.

inland the Great Dividing Range raises its mountain barrier. It is not a high range, but it is not easily crossed, and it was not till 1813 that the first European settlers found their way to the other side.

On the western slopes of the mountains the settlers found good country for growing wheat. The soil was fertile, and rainfall, though not abundant, was sufficient both for wheat and mixed farming. Further west the grassy plains of

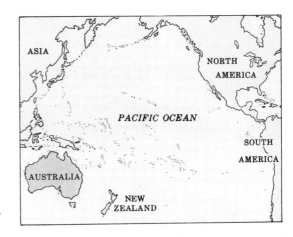

Above: This map shows the position of Australia in the Pacific Ocean.

Australia

| 0 | 100 | 200 | 300 | 400 | 500 miles |
| 0 | 160 | 320 | 480 | 640 | 800 kilometres |

◉ National Capital
◎ State and Territorial Capitals

© Copyright 1960 by Map Projects Inc.

The Nullarbor Plain of South Australia is a 300 mile (480 km) stretch of barren sand, rock, and sparse vegetation.

New South Wales seemed ideal for grazing sheep. To the north in tropical Queensland, the grazing proved suitable for cattle, despite the long winter drought.

As the settlers pushed on further to the west, the country became much drier. Beyond the Darling River, less than 500 miles (800 km) from the coast, the grass became thinner and thinner, and

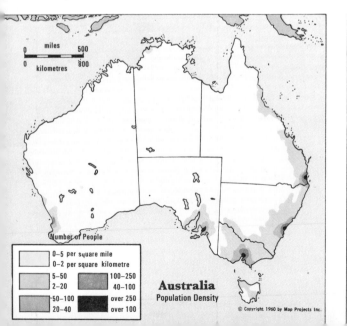

Australia
Population Density

Number of People

0–5 per square mile	
0–2 per square kilometre	
5–50	100–250
2–20	40–100
50–100	over 250
20–40	over 100

© Copyright 1960 by Map Projects Inc.

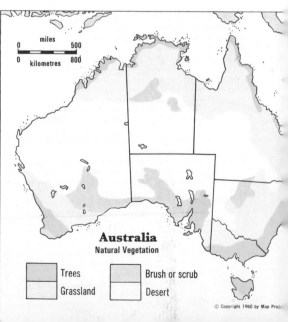

Australia
Natural Vegetation

Trees Brush or scrub
Grassland Desert

© Copyright 1960 by Map Proj

soon the settlers were forced to face the disappointing fact that the interior of their land of promise was nothing more than desert.

The population map demonstrates as plainly as the map of natural vegetation that the interior of Australia, like the Sahara, is a vast area of emptiness. The bulk of the country's population lives in the south-eastern coastal region, where rainfall is adequate. Another populated district, though a much smaller one, is centred on Perth in the south-west. This region has a pleasant Mediterranean-type climate.

Only one railway crosses Australia from east to west, and it avoids the interior of the country. A narrow gauge railway runs up to Alice Springs in the interior, but goes no further. From there on, to Port Darwin on the north coast, the journey has to be made by road.

Roads naturally concentrate round the chief towns. Most of these are sea-ports, however, and much of the traffic between them goes by sea.

In few countries of the world is air travel more important than in Australia. The population is only about 13 million, and the towns are far apart. The world-famous Flying Doctor Service brings medical attention to people living in the most remote areas.

The natural vegetation of Australia is strongly influenced by the prevailing temperature and rainfall. The most common tree is the evergreen eucalyptus. Of this tree there are over 400 species, ranging in size from the giants of the rainy south-eastern uplands, which rise to a height of 200 feet (60 m), to the dwarfed bushlike forms of the dry interior. Another common tree is the acacia. In the deserts there are bushes and tough, spiny grasses.

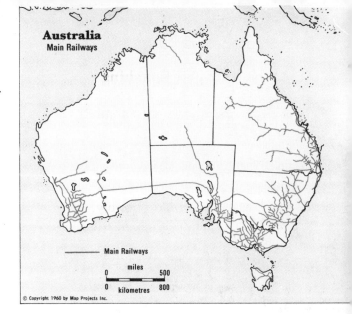

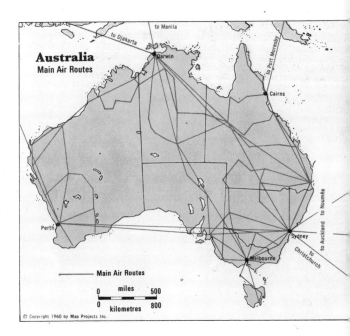

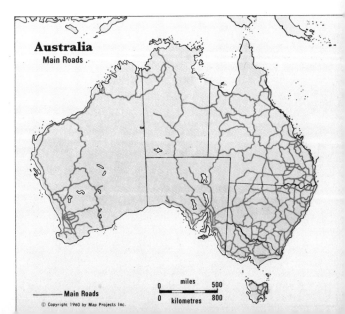

Agriculture and Ranching

We have seen that only a small part of Australia is suitable for farming, yet it is big enough to make Australia one of the great food-producing countries of the world. Far more food is produced than the Australians could possibly consume, and the surplus is shipped overseas.

The rolling plains of Australia are particularly suitable for growing wheat, which can withstand the heat and does not demand a great deal of moisture. Two-thirds of all the cultivated land in the country is used for growing wheat. Wheat can be grown in any area that receives a minimum of 12 inches (300 mm) of rain a year, though more is desirable. With that rainfall the yield can be very low, while with 20 inches (500 mm) of rain, wheat is much more productive. With still more rain, the yield may be even higher. The average yield for the whole country is slightly lower than the average in the United States and Canada, and Argentina, three of the other leading wheat producers.

Australia's wheat farmers use machinery for ploughing, planting, and harvesting.

Ninety-five per cent of Australia's sugar cane is grown on the tropical coastal plain of Queensland.

The dry weather in summer is a great help to Australian farmers. The grain ripens well on the stalk, and the wheat can be harvested and threshed in one operation. Recently nearly 72 million hectolitres of wheat were harvested in a single season.

Some of the wheat farms are very large indeed, and farming is highly mechanised. With proper equipment, one or two men can manage hundreds of acres. Only about a third of the wheat produced is for home consumption, the remainder being exported.

The north-eastern State, Queensland, is largely within the tropics and tropical crops are grown. Sugar-cane was first planted there nearly 100 years ago. At first, workers were brought in from some of the Pacific islands, but later this was stopped. Nowadays all the heavy work of growing and harvesting sugar-cane is done by the Australians themselves. More sugar is grown than is needed for home consumption, and most of the surplus is shipped to New Zealand.

Australia has fine orchards and vineyards. Thousands of hectolitres of apples are grown in Victoria, Western Australia, and Tasmania. Considerable amounts are shipped to Europe, where they are marketed from March to June, at a time when no European apples are available, except those kept in cold storage. This reversal of the seasons in the two hemispheres helps the Australians to get good prices in Europe for their produce. In some years the vineyards produce nearly half a million tons of grapes. More than half are used for making wine, while most of the remainder are dried for sale as raisins, sultanas, or currants.

All this produce comes from slightly over a hundredth part of the total area of Australia. Irrigation is increasing to

A Tasmanian apple orchard in bloom. Refrigerated ships enable Australia to export fruit to Europe.

Hot, dry summers make the irrigated Murray River Valley a leading grape-growing district.

make the land even more productive, especially in Western Australia, on the south-west coastal plain, and in the north.

We get a more typical picture of Australia, however, when we leave the arable and general farming of the coastal belt and turn westwards to the 'outback', the ranching country that extends far into the interior and reappears on the other side of the desert in Western

467

Australian stockmen inspect a 'mob' of Merinos on one of the vast sheep stations of New South Wales. Merino sheep are bred specifically for wool.

Australia. The outback is the home of the great sheep ranches of Australia, known locally as stations. Some sheep stations on the drier pastures of the outback cover many thousands of square kilometres.

Stations in the outback are often many miles apart, and the people who live on them keep in touch with their neighbours by radio. Lessons are broadcast for children who live hundreds of kilometres from the nearest school.

The first European settlers brought a few sheep with them when they arrived at Botany Bay, on the east coast of Australia. Nowadays, in a good year, the number of sheep in Australia exceeds 140 million. Three-quarters are merinos, famous for their fine wool. The rest are crossbreeds, reared for meat and wool.

Nearly half the sheep in Australia are reared in New South Wales. Most of the remainder are found on stations in south Queensland, Victoria, the coastal parts of South Australia, and Western Australia.

Shearing time is anxiously awaited by the sheep-breeders, for that is when the crop of wool can be estimated. Shearing is done at different times in different parts of Australia. It begins in April in Queensland, and by October has reached New South Wales. Shearing is very skilled work. The shearers travel across the country in groups called shearing gangs. The variations in the shearing periods give them time to move across the country from station to station and from state to state.

When the shearers arrive, the sheep are herded into narrow pens. They pass the shearers one by one and each is sheared in a matter of minutes. Each sheep yields about nine pounds (four kilograms) of wool, and an expert shearer can clip 150 sheep a day. Australia is the leading wool-producing country in the world. Altogether Australia produces about 1,000 million pounds (454 thousand kilograms) of wool each year, which is more than a quarter of the world's total

wool production.

In the vast, sparsely populated plain of the Northern Territory are some of the world's largest cattle ranches. One of them alone covers 12,686 square miles (32,855 sq km). Cattle and beef products are the most valuable export commodity of the Northern Territory. Progress in experiments with tick and heat resisting strains of tropical livestock is good, so their value is likely to increase. A buffalo industry is growing in the wet coastal plains, and many live buffalo are now exported.

The Northern Territory is still what is known as pioneer country. Almost everything has still to be developed. But the rewards are great for those who know how to conquer the loneliness and rigours of pioneer life.

Australian sheep shearers use mechanical clippers to remove the heavy fleece. Australia is a leading wool producer.

Cowboys drive a herd of beef cattle near Alice Springs, an oasis in the dry Northern Territory.

The Problems of the Land

So dry is the ranching country of Australia that at times the sheep and cattle are in acute need of water. During a dry year flocks and herds may have to be reduced by as much as a quarter; even then millions may still die of thirst. Once, long ago, Australia had a drought that lasted ten years, during which the flocks were reduced by half. When the drought finally came to an end, it took thirty years to rebuild the flocks to their original strength.

Looking at a map of Australia, one gets the impression there is far more water than there is. The rivers shown on the map are, in fact, often dry. In South Australia there are great lakes like Lake Eyre and Lake Torrens, but they are really only depressions which fill with water on rare occasions after it has rained, but which at other times are completely dry and covered with a glistening layer of salt. In Western Australia the big lakes, Lake Austin, Lake Macdonald, and Lake Mackay, are dry most of the year.

Fortunately some portions of Australia have large stores of underground water which can be reached by drilling deep wells, or 'bores' as they are called in Australia.

Thousands of bores have been drilled, too many perhaps, for in some parts of Australia so much underground water has been drawn off that the supply has diminished. More water must be found and more economical ways of using it be discovered if Australia is to continue to supply the world with large quantities of wool and meat.

Like farmers in many other parts of the world, Australians are learning by experience to conserve their land better.

Where forest cover has been removed, rainstorms leave deep gullies in the earth.

A windmill pumps water for irrigation in the dry outback near Alice Springs.

The wheat farmers, for instance, for many years ploughed up the soil west of the Great Dividing Range. During drought, the covering of grass that once held the soil in place was gone and the soil blew away. Great clouds of dust swirled over the countryside. Once gone, this wind-blown soil could never be recovered. Australian farmers are planting tough perennial grasses, contour ploughing, and planting tree windbreaks to prevent the same thing happening again.

Artesian bores tap underground water supplies. Over-use makes many wells run dry each year.

In southern Australia, with a good climate for arable growth, some parts have remained barren. Experiments have shown that vital trace elements were missing. These, applied on a large scale, have now reclaimed much soil which is now fertile.

Plants and animals, too, provide problems for the farmers. Great damage was caused at one time by the prickly pear cactus. Settlers brought some when they first came to Australia. By 1920 the plants had spread thickly over 60 million acres (24 million hectares) of good grazing land, making grazing impossible. Finally in 1925 an insect called *Cactoblastis*, which kills prickly pears, was introduced from Argentina. Within a few years more than half the ruined land was again available for grazing.

The stock-breeders' worst enemy, however, is the rabbit. There are millions in Australia, and they eat the grass and brush on which the sheep graze. The rabbit was introduced by settlers, who enjoyed hunting it. Since then the Australians have worked hard to get rid of their rabbits. As many as 25 million have been killed in a single year and thousands of miles of fences have been built to keep rabbits out of good pastures.

New hope came a few years ago with the introduction of the rabbit disease, myxomatosis. In the first year it killed three-quarters of all the rabbits in Australia. Some survived, to build up a resistance to the disease, and Australia is still infested.

Kangaroos are also something of a pest. They, too, feed on grass, and in their case, building fences will never keep them off grazing ground, for they can leap 20 feet (6 m) into the air. Unfortunately kangaroo hides and meat are in demand and as a result they have been hunted so extensively that the species is now threatened with extinction.

A solitary acacia tree and barren red sand: a typical Australian desert scene.

A heavy dredge bringing up huge quantities of gold-bearing mud in New South Wales.

Mineral Resources

In 1849 men went from all over the world to the newly discovered gold-fields of California. Two years later another gold rush started, this time in the wilds of Australia.

The first gold was discovered in New South Wales. Then, still richer deposits

A zinc refinery at Hobart, Tasmania.

were discovered in Victoria. Within ten years the population of Australia had increased five-fold.

Gold is mined in every Australian state and territory. Gold worth hundreds of millions of pounds has been mined in Victoria alone. Until the mid 1960s the great gold mining state was Western Australia, and the chief centre, Kalgoorlie in the Coolgardie gold-fields, but now gold is overtaken by oil, bauxite, nickel, and iron ore in value.

Australia is one of the leading countries in the production of lead and zinc, and the mines at Broken Hill in the dry western part of New South Wales are among the greatest in the world. After being worked for nearly eighty years the deposits are far from being exhausted. Recently large nickel deposits have been discovered in Western Australia.

Australian copper mines can produce enough to satisfy home consumption. Small amounts of tin are also mined. But far more important are the great deposits of coal and iron ore, which have formed the basis of Australia's development as a manufacturing country.

For many years Australia had to depend on imported manufactured goods, which was very costly. Now, with coal and iron of her own, Australia can manufacture for herself.

The most important coal-fields are in eastern New South Wales, which produces four-fifths of all the coal mined in the country.

The iron mines are centred at Iron Knob, near Spencer Gulf in South Australia. The ore is taken by rail to docks at Whyalla. From there it is shipped to the blast furnaces of Newcastle and Port Kembla.

Iron mines are worked near Yampi Sound on the north-west coast of Australia. These new deposits assure Australia of a continuing supply of iron ore.

Today, coal provides a great deal of power, but recently oil and natural gas

Coal is pulverised and pumped with water through this pipeline to the steelmaking centre of Port Kembla.

Iron ore is unloaded at Port Kembla's docks. Railway trucks carry the ore to the steel plants.

have been found off-shore in the East Gippsland area of Victoria. The oil provides 62 per cent of Australia's refining requirements and the natural gas is piped to householders and industry in Victoria. Oil and gas found in Queensland is piped to Brisbane.

If nuclear power is developed, it will have the benefit of the important uranium fields that have been discovered in the Northern Territory. Ore from these fields is refined at Port Pirie, in South Australia. Hydro-electricity is restricted to the south-eastern mountains, where rainfall is reliable. Here, the Snowy Mountain Scheme and the Hume Power Station give power to Victoria and New South Wales.

The exploitation of Australia's mineral wealth has led to an expansion of the economy. This is an iron-ore mine in western Australia.

Truck assembly in Brisbane.

The Growth of Australian Industry

The two World Wars greatly affected the development of industry in Australia. During the First World War, Australia was cut off from overseas supplies of manufactured goods. This gave a great incentive to the expansion of the iron and steel industry.

The situation in the Second World War was somewhat different, for this time the war had come to the Pacific. There was a time when Australia feared invasion, and the factories set to work urgently, manufacturing guns, ships, and aircraft. The electrical, chemical, and engineering industries grew rapidly. By 1945 Australia had really become an industrial country.

At present a third of all the Australian labour-force is employed in manufacturing industries. The value of the manufactured goods produced is actually greater than that of all the produce of the land and the mines put together, though agricultural produce makes up the bulk of exports.

The chief manufacturing states are New South Wales and Victoria, and industry has concentrated in the towns along the coast. Raw materials come by ship, or by rail from the outback. The towns provide manpower for the factories and in many cases a local market.

The most important Australian industries are meat-packing, fruit-processing, and flour-milling. Australian iron and steel are used to make farming implements, machinery and cars, and Australian copper for electrical equipment.

Australia's chief export is wool, most of which is shipped from Sydney. Most of the other exports are the produce of the

Australian farms supply food-processing plants like this one, where soup is made.

land (food, wine, etc.) or of the mines. Many manufactures are for home use. Tasmania exports newsprint and refined metal.

Fat being removed from wool. When refined it makes lanolin, a valuable by-product.

475

Below: This map shows the position of New Zealand in the Pacific Ocean.

New Zealand

The Dominion of New Zealand consists of two large islands and several small ones. Altogether they have an area of slightly more than 100,000 square miles (258,000 sq km), which is a little more than the area of Great Britain and Northern Ireland. But the population is only about 3 million.

Australia and New Zealand are often coupled together, but in many ways they are utterly dissimilar. Australia is relatively flat, New Zealand mountainous; Australia is on the whole a dry country, New Zealand a very rainy one, which, when first discovered, was thickly forested. The aboriginal populations of the two countries are also very different – the Maoris of New Zealand having a much higher culture than the aborigines on the Australian continent.

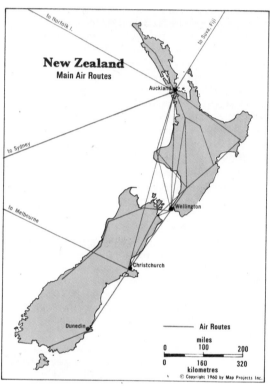

New Zealand
Main Air Routes

On the whole, New Zealand has a cool, maritime climate. On the western side of the mountains, which receive warm, westerly winds, the climate is similar to that of the south coast of Ireland. On the other side of the mountains it is much drier. Summer is mild on both islands, but the southern portion of South Island and the central and southern areas of North Island have cooler winters with snow and frost in many parts.

South Island has high, rugged moun-

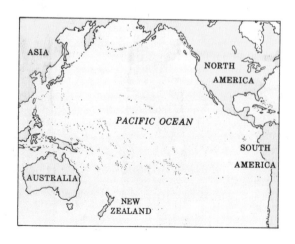

Forest-clad mountains look down on Doubtful Sound in Fiordland, South Island, New Zealand.

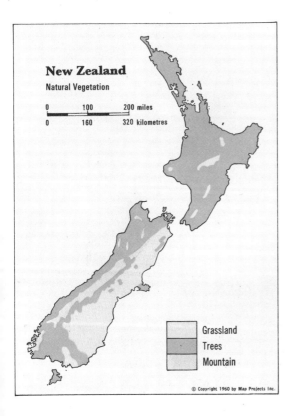

New Zealand

Natural Vegetation

| 0 | 100 | 200 miles |
| 0 | 160 | 320 kilometres |

Grassland
Trees
Mountain

© Copyright 1960 by Map Projects Inc.

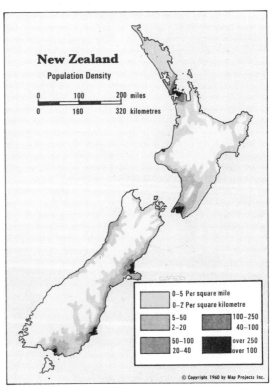

New Zealand

Population Density

| 0 | 100 | 200 miles |
| 0 | 160 | 320 kilometres |

0–5 Per square mile
0–2 Per square kilometre

5–50
2–20

50–100
20–40

100–250
40–100

over 250
over 100

© Copyright 1960 by Map Projects Inc.

tains, running the whole length of the island and completely filling up the centre. The highest peak is Mount Cook, which is more than 12,000 feet (3,700 m) above sea-level. Altogether, South Island has nineteen peaks over 10,000 feet (3,000 m).

The south-western corner of South Island is called Fiordland, because of the many deep fiords that have been scoured out of the rocks by former glaciers. These beautiful fiords, together with the mountains of the Southern Alps, lakes, and wonderful snowy slopes make South Island popular with tourists.

The mountains of North Island are not so high as those of South Island, but they are interesting for their active volcanoes and many hot springs.

For many ages New Zealand, like Australia, was cut off from any other land. However, unlike Australia, New Zealand is not rich in animal life. There are some species of plants and animals which are endemic, but most animals were introduced by Europeans. The most famous animals are the flightless birds, particularly the kiwi. The moa, an ostrich-like bird, is now extinct.

New Zealand's only land mammal is the bat. Some of the animals introduced by the Europeans have become pests. Rabbits have caused much damage, and deer browse on pastures meant for sheep.

Turning to plants, some interesting trees are the giant tree-fern and the rimu, totara, and kauri trees, which are valuable for their timber.

The first European to sight New Zealand was Abel Tasman, the greatest of the Dutch navigators, from whom Tasmania derives its name. He sailed along the coast of New Zealand in 1642, but it was almost 200 years before Europeans came to settle in any number in the country. The majority of these settlers came from Great Britain.

At first the native Maoris welcomed the settlers. Later they rose against them, and many years of fierce, though often extraordinarily chivalrous, fighting followed. Eventually the war came to an end, and the Maoris kept some of their land.

Volcanic peaks, surround Lake Wanaka in South Island.

A Maori mother bathes her son in one of the volcanic hot springs on North Island.

A typical New Zealand farm, among rolling fields. Most New Zealand farms are family-owned and highly efficient.

The Produce of the Land

New Zealand's abundant rainfall and mild all-year temperatures have produced some of the finest pasture in the world. On them graze pure-bred sheep and dairy cattle whose produce has made the country prosperous. Two-thirds of all the land is cultivable.

The farmlands of North Island are largely devoted to grazing. The dairy farms of North Island produce milk of the finest quality, while the province of Hawkes Bay, where they breed Romneys, is generally regarded as the finest sheep country in the world.

The quality of the grazing land of New Zealand is not due to natural conditions alone. The farmers themselves deserve much of the credit for it. They have planted the best grasses, fed the soil with fertilisers, and taken care that no pasture should be over-grazed.

South Island has a larger area of farming country and here farming is more mixed. Wheat and fruit are grown and many vegetables, but the rearing of livestock is in no way neglected.

So mild is the climate that neither cattle nor sheep require shelter. They can be left to graze in the open all the year round.

Dairy herds are not large. Most dairy farmers have about one hundred cows. There are, nevertheless, more than 9 million head of cattle in the country.

The number of sheep is even greater. There are 55 million. Except for those in the High Country, they are not generally the merinos reared on the dry Australian outback. The rich meadows of New Zealand make it more profitable to rear fat lambs – the Canterbury lamb we buy in our butchers' shops. Nevertheless, 10 per cent of the world's total wool production is from New Zealand.

With so much produce from the land, it is only to be expected that many of the factories of New Zealand are engaged in processing food: meat, butter, cheese,

Trained dogs are used on New Zealand's cattle and sheep ranches to help herd the animals.

New Zealand's mild summers, moist climate and rich grasslands are ideal for raising high-quality sheep.

processed milk, and other dairy products.

New Zealand is the world's greatest exporter of lamb and cheese, and it is second only to Denmark in the export of butter. The country rose to this position at the beginning of this century when refrigeration plants began to be installed in ships, making it possible to send food to every part of the world. Britain is New Zealand's most important customer, but EEC restrictions are making New Zealand look elsewhere for custom.

In the export of wool, New Zealand ranks second only to Australia. Altogether, animal produce – meat, wool, hides, and dairy produce – make up more than 90 per cent of her exports. Auckland lies to the north of the rich Waikato dairy region, and in it some of the country's dairy produce is processed, making it one of the chief industrial towns. With the country's great forests, the lumber trade is naturally important, and timber exports are considerable.

Other Industries

About one-fifth of the working population of New Zealand works in factories. They are not all engaged in food processing, but the other products are chiefly for home consumption. The manufacture of clothing and woollen cloth and the milling of flour have long been important industries. Newer industries are the assembly of motor-cars from parts made in other countries (Europe, the United States and Japan), carpets, printing, papermaking, and the manufacture of chemicals and fertilisers.

The country's mineral resources are varied but not large. There are deposits

Water from melting glaciers supplies the rivers which drives the Roxbrough hydro-electric power station in South Island.

of coal and gold on both North and South Island, and on the latter, iron is mined. Other mineral products include mercury, manganese, tin, platinum, silver, tungsten, and oil. A steel plant at Auckland uses local ore and coal. The chief mineral export is gold.

New Zealand's coal would soon be exhausted if water-power was not freely used. The many mountain steams, fed by a large and regular rainfall, mean that building hydro-electric power-stations is easy, electricity is plentiful and their capacity is doubling. Two aluminium smelters use it in South Island. Natural gas from the North Island is piped to Auckland and Wellington.

Government re-forestation schemes are doing much to stop soil erosion, and maintain the supply of timber.

The beauty of the South Sea islands is justly celebrated as this photograph shows.

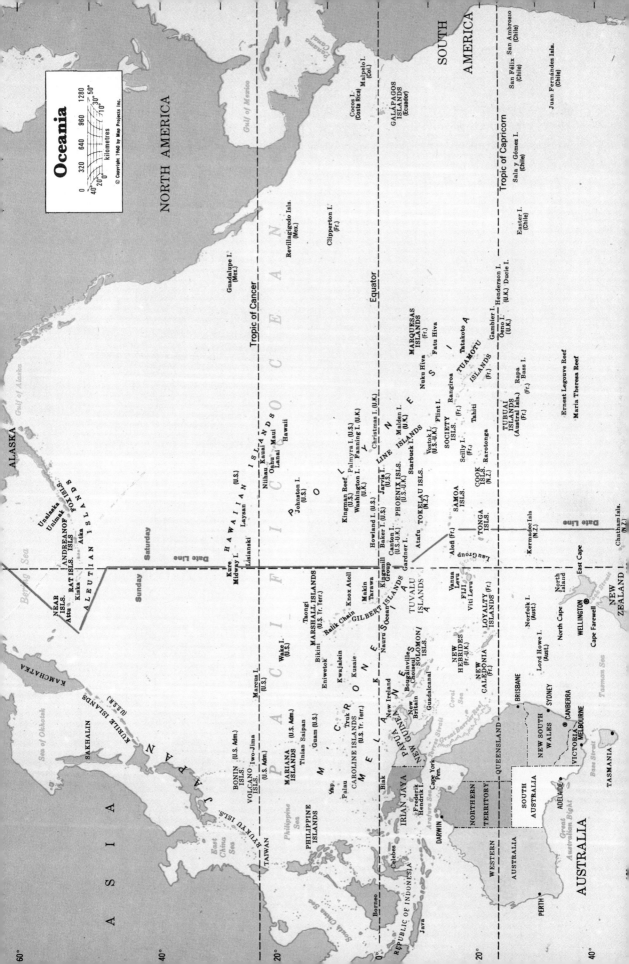

Oceania

© Copyright 1960 by Map Projects Inc.

kilometres
0 320 640 960 1280
0° 10° 30° 50°
40° 20°

NORTH AMERICA

SOUTH AMERICA

Gulf of Alaska

ALASKA

Gulf of Mexico

Guadalupe I. (Mex.)

Tropic of Cancer

Revillagigedo Isls. (Mex.)

Clipperton I. (Fr.)

Cocos I. (Costa Rica)

Malpelo I. (Col.)

GALÁPAGOS ISLANDS (Ecuador)

San Félix San Ambroso (Chile)

Equator

KAMCHATKA

Bering Sea

NEAR ISLS.
Attu Kiska
RAT ISLS. ANDREANOF ISLS.
Atka FOX ISLS.
Unalaska
Unimak
ALEUTIAN ISLANDS

Saturday

Sunday

SAKHALIN

Sea of Okhotsk

KURILE ISLANDS (U.S.S.R.)

J A P A N

TAIWAN

East China Sea

Ryukyu Isls.

BONIN ISLS. (U.S. Adm.)

VOLCANO ISLS. (U.S. Adm.)
Two-Jima

Marcus I. (U.S.)

Date Line

Kure
Midway I. (U.S.)

Lisianski

Laysan

H A W A I I A N   I S L A N D S (U.S.)
Niihau Kauai
Oahu Maui
Lanai Hawaii

Johnston I. (U.S.)

Kingman Reef (U.S.)
Palmyra I. (U.S.)
Washington I. (U.K.) Fanning I. (U.K.)

Christmas I. (U.K.)

L I N E   I S L A N D S
Jarvis I. (U.S.)
Malden I. (U.K.)
Starbuck I. (U.K.)
Vostok I. (U.S.-U.K.)
Flint I.

P A C I F I C   O C E A N

Philippine Sea

PHILIPPINE ISLANDS

MARIANA ISLANDS (U.S. Adm.)
Saipan
Tinian
Guam (U.S.)

M   I   C

Yap
Palau
CAROLINE ISLANDS (U.S. Tr. Terr.)
Truk
Kusaie

Biak

Frederik Hendrik I.

R O N E S I A

Thongi
MARSHALL ISLANDS (U.S. Tr. Terr.)
Bikini
Eniwetok
Kwajalein
Ralik Chain

Wake I. (U.S.)

Nauru Ocean I.
Makin
Tarawa
GILBERT ISLS.
Kingsmill Group
Knox Atoll

Howland I. (U.S.)
Baker I. (U.S.)
Canton (U.S.-U.K.)
Gardner I.
PHOENIX ISLS. (U.S.-U.K.)

Atafu
TOKELAU ISLS. (N.Z.)

SAMOA ISLS.

M   E   L   A   N   E   S   I   A

Celebes

REPUBLIC OF INDONESIA

Borneo

Java

IRIAN JAYA

PAPUA
NEW GUINEA
Cape York Pen.

New Ireland
New Britain
Bougainville
Choiseul
Guadalcanal
SOLOMON ISLS.

TUVALU ISLANDS

NEW HEBRIDES (Fr.-U.K.)

Vanua Levu
FIJI
Viti Levu

Lau Group

TONGA ISLS.

Alofi (Fr.)

Coral Sea

LOYALTY ISLANDS (Fr.)

NEW CALEDONIA (Fr.)

Norfolk I. (Aust.)

Lord Howe I. (Aust.)

Kermadec Isls. (N.Z.)

Date Line

DARWIN

NORTHERN TERRITORY

WESTERN AUSTRALIA

SOUTH AUSTRALIA

QUEENSLAND

NEW SOUTH WALES

VICTORIA

TASMANIA

A U S T R A L I A

BRISBANE

SYDNEY
CANBERRA
MELBOURNE

ADELAIDE

PERTH

Great Barrier Reef

Great Australian Bight

Bass Strait

Tasman Sea

North Cape
North Island
WELLINGTON
Cape Farewell

NEW ZEALAND

East Cape

Chatham Isls. (N.Z.)

MARQUESAS ISLANDS
Nuku Hiva
Fatu Hiva

Tatakoto

Rangiroa
TUAMOTU ISLANDS (Fr.)

SOCIETY ISLS.
Scilly I.
Tahiti

COOK ISLS. (N.Z.)
Rarotonga

TUBUAI ISLANDS (Austral Isls.) (Fr.)
Rapa
Bass I.

Tropic of Capricorn

Ernest Legouve Reef
Maria Theresa Reef

Gambier I. (Fr.)
Oeno I. (U.K.)
Henderson I. (U.K.) Ducie I.

Easter I. (Chile)

Sala y Gómez I. (Chile)

Juan Fernández Isls. (Chile)

A S I A

20°
40°
60°

20°
40°

The Pacific Islands

A vast area of water, tiny specks of land: that is the picture presented by Oceania. Scattered so widely, the islands naturally

This aerial view shows clearly the coral reefs surrounding a typical South Pacific atoll.

Craggy rock formations reveal the volcanic origin of Moorea, one of the Society Islands.

show us a great variety of landscape, people, vegetation, and, of course, animals.

Looking at the map you will see that most of the islands appear in clusters. These clusters usually occur where the sea is relatively shallow. From that relatively shallow ocean floor the peaks of mountains rise above the surface – for the floor of the ocean is quite uneven, and has folded into mountains, hills, and valleys, just like the dry land. Some of the depressions are very deep, and they are called troughs or deeps. Any area over 3,000 fathoms (18,000 feet) (5,500 m) in depth is called a deep. The deepest of all is a strip just to the east of the Philippine Islands, in which a depth of 6½ miles (10.5 km) has been recorded. In other words it is a mile (1.5 km) deeper than Mount Everest, the world's highest mountain, is high.

Some of the islands rise high out of the Pacific. In Western New Guinea, for instance, there are peaks that tower more than 15,000 feet (4,600 m) · above sea-level. These peaks are topped by perpetual ice and snow, despite the fact that New Guinea lies just south of the Equator. Of course few islands are high enough to be snow-capped, though there

Samoan boys learn how to handle outrigger canoes at a very early age.

are many fine mountains with craggy peaks. At the other extreme, some islands are so low on the horizon that, as you approach them, the coconut trees seem to be growing out of the sea. These are the coral islands or atolls.

Coconut palms shade the thatch-roofed huts of Nandi, a typical Fijian village.

Rugged mountains and palm-clad shores are a frequent sight on volcanic islands like Huahine.

Sleek, swift canoes like this one are both a necessity and a source of pleasure to Polynesian islanders.

Life on the Islands

On the whole the life of the coral islanders is simple. Their wants are few.

From the air, the atolls look like tiny beads of coral strung round a reef-

These natives of Maupiti, in the Society Islands, are netting fish in the shallow lagoon.

enclosed lagoon. The quiet water of the lagoon provides a safe harbour for the islanders' outrigger canoes, and a good supply of fish.

At night the islanders wade out into the still water of the lagoon, some carrying torches. Fish are attracted by the torch light, and as soon as they appear, a net is thrown across the water and men, women, and children all help to drag it in.

The islanders farm as well as fish, though the soil of the atolls is poor, and only a few plants will grow. The most important is the coconut. The flesh of the coconut contains an oil and is highly nourishing; so is the milk. On some waterless atolls coconut milk is the islanders' only drink.

The coconut palm plays a very big part in the life of these people. Not only

The stone traps in this lagoon are 200 years old. Fish are driven into the traps and then netted.

Fish are wrapped in leaves, cooked over white-hot stones, and then eaten with the fingers.

This Samoan father is teaching his young son how to spear fish with the traditional wooden spear. Fish canning is an important industry and tuna and local inshore fishing are expanding.

does it supply them with food and drink but the hollow shell becomes a flask, a cup, or the material for carved ornaments. The fibre of the husk is spun into cord. The trunk of the tree is used as building material and for making furniture, while the broad leaves can be used

487

This island boy has climbed the trunk of a coconut palm tree and is now selecting nuts to pick.

The island boys soon learn how to split open a newly picked coconut with one stroke of their sharp knives.

After the coconuts are picked, they are cracked open. The meat is then prised from the shell and spread out to dry in the sun. Dried coconut meat, called copra, is a valuable export. Coconut oil is extracted from copra.

The taro grows best if it is planted in fertile, swampy soil.

Selected stalks of taro are replanted in the plantations, to ensure a good crop in future.

as thatch or for making baskets. The coconut palm is indeed almost a universal provider.

It also provides copra, which is an important article of commerce. Copra is the dried flesh of the coconut, from which the oil is pressed to make margarine, salad oil, fine soaps, and cosmetics.

Preparing copra for shipping is one of the most important occupations on the atolls. The coconuts are opened and the flesh is scraped out of the shell and spread out to dry in the sun. This sun-dried copra is clean, and thus more valuable than the darker, smoke-dried copra of the high, rainy islands.

Here and there among the coconut palms are banana and breadfruit trees, or a small patch of taro – a plant with a starchy root that forms an important part of the diet of the coral islanders.

A few pigs and chickens wander in and out of the palm-thatched huts. Fish from the lagoon, and bonito and tunny fish caught in the open sea, provide most of the proteins that the islanders ever get.

Even the appearance of modern developments like the aeroplane and the radio have not profoundly changed this simple way of life.

Watermelons, grown on the low coral island of Maupiti, find a ready market in nearby Tahiti.

The Resources of the Pacific Islands

When European traders began coming to the islands, they found the people still living in the Stone Age. When the traders displayed their wares, the islanders were anxious to acquire them but the problem was: what could they give in exchange? It was the traders who found the answer: they discovered gold, nickel, bauxite, and chromium. Sometimes the native islanders were engaged to work in the mines, but more often foreign labour was brought in from China, Java, or Japan. For one thing, the rough life and hard work of mining did not appeal to the islanders. In general the islanders gained very little from these mining operations.

Some of the most important of the mining operations were those on the 'guano islands'. Guano, as we saw when we were dealing with Peru, is a valuable fertiliser,

A fire walking ceremony on Bega Island, in the Fiji group.

consisting of phosphates formed of birds' droppings. The life of the guano diggers was hard and lonely. The best deposits were found on barren, treeless rocks where there was no protection from the sun. Almost all supplies came by ship and the food was often poor. The men often became sick and many died. As soon as the deposits were worked out, the islands were abandoned to the sea bird, who had been, of course, responsible for the deposits in the first place.

Along with copra, bananas are a major Samoan export. They grow well on many Pacific islands.

Two islands are especially important sources of phosphates. They are Ocean Island and Nauru, where there are some of the world's richest phosphate deposits, vital to the farmers of Australia, New Zealand, and Japan. Papua New Guinea has copper, gold and silver.

Far more important than mining, however, are the plantations. Coffee, cocoa-beans, citrus fruits, bananas, pineapples, and cotton are all produced.

The Fiji, Hawaiian, and Mariana islands have enormous sugar plantations. The introduction of sugar-cane has brought great changes to these islands. Thousands of Asians were brought in to work on the plantations, and, even where the plantations have been abandoned, many of them have remained and now live side by side with the islanders.

More sugar than copra is produced in Oceania. But the production is concentrated in a few places, while the coconut is important almost everywhere. In some

Fijian copra is boxed at a company plantation and then shipped overseas from the port of Suva.

places the coconut palm, too, is grown on plantations. Sometimes these are small and privately owned. But on the Solomon and Fiji islands, and in Papua New Guinea, copra is produced on a large scale, the plantations being owned by companies. Regardless of how it is produced, copra is a very important product to nearly all the people of Oceania.

A schooner unloads cattle at Tahiti.

Cheap electricity derived from water-power is attracting new industries to Tasmania.

The Future of Oceania

What does the future hold for Australia and New Zealand and the thousands of Pacific islands? Many parts of the Pacific

Children in Fiji learn to read in an outdoor classroom. Today all Fijian children go to school.

have already acquired a new importance in communications. Islands that a few years ago were so isolated that they hardly ever saw a visitor, are now provided with landing strips and refuelling bases for aircraft. The air services of the Pacific are becoming more and more important with the development of communications between North America, Australia, and Asia.

Australia and the 'continental' islands contain some very ancient crystalline rocks in which mineral deposits are occasionally found. Sedimentary rocks (those formed by the building up of sediment deposited on the sea bottom) are also found in this region, and sometimes contain oil, so that besides the valuable minerals that have for years been mined in the Pacific, there are now a few oilfields

492

being exploited both in New Guinea and Australia.

More minerals are almost certain to be discovered in the continental islands, and for them the future is particularly promising. Also, the people of this area have hardly begun to exploit their resources of fish. Echo-sounding equipment will help fishermen to detect large shoals, and improved methods of preparing tropical fish for marketing will certainly be developed. Quick-freezing, packing, and floating tinning factories will do a lot to develop the industry.

Australia and New Zealand have always looked to Great Britain for their market. As the standard of living improves and the desire for consumer

A new house being built on one of the Society islands. Concrete is gradually replacing bamboo and thatch.

Frequent air services operate to and from Papua New Guinea to Australia. Fiji, the Solomon Islands and Irian Jaya are also connected.

goods increases in South-east Asia and elsewhere, and with EEC restrictions, they are finding many fresh markets near at hand. In fact Japan is Australia's biggest customer.

In the past Australia, New Zealand, and the Islands have been too distant from the great centres of population to attract many tourists, yet they have many attractions: Australia's Great Barrier Reef, the fiords, snow-capped peaks, and lovely mountain lakes of New Zealand, and the coral beaches of the Pacific islands. The development of fast, cheap, air travel has brought Oceania more within reach of holidaymakers.

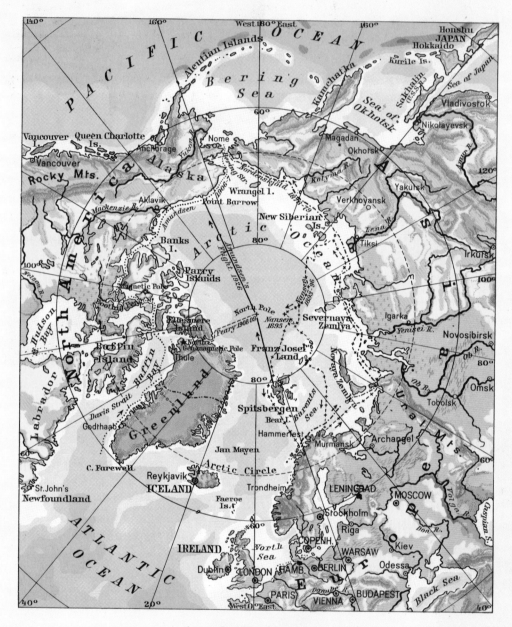

Arctic Regions

Scale 1 : 60 000 000

| 0 | 500 | 1000 | miles |

| 0 | 800 | 1600 | kilometres |

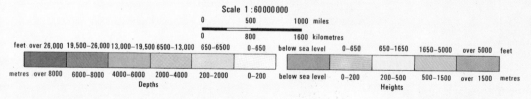

| | feet | over 26,000 | 19,500–26,000 | 13,000–19,500 | 6500–13,000 | 650–6500 | 0–650 | below sea level | 0–650 | 650–1650 | 1650–5000 | over 5000 | feet |

| metres | over 8000 | 6000–8000 | 4000–6000 | 2000–4000 | 200–2000 | 0–200 | below sea level | 0–200 | 200–500 | 500–1500 | over 1500 | metres |

Depths   Heights

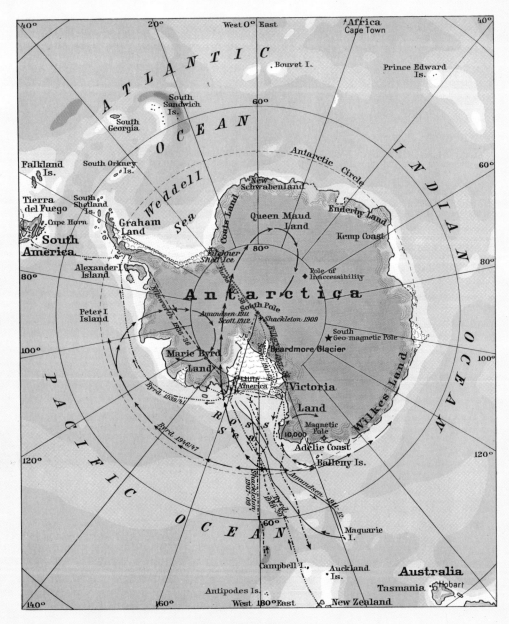

ATLANTIC

OCEAN

West 0° East

Africa
Cape Town

Bouvet I.

Prince Edward
Is.

South
Sandwich
Is.

South
Georgia

60°

Antarctic Circle

INDIAN

Falkland
Is.

South Orkney
Is.

60°

New
Schwabenland

Enderby Land

Tierra
del Fuego

South
Shetland
Is.

Weddell

Coats Land

Queen Maud
Land

Kemp Coast

Cape Horn

Graham
Land

Sea

80°

Filchner
Shelf Ice

80°

South
America

Alexander I
Island

Pole of
Inaccessibility

OCEAN

80°

Antarctica

Peter I
Island

Amundsen 1911
Scott 1912

South Pole

Shackleton 1909

South
Geo-magnetic Pole

100°

Ellsworth 1935-36

Beardmore Glacier

100°

Marie Byrd
Land

Byrd 1933/34

Byrd 1939/41

*Little
America*

Victoria
Land

Wilkes Land

P A C I F I C

Byrd 1946/47

R O S S

10,000

Magnetic
Pole

120°

S E A

Adélie Coast

120°

*Shackleton
1907-09*

*Byrd
1928-30*

Balleny Is.

Amundsen 1911-12

O C E A N

160°

Maquarie
I.

Campbell I.

Auckland
Is.

Australia

Antipodes Is.

Tasmania

Hobart

140°

160°

West 180° East

New Zealand

Antarctica

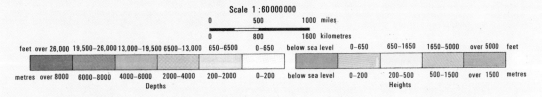

Scale 1 : 60 000 000

0	500	1000 miles
0	800	1600 kilometres

feet	over 26,000	19,500–26,000	13,000–19,500	6500–13,000	650–6500	0–650	below sea level	0–650	650–1650	1650–5000	over 5000	feet
metres	over 8000	6000–8000	4000–6000	2000–4000	200–2000	0–200	below sea level	0–200	200–500	500–1500	over 1500	metres

Depths — Heights

The Polar Regions

An imaginary line called the Arctic Circle is drawn on the globe in latitude 66° 30′ north. Within that circle lies the Arctic, one of the two polar regions. In the southern hemisphere, a similar line is drawn in latitude 66° 30′ south. This region is called the Antarctic. The lines are drawn in those particular latitudes because within those circles the sun never sets on midsummer's day, this being the phenomenon often called the midnight sun. Similarly, within those circles, the sun never rises in the middle of winter. The deeper you go into the polar regions, the longer is the period of continual daylight in summer and continual darkness in winter.

The chief characteristic of the polar regions is of course the extreme cold in the six month long winter. At the South Pole, a temperature of −101 °F (−73 °C) has been recorded. In summer temperatures do rise above freezing.

To such an extent do ice and snow dominate the landscape of the two polar regions that we often fail to realise how very different they really are. The Arctic is a 'hollow', a deep ocean basin. The Antarctic is a great mass of high land, which is in fact a continent, called Antarctica. Larger than Europe, this

The midnight sun lights up the sky over Narvik fiord, Norway, north of the Arctic Circle.

Vast snow-covered plateaus and towering mountains characterise Antarctica's frozen landscape.

This huge iceberg was once part of a glacier. The hole in it was carved by an underground river in the glacier.

continent covers an area of more than 5 million square miles (13 million sq km). Its average height of over 5,000 feet (1,500 m) is higher than that of any other continent. The Arctic Ocean is about as deep as the Antarctic continent is high.

The land surrounding the Arctic Ocean has been inhabited – even if very thinly – for at least 1,000 years by sturdy Eskimos who live by hunting and fishing. No people have ever made permanent homes in Antarctica.

A herd of walruses sun themselves on the rocky Alaskan coast. These warm-blooded animals spend most of their lives in the water. Eskimos hunt them for their meat, blubber, hides, and ivory tusks.

Animal Life

The Arctic is rich in animal life. There are great herds of reindeer in northern Europe and Asia, while the caribou, the North American reindeer, roams the Arctic plains of that continent. A peculiar animal found in North America and in Greenland is the musk ox. Standing 5 or 6 feet high (2 m) at the shoulder, in

Penguins live in colonies in the Antarctic. Their wings have turned into flippers, and they are powerful swimmers.

some ways it is half-way between an ox and a sheep. It has a long shaggy coat, reaching almost to the ground, which enables it to withstand the coldest Arctic winter.

Wolves and foxes sometimes follow reindeer, caribou, or musk ox, attacking stragglers from the herd.

But the best known of all the Arctic animals is the polar bear, which feeds on all sorts of marine animals from fish to seals and walruses.

Both birds and insects are found in great numbers on the land within the Arctic Circle. Millions of birds fly north each year to nest there during the summer months, and there is plenty of food for all, as swarms of mosquitoes and flies hatch in the pools of stagnant water that collect on the Arctic plain in summer.

The Antarctic is a complete contrast to this. A tiny wingless mosquito is the only land animal, and it is only found in a few sheltered areas of Antarctica. There are no land mammals at all, and the continent itself has no birds. The famous Antarctic penguins live on the pack ice around the edges of the continent, near the only source of food – the sea. Penguins are sea birds. They have adapted themselves so that their wings have become large flippers. They are superb swimmers and divers, but are, of course, completely flightless, and rather awkward on land.

The Arctic and Antarctic differ also in their plants. In the Antarctic, only a few mosses and lichens and hardy grasses grow on the rocky, ice-free slopes that catch the sun. Most of Antarctica is buried beneath a mantle of snow and ice, often more than 10,000 feet (3,000 m) thick.

Summer months in the Arctic are less cold than in the Antarctic, though temperatures are not high enough for trees to grow. This treeless region in the Arctic is called the tundra. But in summer, the tundra bursts into bloom. Travellers are

A polar bear cub prowls over an Arctic ice floe searching for food.

often amazed to find beautiful meadows of rich mosses and flowering lichens within the Arctic Circle. The tundra is fine summer grazing land for reindeer, caribou, and the musk ox. Even in winter these animals can paw through the snow to find food on the tundra. This area is also the home of Arctic hares and lemmings.

The caribou, wild cousin of the European reindeer, ranges the North American tundra in search of lichens and grass. The caribou is a principal source of food for the Indians and Eskimos.

Life in the Polar Regions

Nowhere in the inhabited world is life so hard as in the Arctic. The only people who have succeeded in making a permanent home there are the Eskimos. People of other races come on to the tundra in summer, driving their herds of reindeer. But when the winter closes in they move back to the more friendly forests further south.

The Eskimos live all along the extreme north of north-eastern Siberia, North America, and Greenland. Their total number has been estimated at 50,000.

Gambell, on St Lawrence Island off the Alaskan coast, is a typical modern Eskimo village.

Ages ago the Eskimos learned how to live in the Arctic. Since it was impossible to grow crops in the frozen soil of the tundra, they became skilled hunters and fishermen. Seals were their chief quarry, providing almost all their food. Seal skins were made into clothing. Tools and implements were made from the bones, and seal oil was used for fuel and light.

The threat of starvation was always present in the Arctic. By experience the Eskimos learned that if they killed too many seals in one place their source of food would be gone. Therefore they moved frequently to new hunting grounds. They travelled on dog sleighs over the frozen surface of the sea, or the snow-covered tundra. The most well-known Eskimo boat is the one-man kayak, but for travelling in summer and for whale hunting the Eskimos preferred the larger umiak.

Today only in a few isolated places do Eskimos still live like their ancestors. For most Eskimos the old ways of life are changing rapidly. Contact with Americans and Europeans is causing these changes.

Fur traders started some of the changes in the Eskimos' way of life. To help them kill more seals, fur traders gave the Eskimos rifles, which were, naturally, much more effective than the traditional harpoon and bow-and-arrow.

Using their new rifles the Eskimos, at first, easily secured great supplies of seal meat and furs. But they killed too many seals. Soon no seals were to be found in the old, familiar hunting places. And with the seals gone, the Eskimos had nothing to trade and nothing to eat. In some parts of the Arctic, whole villages of Eskimos starved.

Some Eskimos have completely changed their way of life. They have given up all of the ways of their ancestors. The children go to school. Some Eskimos have become radio operators and pilots; others teachers and skilled mechanics. Probably no people on earth have changed their way of life so rapidly as the Eskimos.

In Greenland, which is administered as a county by Denmark, many Eskimos have left their igloos and kayaks. They fish from motor-boats and have moved into fishing villages of wooden houses on the coast. The south-western coast is the most settled. The interior is a vast ice plateau surrounded by peaks and glaciers. In the north-east there is a vast Arctic desert with very little but ice.

If we ignore the desolate icebound South Shetland Islands, Antarctica is a very isolated continent. The tip of South America, the nearest of the other continents, is about 1,000 miles (1,600 m) away.

Releasing weather ballons at Thule, Greenland, one of the world's most northerly weather stations.

Brightly patterned sweaters of intricate design made by Eskimos in Greenland.

As penguins play in the foreground, a ship passes through a fog bank beneath towering Antarctic ice peaks.

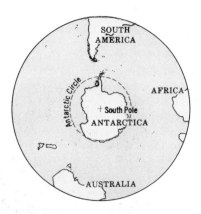

This great continent of Antarctica was almost unknown until modern times; much of it is still unexplored. That is not surprising for it is no easy task to approach the continent by ship. Sometimes great belts of pack-ice extend for hundreds of miles beyond the coast, and even the open seas themselves are dangerous. Rough and stormy, they are also beset by drifting ice and giant icebergs. The coast of Antarctica itself is flanked by towering cliffs of ice, 50 to 200 feet (15 to 60 m) high. Therefore it is hardly surprising that most of the exploration of Antarctica had to wait until suitable aircraft were developed, which could land men and equipment directly on to the continent.

Thrust up beneath the Antarctic icecap are some of the world's great mountain ranges. In Graham Land are peaks that rise more than 10,000 feet (3,050 m), while near the Ross Ice Shelf, the mountains can tower 15,000 feet (4,570 m) above sea-level.

Eastern Antarctica is a high plateau. Geologists say that its composition is much like that of the African plateau. Since the latter is rich in minerals, they now believe that great mineral wealth lies trapped beneath the Antarctic icecap.

Recent research at the South Pole has

confirmed this, but it is extremely difficult to study rocks buried beneath thousands of feet of ice. But in a few places there are rocks that outcrop the ice, and these have been found to contain coal, copper, nickel, and other minerals.

However, no large or valuable deposits have been discovered as yet and even if they were, the problems of mining under polar conditions would be great. Moreover, the transport of even the most valuable minerals to any market would probably be far more costly than their worth today. Therefore, Antarctica is unlikely to become a great mining centre in the near future.

The first men to be drawn towards the Antarctic were those who went for whaling. Whaling ships were sailing in the Antarctic as long ago as 1820. In those days whales were attacked with harpoons, hand-thrown from the ship's boats. Nowadays, whaling has been mechanised. Harpoons are fired from harpoon-guns mounted on the whaler itself. The whalers are accompanied by giant factory ships. As soon as two or three whales are caught, they are towed to a factory-ship where they are hoisted on board and dealt with. Almost every part of the whale's carcass has some value. The most important product is whale oil, which is extracted chiefly from the blubber, the layer of fat under the skin. Some of the flesh goes into cold storage to be used as whale meat, while the bones are crushed up into bonemeal, a valuable fertiliser.

So efficient did modern whaling methods become that it looked at one time as though whales would be completely exterminated. In order to prevent this strict regulations were drawn up to restrict whale-fishing. It is confined to certain months of the year; no young whale may be killed; and there is a limit

SS Manhattan breaking ice in Melville Sound.

This observation tower at 'Little America' is part of an Antarctic weather station.

attempts, but the first man to succeed in reaching the Pole was a Norwegian, Roald Amundsen, who reached it by a swift dash on skis, hoisting his country's flag over the Pole on 14 December, 1911. Meanwhile on 6 April, 1909, an American, Robert E. Peary, had reached the North Pole.

In recent years many scientists have gone to the Antarctic, building scientific stations, both on the continent and the surrounding islands. One of their aims is to discover the influence of this great frozen continent on the weather in other parts of the world, an influence which is believed to be considerable. Other scientists have been measuring the depth of the ice-cap, studying rock formation, and measuring the flow of off-shore ocean currents.

Surveying has also been proceeding, the work being greatly helped by aerial photography. This work has been done by many nations, scientific stations having been established by the United States and the USSR, Britain, and many others.

to the total number that may be captured.

It was not until this century that explorers set out to cross Antarctica to reach the South Pole. There were several

An aeroplane is unloaded for use in Operation Deep-freeze, an Antarctic exploration project.

This titanium mine in Greenland exploits one of the barely touched mineral resources of the polar lands.

The Future of the Polar Regions

So far man has done little to change the natural landscape of either the Arctic or the Antarctic. It is hard to believe that he will ever be able to change much. Even where quite large communities have been established, they are dug into the snow and virtually invisible from the surface. Small populations will no doubt go on living in the Arctic, but it is difficult to see how a population could maintain itself in Antarctica. The number of scientific teams working in the Antarctic and maintained from outside will probably increase, and important work is likely to be done there (making Antarctica the only continent to be used solely as a laboratory). However, it is hoped by many people that eventually the separate national research teams will give up their competing claims and merge together in a common effort directed by the United Nations, or some other international authority.

The outlook in the Arctic is different. Valuable minerals like uranium have already been discovered within the Arctic Circle. The day will come when these minerals are wanted, as the more accessible sources become used up. In the future small mining communities may well be established, scattered across the Arctic. As things are at present, the provision of heat and power for the men working in them would be a very serious problem, but before long nuclear reactors will be more generally available, and they will provide the ideal solution.

A base for scientific teams in Antarctica.

Pollution and Conservation

Since the beginning of the 1960s these two words have been used more and more. People have become aware that as countries scramble for industrialisation and modern living, more and more waste in every form is being accumulated and that our environment is becoming less pleasant. For example factory chimneys pass fumes into the atmosphere, industrial waste flows into our rivers and seas killing people and fish, the waste from mineral extraction is dumped in spoil heaps, indestructible plastics are left everywhere, and juggernaut lorries roar through narrow streets.

Dense black smoke caused by oil gas release. An example of air pollution in Bahrein (above). Low-lying land reclaimed through efficient drainage in Schleswig-Holstein, Germany (below).

Governments, realising how we are destroying our environment, are passing laws and giving grants to help conserve our surroundings. Old industrial lakes are being turned into reservoirs or boating lakes, spoil heaps are being flattened for farming, or forested; industrial effluent is being limited, and many restrictions are now put on the building of motorways and housing schemes to keep the landscape tidy.

Soil conservation has been mentioned many times in this atlas, and there are schemes all over the world to conserve our most precious resource.

Conservation of the world's water resources has become more vital as the population and its needs increase. Dams for irrigation, desalination of water and recycling of industrial water are just a few of the ways water can be saved.

Conservation of energy resources is very important today, with more and more countries becoming industrialised and with living standards becoming higher. Experiments in solar energy are taking place in several parts of the world, as countries assess how long the world's oil and coal will last. Atomic power is being used more and more, but there are fears that if incorrectly managed it could pollute the atmosphere.

Conservation of minerals is important also. In many mining areas old spoil heaps are being searched for overlooked minerals and many old mines are being reworked for minerals associated with the original ones. Scrap metals are resmelted and shipped between countries for specific uses.

In all these ways, and many more, our environment can be saved.

The Aswan dam in Egypt. This irrigation scheme has led to a vast area being made fertile.

These terraces on the Greek island of Naxos have made cultivation of the hillsides possible.

Plate Tectonics

Those who study maps have for a long time been fascinated by the idea that the continents of the earth, now so widely separated, may once have been part of the same land mass. The eastern bulge of Brazil, for instance, fits fairly neatly into the Gulf of Guinea, which forms the great inward curve of the West African coast. Similarly, though less obviously, the western coasts of India and Australia can be made to fit on to the east coast of Africa.

Recent research with seismological equipment, deep drilling experiments, and the study of magnetic fields, has shown that these theories were correct. Through a study of the structure and movements of the earth's crust today, an assessment has been made of how our pattern of continents has evolved with little distortion of their shapes subsequent to their dispersal from a single land mass.

Along the middle of our present day oceans there are volcanic ridges, from which molten rock is ejected from deep inside the earth. This has happened in Iceland where the mid-Atlantic ridge extends above the level of the sea. Iceland has frequent volcanic eruptions and recently a whole new volcanic island, Surtsee, was formed near it. The ocean floor moves outwards at the rate of a few centimetres a year to accommodate the extra volcanic material from the ridges, in a process known as sea-floor spreading. The earth's crust is formed of segments or plates, which move outwards away from the ridges in this way. This explains in part how some of the continents have moved apart whilst still maintaining their shape.

Some of the plates exist beneath the oceans, but some rise close to the ocean surface or rise above it and form our continents; for example: Africa, India, and Australia are all separate plates. There are six large plates on the earth's crust today and six smaller ones; some of these are entirely oceanic, some continental and some a mixture of both.

As these plates, which are internally rigid, but which can move freely on the material below the earth's crust, move

507

All the mountains in the world are associated with plate margin activity. This is a view of Grindelwald in the Alps.

around the surface of the earth away from the mid-oceanic ridges, they collide. When this takes place the plates either slide past each other, or one plate moves underneath another plate. During this movement, material moves back into the earth's interior and compensates for the loss of material to the earth's crust at the mid-oceanic ridges.

When plates slide past each other, faulting occurs, as at the famous St Andreas fault line along the west coast of the USA.

Where one plate moves under another, deep trenches, and in close proximity, high, crumpled mountain ranges are formed. These occur in linear bands and are associated with intensive earthquake and volcanic activity.

Where the Indian continental plate has collided with the Asian plate, a trench, which is now filled by the Ganges alluvial basin, and the Himalayan mountain range were formed.

Where the oceanic plate off the West coast of South America has moved beneath the South American continental plate, a deep trench is found off the western shore of South America, and the Andes mountains and their volcanic peaks have formed.

A similar picture exists in the Pacific ocean where an oceanic plate has pushed under a continental plate and given rise to the Java and Japanese volcanic mountain ranges; the deepest ocean trench in the world; and intense earthquakes.

Most of the volcanic activity and earthquakes that have been recorded in history have occurred along the oceanic ridges and trenches, and they demonstrate that the movement of the earth's crust over the last 200 million years is still in progress.

World Air
and Sea Routes

—— Major Air Routes

—— Major Shipping Routes

☐ Countries not using
Greenwich Time

World
Time Zones

Countries using
Greenwich Time;
one hour zones

odd

even

Greenwich Time;
half after the hour

Facts and Figures

Europe

PRINCIPAL COUNTRIES: AREA, POPULATION

KM = Kilometre
M = Metre

COUNTRY	AREA IN SQ KM	AREA IN SQ MILES	POPULA-TION
Sweden	411,479	173,430	8,144,428
Norway	323,886	125,100	3,973,000
Denmark	43,074	16,576	5,036,184
Finland	305,745	130,100	4,655,250
Iceland	103,000	39,750	213,500
Great Britain and N. Ireland	243,998	94,250	56,000,000
Ireland (Eire)	68,893	26,600	2,980,250
Belgium	30,513	11,778	9,756,600
Netherlands	33,812	13,054	13,733,578
Luxembourg	2,586	998	352,700
France	551,601	212,660	52,000,000
West Germany	248,600	95,300	62,000,000
East Germany	108,178	41,700	17,000,000
Austria	83,850	32,500	7,456,400
Switzerland	41,288	15,944	6,269,800
Spain	504,880	194,945	34,000,000
Portugal	91,631	35,400	8,700,000
Italy	301,245	116,270	55,000,000
Greece	131,986	51,182	8,768,600
Poland	312,677	120,759	33,500,000
Czechoslovakia	127,877	49,370	14,635,000
Hungary	93,032	35,912	10,510,000
Yugoslavia	255,804	98,900	20,000,000
Albania	28,748	11,800	2,400,000
Romania	237,500	91,700	21,000,000
Bulgaria	110,911	42,796	8,706,000
Turkey (in Europe)	23,721	9,155	3,000,000
Soviet Union	22,400,000	8,650,600	255,500,000

PRINCIPAL TOWNS

TOWN	POPULATION*
Paris (France)	8,424,000
London (Britain)	7,167,600
Moscow (USSR)	7,528,000
Leningrad (USSR)	4,243,000
Madrid (Spain)	3,146,071
Rome (Italy)	2,833,103
Berlin, West (W. Germany)	2,047,948
Budapest (Hungary)	2,039,000
Athens (Greece)	2,540,240
Hamburg (W. Germany)	1,751,620
Istanbul (Turkey)	3,019,032
Barcelona (Spain)	1,745,142
Vienna (Austria)	1,734,800
Milan (Italy)	1,743,400
Kiev (USSR)	1,887,000
Bucharest (Romania)	1,642,800
Copenhagen (Denmark)	1,392,200
Lisbon (Portugal)	1,568,000
Warsaw (Poland)	1,388,000
Stockholm (Sweden)	1,485,600
Munich (W. Germany)	1,336,600
Naples (Italy)	1,221,859
Baku (USSR)	1,359,000
Gorki (USSR)	1,260,000
Brussels (Belgium)	1,063,274
Birmingham (Britain)	1,086,500
Berlin, East (E. Germany)	1,088,828
Prague (Czechoslovakia)	1,091,000
Marseilles (France)	1,005,000
Glasgow (Scotland)	893,790
Sofia (Bulgaria)	946,305
Amsterdam (Netherlands)	1,001,052
Belgrade (Yugoslavia)	1,204,270
Kazan (USSR)	931,000
Helsinki (Finland)	844,826
Dublin (Eire)	823,00
Oslo (Norway)	468,515
Zurich (Switzerland)	715,300
Belfast (N. Ireland)	362,100
Rotterdam (Netherlands)	1,040,230
Luxembourg (Luxembourg)	78,000
Reykjavik (Iceland)	84,300
Tiranë (Albania)	175,000

*These are the figures for the conurbation, not for the city alone.

HIGHEST MOUNTAINS

MOUNTAIN	HEIGHT IN M	HEIGHT IN FEET
Mount Communism (USSR)	7,470	24,500
Lenin (USSR)	7,126	23,380
Elbruz (USSR)	5,651	18,540
Klyuchevskaya (USSR)	4,850	15,912
Mont Blanc (France)	4,809	15,780
Monte Rosa (Italy)	4,638	15,217
Weisshorn (Switzerland)	4,511	14,800
Matterhorn (Switzerland – Italy)	4,504	14,780
Gross Glockner (Austria)	3,800	12,450
Mulhacen (Spain)	3,481	11,421
Aneto (Spain)	3,400	11,168
Olympus (Greece)	2,971	9,750

GREAT RIVERS

RIVER	LENGTH IN KM	LENGTH IN MILES
Lena (USSR)	4,506	2,800
Amur (USSR)	4,345	2,700
Yenisei (USSR)	3,910	2,430
Ob (USSR)	3,637	2,260
Volga (USSR)	3,621	2,250
Danube (Western and Eastern Europe)	2,730	1,770
Ural (USSR)	2,462	1,530
Dnieper (USSR)	2,285	1,420
Rhine (Switzerland – France – Germany – Holland)	1,370	850
Elbe (Western and Eastern Europe)	1,159	720
Loire (France)	1,011	628
Ebro (Spain)	925	575
Rhône (France)	812	505
Seine (France)	774	482
Po (Italy)	676	420

INLAND SEAS AND LAKES

SEA OR LAKE	AREA IN SQ KM	AREA IN SQ MILES
Caspian Sea (USSR)	433,430	169,380
Aral Sea (USSR)	65,783	25,400
Baikal (USSR)	32,814	12,670
Ladoga (USSR)	18,388	7,100
Balkhash (USSR)	17,870	6,900
Onega (USSR)	8,534	3,800
Wener (Sweden)	6,422	2,480
Peipus (USSR)	3,626	1,400
Geneva (France – Switzerland)	583	225
Constance (Switzerland – Austria – Germany)	532	208

Asia

PRINCIPAL COUNTRIES: AREA, POPULATION

COUNTRY	AREA IN SQ KM	AREA IN SQ MILES	POPULA-TION
Turkey (in Asia)	756,855	295,000	39,000,000
Lebanon	10,400	4,000	2,854,636
Israel	20,700	8,000	3,200,000
Jordan	95,000	37,000	2,577,000
Yemen Arab Republic	195,000	75,000	7,000,000
Iraq	438,446	171,267	10,410,000
Syria	185,680	71,229	6,000,000
Saudi Arabia	2,400,000	927,000	7,800,000
Bahrain	595	230	216,815
Kuwait	24,280	5,990	862,200
Oman	271,940	105,000	750,000
People's Democratic Republic of Yemen	160,300	61,890	1,390,000
Iran	1,648,000	630,000	30,000,000
Afghanistan	657,500	250,000	19,580,000
India	3,053,600	1,259,000	547,000,000
Pakistan	801,408	310,403	65,000,000
Bangladesh	142,800	55,126	71,000,000
Sri Lanka	64,640	25,300	13,000,000
Nepal	141,400	54,000	11,700,000
Bhutan	46,600	18,000	1,100,000
Burma	678,000	262,000	28,900,000
Thailand	514,000	198,456	40,000,000
Kampuchea	181,000	67,000	6,800,000
Laos	235,700	91,450	2,900,000
Vietnam	336,000	130,000	44,000,000
China	9,738,350	3,760,000	800,000,000
Mongolia	1,565,000	604,095	1,400,000
Taiwan (Nationalist China)	35,980	13,885	15,570,000
Hong Kong	1,030	398	4,250,000
North Korea	122,370	47,000	15,000,000
South Korea	98,430	37,000	34,000,000
Japan	372,500	142,000	110,000,000
Philippines	297,800	115,000	37,000,000
Indonesia	1,900,000	575,890	130,000,000
Malaysia	329,640	127,281	10,400,000

PRINCIPAL TOWNS

TOWN	POPULATION*
Tokyo (Japan)	18,000,000
Shanghai (China)	11,000,000
Peking (China)	10,000,000
Bombay (India)	6,000,000
Calcutta (India)	7,000,000
Tientsin (China)	4,000,000
Hong Kong (Br. Crown Colony)	4,250,000
Lu-ta (China)	3,600,000

Osaka (Japan)	3,200,000
Canton (China)	3,000,000
Jakarta (Indonesia)	4,700,000
Delhi (India)	3,630,000
Tehran (Iran)	3,150,000
Karachi (Pakistan)	3,470,000
Bangkok (Thailand)	3,967,080
Wuhan (China)	3,000,000
Chungking (China)	2,121,000
Singapore (S.E. Asia)	2,185,000
Nagoya (Japan)	2,051,000
Yokohama (Japan)	2,377,000
Madras (India)	2,470,000
Baghdad (Iraq)	1,934,000
Lahore (Pakistan)	2,148,000
Harbin (China)	1,600,000
Sian (China)	1,500,000
Saigon-Cholon (Vietnam)	1,800,000
Pusan (South Korea)	1,878,785
Nanking (China)	1,500,000
Manila (Philippines)	1,500,000
Kyoto (Japan)	1,440,000
Hyderabad (India)	1,798,900
Kobe (Japan)	1,300,100
Taipei (Taiwan)	1,830,000
Surabaya (Indonesia)	1,300,000
Bandung (Indonesia)	984,000
Pyongyang (North Korea)	1,500,000
Hanoi (Vietnam)	1,378,335
Quezon (Philippines)	760,000
Cabul (Afghanistan)	435,000
Tel Aviv-Jaffa (Israel)	362,900
Jerusalem (Israel)	304,500
Amman (Jordan)	583,000
Kuala Lumpur (Malaysia)	451,728
Mecca (Saudi Arabia)	250,000
Katmandu (Nepal)	195,000
Ulan-Bator (Mongolia)	282,000
Beirut (Lebanon)	702,000
Damascus (Syria)	840,000
Manama (Bahrein)	90,000
Seoul (South Korea)	5,525,282
Colombo (Sri Lanka)	562,160
Rangoon (Burma)	3,186,886
Dacca (Bangladesh)	1,310,972
Phnom Penh (Kampuchea)	1,800,000
Islamabad (Pakistan)	235,000
Vientiane (Laos)	150,000
Lhasa (Tibet)	40,000

HIGHEST MOUNTAINS

MOUNTAIN	HEIGHT IN M	HEIGHT IN FEET
Everest (Nepal – Tibet)	8,847	29,028
K2-Godwin Austen (India)	8,611	28,250
Kanchenjunga (Nepal – Sikkim)	8,580	28,150
Makalu (Nepal – Tibet)	8,470	27,790
Cho Oyu (Nepal – Tibet)	8,190	26,867
Ararat (Turkey)	5,165	16,945
Kinabalu (Borneo)	4,101	13,455
Fujiyama (Japan)	3,780	12,395

GREAT LAKES

LAKE	AREA IN SQ KM	AREA IN SQ MILES
Urmia (Iran)	5,957	2,300
Koko Nor (China)	5,957	2,300
Hamun-i-Helmand (Afghanistan–Iran)	5,180	2,000
Van (Turkey)	5,180	2,000
Tungtin (China)	3,755	1,450
Tonlé Sap (Kampuchea)	1,994	770

LONGEST RIVERS

RIVER	LENGTH IN KM	LENGTH IN MILES
Yangtze Kiang (China)	5,480	3,400
Hwang Ho (China)	4,670	2,900
Mekong (China – Thailand)	4,184	2,600
Indus (Pakistan)	3,058	1,900
Brahmaputra (India)	2,897	1,800
Amur (China – Russia)	2,848	1,770
Salween (China – Burma)	2,817	1,750
Euphrates (Turkey – Syria – Iraq)	2,736	1,700
Ganges (India)	2,510	1,560
Irrawaddy (Burma)	2,092	1,300
Tigris (Turkey – Iraq)	1,850	1,150

*These are the figures for the conurbation, not for the city alone.

Africa

PRINCIPAL COUNTRIES: AREA, POPULATION

COUNTRY	AREA IN SQ KM	AREA IN SQ MILES	POPULA-TION
Morocco	458,730	166,000	16,300,000
Algeria	2,300,000	878,000	14,600,000
Tunisia	125,096	48,300	5,270,000
Libya	1,759,540	679,203	2,300,000
Egypt	1,000,000	386,110	36,000,000
Sudan	2,500,000	967,500	15,200,000
Chad	1,284,000	485,750	3,900,000
Niger	1,187,000	449,400	4,243,000
Mali	1,204,021	448,200	5,000,000
Mauritania	1,030,700	449,800	1,180,000
Senegal	197,777	75,750	3,900,000
Gambia	11,000	4,000	494,300
Guinea	245,857	94,927	4,010,000
Sierra Leone	73,326	27,925	3,100,000
Liberia	112,600	43,000	1,500,000
Ivory Coast	322,463	124,510	5,000,000
Upper Volta	274,002	113,100	5,210,000
Ghana	238,537	91,842	8,900,000
Nigeria	923,773	356,669	58,000,000
Togo	56,000	21,616	2,100,000
Benin	112,600	42,946	3,200,000
Zaire	2,345,400	905,564	24,300,000
Cameroun	474,000	183,570	6,000,000
Gabon	267,000	103,089	600,000
Congo Republic	342,000	132,100	1,250,000
Central African Republic	625,000	238,220	2,500,000
Rwanda	26,300	10,166	5,500,000
Burundi	27,834	10,747	3,600,000
Ethiopia	1,000,000	395,000	26,000,000
Somalia	700,000	246,200	2,930,000
Kenya	582,600	224,960	11,100,800
Uganda	236,860	93,891	11,171,000
Tanzania	938,010	362,180	13,750,000
Malagasy Rep.	594,180	229,233	7,700,000
Rep. of S. Africa	1,221,042	472,685	21,500,000
Zambia	752,262	290,323	4,500,000
Angola	1,246,700	481,353	5,673,000
Zimbabwe Rhodesia	390,622	150,333	6,100,000
Malawi	119,310	46,066	4,550,000
Botswana	575,000	222,000	750,000

PRINCIPAL TOWNS

TOWN	POPULATION*
Cairo (Egypt)	8,300,000
Alexandria (Egypt)	2,000,000
Johannesburg (South Africa)	1,600,000
Casablanca (Morocco)	1,894,000
Algiers (Algeria)	1,015,000
Cape Town (South Africa)	1,200,000
Kampala (Uganda)	400,000
Brazzaville (Congo Republic)	250,000
Lusaka (Zambia)	350,000
Abidjan (Ivory Coast)	500,000
Tunis (Tunisia)	944,000
Lagos (Nigeria)	740,000
Durban (South Africa)	950,000
Ibadan (Nigeria)	710,000
Addis Ababa (Ethiopia)	912,000
Kinshasa (Zaire)	1,430,000
Nairobi (Kenya)	520,000
Dakar (Senegal)	581,000
Pretoria (South Africa)	650,000
Salisbury (Zimbabwe Rhodesia)	522,000
Oran (Algeria)	410,000
Marrakesh (Morocco)	1,642,300
Accra (Ghana)	848,825

HIGHEST MOUNTAINS

MOUNTAIN	HEIGHT IN M	HEIGHT IN FEET
Kilimanjaro (Tanzania)	5,963	19,565
Kenya (Kenya)	5,200	17,000
Ruwenzori (Zaire)	5,119	16,795
Ras Dashan (Ethiopia)	4,621	15,160
Elgon (Kenya)	4,321	14,178
Bale (Ethiopia)	4,307	14,131
Guna (Ethiopia)	4,231	13,881
Gughe (Ethiopia)	4,200	13,780
Toubkal (Morocco)	4,165	13,665
Talo (Ethiopia)	4,099	13,451
Cameroun (Cameroun)	4,069	13,350

LARGEST LAKES

LAKE	AREA IN SQ KM	AREA IN SQ MILES
Victoria (Central Africa)	69,482	26,828
Tanganyika (Central Africa)	32,892	12,700
Malawi (Central Africa)	28,490	11,000
Chad (Central Africa)	20,720	8,000
Turkana (Central Africa)	9,064	3,500
Mabutu (Central Africa)	5,345	2,064
Tana (Central Africa)	3,626	1,400
Mai Ndombe (Central Africa)	2,330	900

GREAT RIVERS

RIVER	LENGTH IN KM	LENGTH IN MILES
Nile (N. and C. Africa)	6,678	4,150
Zaire (Central Africa)	4,700	2,900
Niger (Central Africa)	4,200	2,600
Zambezi (Southern Africa)	3,540	2,200
Ubangi-Uélé (Central Africa)	2,253	1,400
Orange (Southern Africa)	2,100	1,300
Kasai (Central Africa)	1,770	1,100
Limpopo (Southern Africa)	1,609	1,000
Okovango (Southern Africa)	1,609	1,000

North America

PRINCIPAL COUNTRIES: AREA, POPULATION

COUNTRY	AREA IN SQ M	AREA IN SQ MILES	POPULA-TION
*Canada	9,974,000	3,851,113	22,000,000
USA	9,212,300	3,557,098	212,000,000
Mexico	1,967,183	760,373	56,240,000
Nicaragua	148,000	57,145	2,210,000
Cuba	114,524	44,206	9,170,000
Honduras	112,088	43,227	2,800,000
Guatemala	108,889	42,042	5,200,000
Panama	75,650	28,571	1,584,000
Costa Rica	50,900	19,695	1,870,000
Dominican Rep.	48,442	19,303	4,250,000
Haiti	27,750	10,714	4,450,000
Belize	22,960	8,867	120,000
El Salvador	21,360	8,259	3,680,000

*Land and fresh water area

PRINCIPAL TOWNS

TOWN	POPULATION*
New York (USA)	11,572,000
Los Angeles (USA)	7,091,000
Chicago (USA)	6,977,000
Mexico City (Mexico)	8,600,000
Philadelphia (USA)	4,824,000
Detroit (USA)	4,435,000
Boston (USA)	3,376,000
San Francisco (USA)	3,010,000
Washington D.C. (USA)	2,909,000
Montreal (Canada)	2,750,000
Pittsburg (USA)	2,401,000
St Louis (USA)	2,360,000
Toronto (Canada)	2,628,000
Cleveland (USA)	2,063,000
Baltimore (USA)	4,800,000
Houston (USA)	1,999,316
Havana (Cuba)	1,864,000
Milwaukee (USA)	1,403,000
Panama City (Panama)	418,000
Santo Domingo (Dominican Rep.)	900,862
Port au Prince (Haiti)	500,000
Santa Ana (El Salvador)	180,000

HIGHEST MOUNTAINS

MOUNTAIN	HEIGHT IN M	HEIGHT IN FEET
Mount McKinley (Alaska)	6,193	20,320
Logan (Canada)	6,052	19,850
Orizaba (Mexico)	5,712	18,700
St Elias (Alaska – Canada)	5,489	18,008
Popocatepetl (Mexico)	5,452	17,887
Ixtacihautl (Mexico)	5,286	17,342
Foraker (Alaska)	5,267	17,280
Lucania (Canada)	5,237	17,150
Steele (Canada)	5,012	16,439
Bona (Alaska)	5,002	16,420
Sanford (Alaska)	4,940	16,208
Blackburn (Alaska)	4,920	16,140
Wood (Canada)	4,840	15,880
Whitney (California)	4,420	14,495

LARGEST LAKES

LAKE	AREA IN SQ KM	AREA IN SQ MILES
Superior (Canada – USA)	82,411	31,820
Huron (Canada – USA)	59,594	23,010
Michigan (USA)	58,014	22,400
Great Bear (Canada)	31,068	12,000
Great Slave (Canada)	28,929	11,170
Erie (Canada – USA)	25,744	9,940
Winnipeg (Canada)	22,157	8,555
Ontario (Canada – USA)	19,528	7,540
Nicaragua (Nicaragua)	8,028	3,100
Athabaska (Canada)	7,940	3,066
Winnipegosis (Canada)	5,402	2,086
Manitoba (Canada)	4,650	1,817

GREAT RIVERS

RIVER	LENGTH IN KM	LENGTH IN MILES
Missouri (USA)	4,367	2,714
Mackenzie (Canada)	4,046	2,514
Mississippi (USA)	3,782	2,350
St Lawrence (Canada – USA)	3,782	2,350
Yukon (Canada – USA)	3,185	1,979
Rio Grande (USA – Mexico)	2,897	1,800
Arkansas (USA)	2,334	1,450
Colorado (USA – Mexico)	2,253	1,400
Ohio (USA)	2,102	1,306
Red (USA)	2,092	1,300
Saskatchewan (Canada)	1,940	1,205
Columbia (USA)	1,931	1,200
Peace (Canada)	1,696	1,054
Snake (USA)	1,670	1,038

*These are the figures for the conurbation, not for the city alone.

South America

PRINCIPAL COUNTRIES: AREA, POPULATION

COUNTRY	AREA IN SQ KM	AREA IN SQ MILES	POPULA-TION
Guyana	215,000	83,000	750,000
Guiana	91,000	35,135	50,000
Surinam	163,265	63,037	384,900
Venezuela	912,050	352,100	10,700,000
Colombia	1,138,914	439,600	24,000,000
Ecuador	270,670	106,200	6,090,000
Peru	1,285,215	496,200	14,100,000
Chile	741,767	286,400	10,044,000
Argentina	2,807,804	1,084,100	23,000,000
Uruguay	186,479	72,200	3,110,000
Brazil	8,511,965	3,287,700	93,000,000
Bolivia	1,098,580	421,400	5,062,000
Paraguay	406,752	157,000	2,354,670

PRINCIPAL TOWNS

TOWN	POPULATION*
Buenos Aires (Argentina)	8,700,000
São Paulo (Brazil)	5,925,000
Rio de Janeiro (Brazil)	4,300,000
Santiago (Chile)	3,700,000
Bogota (Colombia)	2,978,300
Lima (Peru)	3,317,650
Caracas (Venezuela)	2,200,000
Montevideo (Uruguay)	1,450,000
Belo Horizonte (Brazil)	1,235,000
Recife (Brazil)	1,060,700
Medellin (Colombia)	1,269,900
Porto Alegre (Brazil)	905,545
Salvador (Brazil)	1,007,195
Rosario (Argentina)	807,000
Guayaquil (Ecuador)	835,812
Maracaibo (Venezuela)	650,050
La Paz (Bolivia)	562,000
Georgetown (Guyana)	172,000
Quito (Ecuador)	551,163
Asunción (Paraguay)	392,753

HIGHEST MOUNTAINS

MOUNTAIN	HEIGHT IN M	HEIGHT IN FEET
Aconcagua (Argentina)	6,960	22,835
Ojos del Salado (Argentina – Chile)	6,873	22,550
Tupungato (Argentina – Chile)	6,800	22,312
Huascarán (Peru)	6,769	22,205
Tocorpuri (Chile – Bolivia)	6,761	22,182
Llullaillaco (Argentina – Chile)	6,750	22,146
Mercedario (Argentina)	6,668	21,878
Yerupaja (Peru)	6,632	21,760
Incahuasi (Argentina – Chile)	6,620	21,720
Tres Cruces (Argentina – Chile)	6,620	21,720
Illampú (Bolivia)	6,551	21,490
Sajama (Bolivia)	6,520	21,390
Illimani (Bolivia)	6,457	21,185
Antofalla (Argentina)	6,440	21,129
Chimborazo (Ecuador)	6,272	20,577

LARGEST LAKES

LAKE	AREA IN SQ KM	AREA IN SQ MILES
Maracaibo (Venezuela)	16,316	6,300
Titicaca (Bolivia – Peru)	8,287	3,200
Poopó (Bolivia)	2,512	970
Buenos Aires (Argentina)	2,240	865
Argentino (Argentina)	1,414	546
Mar Chiquita (Argentina)	1,165	450
Viedma (Argentina)	1,087	420
Colhué Huapi (Argentina)	803	310
Llanquihue (Chile)	622	240
Nahuel Huapi (Argentina)	543	210

GREAT RIVERS

RIVER	LENGTH IN KM	LENGTH IN MILES
Amazon (Andes – Brazil)	6,276	3,900
Madeira (Brazil)	3,379	2,100
Parana (Brazil – Paraguay – Argentina)	3,299	2,050
São Francisco (Brazil)	2,896	1,800
Orinoco (Venezuela)	2,900	1,800
Tocantins (Brazil)	2,639	1,640
Araguaia (Brazil)	2,623	1,630
Pilcomayo (Bolivia – Paraguay)	2,493	1,550
Negro (Brazil)	2,253	1,400
Paraguay (Brazil – Paraguay)	2,092	1,300
Juruá (Brazil)	2,017	1,250
Tapajóz (Brazil)	2,017	1,250
Zingú (Brazil)	1,979	1,230
Magdalena (Colombia)	1,609	1,000
Uruguay (Brazil – Uruguay)	1,609	1,000

Oceania

PRINCIPAL COUNTRIES: AREA, POPULATION

COUNTRY	AREA IN SQ KM	AREA IN SQ MILES	POPULA-TION
Australia	7,678,700	2,971,081	13,131,000
Papua New Guinea	461,680	178,260	2,580,000
New Zealand	268,704	103,740	3,042,800
Polynesia			
Cook Is.	241	89	21,227
Tuvalu Is.	24	9	5,887
Marquesas Is.	1,274	492	5,593
American Samoa	197	76	27,160
Society Archipelago	1,683	650	100,270
Tokelau Is.	15	6	1,587
Tonga Is.	700	270	92,360
Tuamotu	854	330	8,221
Micronesia			
Caroline Is.	1,193	461	43,050
Gilbert Is.	258	100	47,714
Mariana Is.	958	370	14,355
Marshall Is.	1,812	70	25,044
Nauru	20	8	6,768
Melanesia			
Bismarck Archipelago	49,726	19,200	170,000
Fiji Is.	18,272	7,036	535,357
New Caledonia	19,103	8,560	131,663
New Hebrides	14,700	5,700	82,000
Solomon Is.	41,438	16,000	205,000

PRINCIPAL TOWNS

TOWN	POPULATION*
Sydney (Australia)	2,874,300
Melbourne (Australia)	2,583,900
Adelaide (Australia)	868,000
Brisbane (Australia)	911,000
Auckland (New Zealand)	797,406
Perth (Australia)	739,200
Christchurch (New Zealand)	325,710
Wellington (New Zealand)	349,628
Great Wollongong (Australia)	205,780
Hobart (Tasmania)	157,800
Dunedin (New Zealand)	120,426
Geelong (Australia)	126,500
Canberra (Australia)	185,000
Hamilton (New Zealand)	154,606
Launceston (Tasmania)	65,700
Suva (Fiji)	96,000
Nouméa (New Caledonia)	60,000
Papeete (Tahiti)	22,000
Port Moresby (Papua New Guinea)	77,000

*These are the figures for the conurbation, not for the city alone.

HIGHEST MOUNTAINS

MOUNTAIN	HEIGHT IN M	HEIGHT IN FEET
Carstenz (New Guinea)	4,998	16,400
Idenburg (New Guinea)	4,801	15,750
Wilhelmina (New Guinea)	4,750	15,584
Wilhelm (New Guinea)	4,694	15,400
Victoria (New Guinea)	4,039	13,240
Albert Edward (New Guinea)	3,960	13,000
Cook (New Zealand)	3,764	12,349
Balbi (Bougainville, Solomon Is.)	3,100	10,170
Ruapehu (New Zealand)	2,797	9,176
Egmont (New Zealand)	2,518	8,261
Orohena (Tahiti)	2,322	7,618
Ulawan (New Britain, Bismarck Arch.)	2,300	7,546
Kosciusko (Australia)	2,233	7,328
Panié (New Caledonia)	1,650	5,412

LARGEST LAKES

LAKE	AREA IN SQ KM	AREA IN SQ MILES
Eyre (Australia)	9,324	3,600
Torrens (Australia)	5,776	2,230
Gairdner (Australia)	3,885	1,500
Taupo (New Zealand)	606	234
Te Anau (New Zealand)	344	133
Wakatipu (New Zealand)	293	113

GREAT RIVERS

RIVER	LENGTH IN KM	LENGTH IN MILES
Murray (Australia)	2,575	1,600
Darling (Australia)	1,915	1,190
Murrumbidgee (Australia)	1,689	1,050
Sepik (New Guinea)	1,127	700
Fly (New Guinea)	1,046	650
Macquarie (Australia)	949	590
Flinders (Australia)	837	520
Mamberamo (New Guinea)	805	500
Condamine (Australia)	797	495

The World in Maps

This section of eighteen pages depicts the World, its physical and political organisation, the distribution of its people and their occupations, its vegetation, agriculture, mineral resources, and climate.

A globe is a model of the Earth

Its cover is a map

These gores will cover a globe of the size shown above.

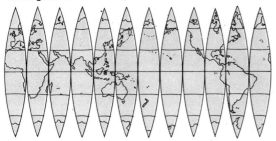

Here the Americas are moved to the left to allow for a more compact form

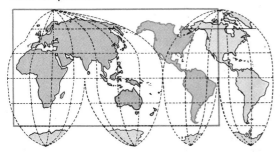

The red line indicates the limits of the maps on pages 520–521 and 522–523

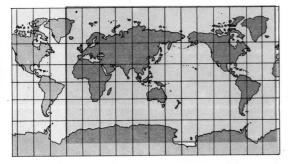

How these Maps were devised

The first thing to know about maps is that they are all distorted or twisted out of shape. Maps of the whole world are the most distorted of all, because the earth is round and maps are flat. To stretch the surface of a globe out on to a flat surface is bound to change the shape of the country represented on it.

The ordinary classroom globe is covered with a map which has first been printed on paper and then cut into 'gores'. Gores fit on to the spherical surface because, though flat, they are narrow enough to involve very little curvature when they are stuck in place.

A set of unmounted globe gores does not make a satisfactory map of the world because it is cut in too many places.

To show the shape of land more accurately, we 'gather' some of the gores in groups so that the distortion comes in the sea area. This is the projection used in this section, except for the physical map of the world on pages 520 and 521. Here it was desired to show the oceans as well as the continents as accurately as possible, and for that purpose another system was used, called the Miller Cylindrical Projection, shown in the bottom diagram on this page.

517

Northern Hemisphere

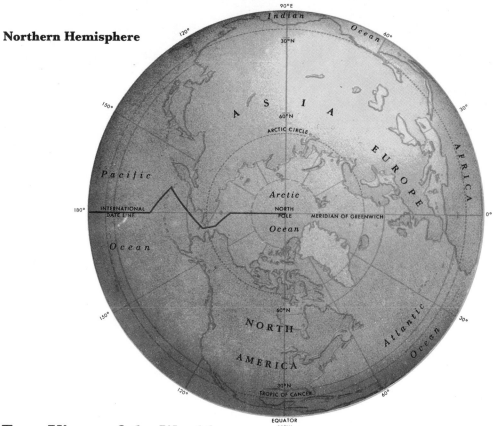

Four Views of the World
(Orthographic Projection)

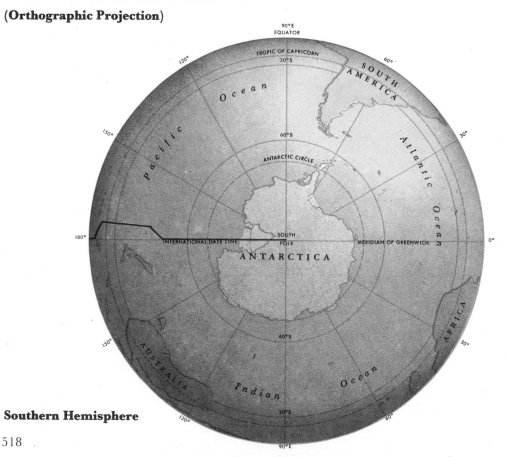

Southern Hemisphere

Western Hemisphere

Eastern Hemisphere

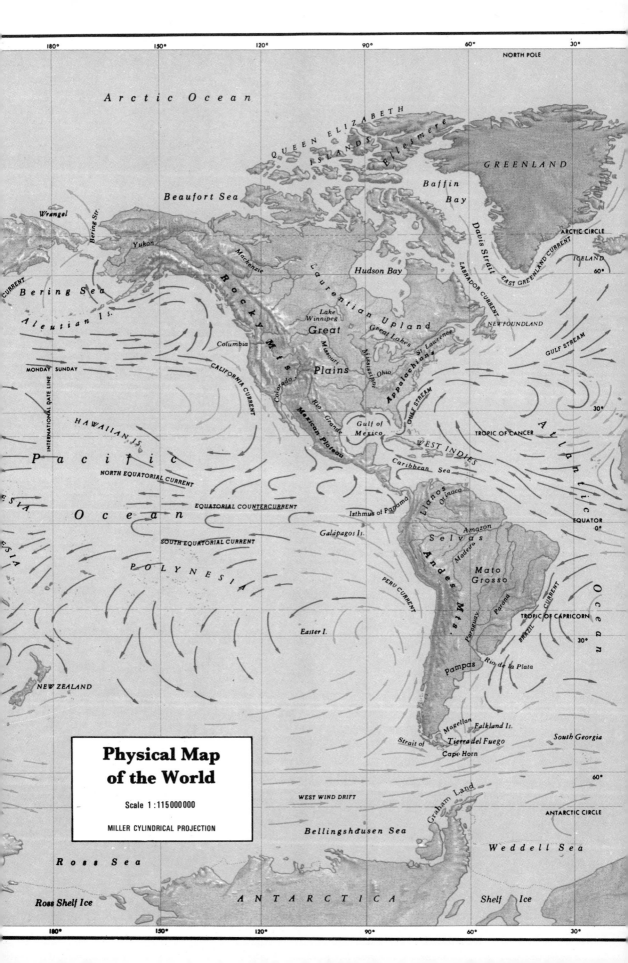

Physical Map of the World

Scale 1 : 115 000 000

MILLER CYLINDRICAL PROJECTION

180° 150° 120° 90° 60° 30°

NORTH POLE

Arctic Ocean

QUEEN ELIZABETH ISLANDS
Ellesmere
GREENLAND

Baffin Bay

Beaufort Sea

Wrangel

Bering Str.

ARCTIC CIRCLE

Davis Strait

EAST GREENLAND CURRENT

ICELAND

60°

Yukon

Mackenzie

Hudson Bay

LABRADOR CURRENT

NEWFOUNDLAND

CURRENT

Bering Sea

Aleutian Is.

Rocky Mts.

Laurentian Upland

Lake Winnipeg

Great

Great Lakes

St. Lawrence

GULF STREAM

Columbia

Plains

Missouri

Mississippi

Ohio

Appalachians

GULF STREAM

MONDAY SUNDAY

CALIFORNIA CURRENT

Colorado

Rio Grande

Gulf of Mexico

TROPIC OF CANCER

Atlantic

30°

INTERNATIONAL DATE LINE

HAWAIIAN IS.

Mexican Plateau

WEST INDIES

Pacific

NORTH EQUATORIAL CURRENT

Caribbean Sea

Ocean

EQUATORIAL COUNTERCURRENT

Isthmus of Panama

Llanos

Orinoco

EQUATOR 0°

Galápagos Is.

Amazon

Selvas

SOUTH EQUATORIAL CURRENT

Madeira

Mato Grosso

POLYNESIA

Andes Mts.

PERU CURRENT

Paraguay

Paraná

BRAZIL CURRENT

TROPIC OF CAPRICORN

30°

Easter I.

Ocean

Pampas

Rio de la Plata

NEW ZEALAND

Magellan

Falkland Is.

South Georgia

Strait of

Tierra del Fuego

Cape Horn

60°

WEST WIND DRIFT

Graham Land

ANTARCTIC CIRCLE

Bellingshausen Sea

Weddell Sea

Ross Sea

ANTARCTICA

Shelf Ice

Ross Shelf Ice

180° 150° 120° 90° 60° 30°

NORTH POLE   0°   30°   60°   90°   120°

Arctic   Ocean

SEVERNAYA
ZEMLYA

NOVAYA ZEMLYA

SPITSBERGEN
(NOR.)

ARCTIC CIRCLE
ICELAND
FAEROE IS.
(DEN.)

60°

UNION OF SOVIET SOCIALIST REPUBLICS

• Leningrad
• Moscow

N. IRELAND   UNITED   DEN.
KINGDOM   Berlin
IRELAND   NETH.   POLAND
London   BEL.   CZECHO.
Paris   W. GER.   HUNG.
FRANCE   3   AUS.   ROM.
YUGO.   BULG   *Black Sea*
SPAIN   Rome   GREECE   TURKEY
PORT.   Madrid   ITALY   CYPRUS   SYRIA   • Tehran
Mediterranean Sea   TUNISIA   1   IRAQ   IRAN
MADEIRA   MOROCCO   Cairo   4   AFGHAN-   PAKISTAN
(PORT.)   EGYPT   ISTAN

MONGOLIAN
PEOPLE'S
REPUBLIC

• Peking
• Tientsin
CHINA   KOREA   JAPAN
Shanghai   • Osaka   Tokyo
Wuhan

30°

CANARY IS.   SP.
(SP.)
W. SAHARA   ALGERIA   LIBYA   SAUDI
CAPE   MAURITANIA   NIGER   CHAD   SUDAN   ARABIA   OMAN   *Arabian Sea*
VERDE IS.   MALI   REP   REP
GAMBIA   1   8   PEOPLE'S DEM. REP. of YEMEN
GUINEA BISSAU   GUINEA   NIGERIA   8   ETHIOPIA
SIERRA LEONE   2   4   CENTRAL   9   SOMALIA
LIBERIA   IVORY   AFR. REP. 10   KENYA

New Delhi   NEPAL   9   BAN.   INDIA   BURMA   VIETNAM   TAIWAN   HONG KONG
Bombay   Calcutta   THAI-   (BR.)
LAND   10   South China Sea
SRI   11   PHILIPPINES   GUAM
Bay of   LANKA   MALAYSIA   (U.S.)
Bengal   12   CAROLIN
SUMATRA   (U.N.—

EQUATOR   EQ. GUINEA
0°   GABON   CONGO   6   11
REP.   ZAIRE
ANGOLA   ZAMBIA   12
ZIMB.   MOZAMBIQUE
NAMIBIA   RHOD.   13
(South West   BOTSWANA
Africa)   REP.   5
OF
SOUTH AFRICA

INDONESIA   NEW GUIN
Jakarta   JAVA   PORT.
TIMOR

ZANZIBAR
TANZANIA   *Indian*
MAURITIUS
REUNION (FR.)   *Ocean*

AUSTRALIA

TASMANIA

MALAGASY REP.
(MADAGASCAR)

TROPIC OF
CAPRICORN
30°

KERGUELEN
(FR.)

60°

ANTARCTIC CIRCLE

ANTARCTICA

0°   30°   60°   90°   120°

Key to Africa
1 Senegal Rep.
2 Upper Volta
3 Togo
4 Benin
5 Lesotho
6 Congo Rep.
7 Cabinda (Ang.)
8 Djibouti
9 Uganda
10 Rwanda
11 Burundi
12 Malawi
13 Swaziland

Key to Europe
1 East Germany
2 Luxembourg
3 Switzerland
4 Albania

Key to Asia
1 Jordan
2 Lebanon
3 Israel
4 Kuwait
5 Bahrein
6 Qatar
7 United Arab Emirates
8 Yemen Arab Rep.
9 Bhutan
10 Kampuchea
11 Brunei (Br.)
12 Singapore
13 Irian Jaya
14 Papua New Guinea

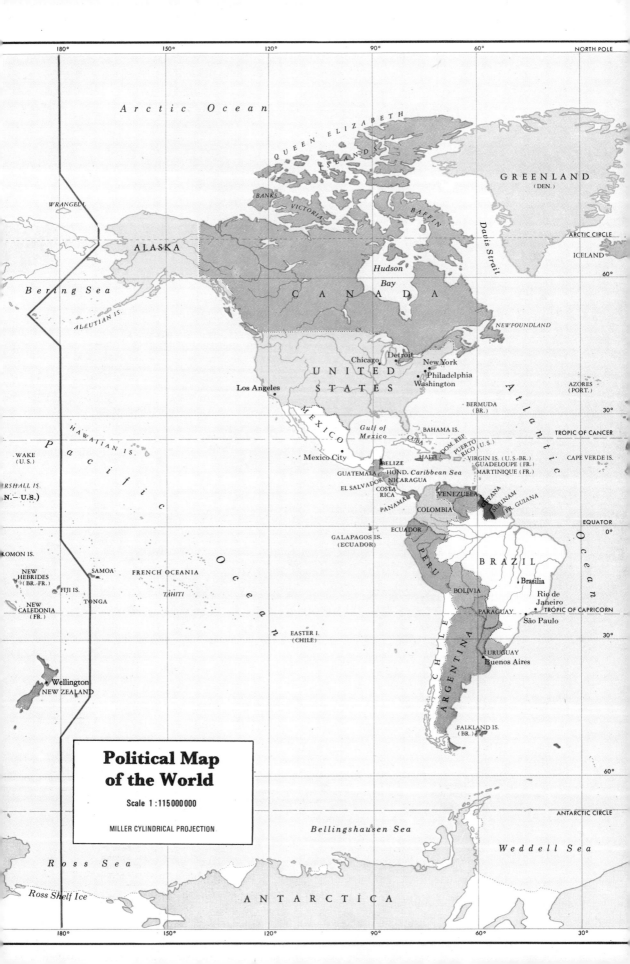

Four thousand million people live in the world today and the population is increasing by more than a million a week. At that rate, by the end of the century, the world's population will number over 8,000 million.

This map shows that the greater part of the world is almost uninhabited. Other vast areas are thinly populated, while in some places great numbers of people are crowded together in small areas.

More than half the world's population is found in the Far East. Yet this portion of the earth represents only one-tenth of the habitable world. Another fifth of the world's population lives in Europe, which is less than one-twentieth of the habitable world. Antarctica is at the other extreme, with an area of over 5 million square miles (13 million sq km) and no permanent inhabitants.

The map shows four principal centres of population. The first is the Far East, the second India and Pakistan, the third Europe, and the fourth the industrial area of North America.

In Asia, the most thickly populated areas are the valleys and fertile plains, where there is good soil and water for

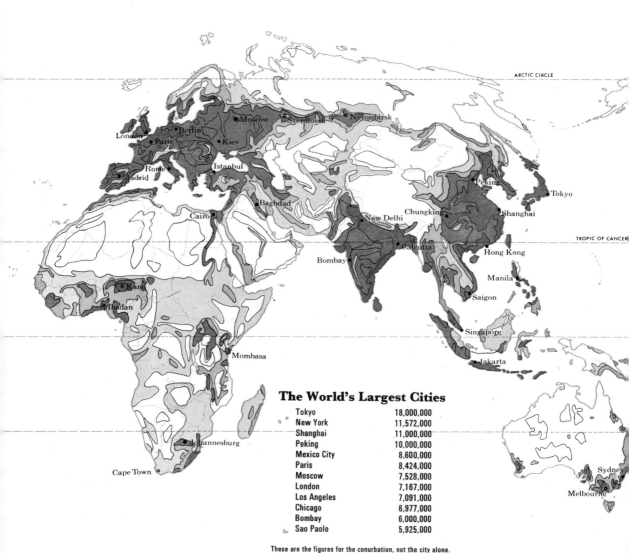

The World's Largest Cities

City	Population
Tokyo	18,000,000
New York	11,572,000
Shanghai	11,000,000
Peking	10,000,000
Mexico City	8,600,000
Paris	8,424,000
Moscow	7,528,000
London	7,167,000
Los Angeles	7,091,000
Chicago	6,977,000
Bombay	6,000,000
Sao Paolo	5,925,000

These are the figures for the conurbation, not the city alone.

irrigation. Asians concentrate in these areas because they live by agriculture. Industry may be growing rapidly, but the bulk of the people are still concentrated in good farming country.

In Europe and North America, the concentration of population follows a different pattern. In these continents the greatest number of people are concentrated in the areas where industry flourishes, and in ports and trading centres.

There seems little chance of solving the problem of overcrowding by sending large numbers of people to the less crowded areas of the earth.

People always move towards areas of greatest opportunity, and those are the more populated areas. Thus crowded areas become more crowded and underpopulated areas even emptier.

The Third World is the name given to the relatively undeveloped parts of the world, where starvation, poverty, disease, and lack of education still exist fairly widely. Asia, Central and South America, and Africa can broadly be termed the Third World, though there are some very highly developed regions within these continents.

Population

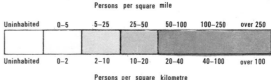

Persons per square mile						
Uninhabited	0–5	5–25	25–50	50–100	100–250	over 250
Uninhabited	0–2	2–10	10–20	20–40	40–100	over 100

Persons per square kilometre

The 33 Most Populous Countries

1	China	800,000,000
2	India	547,000,000
3	U.S.S.R.	250,800,000
4	U.S.A.	212,000,000
5	Indonesia	130,000,000
6	Japan	110,000,000
7	Brazil	93,000,000
8	Germany (E and W)	79,000,000
9	Bangladesh	71,000,000
10	Pakistan	65,000,000
11	Nigeria	58,000,000
12	Mexico	56,240,000
13	United Kingdom	56,000,000
14	Italy	55,000,000
15	France	52,000,000
16	Korea (N and S)	49,000,000
17	Vietnam	44,000,000
18	Turkey	42,000,000
19	Thailand	40,000,000
20	Philippines	37,000,000
21	Egypt	36,000,000
22	Spain	34,000,000
23	Poland	33,500,000
24	Iran	30,000,000
25	Burma	29,000,000
26	Ethiopia	26,000,000
27	Zaire	24,300,000
28	Colombia	24,000,000
29	Argentina	23,000,000
30	Canada	22,000,000
31	Republic of South Africa	21,500,000
32	Romania	21,000,000
33	Yugoslavia	20,000,000

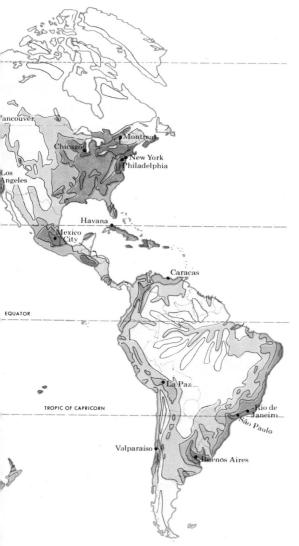

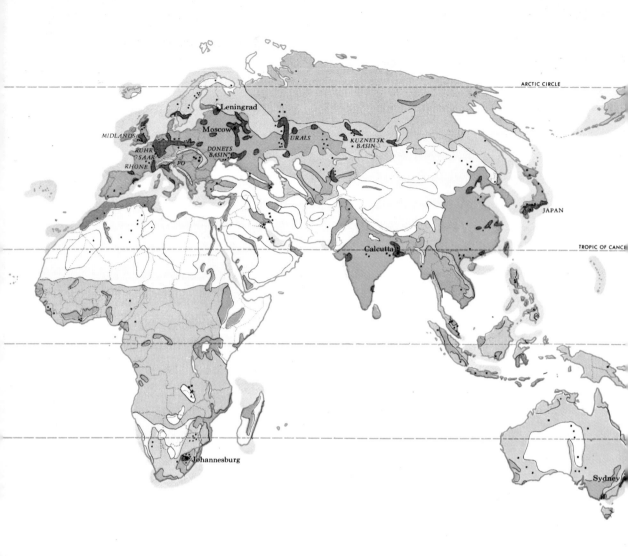

People earn their living in very different ways. The map above shows you how the chief human occupations are distributed over the earth.

Few people live by hunting and fishing. Food procured in this way does not keep long, and has to be eaten quickly. The food supply is uncertain and people are liable to periods of famine.

Nomadic herding is another primitive method of making a living. These people are nomads because they have to keep their flocks and herds moving in search of fresh pastures. It takes a large area of

land to support a single animal so that those who follow this way of life are few.

Livestock bred on farms – usually cattle, sheep, horses, or goats – graze prepared pastures frequently supplemented by special fodder crops.

A small area of arable land can support many people. In the rice-fields of India, China, and Japan, which are intensively cultivated, a square mile (2.5 sq km) can support over a thousand people. In this case the average holding is very small and most of the crop is consumed locally. In contrast just one of the

Occupations

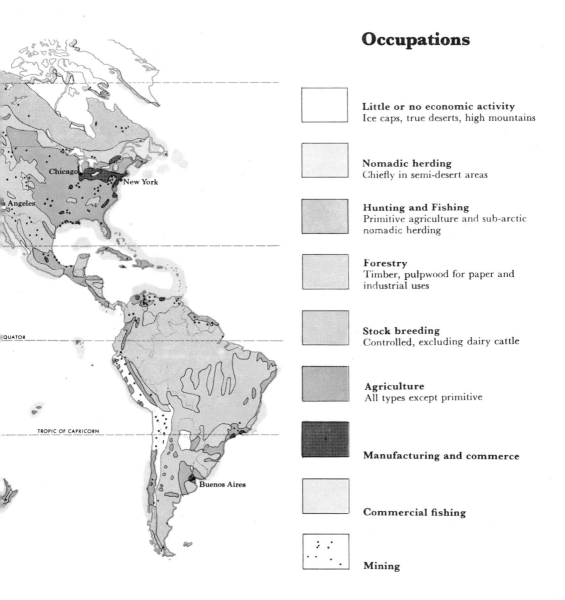

Little or no economic activity
Ice caps, true deserts, high mountains

Nomadic herding
Chiefly in semi-desert areas

Hunting and Fishing
Primitive agriculture and sub-arctic nomadic herding

Forestry
Timber, pulpwood for paper and industrial uses

Stock breeding
Controlled, excluding dairy cattle

Agriculture
All types except primitive

Manufacturing and commerce

Commercial fishing

Mining

huge wheat farms of the Canadian prairies, the American Middle West, or the pampas of the Argentine, may produce enough grain to feed several thousand people.

Forestry, like modern farming and ranching, is often a complex business, demanding skill. Great care is taken in cutting and replanting to ensure continual forest growth and production.

Mining is one of the industries on which the machine age particularly depends. Minerals are often discovered in isolated places, and it is there that the mining community must develop. But the products of the mines soon find their way to the great centres of population, where they are converted into manufactured goods. Fishing on an industrial scale involves quick-freezing and canning to make fresh fish available to people living far inland.

Industry and commerce are of great and growing importance. Millions who once worked on the land are now working in mills, factories, and offices. The greater part of such work is done in large towns.

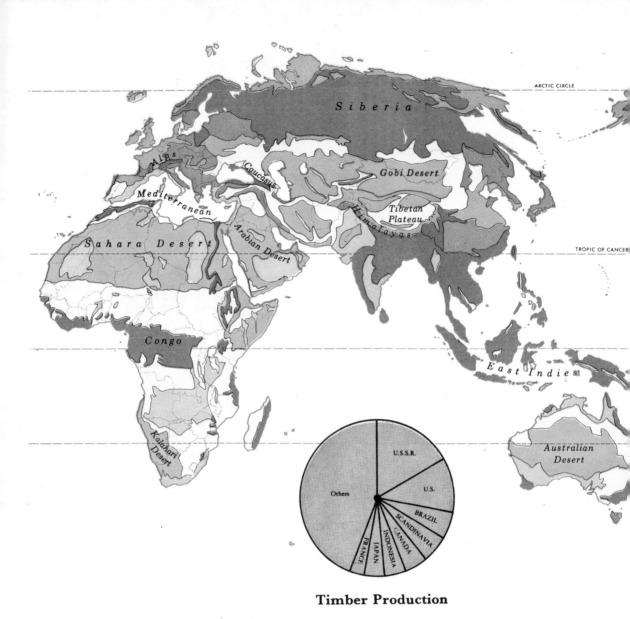

Timber Production

This map of natural vegetation tells an interesting story. Vegetation depends on physical conditions; so the plants that grow in a particular area tell us much about rainfall, temperature, the nature of the soil, etc. Vegetation falls into three main types: forests, grasslands, and deserts. The number of individual species within these groups is vast.

Over large areas of the world, vegetation is determined largely by temperature and moisture.

There are exceptions, however. Plants may be found growing in conditions that would appear to favour another type of vegetation. Desert plants, for example, thrive in many places that have enough rainfall to support a grassland vegetation. The explanation in most cases is that the soil is very porous, and quickly dries out, even after heavy rainfall.

At one time, a quarter of the earth's surface was covered by forests; now it is less than one sixth. Great harm has been

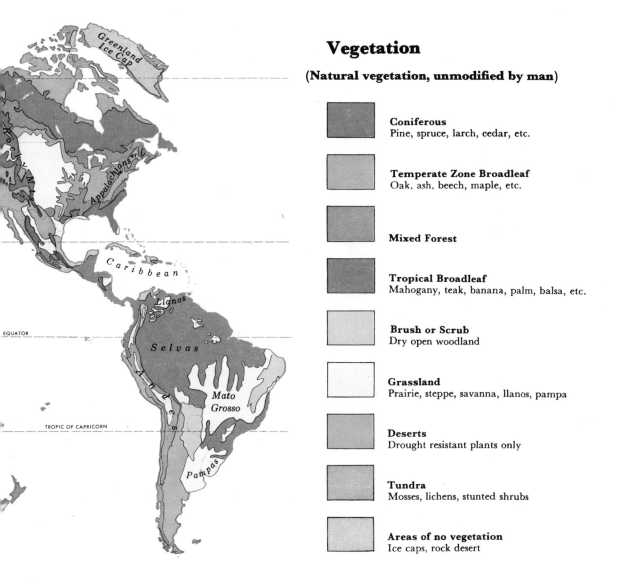

Vegetation

(Natural vegetation, unmodified by man)

Coniferous
Pine, spruce, larch, cedar, etc.

Temperate Zone Broadleaf
Oak, ash, beech, maple, etc.

Mixed Forest

Tropical Broadleaf
Mahogany, teak, banana, palm, balsa, etc.

Brush or Scrub
Dry open woodland

Grassland
Prairie, steppe, savanna, llanos, pampa

Deserts
Drought resistant plants only

Tundra
Mosses, lichens, stunted shrubs

Areas of no vegetation
Ice caps, rock desert

done by the reckless exploitation of forests. In many cases, where the forests have gone, the soil is incapable of supporting anything but the scantiest desert vegetation.

Forests are generally limited to places where summer temperatures average at least 50°F (10°C). The amount of rainfall required depends upon the temperature: where it is cool, the moisture does not evaporate quickly and 15 inches (375 mm) of rain a year are enough. In warmer places much more is needed, tropical forests requiring as much as 90 to 150 inches (2,250 to 3,750 mm) of rain yearly.

Grass requires considerably less rain. In fact grassland is typical of semi-arid conditions.

Originally grassland extended over a third of the earth's surface. As the soil formed on grassland is usually good, most prairies have been ploughed up for the growing of other crops.

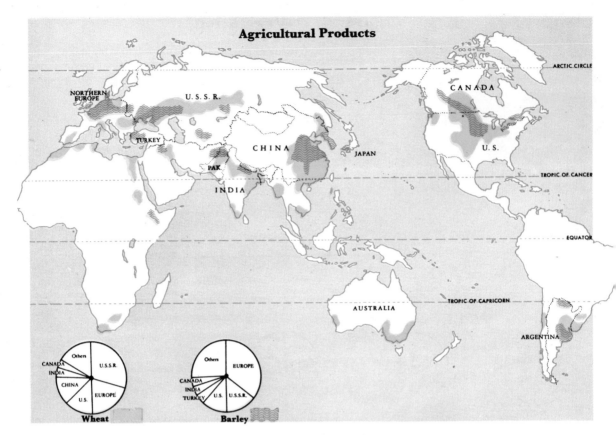

Agricultural Products

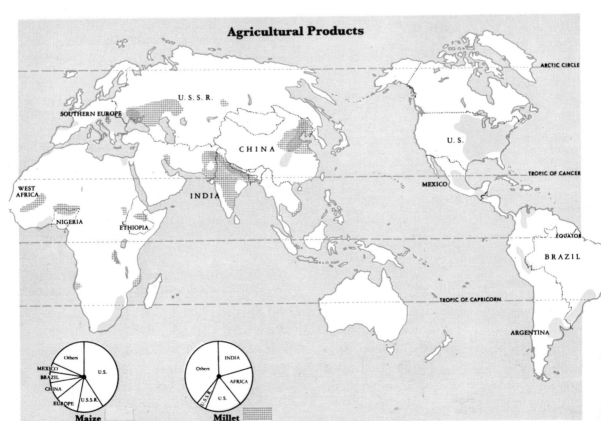

Agricultural Products

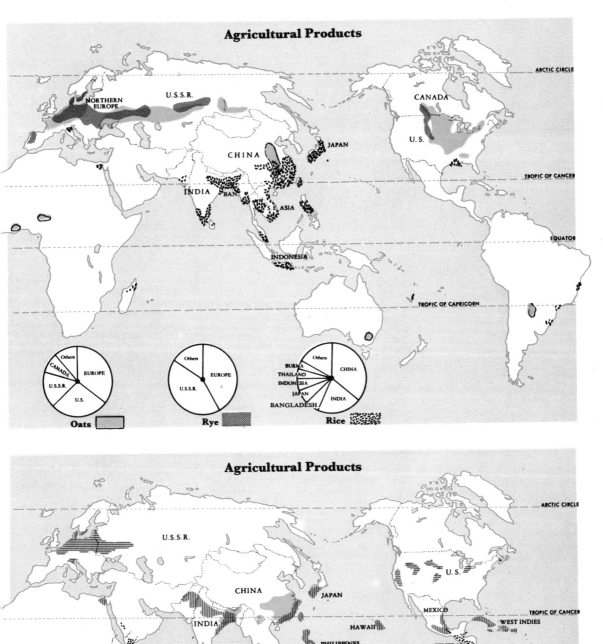

Agricultural Products

Oats ▭   **Rye** ▭   **Rice** ▒

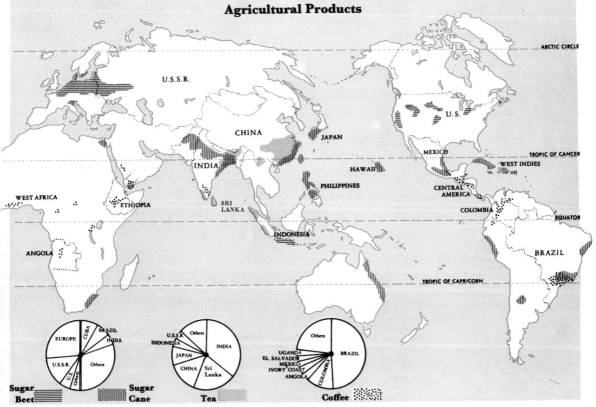

Agricultural Products

Sugar Beet ▤   **Sugar Cane** ▥   **Tea** ▭   **Coffee** ▒

Industrial Minerals

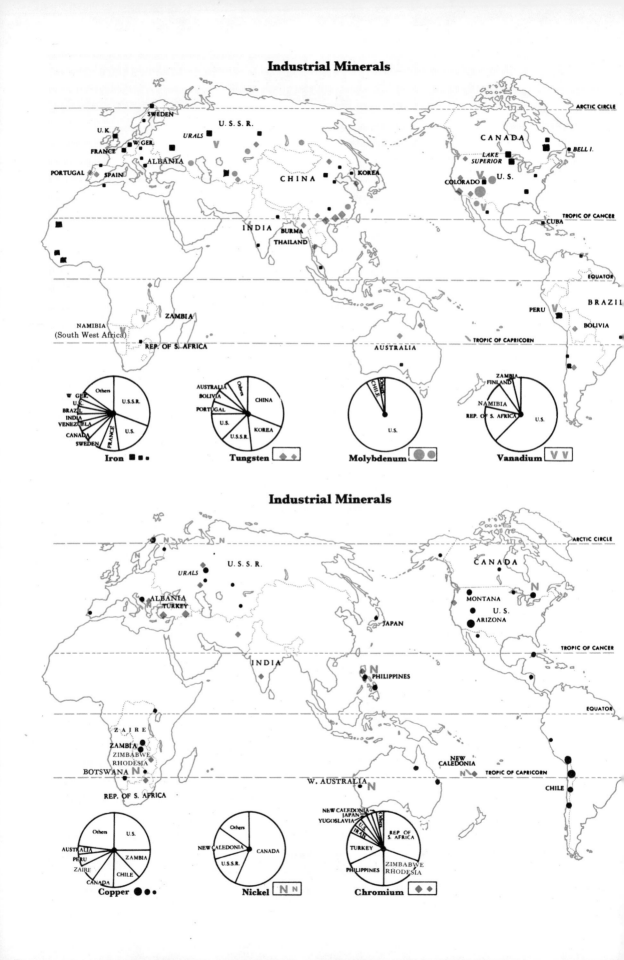

Iron ■ ■ ·

Tungsten ◆ ◆

Molybdenum ● ●

Vanadium V V

Industrial Minerals

Copper ● ● ·

Nickel N N

Chromium ◆ ◆

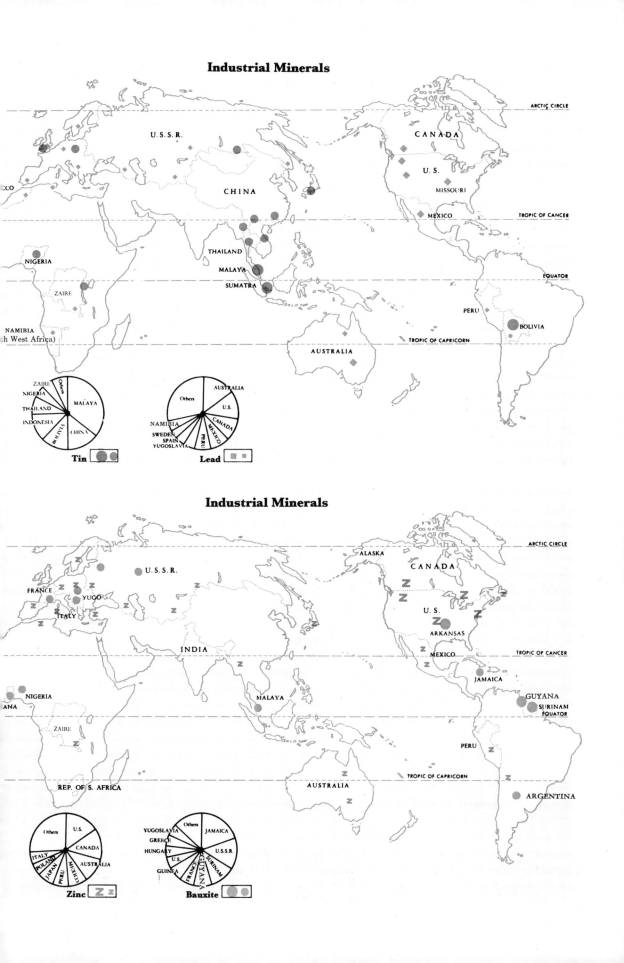

Industrial Minerals

ARCTIC CIRCLE

U.S.S.R.

CANADA

U.S.

CHINA

MISSOURI

TROPIC OF CANCER

MEXICO

NIGERIA

THAILAND

MALAYA

ZAIRE

SUMATRA

EQUATOR

NIGERIA

NAMIBIA
(h West Africa)

PERU

TROPIC OF CAPRICORN

BOLIVIA

AUSTRALIA

ZAIRE
Others
NIGERIA
THAILAND
INDONESIA
MALAYA
BOLIVIA
CHINA

Tin

AUSTRALIA
Others
U.S.
NAMIBIA
CANADA
MEXICO
PERU
SWEDEN
SPAIN
YUGOSLAVIA

Lead

Industrial Minerals

ARCTIC CIRCLE

ALASKA

CANADA

U.S.S.R.

FRANCE
YUGO
ITALY

U.S.
ARKANSAS

INDIA

TROPIC OF CANCER

MEXICO

JAMAICA

NIGERIA
ANA

GUYANA
SURINAM
EQUATOR

ZAIRE

MALAYA

PERU

TROPIC OF CAPRICORN

REP. OF S. AFRICA

AUSTRALIA

ARGENTINA

Others
U.S.
ITALY
CANADA
POLAND
JAPAN
PERU
MEXICO
AUSTRALIA

Zinc

Others
YUGOSLAVIA
JAMAICA
GREECE
HUNGARY
U.S.S.R.
U.S.
SURINAM
GUINEA
FRANCE
GUYANA

Bauxite

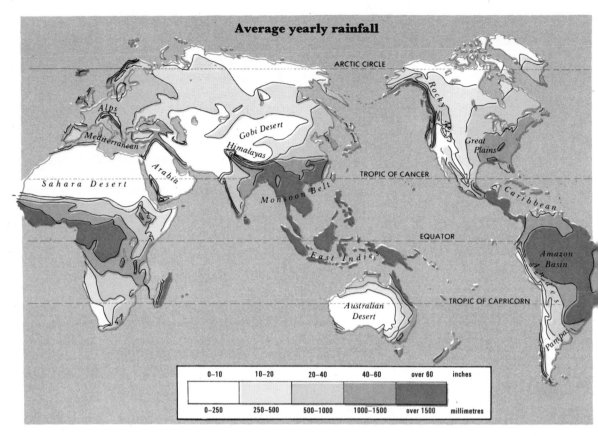

Average yearly rainfall

0–10	10–20	20–40	40–60	over 60	inches
0–250	250–500	500–1000	1000–1500	over 1500	millimetres

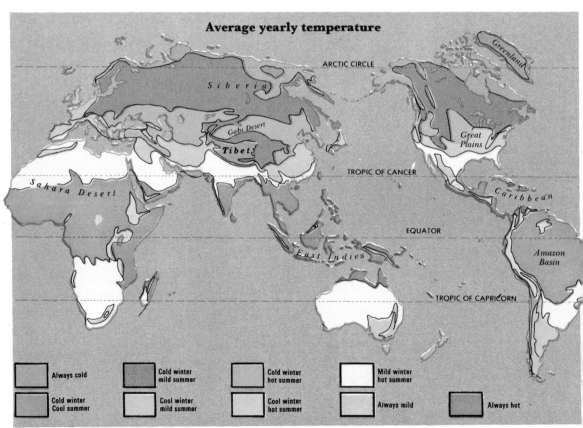

Average yearly temperature

Always cold

Cold winter
Cool summer

Cold winter
mild summer

Cool winter
mild summer

Cold winter
hot summer

Cool winter
hot summer

Mild winter
hot summer

Always mild

Always hot

Index

540

Acknowledgements

AFM 53 top, 54 top right, 61 top, 87, 90 bottom; AFM – De Biasi 89; AFM – Scalfati 82; AMNH-FLO, Bernheim-Conant 241 top left, 250 top, 269, 294 top; APN-Novosti Press Agency 103 top left; Aerofilms, Boreham Wood 37 bottom, 38 top; Alpha – David Forbert 375 bottom left, 375 bottom right; Alpha – Shelly Grossman 226; Alpha – Ewing Krainin 152 bottom left, 267 bottom right, 393 bottom, 398 top, 413; Alpha – Malak 339 bottom left; Alpha – Gerard Oppenheimer 424 bottom; Alpha – Capt. K. C. Torrents 284 bottom left, 285 top left, 314 bottom; Aluminium Ltd., Montreal 345; American Airlines 334 top; American Indian Archives – Royal Lowy 328 top; American Museum of Natural History – Tom Larson 244 top right, 244 centre right; American Museum of Natural History – Elizabeth Morton 237 bottom left, 240 top right. 306 top, 313 top right; American Museum of Natural History – Harold Schultz 432 bottom; Anaconda 414 bottom; Annan Photo Features 409 bottom; Annan Photo Features – Clemson 346 bottom; Annan Photo Features – Bob Crone 242 bottom, 276 left; Annan Photo Features – Richard Harrington 285 bottom left, 454 top left; Annan Photo Features – George Hunter 411 bottom; Annan Photo Features – Malak 43 bottom, 346 top; Annan Photo Features – Martin Simpson 290 bottom, 291 bottom, 303; Ray Atkeson 366 top; Australian Information Service, London 452 left, 458, 459, 460, 462 bottom left, 466 top, 468 top, 469 bottom, 472 bottom, 474 bottom, 492 top; Ruth V. Bair 206 top, 207 top; John Baker 262; André Barsamian, Brussels 44 top right; Sixt Bartholdi 316; Birnback 467 top, 467 bottom, 473 bottom; Birnback – Ernst Baumann 442 bottom; Birnback – Harold Schultz 433; Birnback – Len Sirman 432 top left; Black Star – Frenel Berko 320; Black Star – Max Duk 356 bottom; Black Star – Herbert Lanks 360; Black Star – Constance Stuart 313 top left; Boeing Airplane Company 365; Peter Boxhall 167, 168 top, 228 left, 273, 276 right, 277; Brazilian Embassy, London 436; Raymond Bricon 235 bottom left, 239 top, 240 bottom right, 255 top, 268 top, 271 top left, 271 top right, 271 centre, 271 bottom; British Information Service 225 bottom, 251 bottom; British Petroleum Ltd., London 40; Camera Clix, London 72 top, 207 bottom; Camera Clix – Charles Trieschmann 243 bottom left, 256 bottom left, 267 top left, 280 top, 289 bottom; Camera Press Ltd., London 240 top left, 245 top, 272 bottom, 294 bottom, 314; Mary Carrick 499 top; J. Allan Cash, London 41 bottom, 231 top; Conzett and Huber 230, 232; Jack Couffer 498 bottom, 502; Herb and Lois Crisler 499 bottom; Daimler-Benz, Stuttgart 56 top; De Biasi 60 top, 72 bottom; Howard Doris Ltd. – Chevron and Ninian 41 top left; Eastfoto 84 top, 85, 86 top left, 86 bottom, 197 bottom left, 202 top, 209 centre; Educational Productions Ltd., Wakefield 23, 55, 57 bottom; FLO – Paul Byers 88 top right; FLO – Stephanie Dinkins 285 bottom right; FLO – Ferreira 176 bottom right; FLO – Arne Normann 29 bottom; FLO – Eric Pavel 386, 412, 420, 421 top, 439 top, 443 bottom left; FLO – Vidyavrata 172, 173, 176 bottom left, 181 bottom left, 181 bottom right; FPG 244 top left, 248 bottom; FPG – Samy Abboud 161 bottom right; FPG – Jack Breed 363 bottom; FPG – Homer L. Dodge 120; FPG – Otto Done 370 top; FPG – Gordon Douglas 299, 305 top right, 308 top, 319 top; FPG – Duncan Edwards 33; FPG – Gatti 235 bottom right; FPG – George Hunter 369; FPG – G. H. Jarett 342, 343 bottom; FPG – Rupert Leach 161 top, 478 left, 480 top left, 480 bottom; FPG – Helen Joy Lee 306 bottom; FPG – Terry S. Lindquist 74 top; FPG – W. D. McKinney 339 top; FPG – Frank Newton 449 bottom, 456 top, 456 bottom, 484 top; FPG – E. P. Norwood 338; FPG – Bob Taylor 359 top right; Fasoloi 32 top left; Fiat Company 71, 73 bottom; Firestone Tyre and Rubber Company 250 bottom right; F. Florence 77 bottom; Florida State News Bureau 358; William Fortin 501 bottom, 505 top; Fox Photos, London 22; Ewing Galloway 212 bottom right, 357 top left; Ewing Galloway – Herbert Lanks 408; Sheridan H. Garth 243 top, 301 top; Philip D. Gendreau 74 bottom, 160; Gendreau – Herbert Lanks 371 bottom left; General Mills Co. Inc. 357 top right; Government of Gibraltar 69 bottom; Gilloon Photo Agency 222 top, 223 top; Gilloon Photo Agency – B. E. Lindroos 270 bottom, 287 top; The Great Northern Paper Company 353 bottom; R. Guerand 76, 80 bottom, 83 bottom; Elvajean Hall 244 bottom right, 491 top, 492 bottom; Hamlyn Group Picture Library 21; H. Harrer, Leichenstein-Verlag, Verduz 196 top; Hawaii Natural History Association 448 top; Ernst A. Heiniger 63 bottom, 145 bottom, 217, 218 top left; John Herdman 39 top; Lucien Hervé, Paris 49 top; A. G. Hervey, Northwood 275; House of Photography 158; House of Photography – Jerome W. Bedford 224 top left; House of Photography – Stephanie Dinkins 241 bottom right, 251 top left; 253 top, 286; House of Photography – S. F. Dorsey 183; House of Photography – Wayne Fredericks 291 top, 304 top; House of Photography – Pierre Massin 301 centre, 301 bottom; House of Photography – Kerwin B. Roche 235 centre right; House of Photography – Charles Perry Weimer 394 bottom, 405, 415, 416, 417, 428, 430; Alan Hutchison Library, London 149 top, 149 bottom; Indian Government Tourist Office 177 bottom left; Iranian Oil Participants Ltd. 165 bottom left; Johnson Motor Company 68 bottom; Elmo Jones 496 bottom; K. Kayser 310; Keystone Press 39 bottom, 212 bottom left, 213 bottom; Martin S. Klein 231 bottom, 234 top left, 234 bottom, 257 bottom, 312 top left, 313 bottom, 315 bottom, 449 top, 460 bottom; Herbert Knapp 137 top, 147 top left, 186, 189 top right, 457 top, 484 bottom right, 486, 487 bottom left, 487 bottom right, 488 top left, 488 top right, 488 bottom, 490 right; A. Kolb, Hamburg 129, 189 bottom, 220 top, 479; W. Kuls 229; Jane Latta 328 bottom left; D. Lex 105 bottom; Wolfgang Linke 25; Pierre M. Martinot 375 top; Matson Lines 455 top; A. Mayer 200 top; Steve McCutcheon 498 top; H. Mensching 261, 274 top; E. W. Mercier 46; Paul F. Milhollan 268 bottom; Alfred G. Milotte 236 top left, 236 bottom, 237 top left, 237 top right, 237 bottom right, 238 bottom, 296 top; Alfred and Elma Milotte 452 right, 453 top left, 453 top right, 453 bottom left, 453 bottom right; A. Modl 53 bottom; Monkmeyer – E. Boubat 164 top; Monkmeyer – Tony Chapelle 159 top, 177 top right, 180 bottom; Monkmeyer – Dick Dempewolff 504 bottom; Monkmeyer – Edward M. Edwin 370 bottom; Monkmeyer – Fujihira 146 bottom, 190 top, 191 top right, 191 top left, 193 bottom left, 393 top, 404 bottom left; Monkmeyer – Fitz Goro 473 top; Monkmeyer – Wendy Hilty 151 top; Monkmeyer – Kofod 189 top left; Monkmeyer – Ewing Krainin 170 top; Monkmeyer – Herbert Lanks 418; Monkmeyer – Lew Merrim 501 top; Monkmeyer – Patrick Morin 31 bottom, 32 top right; Monkmeyer – Katherine Tweed Robertson 477, 480 top right, 481 top, 481 bottom, 485 top; Monkmeyer – Lowber Tiers 146 top right; Joseph Muench 67 bottom, 335, 360 top, 363 top; Müller – Miny 12; Multi-photo 48; National Academy of Sciences – IGY Photo 504 top; Novosti Press Agency, London 121; K. Paffen 134; Palmer Photo Agency – Marilyn Silverstone 109 bottom, 137 bottom; Panagra 390 bottom, 398 bottom, 414 top; Pan American Coffee Bureau 329 bottom, 376 top, 392 bottom left, 409 top, 437 top; Pan American World Airways 379; Photo Library – Baroli 73 top right; Photo Library – J. C. Burke 188; Photo Library – Gordon Douglas 298, 304 bottom; Photo Library – George Holton 143 bottom, 185 top left, 185 top right; Photo Library – Cy La Tour 351; Photo Library – Roy Pinney 10, 28 bottom; Photo Library – Harrison Salisbury 123 top; Photo Researchers – Aramco 135 top, 162, 165 bottom right; Photo Researchers – Bips 454 top right; Photo Researchers – E. Boubat, Réalités 161 bottom left; Photo Researchers – Bill Brindle 475 bottom; Photo Researchers – Julian Bryan 103 top right, 122 top right, 140, 391 left, 427 centre right, 427 bottom; Photo Researchers – Van Bucher 136 bottom, 152 bottom right, 197 top right, 223 bottom; Photo Researchers – J. P. Charbonnier 141 bottom right; Photo Researchers – Jerry Cooke 50, 88 bottom left, 110 right, 116, 117 bottom, 127 bottom, 159 bottom left, 159 bottom right, 406 bottom left; Photo Researchers – Ed Drews 69 top, 179 top, 206 bottom, 220 centre.

267 top right; Photo Researchers – Fritz Henle 328 bottom right, 392 bottom right, 404 top, 404 centre, 404 bottom right, 406 top, 406 bottom right; Photo Researchers – C. W. Herbert 373 top; Photo Researchers – Tom Hollyman 37 top left, 54 bottom left, 54 bottom right, 264 bottom, 347, 390 top, 411 top, 442; Photo Researchers – Russ Kinne 238 top right, 500; Photo Researchers – Ewing Krainin 20 bottom, 75 bottom, 145 top, 157 top, 179 bottom, 192, 391 right, 440, 461 bottom, 484 bottom left; Photo Researchers – George Leavens 455 bottom, 462 top, 475 top, 493 top; Photo Researchers – Helen Joy Lee 457 bottom; Photo Researchers – Charles May 253 bottom, 264 top; Photo Researchers – John and Bini Moss 305 bottom, 307 top; Photo Researchers – Roland Paskoff 263 bottom left; Photo Researchers – Scott Polkinghorne 445, 471 bottom; Photo Researchers – Safari Productions 246, 297 top, 297 centre; Photo Researchers – Carl Sherman 353 top; Photo Researchers – Hans Von Meiss 255 bottom, 281 centre left, 294 centre, 296 bottom, 297 bottom, 308 bottom, 315 top; Pixfeatures 56 bottom, 57 top; Rutherford Platt 322, 497; Polish Tourist Information Centre, London 78; Paul Popper Ltd., London 233, 243 bottom right; The Port of New York Authority 352; A. C. Previté, London 380; Puerto Rico News Service 329 top, 381, 382 top; Quebec Province – Photo Driscoll 337; Jim Quigney Associates – Robert Lackenback 104 bottom right; Rapho, Paris 125, 254 bottom, 280 bottom; Rapho – Breton 91 top left, 91 top right, 92 top, 92 bottom; Rapho – John Peter Taylor 263 bottom right; Rapho – Dan Weiner 319 bottom; Rapho Guillumette – A. L. Goldman 141 bottom left; Rapho Guillumette – Patrice Hartley 419; Rapho Guillumette – Ergy Landau 199 bottom; Rapho Guillumette – Kay Lawson 157 bottom; Rapho Guillumette – Davis Pratt 168 bottom, 426 bottom, 443 bottom right; Rapho Guillumette – Michael Serraillier 147 bottom left; Rapho Guillumette – Bill Stapleton 222 bottom; Rapho Guillumette – Stutts 282 top, 285 top right; J. Rifaux 77 top; P. Rose, Leighton Buzzard 30 bottom left, 30 bottom right, 38 bottom; Valentina Rosen 142, 174 top right; Rosignoli 43 top, 54 top left; Kulwant Roy 174 bottom right, 175 top left, 175 top right, 178 top, 178 bottom; G. Sanger 105 top left; J. Sauger 123 bottom; M. M. Schechter 236 top right, 317 top, 318 top, 318 bottom; Jack Scheerboom 146 top left, 146 top right, 147 bottom right; Shostal 274 bottom; Shostal – Joe Barnell 32 bottom, 60 bottom, 73 top left, 184, 217 bottom, 247, 272 top, 343 top, 397 bottom, 421 bottom, 423 bottom, 424 top left, 427 centre left, 429, 434, 437 bottom, 439 bottom left, 439 bottom right; Shostal – Thomas Benner 212 top; Shostal – Tomas Berner 95; Shostal – George E. Brown 41 top right; Shostal – C. J. Coulson 175 bottom, 180 top; Shostal – Art d'Arazien 424 top right, 426 top; Shostal – Thomas d'Hoste 190 bottom; Shostal – W. R. Donagho 251 top right; Shostal – Gordon Douglas 249; Shostal – Harry Edwards 67 top; Shostal – Charles Erikson 239 bottom; Shostal – David Forbert 49 bottom, 219 top, 219 bottom left, 219 bottom right; Shostal – Harrison Forman 103 bottom right, 143 top right, 177 top left, 177 bottom left, 220 bottom; Shostal – Keith Gillett 448 bottom, 462 bottom right; Shostal – Ray Halin 153 bottom right; Shostal – Paul Hufner 19, 153 top, 241 top right, 250 bottom left; Shostal – George Hunter 344; Shostal – Doris Jacoby 427 top; Shostal – Erich Kolmar 242 top, 265; Shostal – Margaret Land 224 bottom; Shostal – B. A. Lang Sr 361 top right; Shostal – Margaret Lang 224 top right; Shostal – Herbert Lanks 42, 270 top, 377 bottom; Shostal – Rupert Leach 305 top left; Shostal – Robert Leahey 407; Shostal – Gene Lett 472 top; Shostal – Ed Lettau 143 top left; Shostal – Ralph Luce 444, 461 top, 485 bottom, 486 bottom, 487 top, 489 top left, 489 bottom, 491 bottom, 493 bottom; Shostal – McKelzie 478 right; Shostal – Ray Manley 372 bottom; Shostal – Charles May 248 top, 284 bottom right; Shostal – Otto Mayer 367; Shostal – Frank E. Meitz 361 bottom; Shostal – Edmund N. Paige 213 top; Shostal – Charles C. Ray 366 bottom; Shostal – Jane M. Singer 403; Shostal – Sidney Press 466 bottom; Shostal – H. E. Street 307 bottom, 312 top right; Shostal – Max Tatch 44 top left; Shostal – Turck 30 top; Shostal – A. M. Wettach 356 top; Shostal – Maynard Williams 141 top; Shostal – J. D. Winbray 106, 216; Shostal – Norman B. Young 128; James R. Simon 432 top right, 438; William Neil Smith 371 bottom right; H. Smotkine 59 top, 59 bottom; South African Tourist Corporation, London 235 top, 238 top left, 244 bottom left, 256 top, 311, 317 bottom; Sovfoto – USSR Magazine 107 bottom, 108 top, 108 bottom, 109 top, 111, 114, 126; Soviet Information Bureau 105 top right, 113 bottom right; H. Spreitzer 135; Dr. Stodter, Düsseldorf 51; John Strohm 83 top, 102 top right, 104 top left, 104 bottom left, 107 top, 113 top left, 113 top right, 113 bottom left, 115 bottom, 122 top left, 144 top left, 144 top right, 144 bottom, 153 bottom left, 164 bottom, 181 top, 201 top, 202 bottom left, 202 bottom right, 204 left, 204 right, 205 top left, 205 top right, 205 centre, 205 bottom, 209 top, 209 bottom left, 209 bottom right, 377 top left, 423 top; Suzuki Motor Company, Hammatsu 218 bottom left; Swiss National Tourist Office, London 63 top, 508; Charles Swithinbank, Cambridge 503; Richard Tegstrom 27 bottom; Wolffe Tietze 28; Trans World Airlines 47, 52 top, 62 bottom, 68 top, 136 top, 156 top, 156 bottom, 160, 166, 170 bottom, 174 top left, 257, 266, 267 bottom left, 336 top; Triangle – Richard Stockwell 122 bottom; C. R. Twidale 102 bottom left, 464, 470 top; USDA 323 top, 350, 354, 355, 359 top left, 359 bottom, 364; United Fruit Company 377 top right, 382 bottom; United Kingdom Atomic Energy Authority, London 36; United States Information Service 361 top left; VEB Leuna-Werke 'Walter Ulbricht', Merseberg 58; Andy Vargo, Weston Turville 323 bottom, 326 top, 326 centre, 326 bottom left, 327, 332 bottom, 333 top, 336 bottom, 357 bottom right; Vautier-Decool, Paris 376 bottom, 378; Erwin Verity 384; H. Verstappen 193 bottom right; Jane Werner Watson 435 top; H. Wilhelmy 254 top; Wolfe Worldwide Films, Los Angeles 24, 174 bottom left, 221, 224 centre left, 373 bottom, 394 top; Hamilton Wright Organisation Inc. 210 top, 210 bottom, 211 top, 211 bottom, 399 bottom; Zaire Tourist Bureau 290 top; ZEFA – 396 top; ZEFA – Dr K. Biedermann 507 left; ZEFA – J. Bitsch 151 bottom, 201 bottom, 208; ZEFA – E.G. Carlé 339 bottom right, 443 top; ZEFA – R. Crispijn 17 bottom left; ZEFA – B. Crader 88 bottom right, 482; ZEFA – Brahm Dev 185 bottom; ZEFA – R. Dorman 468; ZEFA – Hermann Engel 200 bottom; ZEFA – V. Englebert 295; ZEFA – R. Everts 45; ZEFA – A. Foley 245 bottom; ZEFA – Kurt Goebel 93, 333 bottom, 352 bottom; ZEFA – H. Grathwohl 75 top, 326 bottom right; ZEFA – R. Halin 66, 228 right, 256 bottom right, 287 bottom, 397 top left, 474 top, 490 left; ZEFA – W. Hasenberg 425; ZEFA – D. Hecker 288 bottom right; ZEFA – Gunter Heil 182, 234 top right; ZEFA – Konrad Helbig 397 top right, 399 top, 507 right; ZEFA – Hungarian Fotostudio 86 top right; ZEFA – Dr. Hans Kramarz 16, 80 top, 84 bottom, 90 top, 98, 115 top, 203 top; ZEFA – H. J. Kreuger 332 top; ZEFA – S. Kübe 17 bottom right; ZEFA – Bert Leidmann Introduction, 112, 288 top, 292 top; ZEFA – L. Mau 435 bottom; ZEFA – J. Nowack title page; ZEFA – Orion Press 150; ZEFA – Ben Partner half title page; ZEFA – J. Pfaff 58 top; ZEFA – P. Phillips 506 top; ZEFA – M. Pitner 334 bottom; ZEFA – D. Pittius 24 bottom right; ZEFA – E. Rekos 505 bottom; ZEFA – G. Ricatto 103 bottom left, 152 top, 460 top; ZEFA – W. Saller 29 top right; ZEFA – Hans Schmied 191 bottom; ZEFA – Kurt Scholz 94, 110 left, 283 top, 289 top, 395, 396 bottom; ZEFA – W. Schön 288 bottom left; ZEFA – Phil Selfe 282 bottom; ZEFA – G. Sirena 88 top left, 281 centre right, 292 bottom, 293; ZEFA – Starfoto Contents page, 20 top, 27 top, 81, 309; ZEFA – I. Steinhoff 117 top; ZEFA – R. G. Theissen 52 bottom; ZEFA – E. Vetter 506 bottom; ZEFA – Vontin 37 top right; ZEFA – F. Walther 357 bottom left; ZEFA – Werbestudio 163; ZEFA – A. Wesselow 31 top; ZEFA – K. Heinz Zawodsky 387.